The begetters of Revolution

The begetters of Revolution

England's involvement with France, 1759-1789

Derek Jarrett

Rowman and Littlefield

Totowa, New Jersey

First published in the United States, 1973
by Rowman and Littlefield, Totowa, New Jersey

© Longman Group Limited 1973

ISBN 0-87471-136-3

Printed in Great Britain by
Clarke, Doble & Brendon Ltd,
Plymouth

For Betty

Contents

Acknowledgements

We are grateful to the following for permission to reproduce copyright material:

Edward Arnold Ltd. for an extract from *Documents of European Economic History* Vol. I by Pollard and Holmes; Witt Bowden for original letter of James Watt in *Industrial Society in England towards the end of the Eighteenth Century* by W. Bowden, original source: The Boulton and Watt MSS; The University of Chicago Press for short extracts from *The Correspondence of Edmund Burke* ed. T. W. Copeland et. al. 1958070, Vol. I and Vol. V; Cassell and Company Ltd. for letters from *The Letters of Edward Gibbon* ed. J. E. Norton, 3 vols. 1956; The Clarendon Press Oxford for an extract as cited on p. 353 of *The Lunar Society of Birmingham* by Robert E. Schofield 1963, from a letter from Wedgwood to Boulton; Cornell University Press for a phrase from a letter reprinted from Michael G. Kammen: *A Rope of Sand; The Colonial Agents, British Politics, and The American Revolution;* copyright © 1968 by Cornell University; Manchester University Press for an extract from *Diplomatic Correspondence of the Fourth Earl of Sandwich*, 1763/5 ed. Frank Spencer.

Preface

There are few periods less amenable to 'country-by-country' history than the late eighteenth century. While other periods tend to be named after the kings or other great figures who dominated them—'The Tudor Age', 'The Age of Metternich', and so on—this one has come to be called 'The Age of Revolution'. And revolutions, unlike kings or statesmen, are international and amorphous at the same time. They have a way of turning up in one country just when they seem to have been pinned down in another. If it is to be studied at all the Age of Revolution must be studied at an international level, taking into account the whole community, American as well as European, in which the revolutions had their being and their origins.

Yet there is a difficulty. However internationalist our approach, we cannot establish the pedigree of revolutions as easily as we can draw the family tree of a line of kings. Some have seen a family likeness in the revolutions of this period, as though they were all siblings begotten of the same aspirations or the same social forces. Others have thought in terms of polarity rather than similarity, of repulsion rather than attraction. The so-called 'industrial revolution' in Britain, for instance, has been portrayed as a kind of negative image of the French revolution, the healthy response of an adaptable society to the changes which in the rigid society of France caused an explosion. The challenge presented by the Age of Revolution is clear and unmistakeable, but the response has sometimes been a little discordant.

I am concerned in this book to examine not the revolutions themselves but the problems and tensions that caused them. I believe that most of these problems and tensions sprang from the conflict between England and France and that an examination of this conflict is therefore an essential preliminary to an understanding of the Age of Revolution. Whatever we may think about

the relationship between one revolution and another, however
differently we may sketch in the collateral lines in our family tree
of revolutions, we should first make sure that we are in agreement
about the main line of descent. If there are areas of disagreement
—and of course there are bound to be—then these should be
defined at the outset and not left unrecognized to cause confusion
and misunderstanding when the revolutions themselves are under
discussion. Two governments, one based on Westminster and one
on Versailles, controlled the destinies of a large part of the western
world in the late eighteenth century. By their achievements and
their mistakes, by the differing political traditions which they
formed and which formed them, they influenced the American
revolution, the French revolution, the 'industrial revolution' and
many other manifestations of this turbulent age—including, for
instance, the upheavals in Geneva and in the United Provinces.
If we are to agree about the Age of Revolution we must first
agree about the significance of what those two governments did.

The actions of governments are not in themselves sufficient to
explain the development of the societies they sought to rule—
especially at a time when localism was as important as it was in
the eighteenth century. I have therefore tried to explore the
context in which those governments worked, the pressures to
which they were subjected and the prejudices and convictions
which they had to take into account. This is not just a book
about 'Anglo-French relations' in the traditional diplomatic and
military and naval sense of that phrase: it is a book about the
interaction of two societies at all levels. I have tried to examine
attraction as well as repulsion, to show that in some respects the
two countries were partners rather than rivals. I have also tried
to avoid the long shadow of the 'compare-and-contrast' approach
to English and French history, the approach that led Lord John
Russell, for instance, to remark that if the French aristocracy
had been as sober and conscientious as his ancestor the fourth
Duke of Bedford there might not have been a revolution.[1] Antithetical judgements of this sort tell us more about those who make
them than about those they claim to judge. During the nineteenth

[1] 'The want of practical religion and morals, which Lord Chesterfield held
up to imitation, conducted the French nobility to the guillotine and
emigration; the honesty, the attachment to his religion, the country habits,
the love of home, the activity in rural business, in which the Duke of Bedford
and others of his class delighted, preserved the English aristocracy . . .'
Correspondence of John, Fourth Duke of Bedford, ed. Lord John Russell,
3 vols, 1842–46, i, p. iv.

century many Englishmen wanted to feel themselves part of a tradition that had always guaranteed continuity and stability, just as many Frenchmen wanted to justify their own revolutionary tradition by showing that the society which the revolution had overthrown had always been inherently bad. Thus there arose and flourished the history of hindsight, the history that claimed that because the two countries had ended differently they must therefore have been different all along, almost mirror images of one another. I have done my best to avoid this kind of thinking, while at the same time avoiding also the temptation to put too much emphasis on the similarities which such antithetical historians have ignored in the past.

I have chosen to begin with England's 'Year of Victories' in 1759 because those victories gave a new dimension to the relations between the two countries, involving them in a strange mixture of confrontation and emulation which Goldsmith summed up neatly with his phrase about 'fear and admire'.[2] This was the mixture that led to revolutionary changes in both countries, to the dismemberment of the British empire and the industrialization of British society as well as to the French revolution itself, the event with which the book ends. Ends and beginnings are not easy to justify and I am well aware that this thirty-year slice of Anglo-French history may seem to many people to be unrepresentative and even distorting. I have therefore tried to set it in its context by giving some account of the involvement of the two countries in more general terms in the first chapter. Limitations of space, like those of time, are difficult to justify and yet they have to be made: I have not been able to deal with the British empire as a whole and I have indicated this by intentionally using the term 'England', rather than 'Britain' or 'Great Britain'. This is a book about Englishmen (and Frenchmen also) reacting to problems raised by the American colonies, by Ireland and by other territories which were in effect ruled from England; but it does not claim to be a history of those problems or those territories.

The thesis out of which this book grew was completed between 1952 and 1955, under the supervision of Mr (now Professor) A. Goodwin. I am indebted to him and to many others who helped me at that time, including especially Monsieur l'abbé Bénétruy, Mr Charles Blount, Professor C. W. Everett, Dr Bernard

[2] See below, p. 40.

Gagnebin, Mr Maurice Hutt and Monsieur Jean Martin. Since I returned to the subject in 1965 I have received advice and assistance from Professor J. H. Burns and Professor I. R. Christie and I have had many fascinating talks with Mr John Brooke, whose penetrating understanding of the eighteenth century has been a constant inspiration. Librarians and keepers of archives, in Geneva and Paris as well as in London, have provided services and kindnesses without which my researches would have been impossible. My colleagues and pupils at Goldsmiths' have helped me to clarify my ideas, while my wife and children have helped me to keep my sense of proportion. I owe a particular debt of gratitude to Professor John Bromley, whose interest in my work has extended over more than twenty years and who has done me the great kindness of reading this book in manuscript and making many valuable suggestions for its improvement. The faults that remain are of course my own; but without his help they would have been a great deal more numerous and a great deal more serious.

J.D.J.

London, 1972

Abbreviations

Add.	Additional Manuscripts, British Museum.
A.H.R.F.	*Annales Historiques de la Révolution Française.*
Am.H.R.	*American Historical Review.*
A.N	Archives Nationales, Paris.
Bachaumont	L. Petit de Bachaumont *et al.*, *Mémoires secrets*, 36 vols, London and Amsterdam, 1777–89.
Browning i and ii	O. Browning, ed., *Despatches from Paris, 1784–90, Camden, Third Series* xvi, xix: vol i (1784–87) 1909; vol ii (1788–90) 1910.
C.H.O.P. i–iv	*Calendar of Home Office Papers, 1760–75*: vol i (1760–65), ed. J. Redington, 1878; vol ii (1766–69), ed. J. Redington, 1879; vol iii (1770–72), ed. R. A. Roberts, 1881; vol iv (1773–75), ed. R. A. Roberts, 1899.
C.J.M.	Collection Jean Martin, Cartigny, Geneva.
Commons, 1754–90	Sir Lewis Namier and John Brooke, *The History of Parliament: the House of Commons, 1754–90*, 3 vols, 1964.
Doniol	H. Doniol, *Histoire de la participation de la France à l'établissement des Etats-Unis d'Amérique*, 5 vols, 1886–99.
Ec.H.R.	*Economic History Review.*
E.H.R.	*English Historical Review.*
F.H.S.	*French Historical Studies.*
Fortescue	*The Correspondence of George III*, ed. J. Fortescue, 6 vols, 1927–28.
Gent.Mag.	*Gentleman's Magazine.*
H.J.	*Historical Journal.*
H.M.C.	*Historical Manuscripts Commission Reports.* All references to these are given in the form recommended in the *Sectional Lists* published by the Stationery Office.

J.M.H.	*Journal of Modern History.*
Lescure	*Correspondance secrète inédite sur Louis XVI, Marie-Antoinette, la Cour et la ville, 1777–92,* ed. M. F. A. Lescure, 2 vols, 1866.
Lüthy	H. Lüthy, *La Banque Protestante en France,* 2 vols, 1959–61.
MSS Dumont	Dumont Manuscripts, Bibliothèque de Genève.
P.H.	*Parliamentary History.*
P.R.O. S.P.	Public Record Office: State Papers Foreign.
R.H.	*Revue Historique.*
R.H.D.	*Revue d'histoire diplomatique.*
R.H.E.S.	*Revue d'histoire économique et sociale.*
R.H.M.	*Revue d'histoire moderne.*
R.H.M.C.	*Revue d'histoire moderne et contemporaine.*
Romilly	*The life of Sir Samuel Romilly, written by himself, with a selection from his correspondence; edited by his sons,* 3rd ed., 2 vols, 1842 (This edition is to be preferred to the earlier three-volume editions, as it contains important additional material.)
Stevens	B. F. Stevens, ed., *Facsimiles of MSS in European archives relating to America, 1773–83,* 25 vols, 1889–98.
T.R.H.S.	*Transactions of the Royal Historical Society.*
U.B.H.J.	*University of Birmingham Historical Journal.*
UCL MSS.	Bentham Manuscripts, University College, London.
Walpole, *Last Journals*	H. Walpole, *Last Journals,* ed. J. Doran, rev. by A. F. Stewart, 2 vols, 1910.
Walpole, *Letters*	*Letters of Horace Walpole,* ed. Mrs Paget Toynbee, 16 vols, Oxford, 1903–5. (Since the fuller and more recent edition by W. S. Lewis is still incomplete, I have cited the 1903–5 edition throughout for the sake of consistency.)
W.M.Q.	*William and Mary Quarterly.*

In all references to works published in English, the place of publication is London unless otherwise stated; in the case of works published in French it is Paris unless otherwise stated.

1   *The background*

*I*t was not only the French who were concerned about the prospect of revolution in 1789. On midsummer day of that year, just three weeks before the fall of the Bastille changed the history of the world, a middle-aged English nobleman committed to paper his own private fears. He wrote gloomily:

> Noblemen and gentlemen have almost abandoned the country, so amongst the first great people now residing there may be reckoned the innkeepers, the tax gatherers and the stewards of great estates who with the lawyers rule the country . . . the poor must plunder because not provided for . . . corporations are venal; trade and manufactories are overstrained; banks and bankruptcies in and over every town; laws, from being multiplied beyond comprehension, cannot be enforced . . . and as that increasing wen the metropolis must be fed the body will gradually decay: all the canals, all the roads must be forced to supply it; and when they have brought all they can, and it should by oversize, or particular seasons, want more—why then there will come a distress, a famine and an insurrection; which the praetorian guards, or the whole army cannot quell; or even the parliament pacify; the latter because they have con-

nived at the (now general) alarm, from having been constantly
employed in struggles for power; and regardless of the peace
and interior happiness of their country![1]

There is something almost uncanny about this prophecy. Sir
Lewis Namier pointed out nearly forty years ago its relevance to
the French Revolution—a relevance which forty more years of
scholarly study have done nothing to diminish.[2] At almost every
stage, from long-term social causes to specific political events, the
prophet places his emphasis just where modern scholarship would
wish to have it placed. The only trouble is that he is writing
about the wrong country, about England and not about France.
This lessens his stature as a prophet, but it does not lessen his
importance as a historical phenomenon. On the contrary, it
increases it. It is extremely significant that one of the most
perceptive contemporary analyses of what actually happened in
France should be found in the midsummer day's dream of an
English nobleman about what did not happen in his own country.

This is not because the prophet knew or cared much about
France's troubles and their possible repercussions in England. The
passage comes from the diaries of John Byng, later viscount
Torrington, who was as insular and as chauvinistic as most
Englishmen of his time. He was not the man to analyse developments in France and weigh their importance for his own country.
His forebodings, like the similar forebodings entertained by many
of his contemporaries, were home-produced and self-generated:
they owed little either to comprehension or to apprehension of
what was happening on the other side of the Channel. In later
years the advantages of hindsight were to enable Englishmen to
assert that their own country had always been stable and that it
could only be rendered unstable as a result of contagion from
revolutionary France. But on midsummer day 1789 all that was in
the future. To English eyes it seemed that the long awaited Estates
General of France had turned out to be a harmless and lifeless
body stuck fast in its own procedural squabbles: it was the
parliament at Westminster, incited by George III's illness to
unprecedented insolence and factiousness, that looked really
dangerous. Even hindsight did not always succeed in obscuring
this fact. As late as 1815, after all the upheavals of the revo-

[1] *Torrington Diaries*, ed. C. B. Andrews, 4 vols, 1935, ii, 87–8.
[2] See Namier's review in the *Manchester Guardian*, 13 September 1934
and 24 June 1935, reprinted in *Crossroads of Power*, 1962, pp. 187–93.

lutionary and Napoleonic era, a man as well informed and
politically aware as Sir Nathaniel Wraxall could still write that
the year 1789 had been important firstly for the crisis over the
king's illness and only secondly for the revolution that had taken
place in France.[3]

The close parallel between France's experiences and Byng's
fears is significant precisely because it was *not* the result of
detached observation of the one by the other. It was, on the
contrary, yet another product of the inextricable involvement of
the two countries with one another, an involvement so deep and
so long-standing that it made detached observation almost impossible. It was as difficult for Englishmen and Frenchmen to examine
one another objectively as it would have been for them to measure
their own shadows. Each country cast its shadow over the other,
a shadow all the more potent for being resented rather than
recognized. The more the two nations repudiated one another,
claiming to stand for different ways of life and opposing systems
of government, the more binding their strange relationship
became. At its core was the phenomenon which later came to
be called 'feedback', but which Byng's generation had not yet
recognized either in the physical or in the political sciences. This
did not stop them from contributing to it, with gusto if not with
understanding. By 1789 there was very little in the politics of either
country that did not spring, directly or indirectly, from interaction with the other. Byng's fears were relevant to France not
because he saw from the outside a revolutionary process in which
France alone was involved, but because he saw from the inside
a revolutionary process which embraced both countries and to
which their mutual dislike had contributed in no small measure.

In so far as it was revolutionary this process was comparatively
recent. It was only during Byng's own lifetime—he was born
in 1742—that the rivalry between the two countries produced
stresses and strains that tore apart the British empire in 1776 and
brought down the French monarchy in 1792. The Seven Years
War, waged between 1756 and 1763, was perhaps the real turning
point in the history of both countries: it set them apart as
opposites, England as the champion of commercial expansion and
France as the archetype of a settled agrarian society, while at the
same time involving them in problems that brought them closer

[3] Sir N. W. Wraxall, *Historical Memoirs*, 2nd edn, 2 vols, 1815, i, preface,
p. iii.

together in a common need to reorganize their government and their society. Their problems were convergent and yet their solutions to those problems became more and more divergent. Any course of action adopted in one country became, almost automatically, an object of suspicion and distrust in the other; any debate on any issue came to look like an inverted copy, a kind of mirror image, of the comparable debate going on in the other country. It was this paradoxical polarity between the two most powerful countries in the world that lay at the root of the 'Age of Revolution' of the late eighteenth century.

But if the revolutionary process itself was relatively new, the involvement from which it sprang was very old—as old, perhaps, as the narrow strip of water which divided the two nations and dictated their attitudes to one another. Ever since the melting ice had first flooded the land bridge between them, England and France had been like a pair of separated Siamese twins, each determined to live its own life and yet resentfully conscious of the other self that had been taken from it. The medieval imperialism of the Angevin kings had merely deepened the gulf it sought to bridge, leaving behind an ugly sediment of prejudice and chauvinism which Shakespeare in due course stirred up in order to give colour to his historical dramas. Like John of Gaunt, the English settled down in their fortress built by nature for herself and looked out with amused contempt on the envy of less happier lands—especially the land of France. But the fortress was not as detached and self-sufficient as it seemed: dissidents and malcontents in England looked instinctively to France, while the close links between that country and the Scots meant that the rear of the citadel was almost always in danger. The sixteenth and seventeenth centuries brought new and deeper issues to tangle the situation still further. England became officially committed to the Protestant religion, to some sort of partnership between king and parliament and to a policy of colonial and maritime expansion—with the inevitable result that those who disapproved of these things gave part of their loyalty to the values represented by the Catholic king of France and the hierarchical agrarian society which he ruled. Across the Channel the same process took place in reverse: just as traditionally minded Englishmen were attracted to France, so commercially minded Frenchmen were attracted to England. The more opposed the two countries became, the more important each was in the internal conflicts of the other. It was a polarity in which unlike poles served both to attract and to repel.

In 1667 Louis XIV of France suggested that with goodwill on both sides the unlike poles ought to be able to revert to their natural function of attraction. 'If the English would be content to be the greatest merchants of Europe,' he told his ambassador in London, 'and let me have for my share whatever I could conquer in a just war, it would be as easy as anything for us to get on together.'[4] It was a disingenuous suggestion, since Louis and his ministers were in fact doing their utmost to secure for France the commercial supremacy which he said he was prepared to leave to the English; but it was important nevertheless because it was one of the earliest and clearest statements of the myth that was increasingly to dominate relations between the two countries. This was the myth of symbiosis, the idea that England and France were developing along lines so diametrically opposed to one another that they could lead only to harmony if they were properly respected. Governments made use of this myth as and when it suited them for propaganda purposes: the English asserted that all would be well if only the French did not dispute with them their sugar islands and their fishing grounds and their trading concessions, while the French insisted that the peace could be kept as long as the English did not make unwarranted interventions in European affairs. Neither government believed what it said, since it was by this time clear that the two spheres overlapped and that security in one could not be maintained without a certain amount of activity in the other. But subjects were often more naïve than governments. There were many Frenchmen who felt that their country would be better off if it left the sordid business of trade and colonialism to the English, just as there were many Englishmen who saw no need to dispute France's hegemony in Europe. Such attitudes were born of contempt for the other country rather than secret sympathy with it; and thus they complicated the cross-connections still further. While some Frenchmen were reluctant to fight English commercialism because they wanted to cooperate with it, others were reluctant because they wanted to turn their backs on it. Similarly in England opposition to the wars against France came partly from those who sympathized with the things for which she stood and partly from

[4] Louis XIV to Colbert de Croissy, 1667, cited C. G. Picavet, *La Diplomatie française au temps de Louis XIV*, 1930, p. 171.

those who disliked them so much that they would not make use of them even to defeat the country from which they sprang.

Whatever its motives, opposition to war was not very successful in either country. In 1688 William III, the protestant ruler of the Dutch and the acknowledged European rival of Louis XIV, led an expedition to England which ended in his being raised to the English throne while the Catholic James II fled to France. The war that followed sprang originally from Louis's determination to put James back on his throne, but before it was over it had caught up in its train almost all the great issues of the time. William was the champion not only of Protestantism but also of national sovereignty: he regarded Europe as a concert of independent powers while Louis saw it as a dismembered Christendom which should be reunited under the Catholic leadership of France. William forced his new English subjects to see that their trade and their security depended on the balance of power in Europe, while Louis for his part maintained that this impertinent eruption of England into European affairs threatened not only his personal honour and glory but also the sacred monarchical principles for which he stood. As the two rulers piled the stakes higher and higher their subjects resented the widening wars more and more; but they found it increasingly difficult to find firm ground on which to oppose them.

The tremendous importance of the Anglo-French confrontation was seen very clearly in 1700, when Louis's grandson Philip inherited the vast and unwieldy Spanish empire. The French royal house of Bourbon now controlled not only France and Spain but also large areas of central and southern America, as well as key points in the Mediterranean and the Netherlands and the East Indies. The other powers of Europe tried to contest this catastrophic upset in the balance of world power, but they proved incapable of doing so: it was only when the English parliament passed the Act of Settlement in the following year that events began to move towards a European alliance system which eventually forced Louis to accept a partition of the Spanish empire. If the young Duke of Gloucester had not died in the summer of 1700, thus forcing the English to settle their crown on the bitterly anti-French royal house of Hanover, the French acquisition of Spain might well have gone unchallenged. The whole balance of world power had come to depend on the actions of the English parliament, as William himself told that body with somewhat embittered flattery. All the complex issues that were at stake between England and France were subordinate to one central issue, the success or failure of England's revolutionary policy of choosing her own kings. Revolution, which was to be the final outcome of the Anglo-French relationship at the end of the eighteenth century, was also the chief determining factor in that relationship at the beginning of the century.

It was revolution in a very different sense: whereas the French in 1789 made a revolution that shook the whole fabric of society, the English in 1688 made certain limited political adjustments intended to keep society as it was. For most of the eighteenth century the word 'revolution' meant what the English had made it mean in 1688 and not what the French were to make it mean a hundred years later. Hence Byng's avoidance of the word in his prophecy in 1789: he was envisaging something far more cataclysmic than the self-contained political shufflings which most of his contemporaries had in mind when they spoke of 'revolutions'. But however limited it might be, the word still had enough meaning to worry Louis XIV and the majority of his subjects. From 1688 onwards a king of England could only validate his claim to the throne by admitting that in certain circumstances—such as, for instance, his conversion to the Catholic religion—his subjects had the right to take it away from him. To deny this right was tantamount to accepting James II and his heirs as rightful kings. In French eyes a monarchy based on such principles was not only contemptible and heretical but also dangerous to its neighbours. It was dangerous because it was totally unreliable—no king of England could keep his word when he was subjected to the capricious pressures of an irresponsible parliament—and it was dangerous because it might infect its neighbours with its own pernicious doctrines. The Huguenots, French Protestants who had had their religious liberties taken away from them in 1685, were already flocking to England in order to support the revolution there and work for its extension to France. 'Is not this auspicious revolution in England a prelude to our own,' wrote one of their publicists, 'a portent to give us hope and a pathway to give us guidance?'[5] As the Huguenot exiles became steadily more influential in English politics, scaring their hosts with stories

---

[5] I. de Larrey, *Réponse à l'avis aux réfugiéz*, 1709, p. 22, cited W. J. Stankiewicz, *Politics and Religion in Seventeenth Century France*, Berkeley, California, 1960, p. 206.

of French persecution and supporting the war against France with
their very considerable financial resources, French Catholics began
to fear that by this means England's 'revolution principles' might
one day be exported to their own country.

Within a few years of the English revolution the Jacobites,
supporters of the dethroned James, had been driven out of
Ireland and Scotland as well as out of England. Many of them
congregated in France, there to act the same part that the
Huguenots acted in England. They scandalized their French hosts
with accounts of the insubordination and irreligion which the
revolution had produced in England; and in some cases they even
outdid the French themselves in their efforts to keep such things
at bay. Charles O'Brien, a Catholic refugee from Ireland who was
made Louis XIV's *gouverneur du roi* in Languedoc and Guyenne,
became renowned for his ferocious persecution of the Huguenots
there.[6] The activities of the Jacobite exiles in France produced
suspicions which mirrored those excited by the Huguenots in
England. Just as Louis thought that the English were harbouring
Frenchmen who had revolutionary designs on his own absolute
authority, so the English thought—on the whole with more
justification—that Louis wished to lead the Jacobites back to
England to overthrow the English revolution.

As well as engendering suspicions in the countries they had
left behind the exiles complicated still further the domestic
discontents of the countries that welcomed them. From about
1709 onwards Louis XIV's war against the English produced
serious crises in both countries: in France there was famine and
commercial depression, leading to the bankruptcy of the government's bankers, while in England opposition to the war reached
such a pitch that the revolution settlement itself came under
attack. The politicians who were running the war were accused
of selling the country to Hanoverian militarists and Huguenot
moneylenders; and there was an attempt to revive the doctrine
of 'passive obedience', which would have meant the recognition
of the Jacobites instead of the Hanoverians as future kings of
England. Both countries started to put their policies into reverse:
in England a Tory administration came to power dedicated to
ending a war which it said was nothing but a Whig confidence

---

[6] Lüthy, ii, 240. For further information on O'Brien and other Irish
Jacobite exiles, see R. Hayes, *Biographical Dictionary of Irishmen in France*,
Dublin, 1949.

trick, while in France the government began to take advice from men who had previously been its clandestine critics. Louis XIV even sent Nicolas Mesnager, a long-standing opponent of the war and of the aggressive economic policies it entailed, to sound out the English about a possible commercial treaty.[7] The belligerence of the Huguenot and Jacobite exiles remained, but it evoked less and less response from their respective hosts.

Peace was signed between the two countries in 1713; and for a time it looked as though it might serve to disentangle some of the complex cross-connections between them. The Tory ministers in England were genuinely anxious for good relations with France, both diplomatic and commercial, and they also seemed ready to bring English government and society more closely into line with her. They passed laws aimed at reducing the influence of the Calvinists and Huguenots who had come over with Dutch William, and also of the English dissenters and monied men who were the natural allies of these subversive foreigners. They announced their intention of re-establishing the hierarchical agrarian society which had existed (or which they and their supporters thought had existed) before 1688; and they declared that they would keep foreign trade in its proper place, so that it could be engaged in freely by English gentlemen and not be monopolized by Huguenot moneylenders who led the country into aggressive mercantilist wars. Having attacked the social and economic and diplomatic consequences of the 1688 revolution in public, the Tories attacked the revolution itself in private: they contacted James II's son and begged him to return to the Anglican faith, so that in his person the Stuart dynasty could continue with its rightful task of defending Englishmen not only against Catholics on the one hand and Calvinists and Lutherans on the other, but also against the theory of elective monarchy to which the events of 1688–89 had opened the door. Louis added his voice to theirs, since a Jacobite restoration could be expected to bring to a satisfactory conclusion that process of convergence between the two countries which most of his ministers now saw as beneficial to France.

But James III would not change his religion; and in the summer of 1714 events began to move in a direction that suggested

[7] On Mesnager's mission and its significance see L. Rothkrug, *Opposition to Louis XIV*, Princeton, 1965, p. 260, and the review of Rothkrug's book by R. Hatton in *Government and Opposition*, i, 1965–66, 567–71.

divergence rather than convergence. Queen Anne, William III's successor and the last of the Anglican Stuarts, died before her Tory ministers could complete their plans for a restoration. George of Hanover, who now arrived in England to take up the crown promised him by the Act of Settlement, was a staunch opponent of Louis XIV and had bitterly resented the action of the Tories in pulling his future kingdom so precipitately out of the war against France. He was in sympathy with many of those against whom the Tories had discriminated, particularly with the dissenters, and he had good reason to reverse Tory policies at all levels. His succession might well have been expected to produce a move away from France as pronounced as the move towards her would have been if James III had come to the throne.

George I was not, however, an admirer of those 'revolution principles' to which he owed his crown. He wanted to be a strong king and to rule over a kingdom in which people knew their place and kept to it. He was suspicious of the Tories, especially after some of them involved themselves in the Jacobite uprising of 1715, but he was also suspicious of the English parliament and of the Whigs who so zealously championed its rights. He never forgot that the English had once killed one of their kings and that he must be on his guard against their constant attempts to whittle down the royal prerogatives. By the autumn of 1719 he had provided himself with ministers who planned to buttress his power and their own by establishing permanent control of the Church, the universities, the City of London and both Houses of parliament. He had already swallowed his dislike of France and signed a treaty of alliance with her; and now, it seemed, he was moving closer to her absolutist system of government in his attempts to transcend the weak and divisive structure of politics which he had inherited. England seemed to be looking to France after all, even if not quite in the way the Tories would have liked.

France for her part was moving closer to England, though not for reasons that would have pleased Louis XIV. He had died in 1715, leaving his country in a situation which more or less forced her to seek an English alliance. She was disliked by most of the powers of Europe, either because they had fought against her and were unreconciled or because they had fought beside her and were unforgiving of the peace treaty which she had forced upon them without consulting their interests. Spain was particularly resentful, since the treaty had involved the partition of her empire; and she was also particularly dangerous, since her king Philip V had a claim to the French throne. He had been excluded from it in 1700, when he succeeded in Spain, but even at that time his grandfather, Louis XIV, had contested the validity of the exclusion. Now that Louis XIV was dead and the king of France was his great-grandson Louis XV, a sickly little boy of five, it could well be argued that in the event of the child's death Philip of Spain would have more right to the French throne than the duc d'Orléans, head of the cadet branch of the Bourbons and at present Regent for the young king. Having exploited the dynastic difficulties of others and fought a War of the English Succession as well as a War of the Spanish Succession, France now found herself faced with the possibility of a disastrously divisive War of the French Succession. In these circumstances it was hardly surprising that the Regent Orléans dropped his support of the Jacobites and made common cause with George of Hanover.

The Regency of the duc d'Orléans, which lasted from 1715 to 1723, saw something deeper than a mere diplomatic *rapprochement* with England. It also saw France adopting many of the political and economic devices which had hitherto been regarded with suspicion because they were associated with England. On 24 October 1715, little more than a month after Louis XIV's death, the French *Conseil des Finances* considered a plan for financial and commercial reform which was put forward by a Scottish adventurer called John Law and which proposed in effect to import into France the system of government-sponsored credit which the English had been operating with considerable success since the foundation of the Bank of England in 1694. Traditionalists on both sides of the Channel had always said that national banks would bring national ruin, upsetting the natural balance of society and puffing up the economy with unreal paper money until it burst. But twenty years' experience of the Bank of England seemed to suggest that it promoted healthy growth rather than unnatural inflation. Even the most rabidly prejudiced Tory landowner was coming to see that a credit economy helped him to get the most out of his land by mortgaging part of it in order to get working capital for the development of the whole estate. Opposition to Law's plan came therefore not from the French counterpart of the Tory landowner but from the great private bankers and financiers whose position it seemed to threaten. It

was Samuel Bernard, the banker who had failed to provide for
Louis XIV the financial stability that the Bank of England had
provided for William III and Anne, who got the *Conseil des
Finances* to reject the scheme. But Bernard's victory was shortlived: within a few months he and his associates were dragged
before a special court and fined a total of 219 million livres as a
punishment for the excessive and illegal profits which they were
said to have made from financing Louis XIV's wars. John Law,
meanwhile, brought forward a new version of his scheme and
got it accepted.[8]

On 4 December 1718, only two and a half years after it had
first gone into business, Law's joint stock bank was turned into
the equivalent of the Bank of England, with the title of *Banque
Royale*; and in 1720 it was merged with his *Compagnie
d'Occident*, popularly known as the Mississippi Company, which
had originally been formed to trade with Louisiana but had
subsequently been given exclusive rights to the trade of America,
Africa and Asia. Law himself, now a Catholic and a French
subject, became controller general of finances and began to
draw up plans to use these vast new credit resources in order to
finance unprecedented expansion of French industry and commerce. The English began to get seriously worried. On the face
of things Law was an anglophile, bringing France into line with
England and undermining the position of those forces in her
society which made her hostile to the English. Many of his closest
financial associates were Huguenot bankers, intimately linked
with the great financiers of London. But by bringing the two
countries closer together he was also bringing them more and
more into competition: after a generation of bitter rivalry spring-
ing from the differences between them, England and France
seemed poised now on the brink of an even more bitter rivalry
resulting from their similarities. Not only England's commercial
position but also her financial position was threatened by Law's
success. Even the Dutch, who were large-scale holders of English
government stock, began to sell out and buy stock in the *Compagnie d'Occident*.

[8] Lüthy, i, 284ff, 301–2. In his analysis of the Law affair Lüthy stresses
the links with England, commercial as well as financial. M. Giraud, *Histoire
de la Louisiane française, iii, l'époque de John Law, 1717–1720*, 1966, pp.
4, 14, also points out the importance of the English example and shows the
importance of Law's 1715 scheme in the subsequent evolution of the Mississippi Company. See also M. A. Sallon, 'L'échec de Law', *R.H.E.S.* xlviii, 2,
1970, 145–95.

England's answer to Law was the South Sea scheme. George I's ministers were determined in any case to gain control of the City of London by creating a monopolistic monied corporation which should be dependent on them; and it was the South Sea Company, originally a Tory trading company but now a Whig finance corporation with the king himself at its head, which provided them with their instrument. Having outbid the Bank of England, the company was authorized to create £31 million of new stock and offer it to government creditors in exchange for their government stock. Thus in effect it took over the national debt—and took it over at a bargain price, for a rush of speculative buying pushed the new South Sea stock up to several times its nominal value and thus reduced the amount of it that had to be offered in exchange for a given amount of government stock. By the summer of 1720 the new stock was worth something like £300 million on the market, completely dwarfing the £31 million-worth of government stock which it was buying up. George I's supporters were exultant and his opponents were overawed: the dissident Whigs who had previously seemed so dangerous in parliament now made their peace with the ministry, accepting with humble relief such terms as they could get. By skilful use of the apparently divisive and new-fangled institutions of England George I had put himself in a position of power which even the traditionalist and hierarchical rulers of France might envy.[9]

The Regent Orléans had good reason for envy in the summer of 1720, for the apparent success of George I's schemes coincided with the utter collapse of his own. Confidence in the Mississippi Company began to falter in February and within a matter of weeks Law's proud financial empire had been brought down in a wave of panic selling. There was a violent reaction throughout France not merely against stockjobbing but against the whole business of banking and credit and paper money. It extended even to the Regent's political experiments, which had been in reality very limited: he had revived some of the powers of the Paris *parlement* and he had tried to involve the nobility more in the business of government. These changes were far less ambitious than those which had been proposed in 1711 by the advisers to the then heir to the throne; but now they were magnified by the enemies of the house of Orléans until they became part of a

[9] See J. P. Carswell, *The South Sea Bubble*, 1960, and J. H. Plumb, *Sir Robert Walpole, the Making of a Statesman*, 1956.

deliberate conspiracy to undermine the ancient strength of France by foisting upon her the divisive institutions and the financial folly of her hated rival across the Channel.[10] These charges of 'anglomania' which were levelled originally against the Regent in the 1720s were to be inherited, with momentous political consequences, by his great-grandson in the 1780s.

During the autumn of 1720 South Sea stock ran into the same kind of panic selling that had already brought down the Mississippi Company; but the English company, significantly enough, was able to survive where the French one was destroyed. The speculative bubble burst, with disastrous results for many people, but the South Sea Company itself continued to trade and its shares continued to be worth more or less the same as before the scheme was launched. Confidence in the Bank of England, and in the credit structure in general, was restored by means of a sustained and skilful parliamentary campaign on the part of the king's new minister, Robert Walpole. In hard financial terms Walpole did relatively little, but in political and psychological terms he did a great deal, convincing parliament that it was still in control of things and convincing the nation that it could rely on parliament to regulate the future growth of the credit structure and to prevent any more speculative bubbles. Most important of all, he convinced the king that in the long run ministers who could coax and manipulate parliament were more useful than those who claimed to be able to subdue it. Thus in England the collapse of monopolist and absolutist dreams strengthened rather than weakened the political and financial institutions which they had tried to supersede, while in France the monolithic structure of government and the hierarchical structure of society survived and even profited from the Regent's attempts to modify them. Each country emerged from the traumatic experiences of 1720 with its faith in its own traditions confirmed and its suspicions about alien traditions intensified. Though the two countries were officially at peace with one another until 1743, their contempt for each other's systems of government meant that they were in practice building up, layer after chauvinistic layer, the hostility that was to lead first to war and then, through war, to revolution.

[10] See for instance Barère de Vieuzac, *La Conduite des princes de la maison de Bourbon*, 1835, pp. 14–15. For the proposals of 1711 see *Plans de gouvernement concertés avec le duc de Chevreuse pour être proposés au duc de Bourgogne*, printed in P. Sagnac, *La Formation de la société française moderne*, 2 vols, 1945–46, i, 225–36.

John Byng and his generation were heirs to this relentlessly accumulated xenophobia. Their inheritance was made more durable and more deadly by the spectacular wars which over-shadowed their childhood and brought stories of martial adventure into their nurseries from all over the world. Cradled in sullen chauvinism and bred up in belligerent anticipation, they were finally brought to maturity by the serious business of real fighting: Byng himself, who was an infant in arms when the wars began, was an officer in the army by the time they ended in 1763. Thousands upon thousands of his contemporaries, French as well as English, were subjected to formative influences which were very similar. This was their political apprenticeship, their preparation for the task of managing the most revolutionary period through which western society had yet passed.

It was an apprenticeship which produced nagging doubts as well as dogmatic certainties. Frenchmen saw their highly organized bureaucracy cracking under strains which the more casual and amateurish administrators of England seemed to take in their stride; Englishmen saw their parliament bringing forth a factious chaos which contrasted sharply with the apparent stability of France. Byng himself had a particularly vivid insight into the dangerous combination of hysterical francophobia and irresponsible demogogy which dominated English politics during the Seven Years War. When he was in his early teens his uncle, Admiral John Byng, was court-martialled and shot for his failure to protect the island of Minorca from French attack. Though technically justified, the sentence of the court might not have been carried out if the king's ministers had recommended a pardon because of the mitigating circumstances; but the politicians and the journalists of the opposition had stirred up such a frenetic outcry that the government feared that it might itself be in danger if it tried to save Byng. And so the admiral was shot, a victim of those very freedoms he had failed to defend. Whatever the ministers of an absolute king might have done, the ministers of George II were too frightened of parliament and of the press to do what some of them probably thought right.[11] John Byng the nephew never forgot what had happened to John Byng the uncle. Again and again his ruminations turned to the problem which the admiral's death had illuminated in such a lurid fashion. How

---

[11] But the ministers of Louis XV could on occasion make similar surrenders: see below, p. 101.

could the propertied classes, the freemen in the towns and the freeholders in the country, ensure that the politicians whom they elected to defend their freedoms would not by their factious ambitions put power into the hands of the unpropertied and giddy rabble? What was the point of defending parliamentary monarchy against French despotism and French popery if parliament itself could not be trusted to keep divisive and anarchic forces in check?

As well as making some Englishmen think twice about the dangers of French absolutism, Admiral Byng's death also made some Frenchmen think twice about the attractions of the English parliamentary system. Voltaire, who had been for many years a leader of the anglophile minority in France, had in the past said many flattering things about the benign influence of the English press and parliament; but now he produced a devastating comment on the arbitrary exercise of that influence—a comment which was to be remembered long after the earlier flatteries had been forgotten by all but academics. 'In this country,' his hero Candide was told when he arrived in England, 'it is thought good to kill an admiral from time to time to encourage the others.'[12] The imaginary Candide, moving in bewilderment through a world in which promises of reform and dreams of utopia led only to tyranny and corruption, had some surprising affinities with the saddened and sceptical John Byng, prophesying gloomily about the unscrupulous demagogues who had devoured his uncle and would end by devouring the whole country. Shattered naïvety and deepening disillusionment led both of them to similar conclusions: Candide came to think that a man must tend his own garden even if the world around him went mad, while Byng saw the independent landowner as the only hope of stability in a rapidly disintegrating society.

This appearance of convergence was produced not by any similarity of approach—it would be hard to think of anything farther removed from the caustic intelligence of Voltaire than the muddleheaded nostalgia of John Byng—but by the steadily narrowing space within which they and their contemporaries were working. The great Anglo-French disputation about the nature of government and society, which had once seemed to be a genuine clash of opposites, was by this time coming to look more like a discussion about the respective merits of administrative and

[12] Voltaire, *Candide*, ch. xxiii (*Oeuvres complètes*, 52 vols, 1877–85, xxi, 197).

political techniques which in fact differed very little. The Seven Years War revealed the shortcomings of some of them, thus closing some of the remaining options and making it even more difficult for the two countries to tread the razor edge between stultifying bureaucracy and divisive party politics. It was the same razor edge for both of them: in spite of the traditions of chauvinism, in spite of the much publicized polarity between the two systems of government, the truth was that the political debate in which both nations were engaged could never again take place in the context of one nation alone. They were involved with one another; and the upheavals of the Seven Years War were fast producing an involvement that was tighter still, an involvement that could span thirty years of time as well as twenty miles of water. The spectacular English victories of 1759, the year in which *Candide* was published, were to lead step by step to the administrative dislocation and political uncertainty of the year 1789, the year in which Byng wrote down his midsummer forebodings. And at every stage in this process the developments of politics were conditioned by hopes and fears, speculations and expectations, about the parallel developments that were taking place on the other side of the Channel. For the French the process led in the end to cataclysmic change, whereas for the English it seemed only to preserve stability and continuity; and this difference at the end tempts us to postulate differences earlier on, to unplait the whole rope because the end is unravelled. It is a temptation which should be resisted. Politics in England and France during these thirty years were too closely interwoven for the history of either country to be intelligible on its own.

2   *Image and Reality*

'Before the English learn that there is a God to be worshipped,' wrote Fougeret de Montbron in his *Preservative against Anglomania*, 'they learn that there are Frenchmen to be detested.' He then proceeded to demonstrate that his countrymen ought to return this detestation in good measure; and he concluded that the only good things to be said for the English were that they bred excellent horses and dogs and had managed to free their country from both wolves and monks.[1] His book, published in 1757 at the outset of the Seven Years War, is a fairly typical example of the ferocious literature of xenophobia that flourished on both sides of the Channel. The reading public in England was constantly assailed by diatribes against the French and against the dire results of imbibing their customs and their principles. Even *The Craftsman*, an opposition journal which was often tempted to praise the purity of French government as a means of attacking the corruption of Walpole's government in England, dismissed France as 'the perfect mistress of all that is polite and all that is

[1] J. L. Fougeret de Montbron, *Préservatif contre l'Anglomanie*, 'à Minorque', 1757, p. 52.

silly'.[2] French fashions might be seen in London drawingrooms, but the majority of Englishmen regarded France as the home of all that they most loathed: standing armies, royal tyranny, feudal servitude, Catholic bigotry and messy food.

Official publications showed equally clearly, though less hysterically, how little love was lost between the two countries. While English almanacs and other works of reference calmly listed 'King of France' among their royal master's titles, the French *Almanach Royal* relegated the king of England to the lowest position it could devise. After picking their way through all the French and Spanish ramifications of the House of Bourbon, the compilers went on to list the princes of Italy, even down to the Grand Master of the Knights of St John in Malta, and six pages of German rulers, Protestant as well as Catholic and elective as well as hereditary. Only then, on the last page but one of their list of the princes of Europe, did they deign to mention *le Roy d'Angleterre*; and even then they insisted on giving James Stuart, pretender to the English throne, a place of honour among the royal family of England. For proper details of the real royal family, the reader had to look under the heading 'Hanover'. It would have been difficult to illustrate more clearly the gulf of hatred and contempt which lay between one of the oldest monarchies of Europe and a relative newcomer to the ranks of the great powers.

The collapse of Law's financial schemes, and the dramatic reversals of fortune which it brought with it, gave a new edge to anglophobia in France. Previously wealthy families whose riches had disappeared in the bubble of speculation were anxious to assert traditional values and to insist that their lineage still entitled them to respect, even if their lands and their money had been lost. The newly enriched, desperate for acceptance and recognition, were equally ready to idealize the old hierarchy and spurn the new world of business and credit that had brought them their wealth. And everyone agreed, as French society cautiously edged its way back to stability, that the root cause of the whole trouble had been an infection from England. England, whose financial skills had so recently been envied and studied, now became a kind of scapegoat on whom the French could load all those mistaken ideas that had so nearly toppled their whole world. Béat Louis de Muralt, whose *Letters on the English and French*

---

[2] *Craftsman*, no. 609, 11 March 1738.

B

Nations went through several editions from 1725 onwards, both
in the original French and in an English translation, was on the
whole an admirer of the English—since he was himself of Swiss
origin he could stand apart from both nations and note that
whereas the French 'submit to authority, be it never so severe',
the English 'know how to live independently'—but he was highly
critical of the soulless commercialism of English life. It was to
blame, he thought, both for the human misery which he saw in
the debtors' prisons and for the political instability of the country
as a whole.[3]

This conviction that English commercialism was a threat to the
stability of government and society grew steadily during the
thirty years between Law's schemes and the Seven Years War.
Even the Abbé Leblanc, who passed in France for an admirer of
England and was attacked as such by Fougeret de Montbron,
thought that the English middle classes were insubordinate and
that the English political system was falling apart because of the
constant pull of conflicting private interests to which it was
subjected. 'The English are a rational and trading people,' he
wrote, 'who seek only to enrich themselves and have not that
powerful motive which the Romans had to make them act for
the public good preferably to their own.'[4] The marquis de
Mirabeau, archpriest of the anticommercialist cult, spoke of the
English as being torn between two conflicting passions which
would in the end destroy them: the love of liberty and the love
of wealth. By the 1760s his journal, the *Ephémérides du Citoyen*,
was asserting that the English constitution of its very nature made
inevitable a constant civil war between the landed proprietors and
the capitalists. Meanwhile one prominent financial writer, who
was later to become controller general of finance, had declared
that since England's national debt exceeded her supply of bullion
she was in constant danger of bankruptcy and was in fact one
of the poorest, not one of the richest, countries in Europe.[5]

At the beginning of the century those who had criticized

---

[3] B. L. de Muralt, *Letters Describing the Character and Customs of the
English and French Nations*, 1726, pp. 153, 171, 68–9, 61. This is the earliest
and best English version of the work. See also the critical edition by C. Gould
(*Bibliothèque de la revue de littérature comparée*, no. 86), Paris, 1933.

[4] J. B. Leblanc, *Letters on the English and French Nations*, 2 vols, Dublin,
1747, ii, 244.

[5] Marquis de Mirabeau, *L'Ami des hommes*, 3 vols, The Hague, 1758.
iii, 213–14; *Ephémérides du citoyen*, vol. i, no. 4, April 1767, pp. 194–5;
P. Clement and A. Le Moine, *M. de Silhouette, Bouret et les derniers
fermiers généraux*, 1872, p. 25.

Louis XIV's absolutism had been led almost inevitably into an admiration of England and things English; but now things were very different. Even the influential *Club de l'Entresol*, whose members were responsible for many of the subversive political tracts which circulated in manuscript during the first half of the century, contained violent critics of England such as the marquis d'Argenson. In one of his tracts on government he wrote that the English system was corrupt, imperfect and despotic, and all because of the debilitating effect of the National Debt and the universal obsession with monetary gain. 'With them,' he concluded, 'everything is a matter of money: people think of nothing else.' And he made the point which was to be echoed by Leblanc: unlike the pious and patriotic republicans of ancient Rome the English were incapable of putting the public good, the *res publica* or the interest of the *patria*, before their own petty private interests.[6] 'Half a century earlier La Bruyère had written, in a bitter comment on Louis XIV's insatiable thirst for glory, 'In a despotism there is no public interest, no *patria*; other things, such as the honour and glory and power of the prince, take its place';[7] but now it was the French themselves who had preserved their honour along with their monarchy and were claiming to be better patriots than the latterday quasi-republicans of London.

To some extent this radical rereading of the message from England was the result of the channels through which it came. In many cases these were the channels of disillusionment and distaste: for every Frenchman who saw England through the admiring eyes of a Voltaire or a Montesquieu there were probably four or five who knew it from the soured recriminations of exiled Jacobites. Even the scientific theories of Newton, the most unexceptionable of the English intellectual exports of the period, had different implications on different sides of the Channel. In England they were seen as a justification of the English constitution, a proof that the God who had ordained a balanced universe must of necessity smile upon a balanced system of government. John Theophilus Desaguliers, a Huguenot refugee who had become a popular lecturer on scientific matters and also a leading light in English freemasonry, even wrote a poem on the subject

[6] I. Kramnick, *Bolingbroke and his Circle*, Cambridge, Mass., 1968, p. 151. See also *H.M.C.* 68, Denbigh v, pp. 116ff. and I. O. Wade, *The Clandestine Organization and Diffusion of Philosophic Ideas in France from 1700 to 1750*, Princeton, 1938.
[7] J. de la Bruyère, *Oeuvres complètes*, ed. J. Benda, 1951, p. 269.

entitled *The Newtonian System of the World the Best Model of Government*. He compared the king to the sun:

> His power, coerced by laws, still leaves them free,
> Directs but not destroys their liberty . . .
> By his example in their endless race
> The *Primaries* lead their *Satellites*,
> Who guided, not enslaved, their orbits run
> Attend their chiefs, but still respect the sun.[8]

In France, on the other hand, Newton's theories were usually shorn of such political overtones and were eventually accommodated within the context of Catholic orthodoxy. Here, as in so many aspects of the cross-Channel traffic in ideas, the Jacobite exiles played their part: it was an Irish Jesuit, Father Joseph Ignatius O'Halloran, who was credited with introducing Newtonian philosophy into the University of Bordeaux.[9]

By far the most influential of these ambiguous evangelist exiles was Bolingbroke, who was in France between 1715 and 1723 and again from 1735 until his death in 1751. By many he was regarded as an apostle of the age of reason, an enlightened philosopher who had come to teach the French to sweep away superstition and manage their affairs by those same reasonable principles which the English had found so effective; and it is significant that when Burke at the end of the century wanted to attack the rationalists of the previous generation, Bolingbroke's was the name he singled out.[10] And yet Bolingbroke's politics were, to use the phrase of a recent biographer, the politics of nostalgia.[11] He and his Tory friends looked back wistfully to the days when the king's authority was pure and untrammelled, when the corruption and bickering of party politics had not yet warped the constitution. Like d'Argenson and Leblanc, they believed that the English political system militated against truly 'patriotic' conduct; and like them they inclined to the view that the French system was

[8] J. T. Desaguliers, *The Newtonian System of the World the Best Model of Government : an allegorical poem*, 1728, pp. 24, 27.
[9] Hayes, *Biographical Dictionary of Irishmen*, p. 233. For a more general view see P. Brunet, *L'Introduction des théories de Newton en France au xviii* siècle*, 1931—the first and only volume of an uncompleted work —and J. Ehrard, *L'idée de Nature en France dans la première moitié du xviii* siècle*, 2 vols, 1963, i, 125–78.
[10] Burke, *Reflections on the Revolution in France* (*Select Works*, ed. E. J. Payne, 3 vols, Oxford, 1878–1904, ii, 105).
[11] The phrase is used as the subtitle of Kramnick's book—see above, p. 21n.

superior in this respect. 'Those who have examined the trade and revenues of France,' wrote one English opposition journal in 1732, 'have wondered that it should be able to maintain such vast forces; but great things may be done with small revenues and good management. In France there are not perhaps one-fifth of civil officers as in some countries, their salaries are small, nor is the pick-pocket term *perquisites* so much as known among them . . . These things considered, no wonder if some other nations, where everything is managed by bribery and corruption, should raise twice as much on the subject and yet not be able to spare half so much for its just defence.'[12]

Those Frenchmen who saw England in this way, through the eyes of embittered Jacobites and splenetic opposition politicians, saw a distorted picture indeed. Yet it was probably no more distorted than the idealized one produced by such enthusiastic admirers of England as Voltaire. 'There are no arbitrary taxes like the *taille* or the *capitation*,' wrote Voltaire of England in his *Lettres Philosophiques*, 'only a graduated tax on land values. These were all assessed in the reign of the famous King William III, at less than their actual market value. The land tax is still based on this assessment, even though the income from the land has gone up; thus nobody is oppressed and nobody complains.'[13] Certainly there were complaints enough in France, where the two principal direct taxes, the *taille* and the *capitation*, both bore more heavily on the poor than on the rich. Yet it was difficult to see how the situation could be improved by adopting the English system of a hopelessly out-dated assessment which bore no relation to existing land values. The French government did not have much success in its attempts to mitigate the injustices of the tax system, but at least it did try. Assessments for *capitation* took into account a man's liabilities as well as his income, while the *taille* was based on an estimate of the actual value of the year's crop: tax rebates were sometimes allowed in areas where the harvest was especially poor and in some cases government grants and loans were given as well.[14] The English, obsessively anxious to reduce the sphere of

---

[12] *Fog's Journal*, no. 315, 16 November 1732.

[13] Voltaire, *Oeuvres complètes*, xxii, 109.

[14] Assessments for *capitation* may be studied in the *Inventaires sommaires* of the French departmental archives; see, for instance, that for Calvados (série C, tome v, Caen, 1935), p. 314; 'Rôle pour 1771: J. B. de la Beslière, seigneur de Vains, 4000 l, de rentes mais 8 enfants, 35 l.' The assessments show the inadequacies of the popular view that noblemen did not pay direct taxes, a view which has been challenged by Betty Behrens, 'Nobles, privileges

government, deliberately denied themselves the resources and the machinery to change assessments or adjust levels of taxation: when they needed more money they simply raised the overall rate of the land tax, thus multiplying and sharpening the existing inequalities and injustices. And in any case the land tax, even at its emergency wartime rate of four shillings in the pound, only produced a fraction of the total revenue: the rest came from the miscellaneous and multitudinous troop of indirect taxes which bore on rich and poor alike. There was no English counterpart to the *gabelle*, the hated French salt tax, but many other necessities were taxed as heavily in England as in France.[15]

The reason for these distortions, and for similar ones in England's view of France, was that people saw in the other country precisely what they wanted to see. Each country was using the other as a mirror for its own questionings. Sartre, in *Huis Clos*, has portrayed a hell in which the dead are robbed of their looking glasses and have to use instead the eyeballs of their companions; and at a national level, where there are no looking glasses, this practice has always been a favourite though unacknowledged method of self-examination. Like many other hawk-eyed and self-deluding observers before and since, Englishmen and Frenchmen of the eighteenth century stared intently across the Channel, determined to search out their neighbour's secrets and reach a detached assessment of his powers and potentialities. And deep in the pupils of his eyes they saw what they were really looking for all the time: their own reflections.

By the middle of the eighteenth century both Englishmen and Frenchmen had good reason to make such an examination. Years later, when the French revolution had come and gone, almost all those who were old enough to remember the years around 1750 agreed that this was the moment when the old order first started to appear really threadbare and when talk of a new order became common.[16] It was in 1750 that Pinot-Duclos published his influential book, *Considérations sur les moeurs*. He was a

and taxes in France at the end of the *ancien régime*', *Ec. H.R.* 2nd series, xv, 1963, pp. 451–75. See also M. Marion, *Les Impôts directs sous l'ancien régime*, 1910; G. Larde, *Une Enquête sur les vingtièmes au temps de Necker, 1777–78*, 1920; J. Villain, *Le Recouvrement des impôts directs sous l'ancien régime*, 1952; C. Ambrosi, 'Aperçus sur répartition et perception de la taille au dix-huitieme siècle', *R.H.M.C.* viii, 1961, pp. 281–99.
[15] See W. R. Ward, *The English Land Tax in the Eighteenth Century*, Oxford, 1953.
[16] Betty Behrens, *The Ancien Régime*, 1967, pp. 14–16.

Breton, whose father had been a hatter and whose mother, widowed early in life, had developed extensive shipping interests in order to maintain the family fortunes. His book made such an impression that he was given a patent of nobility five years after its publication, on the unanimous recommendation of the Estates of Brittany. '*Grand seigneur*', he wrote, 'is a word which has only historical interest: the reality has gone . . . people of gentle birth have already lost the right to look down their noses at the world of finance, since there are so few of them left whose position depends purely on their breeding.' He shared the general prejudice of his time against pure financiers, mere manipulators of money, but he had a great respect for merchants: financiers, he said, ruin the state with their usuries while merchants support it with their credit.[17] This attempt to separate usury from credit, a division about as practical as Solomon's proposed treatment of the disputed baby, was typical of the whole book, typical of the age itself. It was an age whose attitude to the old was compounded of impatience and nostalgia and whose attitude to the new was compounded of disdain and excitement.

In England there was much the same feeling abroad, an excited consciousness of the need for change combined with a desperate nostalgia for the old order of things. Many people, gulled by opposition propaganda, genuinely expected the fall of Robert Walpole in 1742 to be followed by a sweeping change in the whole fabric of national life: corruption and self-seeking were to be eliminated not only from the House of Commons but from every kind of transaction, private as well as public. 'Patriotism',[18] a noble renunciation of particular interests for the sake of the common good, was to reign instead. When nothing of the sort happened, when it became clear that by forcing the resignation of Walpole the political nation had merely exchanged one set of corrupt place hunters for another, disillusion was the natural result. Some politicians and publicists even allowed themselves to suspect the truth—that the much vaunted constitution of 1688–89 made corruption and placehunting inevitable. If the king's government was to be carried on at all his ministers must

[17] C. Pinot-Duclos, *Considérations sur les moeurs*, ed. F. C. Green, Cambridge, 1939, pp. 83, 133.
[18] I hope that the particular sense in which the eighteenth century used this word will by now have become clear; and the inverted commas used up to now are therefore discarded from this point onwards. The word is given a capital letter when used to mean the party or following that called itself Patriot.

have a body of reliable supporters in the Commons; and if this
body was not to be kept together by sharing a belief in certain
principles—a method which threatened either to revive the divisive
cries and counter-cries of the seventeenth century, or to lead
to a dangerous demand for 'reform'—then it must be kept together
by sharing the spoils of office. Similarly, its rivals in the ranks of
the opposition were kept together by a desire to take over those
same spoils. Caught in this *impasse*, it was natural enough that
idealists and would-be Patriots should look across the Channel for
an answer.

'I say nothing of the exile of the Parlement of Paris,' Horace
Walpole wrote from Paris in the spring of 1753 to his friend
Conway, 'for I know no more than you will see in the public
papers; only as we are going to choose a new parliament, we
could not do better than choose the exiles: we could scarce
choose braver or honester men.'[19] The *parlement* of Paris was not
the counterpart of the parliament of Westminster, even though
it sometimes liked to think it was: it was a court of law which
had extensive powers, administrative as well as judicial, over most
of central France.[20] Other *parlements* were responsible for the
more distant and more recently acquired provinces. All had the
privilege, suspended by Louis XIV but restored by the Regent
Orléans in his bid for support in 1715, of registering their objections, or 'remonstrances', against the laws they were required to
enforce. When they exercised this privilege in a particularly
insolent manner, as the Paris *parlement* had now done, they were
liable to be punished by being exiled to the provinces. By the
autumn many of the opposition journals in London had taken up
Walpole's point and had added morals and conclusions of their
own. 'Almost all the offices of France,' *The Protester* pointed out
on 15 September, 'are, by rule of government, bought and sold
. . . yet no government in Europe is better served than the French
government . . . and it is plain, from the scenes passing with so
much admiration before us, that there is no country but that in
the world where placemen are animated with the true spirit of
patriotism.'[21]

This was strong stuff. For an English journalist to assert that
French government officials were efficient was surprising but not

[19] Walpole, *Letters*, iii, 162.
[20] See J. H. Shennan, *The Parlement of Paris*, 1968.
[21] *The Protester*, p. 96 (15 September 1753). On the *parlements*' opposition
see J. Egret, *Louis XV et l'opposition parlementaire*, 1970.

unprecedented: Bolingbroke's newspapers had said something of
the sort from time to time in the 1730s. But to say that they were
patriotic, that they were readier than their English counterparts
to defy the government and defend the interests of the governed,
was by implication a very grave criticism of the English political
system. The English believed in amateurism in government,
in that they thought posts of responsibility of all sorts, from
secretaryships of state down to positions as justices of the peace,
should go to those whose rank deserved them or whose riches
could buy them. The French had a more professional approach,
at any rate in some departments of government: in the Inspectorate of Manufactures, for instance, every official received a
thorough training and had to pass an examination before being
commissioned as an inspector. Similarly, those who enrolled in the
Department of Bridges and Highways had to attend its special
school in Paris, where they started work at six o'clock in the
morning (eight in the winter months) and could be summarily
expelled if they took any sort of spare time employment.
Throughout their careers they were reported on regularly by
their superiors and there were dire penalties for any kind of
corruption or for collusion between officials and the contractors
they employed.[22] It was this contrast between English amateurism
and French professionalism that caused the Rev John Brown to
remark of the French in his very influential book, *Estimate of the
Manners and Principles of the Times*: 'Their effeminate manners
affect not their national capacity because their youths are
assiduously trained up for all public offices, civil, naval, military,
in schools provided at the national expense: here the candidates
for public employ go through a severe and laborious course of
discipline and only expect to rise in station as they rise in knowledge and ability.'[23]

Advocates of the English system of amateurism could parry
criticisms of this sort relatively easily: efficiency, they argued,
was less important than independence. Trained professional
administrators might possibly do a better job, but it took men of
independent means, men who could view the possible loss of their

[22] F. Bacquié, *Les Inspecteurs de manufactures, 1669–1791*, Toulouse, 1928;
B. Wybo, *Le Conseil de commerce*, 1936; J. Petot, *Histoire de l'administration des ponts et chaussées, 1599–1815*, 1958. See also L. Biollay, *L'Administration du commerce*, in *Le Pacte de famine: études économiques sur le
xviiie siècle*, 1885.
[23] J. Brown, *Estimate of the Manners and Principles of the Times*, 2 vols,
1757, i, 136.

posts with equanimity, to stand up for what was right and prevent
government turning into tyranny. But if *The Protester* was right
this argument fell to the ground: English political corruption
had become so universal and so insidious that it took the servants
of the overregulated and overprofessional French bureaucracy to
teach English placemen a lesson in patriotism.

The two chief sponsors of *The Protester* were an oddly
matched couple: on the one hand that same fourth duke of
Bedford, whose devotion to rural duty was such an effective
prophylactic against revolution[24] and, on the other, Alderman
William Beckford, a merchant of West Indian origin and future
leader of the London radical group in the House of Commons.
Bedford was a Whig, a member of that small clique of 'revolution families' that had come to regard high office as their
particular right, while Beckford was a spokesman for commercial
and financial interests. Yet their newspaper took what could only
be described as a Tory line: devoted to the traditional values of
a landed society, critical of the new monied men and violently
opposed to all foreign immigrants. Its contribution to the campaign against the Jewish Naturalization Bill (a very reasonable
and moderate measure which the government was forced to repeal
in deference to a hysterical outburst of anti-semitism) brought
together all three themes: 'We have, it is true, swarms of them
already amongst us, and from the dirtiest principle that ever
debauched and debased human nature (the sordid homage exacted
and paid to wealth wheresoever lodged and howsoever acquired)
they have met with more countenance here than anywhere else.'
Yet for all its hatred of foreigners *The Protester* made an exception of the French, who were in the eyes of most Englishmen
the most hated foreigners of all. Quite apart from its panegyric
on the exiled *parlementaires*, it lost few opportunities to praise
the French and on one occasion it even reminded its readers that
the great Bolingbroke himself had said that there was less servility in France than in England.[25] In 1754 Beckford even went
so far as to suggest to Bedford that the best leader for their group
in the House of Commons would be Alexander Forrester, a Scots
lawyer of Jacobite descent who was probably born in France of
a French mother.[26] It seemed as though disillusionment with the

[24] See above, p. x.
[25] *The Protester*, pp. 63, 77 (11 and 25 August 1753).
[26] *Commons, 1754–1790*, ii, 451–3.

English political system was beginning to produce political groups which looked to the French system as an alternative.

If this was so, then the Seven Years War certainly stopped them in their tracks. Beckford switched his allegiance to the elder Pitt, a rabid opponent of French power and influence in whatever form it might appear, and the Patriot movement in politics became more and more associated with Pitt's bellicose nationalism rather than with Bolingbroke's search for the ideal form of government. As for Bedford, he had to put his admiration for the French aside for the time being, although when peace came he tried to make it once more a force in English politics.

War against France might curtail the activities of francophile politicians, but it did not prevent thoughtful men from continuing to point out the advantages which they saw, or imagined they saw, in the French way of doing things. Brown's *Estimate* was published in 1757, just as the war was getting under way; but it contained nevertheless some very fulsome praise of French government and society. After commending French professionalism in government in the passage already quoted, Brown went on to say that the undisputed authority enjoyed by the French king was beneficial, in that it gave 'unity and steadiness' to society, while the fact that the French nobility remained true to their feudal and military origins, instead of soiling their hands with making money, was the chief reason why France retained 'her principles and power'.[27]

While Brown thus attacked by implication two of the most cherished tenets of the English, their attachment to limited monarchy and their preference for a flexible social order rather than a feudal hierarchy, another book published in the same year launched an even graver attack on an even more hallowed belief —the belief that England's parliamentary system did more for trade and industry than the economic regulation imposed by the French monarchy. 'Was our African trade ever put on so good a foundation as the French is?' asked Malachy Postlethwayte in his widely read treatise on *Britain's Commercial Interests Explained and Improved.* 'Everyone that is acquainted with its history knows the contrary . . . I profess myself a great admirer of the wisdom and policy of that nation.' What was true of the African trade was also true, he asserted, of all other branches of commerce: the regulations laid down by the French for their

[27] Brown, *Estimate*, i, 140, 203–4.

traders were greatly superior to those which emerged from the confusion and scuffle of the English parliament.

> Of these [the French] laws we shall observe . . . that they are grounded on the representations of the deputies of commerce, made, from time to time, to the royal council of state; that those deputies of commerce are persons well skilled and experienced in those branches of trade about which they lay their sentiments before the royal council; that these laws and regulations in general are derived from a very exact and circumstantial state of the commerce as carried on by the practical merchants and traders.[28]

Postlethwayte was equally impressed with the French government's encouragement of industry. The system of granting exclusive rights or privileges, which to many English observers was a way of putting an intolerable straitjacket on the proper development of industry, seemed to him preferable to the English system of patents.

> The means generally made use of in France to encourage the establishment of manufactures are to purchase at the *public expense* the particular secrets, either for preparing or dying materials, or the engines, whether new or not known there before, and to grant rewards proportioned to the importance of such new undertakings. Those rewards, always judged necessary, are personal distinctions and prerogatives granted to the directors of the undertaking; funds advanced, proper places allotted to save expense at first, till the profits became certain.[29]

One industrialist who would certainly have agreed with Postlethwayte's conclusions was John Kay, inventor of the flying shuttle. Having been ruined by his efforts to protect his patent and get a proper return on his invention, he fled to France, where the government treated him with great generosity. He was paid a substantial pension from government funds and spent most of his time teaching his new techniques of weaving and carding at textile works up and down France. At the time of the publication of Postlethwayte's book he was back in England again, making yet another attempt to get fair treatment; but by June 1758 he had given up the attempt and gone back to France. He spent the

[28] M. Postlethwayte, *Britain's Commercial Interests explained and improved*, 2 vols, 1757, ii, 205, 317, 107–8.
[29] *Ibid.*, ii, 425.

rest of his life there and became closely associated with a cloth factory at Sens which had been established by other disillusioned English industrialists and which was the recipient of particularly generous grants and loans from the French government.[30] An even more influential English exile was John Holker, a Catholic Jacobite refugee whom the *Bureau de Commerce* had made an Inspector General in 1755 with special responsibility for 'those industries which have been established after the manner of foreign ones, and with foreign workmen'. At his own cotton mill at Darnetal near Rouen only a minority of the workpeople were French: the rest were recruited in England either by his agents or by Holker himself during a secret visit which he made to Manchester in 1754. He also provided workers for other manufacturers. Miss Law and Miss Heyes were brought back from England in 1754 to teach spinning in the Bordeaux area and were later paid pensions of 300 livres and 600 livres respectively by the French government.[31]

As well as feeding the skills and secrets of Manchester into the French textile industry, Holker was concerned to feed those of Birmingham into the French hardware industry. To this end he worked closely with another Englishman, Michael Alcock, who had established hardware factories at St Omer near Calais, at La Charité on the Loire, and at St Etienne near Lyon. In May 1756, when it was clear that war with England was imminent, Alcock had asked permission for his friend Mrs Willoughby to go on living at St Omer because she owned land near Birmingham and was useful in getting him the special materials and skilled workmen he needed. By the end of the year Mrs Alcock was asking for a passport to go to England and get workmen for her husband.[32] Daniel Trudaine, commissioner at the *Bureau de Commerce* since 1749 and virtually minister of economic affairs, worked closely with Alcock, getting English prisoners of war released to work in his factories and ensuring that all his skilled

[30] For an account of Kay in France see A. P. Wadsworth and J. de L. Mann, *The Cotton Trade and Industrial Lancashire, 1600–1780*, Manchester, 1931, pp. 457–65. On government grants and loans see E. Depitre, 'Les prêts au commerce et aux manufactures de 1740 à 1789', *R.H.E.S.* ii, 1914, 196–227.

[31] A. Rémond, *John Holker, manufacturier et grand fonctionnaire en France au xviii⁰ siècle*, 1946; Wadsworth and Mann, p. 176; C. Ballot, *L'Introduction du machinisme dans l'industrie française*, 1923. See also W. O. Henderson, *Britain and Industrial Europe, 1750–1870*, Liverpool, 1954.

[32] The two requests, dated 18 May and 9 December 1756, are in A.N. F¹² 1315a.

workmen had exemption from militia service; while Holker arranged government pensions for the workmen who came over and 'gratifications' for Alcock himself for securing them.[38] Meanwhile in England leading men in the iron and hardware industries, such as John Roebuck and Samuel Garbett, were becoming increasingly worried by this drain of skilled workmen to other countries and by the government's failure to take effective measures against it. Garbett finally came to the conclusion that the real trouble was the parliamentary system itself and the fact that industry had to accept as its spokesmen in the House of Commons country gentlemen who didn't understand its needs: 'These old county families,' he wrote to William Burke, 'look upon themselves as the patrons of the trade of the neighbourhood and really have great inclination to serve it when they distinctly understand the subject; but they are seldom troubled; and indeed somebody is sorely wanted who is not only intelligent but hath enlarged views, to take the lead in considering our commerce as a subject of politics.'[34]

This contrast between the attitude of the English government and that of the French did something to justify Postlethwayte's admiration of the latter; but it also bore witness to the fact that the English system, in spite of all the criticisms levelled at it, could at least produce something that the French thought worth stealing. The French government was in fact a great deal more conscious of its own shortcomings, and thus of the need to study and copy the English, than were most of its subjects. Most educated Frenchmen probably had their opinions of England moulded for them by embittered Jacobites or hostile literature; and even when they read literature sympathetic to England they probably drew contrary conclusions from it. Thus the bound volumes of *The Spectator*, which Mornet's researches showed to be one of the most popular works in French private libraries in the eighteenth century,[35] may well have served merely to confirm

[33] Trudaine's correspondence with Alcock and with the army authorities is also in A.N. F[12] 1315a, as are Holker's letters fixing scales of remuneration —150 livres to Alcock for each English workman recruited, plus 100 livres for the man himself.

[34] Garbett to Burke, 4 May 1766; *C.H.O.P.* ii, no. 134. See also nos 82, 203, 309, 314, 320, 329, 350 and *C.H.O.P.* i, nos. 1339, 1359, 1818, 1821, 1919, 1941, 2000 for further material on the suborning of workmen.

[35] D. Mornet, 'Les enseignements des bibliothèques privées, 1750–1780', *Revue d'histoire littéraire de la France*, 1910, pp. 449–96. *The Spectator* was the fifth most popular work in the 500 libraries examined by Mornet. Leblanc and Muralt also came high on his list.

their belief that England was a soulless and mercenary country where honest landed gentlemen like Sir Roger de Coverley had a hard time of it. While most Englishmen who had been to France agreed that the French,[36] for all their faults, were at least a 'social and conversible people', the French found the English ill-mannered and lugubrious. 'A kind of melancholy broods over everything,' reported one observer, 'a sombre and taciturn atmosphere.'[37] Even when they borrowed from the English they quite often finished up by biting the hand that lent to them. The great *Encyclopédie* which Diderot and d'Alembert published from 1751 onwards, and which came later to be seen as one of the great solvents of the old order of things, was inspired by similar works published in England by John Harris, Ephraim Chambers and Thomas Dyche; but many of its contributors, especially Diderot himself, were bitterly critical of the commercialism of English life and the evils to which it led.[38] The French government, on the other hand, knew that English commercial and industrial strength was something to be reckoned with, something to be properly analysed, something to be imitated if at all possible.

A typical and influential anglophile within the ranks of the French bureaucracy was the *Intendant du Commerce*, Vincent de Gournay, an eminent writer on economic theory. While Holker was content to steal English industrial skills and graft them on to the existing French social and economic and administrative structure, de Gournay wanted to change the structure. He believed that government regulation of the economy should be slackened and he was particularly concerned to import into France the social values of England. 'The English constitution is very different from ours,' he once remarked, 'and while her merchants are supported in their determination to make their merchandise as good as possible, in order to maintain a way of life which the whole nation respects, ours are encouraged to make their fortune as soon as possible, without worrying too much about the quality of their goods, in order to buy their way out of business life and into an official position.' While many people in England feared

---

[36] The description is by Robert Adam and is cited by E. Einberg, in the introduction to *The French Taste in English Painting during the first half of the 18th century* (Iveagh Bequest Summer Exhibition catalogue, 1968).

[37] Add. 20, 842, fos. 20–1.

[38] The literature on the *Encyclopédie* is immense: it can usefully be approached *via* J. Lough, *The Encyclopedia of Diderot and d'Alembert: selected articles*, Cambridge, 1954. On Diderot's idealization of the rural life, see below p. 179.

that their social and political system was falling apart because it paid too little attention to the traditional values, there were men in France who thought that those same values were throttling her society and stifling her initiative.[39]

Thus the Seven Years War was a dramatic confrontation between two rival systems which were both beginning to suffer from a nagging unease, a feeling that they had after all something important to learn from their enemies. On the surface there was the clearcut contrast described so vividly by Frederick the Great of Prussia: 'Of all the powers of Europe, France and England had a decided preponderance over the others: the first because of her armies and her great natural resources, the second because of her navies and her commercial wealth. These two powers were rivals, jealous of one another's expansion: they were determined to be arbiters of all Europe and they thought of themselves as captains in whose teams all other kings and princes must enrol themselves.[40] But to some extent the war itself was an attempt to destroy the very contrast out of which it arose. Barnave in the 1790s saw the point, even though he was over-ready to attribute to the Austrian alliance of 1756 a rivalry which in fact ante-dated it by at least a hundred years.

By allying France to Austria the authors of this scheme of things hoped to keep the peace on the continent of Europe so that our resources could be put into building up our navy, weakening England and expanding our own trade. With the same end in view they prepared the ground for the revolt of the English colonies against their mother country, so that when that revolt finally came it had to be given support. Thus arose the war which favoured in three ways the coming of revolution: it filled the nation with ideas of revolt and liberty, it undermined the army's loyalty to the old order and it led to the collapse of the old financial system.[41]

It required considerable acumen to trace this chain of causation backwards from the 1790s: to foresee it all from the 1750s would have needed something like clairvoyance. But the duc de Choiseul, French foreign secretary from December 1758, cer-

[39] These remarks were made to Pradier, an inspector of manufactures, who reported them in a letter dated 21 October 1753: it is cited in Bacquié, *Les Inspecteurs*, p. 25.

[40] Frederic II, *Mémoires*, eds E. Boutaric and E. Campardon, 2 vols, 1866, i, 69–70.

[41] A-J-M-P. Barnave, *Introduction à la Révolution française*, ed. F. Rude (*Cahiers des Annales* no. 15), 1960, p. 54.

tainly foresaw quite a lot of it. In the first place, he understood England a great deal better than either the rabid anglophobes or the starry-eyed anglophiles. He saw that her apparently insatiable commercial and colonial ambitions were a danger not only to France but to the whole of Europe: 'France,' he said in 1760, 'protects the commerce of Europe against English ambition.'[42] Postlethwayte himself had made these ambitions clear enough. For all his praise of France he had nevertheless concluded that it was not only desirable but also possible 'to throw the balance of trade so effectively into the hands of Great Britain as to put the constant balance of power in Europe into her hands'.[43] There was no longer any question—if, indeed, there ever had been—of the English doing as Louis XIV had hoped and keeping out of continental affairs. They had embarked on an irreversible career of maritime expansion and in doing so they had developed techniques of financial manipulation and representative government which helped them on their way. These techniques would sooner or later push their way into Europe and it was no good trying to keep them out with a smokescreen of feudal nostalgia. If France was to keep what was best in the traditional values she could only do so by taking her pick of the new ones now and not by waiting until they swamped her.

Choiseul's enemies accused him of being deliberately subversive, of encouraging revolution not only in America but in France as well. It was said that he was secretly in league with the *parlements* and encouraged them to defy his own colleagues and even his royal master. In modern times he has been acclaimed as a herald of the democratic age. 'He was essentially a Frenchman before being a subject of Louis XV,' wrote one biographer at the beginning of this century, 'and when absolutism and national liberties clashed he took the part of the nation. . . . It is no exaggeration to say that he had the spirit of a constitutional minister, to whom the will of the people is the supreme law.'[44] It is in fact not only an exaggeration but also a distortion to say anything of the sort: Choiseul had an essentially authoritarian turn of mind and he would have had little patience with phrases like 'the will of the people'. He had a great admiration for the English constitution (towards the end of his life he came to think that it

[42] Cited A. Christelow, 'The economic background of the Anglo-Spanish war of 1762', *J.M.H.* xviii, 1946, p. 26.
[43] Postlethwayte, *Commercial Interests*, ii, 551.
[44] R. H. Soltau, *The Duke de Choiseul*, Oxford, 1909, p. 128.

was the best there was, even for the king), but he deplored the insubordination and factiousness that marked English political life. He had one aim—to make France strong enough and efficient enough to beat the English at their own game. In order to do so he was prepared to copy English industrial and commercial techniques, English methods of naval and colonial warfare and even English representative institutions. If a dialogue between the government and the *parlements* made it easier to collect essential taxes and to modernize French society and administration, then a dialogue there must be. 'Under Choiseul,' a recent historian of eighteenth-century France has written, 'capitulation to the *parlements* almost became official policy.'[45] And at the same time there was a quickening interest in new ideas of all kinds, many of them traceable to England. France had never been so deeply influenced by England as she was in her moment of confrontation with her.

The elder Pitt was in many ways the English counterpart of Choiseul. He too came to power in the dark days at the beginning of the Seven Years War and claimed to be a Patriot, to stand for the nation as a whole rather than the aristocratic cliques which, in England as in France, tended to dominate the Court and the upper reaches of the administration. He was, he insisted, 'a man standing single and daring to appeal to his country at large';[46] and he described Newcastle, the most influential politician among the old cliques, as 'the wretch who draws the great families at his heels'.[47] As Choiseul was determined to match and master England's commercial power, so Pitt was determined to stop him: 'France,' he said, 'is chiefly, if not solely, to be dreaded by us in the light of a maritime and commercial power.'[48] As rabid xenophobes, as Patriot ministers and as advocates of commercialism, the two men were well matched.

On the other hand, Pitt did not repay the compliment of emulation which Choiseul paid to England and to English institutions: he could see few if any ways in which England could learn from France. It was only as Pitt started to lose ground in

[45] A. Cobban, 'The *parlements* of France in the eighteenth century', *History*, xxxv, 1950, pp. 64–80. See also the violent attack on Choiseul's *parlementaire* policies by his enemy Favier, printed by Flammermont in *Révolution Française*, xxxvi, 1899, pp. 161–84, 258–76, 314–35, 415–62.
[46] Pitt to Newcastle, 19 October 1764; Add. 32, 962, fo. 349.
[47] Pitt to Bute, 28 June 1757; printed in *Essays presented to Sir Lewis Namier*, ed. R. Pares and A. J. P. Taylor, 1956, p. 125.
[48] Speech of 9 December 1762; *P.H.* xv, 1265.

the latter stages of the Seven Years War, defeated politically by his very successes on the battlefield, that the admirers of France began to make themselves heard again in English politics. Even as early as 1759, at the height of his great 'year of victories', Pitt himself could see that the successes of his commercial war might have divisive and dangerous consequences. 'Some are for keeping Canada, some Guadeloupe,' he observed wryly, 'who will tell me which I shall be hanged for not keeping?'[49] While some sugar planters wanted to bring Guadeloupe into the British empire, others feared competition from it and wanted it kept out. As for Canada, that aroused even deeper and more elemental fears: 'Are we not the only people upon earth, except Spain,' wrote one pamphleteer, 'that ever thought of establishing a colony ten times more extensive than our own . . . if it does not become our master it may soon, very soon, stand our powerful rival in all branches of trade.'[50] In the later years of the war, as the trading boom gave way to depression, a full-scale reaction set in against the war and against those commercial interests which were supposed to have promoted it. Real or imaginary scandals, about private individuals who had furthered their interests under the guise of public enterprises, dominated the political scene. Each new conquest brought new problems: it would be inglorious to give it back, yet it might prove ruinous to keep it. What with the expense of acquiring them, the difficulties of governing them and the impossibility of restraining them—to say nothing of the apparently catastrophic effects they were having on the economy of the home country—these new fields of commercial enterprise seemed to be a great deal more trouble than they were worth.

It was against this background that Bedford, whose admiration for France had been rendered so unfashionable by the outbreak of war, sought to make his comeback. In July 1761 he wrote a letter to Bute, Pitt's fellow secretary of state, pointing out the dangerous consequences which might flow from the determination of Pitt and his commercial friends to hold out for stiff peace

[49] H. Walpole, *Memoirs of the Reign of George III*, ed. G. F. R. Barker, 4 vols, 1894, i, 26.
[50] *Reasons for Keeping Guadeloupe at a Peace, Preferable to Canada*, 1761. The controversy over Canada and Guadeloupe, which produced over sixty pamphlets between 1759 and 1763, is studied in W. L. Grant, 'Canada versus Guadeloupe, an episode in the Seven Years War', *Am.H.R.* xvii, 1912, pp. 735–43. A bibliography of the pamphlets is given in C. W. Alvord, *The Mississippi Valley in British Politics*, 2 vols, Cleveland, 1917 (reprint New York, 1959), ii, 253–64.

terms. 'The endeavouring to drive France out of any naval power is fighting against nature,' he declared, 'and can tend to do no good to this country; but, on the contrary, must excite all the naval powers of Europe against us, as adopting a system—viz, that of a monopoly of all naval power—which would be at least as dangerous to the liberties of Europe as that of Louis XIV, which drew all Europe on his back.'[51] It was a convincing argument and one which became more and more popular as the reaction against Pitt's commercial war grew. When in the following year the comte de Viry, Sardinian ambassador in London, agreed to act as the channel for secret peace talks, he made it clear to the French that the duke of Bedford was swiftly becoming the central figure in English politics. In due course Bedford was sent to Paris to negotiate the definitive peace treaty with the French and when the task was completed, to his own satisfaction though by no means to that of Pitt, he received the most fulsome congratulations and thanks from George III. By the autumn of 1763, after Pitt, Newcastle and Bute had all resigned in steady succession, Bedford remained the most senior and in many ways the most influential figure in the cabinet. The French foreign office regarded him as the prime minister of England—as did many politicians in England as well, for the first lord of the treasury, George Grenville, seemed of little account—and the French ambassador in London was instructed to take great pains to cultivate him.[52]

While the French conducted an inquest on their defeat, trying to find out why they had failed to match England's commercial strength and resolving to build up their industrial and mercantile and naval resources in order to challenge her again, the English conducted an inquest on victory which was just as searching and just as self-critical. The writer in the *Annual Register* who insisted in 1767 that any statesman who would cure England's economic and social ills 'must be deaf to all mercantile applications for opening new inlets of commerce at the public expense',[53] was speaking for a generation which wanted to turn its back once and for all on the expensive and dissipating game of colonial warfare.

---

[51] *Correspondence of John, Fourth Duke of Bedford*, ed. Lord John Russell, 3 vols, 1842–46, iii, 26.

[52] P. Vaucher, ed. *Receuil des instructions données aux ambassadeurs et ministres de France, xxv, 2: Angleterre, tome 3 (1698–1791)*, 1965, p. 415. A précis of Viry's views is in *H.M.C.* ii, 3rd Rep., App. I, *Lansdowne*, p. 131b.

[53] *Annual Register*, 1767, pt ii, 171–2.

The colonies, old as well as new, were already beginning to justify the worst fears of those who had prophesied that they would neither govern themselves nor submit to being governed. There was talk of vast new armies of placemen, both civil and military, to keep them under control—they were becoming, as one ambitious young lawyer wrote hopefully to the patronage secretary at the Treasury, 'every day more and more the object of civil government'[54]—and this at a time when the idealism of the young king George III at last gave reason to hope that the old system of corruption and placehunting would be reformed. The hopes and fears of the time were summed up by Goldsmith in *The Traveller*:

> But when contending chiefs blockade the throne,
> Contracting regal power to stretch their own,
> When I behold a factious band agree
> To call it freedom when themselves are free;
> Each wanton judge new penal statutes draw,
> Laws grind the poor, and rich men rule the law;
> The wealth of climes, where savage nations roam,
> Pillag'd from slaves to purchase slaves at home;
> Fear, pity, justice, indignation start,
> Tear off reserve, and bare my swelling heart;
> 'Till half a patriot, half a coward grown
> I fly from petty tyrants to the throne.[55]

All the doubts which Brown had had back in 1757 when he published the *Estimate*—doubts about the superiority of limited monarchy over absolute rule, doubts about the party system and parliamentary government, doubts about the results of unbridled commercialism—had now become subjects for open political discussion. Logically, therefore, the English should have been prepared to do what Brown himself had done: turn to France to see if they managed things better there. If the French inquest on defeat implied a need to copy England, the English inquest on victory implied just as clearly a need to copy France.

The English, however, were not made that way. Many years earlier Muralt had observed that the English 'are content with thinking their own way of living the best, and allow the rest of the world may govern themselves as they think fit'.[56] Even

[54] James Marriott to Charles Jenkinson 7 April 1765; Add. 38, 204, fo. 186.
[55] O. Goldsmith, *Collected works*, ed. A. Friedman, 5 vols, Oxford, 1966, iv, 265–6.
[56] Muralt, *Letters*, p. 174.

more revealing was the comment of a certain Mr Read, who bought in October 1763 a copy of a play of Favart's called *L'Anglais à Bordeaux*. It had been produced in March of that year by the players in ordinary to the French king and seems to have marked a genuine attempt to promote reconciliation and good relations between the two countries. Read wrote on the fly-leaf of his copy:

> I have preserved *L'Anglais à Bordeaux* not for any merit in the work, but as a mark of the joy which the French received at the Peace: they were so glad of it that the author got a pension for his play of 1200 livres. I think he says somewhere *'Deux nations faites pour s'entre estimer'*—which is vainly begging a foolish question, for the English despise and imitate the French and the French esteem without imitating the English.

A Frenchman into whose hands the book later passed wrote disgustedly under this: *'L'outrecuidance anglaise qui n'est que trop commune.'*[57] And well he might, for Read's self-satisfied remarks had completely missed the point. To him imitation of the French probably meant the rage for French clothes, French etiquette, French hairdressers and French cooks—a rage which according to most Englishmen was something they despised and in which they only indulged in order to please their wives. He appears to have been incapable of understanding the point which Goldsmith had made with incisive clarity in his *Citizen of the World* letters: 'The English and the French seem to place themselves foremost among the champion states of Europe. Though parted by a narrow sea, yet are they entirely of opposite characters; and from their vicinity are taught to fear and admire each other.'[58]

In that phrase 'fear and admire' was the kernel of the whole matter. Intelligent men in each country knew that the other had things which their own country lacked and which it neglected at its peril. The English feared French absolutism and Catholicism, but they also knew that these things gave France a stability and strength which they themselves sometimes envied—and never more than now, when their very victories seemed to have brought their divisive and centrifugal system of politics to the verge of collapse. The French feared English commercialism, but they also

[57] C. S. Favart, *L'Anglais à Bordeaux*, 1763. The comments quoted are in the copy in the British Museum, catalogued under shelf mark 11737 cc. 17(1).
[58] Goldsmith, *Collected works*, ii, 72.

realized that it gave England a dynamism which they found both admirable and desirable, especially now in their moment of defeat and humiliation. Neither country could solve its problems without taking one or perhaps more leaves from the other's book, yet each had to surmount formidable barriers of chauvinism and prejudice before it could do so. As the disintegration of the old order of things gathered pace on both sides of the Channel it became more and more difficult to formulate constructive measures of reform without such borrowings, even though the borrowings themselves might lead to new tensions and further disintegration. It was in this way, constantly tripping up themselves and one another with their ties of fear and admiration, that the two countries shuffled towards their twin revolutions.

3 *The aftermath of war*

The Seven Years War brought the paradoxical problems of
Anglo-French relations into sharper focus than ever before;
and it also projected them onto a wider screen than ever before,
a screen that was as wide as the world itself. As well as being the
first world war, in the sense that it was the first war to be fought
for the domination of the whole globe, the Seven Years War was
also the first war in which the two worlds of land and money
were brought face to face. Two opposing visions of society, one
based on the static hierarchical world of land and one based on
the dynamic mercurial world of money, confronted one another.
It was a confrontation that took place not simply between one
belligerent and another but within the warring nations themselves: it was the central issue in the internal politics of England
and of France, as well as being the central issue in the relations
between them. The two peace treaties of 1763 were in themselves sufficient to point the contrast. That concluded between
the powers of eastern Europe changed almost nothing: after
seven years of bitter fighting all they could do was to put things
back more or less as they had been before. The other, signed by

Britain and France and Spain, changed the face of the whole world. A few campaigns, fought at a fraction of the cost of the great battles in Germany, had sufficed to bring vast tracts of territory under British control. It was hardly surprising, therefore, that those who had managed to sway the rod of maritime empire should be impatient with those who clung to the cool sequestered vale of agrarian life.

And yet the rod of empire was not easy to sway. If the French had had it snatched from their hands they could at least console themselves with watching its dire effects on the English politicians who tried to wield it. George III, the idealistic young king of England who had succeeded to the throne in the middle of the war, made no secret of the fact that he disliked both the war itself and the divisive system of party politics which in his opinion had brought it about. But apart from bringing his personal friend Lord Bute into the government he did little to force his views on his ministers: on the contrary, he stood by patiently while they allowed their wrangles over the peace terms to render them even more impotent and divided than they already were. Pitt resigned in 1761, leaving to others the task of making a peace which was almost bound to be unpopular and which he hoped to oppose successfully in due course. And as Pitt's dashing and colourful brand of warfare grew unpopular so the traditional military and political establishment which it had elbowed aside in 1757 began to make its comeback. The king's uncle, the duke of Cumberland, who had been forced to retire as commander in chief in 1757 and had since spent his time breeding racehorses, now began to stir himself as the defender of the Whig power structure both against the impudence of Pitt and against the real or imaginary reforming zeal of his own nephew. Newcastle and the other Whig leaders left the government to join him in this enterprise. Thus the war, which had already played havoc with the economic and social order of things, finished up by producing political divisions that robbed the king of most of the ministerial talent that he needed if he was to solve the problems it had bequeathed and exploit the victories it had brought. War, traditionally the great testing time for any régime, had certainly tested the English political system to the limits of its endurance.

Like many other less sophisticated but equally ritualistic social groups, the English politicians found that their king was an ideal scapegoat for their sins. With breathtaking obtuseness they con-

vinced themselves and others that the slightest nuances of royal
behaviour were somehow more destructive of political stability
than the effects of the most cataclysmic war the country had ever
fought. The almost impossible position in which the king had
been placed came to be seen not as the result but as the cause of
the confused political situation that the war had left behind it. One
major consequence of the war was that there were very few politicians left with enough in common to form a government; but
when those few tried to cope as best they could with problems
others had created for them they were constantly reviled as the
tyrannous favourites of a king who had excluded all others from
his councils.

In France the king was discredited not because he had
abandoned a war that was too successful but because he had been
responsible for a war that was not successful enough. Most of
the generals who had followed one another into disgrace and
retirement had been personal favourites of the king, and one of
them, Clermont, had been a prince of the blood. It had been
widely supposed in 1756 that the war sprang from a personal
desire of the king to avenge insults offered by Prussia to the family
of his son's wife; and since his son the dauphin was a devout and
rigid churchman the disrepute of the monarchy rubbed off on to
the Church. Anti-clericalism had long been one of the most
powerful disruptive forces in France; and now the war had made
it even more dangerous. The English ambassador in Paris told his
government that France was on the eve of a religious revolution
and the Rev. William Cole, when he visited France in 1765,
thought that 'the present situation of France has much the
appearance of being soon the theatre of civil war'. Though an
Anglican, Cole was one of those who greatly preferred the subordination and conformity achieved by the Catholic Church in
France to the more tolerant religious atmosphere in his own
country; and now he was shocked to find that subordination
threatened. 'That restless republican spirit of Calvin will never
be at quiet till the monarchy and hierarchy are laid level with
their idol of equality', he concluded gloomily.[1]

More specifically, the war had intensified the attack on the
Jesuits. Among the many French commercial enterprises ruined

---

[1] Hertford to Halifax, 21 February 1765, P.R.O. S.P. 78/265, fos 207–8;
W. Cole, *Journal of my Journey to Paris in the year 1765*, ed. F. G. Stokes,
1931, pp. 96, 95.

by the war was one established at Martinique by the Jesuits; and the Paris *parlement* had been only too glad to use the complaints of outraged creditors as an opportunity for a hostile inquisition into the doings of the order as a whole. The king tried to stem the tide by taking the investigation into his own hands and forbidding the *parlement* to take any action against the Jesuits; but the *parlement*, assisted by its counterparts in the provinces, ignored the royal command and issued on its own authority declarations which in effect dissolved the order. The royal council hurried along behind, doing its best to look as though it was leading rather than following, and in February 1763 it issued an edict setting up *bureaux d'administration* to decide what should be done with the schools and colleges previously under Jesuit control. This was the signal for a spate of proposals for a brand new secular system of national education, most of which laid emphasis on technical rather than on classical accomplishments, and advocated modern languages (especially English, 'which has become essential for scientific studies')[2] rather than Latin and Greek. None of these projects came to anything, but one of them gained for its author —La Chalotais, a lawyer of the *parlement* of Rennes in Brittany and author of one of the many hysterical accounts of Jesuit misdoings which had appeared in 1761 and 1762—an acclaim which was to help him in future conflicts with the king's authority. Most important of all, the campaign against the Jesuits gave the *parlements* of France as a whole valuable experience of joint action. Recent research has shown that they were not very good at it (the *parlements* of Aix and Grenoble, in particular, were badly out of step) but to many people they seemed to have justified their proud and potentially revolutionary claim to form one single national assembly of France, representative of her people and guardian of her laws.[3]

George III in England and the Jesuits in France were not the only ones to suffer as a result of the postwar hunt for scapegoats. Popular opinion in England quickly fastened its teeth into its

[2] L. R. Caradeuc de la Chalotais, *Essai d'éducation nationale*, s.l., 1763, p. 70.
[3] For statements of this theory see J. Flammermont, ed. *Remontrances du parlement de Paris au xviii*e *siècle*, 3 vols, 1888–98, especially the remonstrances of 9 April 1753 (i, 506–614), 22 August 1756 (ii, 130–48) and 26 December 1763 (ii, 414–23). On the lack of a consistent policy towards the Jesuits see J. Egret, 'Le procès des Jésuites devant les parlements de France, 1761–1770', *R.H.* cciv, 1950, pp. 1–27. See also L. Mention, *Documents relatifs aux rapports du clergé avec la royauté de 1705 à 1789*, 1903.

usual prey, the swarm of sinecurists and contractors and government creditors who were generally supposed to have diverted into
their own pockets the vast sums that taxpayers had raised to
finance the war. William Aislabie, a typical placeman who made a
great deal of money from his post as auditor of the imprest, provided an introit for these days of judgement when he admitted
openly in the Commons in February 1763 that his place had been
made even more profitable by the 'large and expensive schemes'
which Pitt and his commercial friends had promoted during the
war.[4] One of those friends had been Samuel Touchet, a contractor
and financier who had provided large sums of his own money to
finance expeditions against the French in West Africa. This was
less altruistic than it seemed, since he was concerned to ensure his
supplies of the Senegal gum which was vital for the linen and
calico printing that formed one of his many commercial and
industrial interests. He was clever enough to keep himself in
favour with the new government, even after some of his closest
fellow contractors had been sacked as friends of Newcastle, but
he was not clever enough to resist the tide of unpopularity. He
went bankrupt in the autumn of 1763 and several of his compeers
in the City hurriedly promoted a Bill to stop him from using his
position as an M.P. to shield himself from bankruptcy proceedings. The new attorney general refused to sanction the seven-
year charter for African trade, which Pitt had promised him as a
reward for his money, and an infuriated House of Commons
refused to listen to its own committee when it reported favourably
on his claim for compensation. His friends in the government
finally managed to get his compensation for him and when Pitt
came back to power Touchet regained some of his political
importance, being rewarded with grants of land in the colonies.
But his reputation, like those of many others associated with Pitt's
colonial warfare, never recovered from the accusations of pro-
fiteering which had been made against him.[5] Even the commanders in the field did not escape: Robert Clive, who had done
more than any other man to end French power in India, was to
be hounded for the rest of his life by those who distrusted the
commercialism and self-seeking of the East India Company and its
servants.

    [4] *Commons, 1754–90*, ii, 14.
    [5] *Ibid.*, iii, 533–6. See also Wadsworth and Mann, *Cotton Trade*,
pp. 244–6.

The French, like the English, were eager to turn on those who had lent money to the government; and in France it was easier to do so because a particular set of men, the Company of General Farmers, were popularly thought to have a monopoly of such lending. Every five years they came to an agreement with the government whereby they advanced it a certain sum of money each year in return for the right to collect the indirect taxes for the ensuing year. These consisted of the *traites* and the *aides*, roughly corresponding to the customs and excise, together with the salt tax, the tobacco tax and a host of miscellaneous dues. It was popularly believed that the tax farmers, as well as making exhorbitant profits out of the actual collection of the taxes, were solely responsible for the indebtedness of the government and encouraged it in order to screw up the rates of interest they could charge. In fact the creditors of the government included all kinds of people, often of quite modest means, who held government stocks of one sort or another. Corporations of all kinds, including the Church and the local estates of such provinces as Languedoc and Provence, also lent to the government on a large scale, as did many foreign financiers. Even the king himself had stocks in the Company of General Farmers, so that his private person lent money to his public person at a considerable profit. But in the popular view all this was beside the point: the word *financiers* had had its meaning narrowed down from money-lenders in general to the tax farmers in particular and it was they alone who were thought to hold the nation's fortune in pawn and who must be made to disgorge.[6]

As in the case of the Jesuits, the *parlements* and their pamphleteers launched the attack. On 31 May 1763, just as the Paris *parlement* was being forced to register two new tax edicts against which it had remonstrated violently, there was circulated throughout the city a work called *The Riches of the State*. It was by Roussel de la Tour, who had put his talents to the service of the *parlement* the year before in order to produce a highly coloured report on Jesuit malpractices. It was followed by a deluge of similar works, all of them bitterly critical of the so-

---

[6] See G. T. Matthews, *The Royal General Farms in eighteenth-century France*, New York, 1958. P. Clement and A. Le Moine, *Silhouette, Bouret et les derniers fermiers généraux*, 1872, and H. Thirion, *La Vie privée des financiers au xviii⁰ siècle*, 1895 are still useful for the insights they give into the reasons for the financiers' unpopularity. See also Y. Durand, *Les Fermiers Généraux au xviii⁰ siècle*, 1971.

called *financiers* and culminating in Darigrand's immensely
popular *The Anti-financier*. By November English secret agents
on the continent were passing back to the treasury in London
reports that all the tax farmers were to be dismissed in a matter
of days.[7]

The reports were without foundation. Neither Louis XV nor
his ministers were in the mood to jettison the tax farmers as tamely
as they had jettisoned the Jesuits. Whereas the Society of Jesus
had dealt in spiritual and educational matters, the Company of
General Farmers dealt in hard cash. Their kingdom was of this
world and it could not be allowed to pass away while the
parlements argued among themselves as to how to replace it. An
edict was issued inviting the *parlements* to send in plans for
financial reform and at the same time forbidding anyone else to
publish anything further on the subject (a provision which in the
circumstances was as useful as restricting to cannibals a debate
on the propriety of eating human flesh), but in the meantime the
tax farmers continued to function. Few *parlements* bothered to
send in their plans and those few illustrated once again the divisive
and centrifugal tendencies which lay behind the grandiose talk of
a nationwide representative and consultative body. The *parlement*
of Aix turned in an intelligent and constructive report which
stressed the need to maintain government credit by prompt payment of debts, but from other provinces there came suggestions
for the wholesale repudiation of debts.[8]

English politicians studied the French crisis with interest and
with a good deal of complacency, collecting the pamphlets that
were published and lending them to each other with accompany-
ing comments.[9] Charles Jenkinson, secretary at the Treasury, had
various channels of information on French finances, including an

---

[7] Add. 38, 201, fos 228–9. The pamphlet warfare is best studied in
*Economie et population: les doctrines françaises avant 1800, bibliographie
générale commentée*, published by the Institut National d'études démographiques, 1956, especially items 281, 1625, 3275, 3276, 3356, 3966, 4554,
4556, 4570, 4577, 4605, 4723, 4746, 4802.

[8] The response of the *parlement* of Aix has been published by P. H. Beik
under the title *A Judgement of the Old Regime: being a survey by the
Parlement of Provence . . .* (*Columbia studies in history, economics and
public law*, no. 509), New York, 1944. The reactions of the other *parlements*
are summarized in M. Marion, *Histoire financière de la France depuis 1715*,
6 vols, 1914–31, i, 207, 233–5.

[9] See for instance Add. 35, 636, fo. 418, a letter from Hanbury to Yorke,
30 December 1763, sending him *Les Richesses de l'Etat* (which he had himself
borrowed from another friend) and looking forward to having the next
pamphlet soon. See also Add. 21, 622, fos 30–54.

agent in Rotterdam who forwarded reports from his spies in Paris
—most of whom were remarkably ill-informed and unreliable.
'The French ministers are making useless efforts to improve their
finances,' Jenkinson wrote loftily as one groundless report
succeeded another in his dispatch box, 'I say useless for anything
I have hitherto heard of is either trifling in its nature or not likely
to succeed in the execution of it.' His agent replied dutifully in
the same tone, doubting the French government's ability to offer
any acceptable security for loans as long as it was embroiled with
the *parlements*, and dismissing out of hand reports that it was
about to raise a large loan at low interest on the money market
of Amsterdam.[10]

Yet there was little enough reason for complacency in England,
where the national debt was about three times as much per head
of the population as in France and the difficulties of paying it off
just as great. In the autumn of 1763 there were failures at Berlin,
Hamburg and Amsterdam which led to fears of bankruptcies and
a serious credit crisis in the City of London as well. Opposition
leaders told one another with increasing assurance that the
ministry was on the point of collapse because the financiers could
not or would not give it credit.[11] When Samuel Touchet stopped
payment on 21 October 1763 there were rumours that some of
the government's closest financial backers, in particular George
Amyand, were involved in his collapse. The ministry took these
stories so seriously that when they were repeated in the *Paris
Gazette* the English ambassador in Paris, Lord Hertford, was
instructed to obtain for Amyand an official apology from the
French government. Hertford, who was a great Whig grandee
and no lover of jumped-up financiers, had little heart for the job
and thought it quite sufficient when the French inserted a correc-
tion in the *Gazette*. He was extremely irritated when the secretary
of state told him that Amyand merely regarded this as a fresh

[10] Jenkinson to Wolters (copy) 22 May 1764, Add. 38, 304, fo. 22; Wolters
to Jenkinson 19 October 1764, Add. 38, 203, fo. 194. Jenkinson continued
to receive secret reports on French financial affairs throughout the 1760s:
see Add. 38, 201–38, 206, *passim*. His papers also contain careful analyses
of documents on the same subject—see Add. 38, 373, fos 200–3, an abstract
of the *parlement* of Bordeaux's memoir of 1764. His early efforts to find
sources of information are shown in *H.M.C.* 7, 8th Rep. App. I, *Braybrooke*,
p. 285a.

[11] Newcastle to Cumberland, 10 September 1763; Cumberland to Newcastle, 13 September 1763; Newcastle to Hardwicke, 3 October 1763: Add.
32950, fos 381–2; 32, 951, fos 17–18, 265–70. See also Newcastle to Charles
Townshend, 29 April 1764, *H.M.C.* 49, *Stopford-Sackville*, i, p. 60.

insult. Amyand, he wrote, should be very grateful that 'his interests in this affair have been treated with as great seriousness as if they had involved the greatest national concern'. The truth was, however, that they *were* of the greatest national concern, for the credit of Amyand and men like him was indispensable to the government's stability. But Hertford regarded the matter as closed after he had a final interview with the French foreign secretary Praslin at which the latter showed very clearly what he thought of a government that encouraged the impertinence of upstarts. 'We shall ask the King of England's pardon,' replied Monsieur de Praslin, 'if we have any way offended him, but for Mr Amyand, he must really be so good as to excuse us.'[12]

Most people in England shared the French suspicion and contempt for financiers and wanted to wipe out the national debt as soon as possible in order to free the nation from its enslavement to such men. It was all very well for Jenkinson to look down on the French government's 'trifling efforts' and to be shocked when it issued an edict for the partial repudiation of its debts, but there were those among his masters who envied the French their ability to deal so highhandedly with their creditors. Even though the English had perfected the devices of government credit manipulation and had won an empire as a result of them, they did not necessarily approve of them. Certainly they were very far from the modern view which sees an enormous and unrepayable national debt as something acceptable and even beneficial. Even George Grenville himself, the first lord of the treasury who had to wrestle with the postwar financial problems, wrote later that the recent extension of government credit brought with it terrible risks and that 'France, bankrupt France, had no such calamities impending over her'.[13] Arthur Young, that doughty champion of hardworking farmers against the parasitical world of financial speculation, put the point even more dramatically in his *Letters Concerning the Present State of the French Nation*. Having pointed out somewhat smugly that the French government, because of its despotic nature, could not command the same

[12] Hertford to Halifax, 18 December 1763, 21 December 1763: P.R.O. S.P. 78/259, fos 156, 189. Amyand's correspondence with Jenkinson is in Add. 38, 202, fos 206, 327; 38, 203, fo. 258; 38, 204, fos 30, 62, 85, 90.
[13] (G. Grenville and W. Knox) *Present State of the Nation*, 1768, p. 14. This work, published in France in 1769 and openly attributed to Grenville, played an important part in the French debate on finance as well as in the English. It was probably translated by Israel Mauduit, himself a bitter critic of Pitt's costly wars.

resources of credit as were available in a free country, he nevertheless concluded: 'In short, in whatever light we consider public credit in general, and that of England in particular, we have the strongest reason to give to France in this article the palm of superiority, in the *want* of that which some are so blind as to admire.'[14]

In the House of Commons there was violent opposition to any suggestion of further borrowing by the government and Pitt once declared that if Grenville had recourse to such expedients he would oppose him even if he were so ill that he had to come to the house swathed in blankets.[15] And yet the same people who rejected government borrowing also rejected the ministry's attempts to pursue the alternative policy of additional taxes. Pitt was particularly irresponsible and unconstructive in his opposition to the excise on cider, by means of which the government hoped to raise some £750,000 a year to tide them over their postwar difficulties. When Grenville challenged him to suggest other means of raising the necessary revenue he merely replied with cheap insults; and in his campaign against the tax he had strong support from the cider-producing counties. The Tory gentlemen of Devonshire were even prepared at one stage to make common cause with the Newcastle Whigs whom they had hated for so long, if only it would help to defeat the new tax. Lord Strange, who sat in the Commons for the county of Lancashire and had the reputation of an independent man who 'in or out of employment always acts according to the dictates of conscience', once stated roundly in the House that the campaign against the tax was local and not national in character: 'it was the private interest of the gentlemen of the cider counties which made them against it'.[16] Henry Legge, who had been chancellor of the exchequer during the war and was now in opposition, put the same point from a more hostile angle when he asserted that the ministry was deliberately setting the eastern corn-producing counties against those in the west that grew apples for cider.[17] As in the case of France, the attempt to present a united national opposition to government policies succeeded only in revealing and widening the very cracks

[14] A. Young, *Letters Concerning the Present State of the French Nation*, 1769, 425.
[15] Add. 32, 952, fos 143–6.
[16] Add. 32, 962, fos 329–67; 36, 796, fo. 66; *Commons 1754–90*, iii, 453–5.
[17] Legge to Newcastle, 8 February 1764, Add. 32, 955, fos 393–4.

C

that it tried to ignore. Of all the problems that were exacerbated by the war and its aftermath, this one of the centrifugal and localized nature of eighteenth-century society was the most intractable.

It was manifested in many other ways as well as the hunt for scapegoats and the drive to avoid taxes. Such things were after all only part of the ugly heritage that war left behind it. The comte de Guibert described the full extent of that heritage when he wrote some years later:

> Wars exhaust victor and vanquished alike. The volume of national debts grows. Credit is low and money is short. It is impossible to find sailors for the fleets or soldiers for the armies. Statesmen on either side see that it is time to negotiate. A peace is patched up. A few colonies or provinces changed hands. Usually nothing is done to remove the cause of the conflict and each side is left sitting on its own debris, busily paying back its debts and preparing for the reopening of war.[18]

Thus the real difficulty was not simply that the war had to be paid for, with all the financial and administrative and political strains that this involved; it was that this had to be done against a background of uncertainty. There was uncertainty as to the permanence of the peace and the intentions of the erstwhile enemy, and this brought in its train fierce controversy about defence expenditure. Worse still, there was controversy and uncertainty as to the value of the colonies and provinces that had changed hands. The French government had to convince its critics at home that it had kept what was valuable and conceded what was useless, while the ministry in London had somehow to silence those who said it had thrown away priceless conquests for the sake of acquisitions that would never be profitable and might well be a liability. And on top of all this there was the age-old tendency of the English and the French to use each other as sticks with which to belabour their own governments. Any government that did too little would soon find itself attacked by malcontents who pointed out how quickly the other country was outstripping it; but if it did too much those same malcontents would be sure to accuse it of imposing on its people the hated ways of the other country.

Almost inevitably these problems involved any government

[18] J. A. H. de Guibert, *Oeuvres militaires*, 5 vols, 1803, i, 15–16.

that tried to deal with them in accusations of tyranny and unconstitutional behaviour. The 1760s were marked, on both sides of the Channel, by a universal eagerness to rediscover and idealize ancient constitutions. While the *parlements* of France talked of a hallowed constitution under which they were acknowledged guardians of the 'fundamental laws' of the French monarchy, the English brought to a triumphant climax that favourite game of makebelieve which turned the hurried expedients of 1688 and 1689 into an integrated piece of constitutional wisdom. While politicians, including the king himself, declaimed constantly about the constitution and claimed to be able to smell out breaches of it with the facility of bloodhounds, writers of all kinds published learned expositions of its exact nature. All such accounts, from ponderous legal treatises like Blackstone's to virulent political pamphlets like Burke's, left out the one important point about the constitutional arrangements of 1688–89—the fact that they provided no link between the executive power of the king and legislative power of parliament. The constitution could only be made to work at all by providing such a link—and this had been done by patronage and corruption, by the government's placemen supporting it in parliament. Those who now attacked corruption claimed that they wanted to restore a perfect constitution to its original pristine purity, but in fact they sought to remove from an extremely imperfect constitution the makeshift contrivance that enabled it to function. They also claimed, with quite extraordinary naïvety, that if only the constitution were properly respected the conflict between public good and private interest would somehow disappear. 'Nature inclines men everywhere to love the society they are members of,' wrote one pious optimist in 1764, 'but where a constitution excels, as in Great Britain, the passion ought to be proportionally stronger. Yet even here we find that self-passions and private systems often warp and bias its course.'[19] Such admonitions were powerless to improve a constitution which gave a central place to that House of Commons which even Burke, a devout worshipper of the constitution, feared would soon become 'a confused and scuffling bustle of local agency'.[20]

In France the accusations of tyranny and the appeals to a real or imaginary constitution were sparked off by the edicts of April

[19] Anon, *A View of the Internal Policy of Great Britain*, 1764, p. iv.
[20] Cited R. Pares, *King George III and the Politicians*, Oxford 1953, p. 3.

1763, by which Bertin, the controller-general of finance, sought to turn the temporary wartime tax known as the *vingtième* into a permanent source of revenue. He also decreed the compilation of a *cadastre*, or general register of property throughout the kingdom, so that assessments for *vingtièmes* and other direct taxes could be made more realistic. Even under existing conditions the *vingtième* was a comparatively equable and efficient tax, in the form of a levy of one-twentieth on all sources of income, and assessments for it were made with great care. If a proper *cadastre* could be drawn up the *vingtième* might well become sufficiently productive to replace, instead of supplementing, the older and more unfair direct taxes such as the *taille*. But the *parlements*, perhaps remembering Voltaire's observation that the arbitrary and imperfectly assessed land tax was one of the great guarantees of English liberty, prepared to do battle with their king and earn for themselves once again the eulogies that Horace Walpole had bestowed on them ten years before. The *parlement* of Paris rejected the edicts as being unconstitutional and it was supported by many *parlements* in the provinces, especially in Languedoc, Dauphiné, Normandy and Brittany. The edicts finally had to be registered by force on 31 May 1763 and it was this manoeuvre, carried out by means of a show of royal authority known as the *lit de justice*, that called forth *The Riches of the State* and the deluge of financial pamphlets that followed it.[21]

The province which posed the most difficult problem for the central government was Brittany. It had always been a remote and unruly province, turning outwards towards the Atlantic rather than inwards towards the rest of France. Its bleak central plateau was surrounded by thick forests, in such a way that one official described the province as the tonsured head of a monk, bald in the middle and matted all round.[22] It had suffered in the war more than any other part of France: the English had ruined its trade and its fishing industries, raided its ports on several occasions and occupied Belle Isle, a few miles off the Breton coast, from April 1761 until May 1763. The inhabitants of Belle Isle demanded £15,000 compensation from the government for their losses, while the rest of the province was furious at the neglect of Breton interests, especially Newfoundland fishing interests, in

---

[21] Flammermont, *Remontrances*, ii, 322–39.
[22] Cited H. Freville, *L'Intendance de Bretagne 1689–1790*, 3 vols, Rennes 1953, i, 26.

the peace talks. To make matters worse, the central government in its desperation during the war had come to an agreement with the local estates in Brittany allowing them control over certain aspects of taxation. The Bretons were determined that this arrangement should be made permanent, particularly as they felt that they had suffered enough already in a war that had brought them nothing but loss. La Chalotais, fresh from his successes against the Jesuits and already famous throughout France for his *Essay on National Education*, was able to exploit all these grievances to good effect in a sustained campaign against the tax edicts and against the authority of the royal governor of Brittany, the duc d'Aiguillon.

The royal governors in other provinces found themselves under equally violent attack. The duc de FitzJames, royal governor of Languedoc, referred disdainfully in a private letter to 'these gentlemen of the *parlement* who have forced me to take a firm line with them';[23] but his disdain was shortlived. Within a few months the central government had given in and dismissed him, along with the governors of Dauphiné and Normandy. Only d'Aiguillon in Brittany hung on grimly, forcing the royal administration to make a fight of it with La Chalotais. It was this bitter and protracted struggle, known as 'the Brittany Affair', that lay at the root of later and far more serious confrontations between the king and his *parlements*.[24]

The dismissal of the provincial governors was part of a spectacular and apparently abject surrender by the government. As early as September 1763 Jenkinson's informant in Paris was telling him that Choiseul had decided on the dismissal of Bertin and a few weeks later Hertford told his government that it was said that the ministry had decided to conciliate the *parlements*. There were rumours that the tax farmers were to be dismissed, that a National Bank was to be set up and that an entirely new ministry was to be formed.[25] At the end of November the king issued a declaration promising that in future he would rule not

[23] FitzJames to his sister, 19 September 1763, Add. 29, 760, fo. 142.
[24] J. Rothney, *The Brittany Affair and the Crisis of the Ancien Régime*, New York and London 1969, prints some useful extracts from contemporary sources; but for a proper understanding it is still necessary to go back to B. Pocquet, *Le pouvoir absolu et l'esprit provincial*, 3 vols, 1900–01 and A. Le Moy, *Le Parlement de Bretagne et le pouvoir royal au xviiie siècle*, 1909. See also A. Rebillon, *Les Etats de Bretagne 1661–1789*, Paris and Rennes 1932, and Freville, *op. cit.*
[25] Add. 38, 201, fos 128–30, 228–9; P.R.O. S.P. 78/259 fo. 76

by the exercise of his own personal authority but 'according to justice and in accordance with the rules and constitutional forms which have been wisely established in the kingdom'.[26] Hertford was disgusted with this concession, which he rightly thought would lead to trouble in the future, and insisted that the danger was not as great as the king seemed to think. 'Though the flames break out in every part of the kingdom,' he wrote, 'the nation itself does not as yet appear to be in any general combustion.'[27] However, the policy of surrender continued, culminating in the dismissal of Bertin in December and his replacement by none other than L'Averdy, the leader of the Paris *parlement's* campaign against the government and one of the most popular men in France. It was widely believed that L'Averdy would refuse to cooperate with the government unless it changed its policies radically—in which case, said Hertford, 'he will thereby acquire such a stock of popularity as may render him formidable even to the crown of France'.[28] The tax farmers, said Jenkinson's informant, were terrified by the news of the appointment and thought that it would mean their dismissal as part of a thorough-going purge of the old order of things. Indeed, L'Averdy was reported to have declared that if he was not able to push through the reforms he wanted within six months he would return to his old post as leader of the opposition.[29] It seemed that the *parlements* of France had achieved what the parliament of England had often undertaken but seldom accomplished: the complete replacement of the old order of things by a government of their own choosing.

In England the situation was more complicated, because the opponents of the old order of things had long ago quarrelled violently among themselves. Before the Seven Years War the Whig establishment had been opposed by a reasonably coherent and integrated political group who called themselves the Patriots. At their centre, united by close family ties, stood Pitt and Grenville. Their aim—which might well have been achieved had it not been for the war—was to produce a new and reformed brand of Whiggism which would be acceptable to Tories. Pitt summed up the Patriot ideal when he said later that he 'lay under great obligations to many gentlemen who had been of the denomination

[26] Marion, *Histoire financière*, i, 227.
[27] Hertford to Halifax, 29 November 1763, *P.R.O. S.P.* 78/259 fo. 76.
[28] *Ibid.*, fo. 190.
[29] *Add.* 38, 201, fo. 370.

of Tories but during his share in the administration had supported government upon the principles of Whiggism and of the Revolution'.[30] Traditional establishment Whiggism, epitomized by men like Newcastle and Cumberland and supported by corruption and standing armies, would drive independent gentlemen to flirt with the bad old Tory doctrines of prerogative government and even to wish perhaps that they had the Stuarts back again. The Patriot Whiggism of Pitt and Grenville, on the other hand, would convince them that their interests were being looked after: that the government cared more for England's interests than for those of Hanover, that it cherished local independence and would not snuff it out with armies of placemen. In hard economic terms the Patriots represented all those whose property and prestige did not depend on the government. Whereas the professional placeman and the corrupt government contractor had bought their places and contracts and must rely on them for a living, the independent landed man and the sturdy self-made merchant in the outports had no need to stoop so low. Their income came honestly, from tilling the soil or distributing its produce, and not from squeezing higher fees or higher profits or higher interest rates from some government concession in order to sell it at a profit.

Patriot politics would probably have run themselves into the ground in the end in any case, since they were based on the delusion that pure and incorruptible government was somehow possible without resorting to a salaried civil service: they assumed that amateurism rather than professionalism was the proper antidote to patronage politics. But the immediate cause of their collapse was the Seven Years War. While Pitt went on his self-intoxicated way, conquering one new colony after another with little regard for the cost and even less for the long-term economic and administrative consequences, Grenville became increasingly apprehensive about the whole process. The two men quarrelled violently and the Patriot group split in two, Pitt's following growing steadily smaller and Grenville's steadily larger as the reaction against the unbridled commercialism of the war grew stronger. When George III found himself deserted both by Pitt and by Newcastle—who had in any case become bitterly distrustful of one another as a result of trying to run the war

[30] P. C. Yorke, ed., *Life and Correspondence of the Earl of Hardwicke*, 3 vols, Cambridge 1913, iii, 431.

together—and when he found that Bute had no stomach for high office, Grenville was the only man left. In this way and for these reasons was formed, between April and September 1763, Grenville's administration—the worst, according to Lord Macaulay, in the whole of eighteenth-century history.

Grenville's ministry was in fact very well suited to the job it had to do. He himself was a skilled and painstaking fiscal expert, determined to scale down the accumulated war debts and streamline the tax system, while Lord Halifax, one of the secretaries of state, had had long experience of colonial government. Bedford, as lord president of the council, was the advocate of the new policy of conciliating France and reducing the many barriers to Anglo-French trade. 'For God's sake let us take heed not to hurry ourselves precipitately into a war', he wrote anxiously in 1764 when quarrels over the implementation of the peace terms were threatening relations between the two countries, 'in order to gain a popularity which, could it be obtained, would be of no service to us, and which must I fear be the inevitable ruin of this nation.'[31] And in the following year, when Bedford supported free trade in French silks, he provoked riots among the London silk weavers that almost brought down the ministry.[32] In spite of Macaulay's strictures, the Grenville administration had real and positive policies—policies which looked forward to the nineteenth-century doctrine of free trade and which could well be summed up in the nineteenth century formula of 'peace, retrenchment and reform'.

Such policies were not, however, calculated to help Grenville win a wider measure of support. While the colonists resisted retrenchment and the old Whigs were embattled against reform, Pitt and his brother-in-law Lord Temple (Grenville's own elder brother but now totally alienated from him and committed to Pitt) made it extremely difficult to keep the peace. Though they had been deserted by most of the independent gentlemen—Pitt had no answer when in September 1763 Newcastle mockingly asked him what had happened to 'his Tories'[33]—they were still

[31] F. Spencer, ed., *Diplomatic Correspondence of the Fourth Earl of Sandwich*, Manchester 1961, pp. 210–12.
[32] In May 1765 Bedford got the Lords to reject an attempt by the Commons to reimpose duties; and the weavers believed that he had made secret promises to the French on this score. For a fuller account see my article, 'The Regency crisis of 1765', *E.H.R.* lxxxv, 1970, pp. 282–315.
[33] Newcastle to Devonshire, 11 August 1763, Add. 32, 950, fo. 68.

able to stir up trouble for the government among the commercial men of the City of London. The duc de Nivernois, French peace plenipotentiary in 1762 and subsequently ambassador, had described to his government with some distaste the 'enormous throngs of speculators and merchant venturers who fill the City of London' and had pointed out that it was the support of such people that made the Pitt–Temple faction the most vicious and the most violent in English politics.[34] Its hired journalist John Wilkes made his paper, *The North Briton*, a vehicle not only for a crusade on behalf of those commercial interests which had supposedly been neglected by the peace terms but also for a sustained attack on the government's allegedly tyrannous behaviour and for a squalid racialist campaign against the Scots, sparked off by the fact that Lord Bute came from Scotland. Even James Boswell, though he deplored the persecution that his countrymen suffered in London, could not resist going down to the City every Saturday afternoon to get *The North Briton* hot from the press.[35]

For all its vehemence the opposition to Grenville did not succeed in equalling the feats of the French *parlements*. Although George III in the autumn of 1763 talked gloomily of 'insurrections and tumults in every part of the country' and declared that there was 'no government, no law',[36] there was in fact nothing in England comparable with the commotions in France. A bid to bring Pitt back to power in August failed and he was ready to give up the fight. 'As to the country,' he wrote, 'it is lost beyond the possibility of being restored; the moment thrown away was, in my judgment, the last which offered the smallest gleam of hope. May it never be my fate again to hear anything of taking a share in the affairs of a nation devoted to confusion and ruin!'[37] Newcastle was plunged in a mood of valedictory melancholia which was to be deepened during the next few months as many of his old Whig colleagues—Devonshire, Hardwicke, Henry Legge—died one after another. The men he had loved were gone, either to the grave or to Grenville, and he was left like Tennyson's King Arthur, forgotten by authority. Now that the old Whig system of politics was being jettisoned he could see only

[34] *Oeuvres posthumes du duc de Nivernois*, 2 vols, 1807, ii, 24.
[35] J. Boswell, *London Journal 1762–63*, ed. F. A. Pottle, 1950, pp. 227–8.
[36] Add. 32, 952, fo. 200 (Newcastle's account of an audience the king gave to Charles Yorke on 2 November 1763).
[37] Pitt to Newcastle, 12 September 1763, Add. 32, 951, fos 7–8.

two possible results: revolution on the one hand or tyranny on the other. But when he pointed this out to Pitt, saying that unless they got together to oust Grenville 'we might see either Anarchy, Confusion and even Rebellion; or a total subversion of our Constitution by power and force', Pitt merely replied hopelessly that 'if things were to miscarry, he had rather see them fail in the hands of the present ministry than in ours'.[38]

Meanwhile the attempt to use Wilkes as bait had failed: the ministers had indeed acted vigorously against him, but all the opposition's efforts to get parliament to declare their acts unconstitutional had been in vain. Even over the question of the 'general warrant', under which Wilkes had been arrested, there was difficulty and embarrassment. Most of the old Whigs had used such warrants constantly when they were in office and they were thus rather disconcerted by the sudden discovery by Pitt and his friends that they were illegal. As for Cumberland, the acknowledged royal leader and figurehead of the Newcastle Whigs, he deplored the whole business and declared that it was extremely dangerous to pretend that it raised vital constitutional issues.[39] Wilkes himself had to flee to France and the efforts made on his behalf in his absence—including one debate on general warrants where the opposition were only defeated by fourteen votes— could not conceal the fact that his supporters were deeply divided. For all their concern about constitutional principles, most of them were more frightened by Pitt's bellicose slogans or by Newcastle's traditional Whiggism than they were by Grenville. The backbenchers of the Commons were in no mood to throw away the chance of reasonably firm and conscientious government for the sake of commercial opportunism or corrupt oligarchy. They were, indeed, so lethargic that opposition politicians had to brandish the example of France in their faces to try to rouse them. 'Shall France deride our langour,' cried the fiery Colonel Barré, 'when her parliaments are making such strides towards liberty?'[40]

By this time France was certainly in a derisive mood, for the year 1763 had been a turning point in her view of England and thus in her view of herself. When Edward Gibbon arrived in Paris at the beginning of the year, when the ink was scarcely dry on the peace treaty, he found that the French regarded the English

[38] Newcastle to Devonshire, 11 August 1763, Add. 32, 950, fo. 67.
[39] Cumberland to Newcastle, 31 October 1763, Add. 32, 952, fo. 141.
[40] Cited P. Brown, *The Chathamites*, 1967, p. 199.

with something like awe. 'The name of Englishmen inspires as great an idea at Paris,' he wrote home, 'as that of Roman could at Carthage after the defeat of Hannibal . . . from being very unjustly esteemed as a set of pirates and barbarians we are now by a more agreeable injustice looked upon as a nation of philosophers and Patriots.'[41] Frenchmen in general, it seemed, were now beginning to value those things in English society that anglophiles like Voltaire or Gournay had admired for so long already. Having been defeated and humiliated by English seapower, they wanted to learn its secrets and copy its methods. Books like Châteauveron's *The School of Naval Administration; or, The Public-Spirited Sailor* popularized the study of English seamanship and naval organization, which previously had been restricted to the French naval administrators themselves.[42] Furthermore, the French saw that seapower was not just a weapon, to be seized in an emergency and honed in a hurry: it was more a way of life, based on a thriving commerce and industry which was given proper respect by society as a whole. The Abbé Coyer's book, *The Commercial Nobility*, arguing that the French nobility, like the English, should cease to rely purely on landed revenues and should be prepared to take part in trade and industry, had had a considerable vogue since its publication in 1756 and the number of noblemen engaged in business, often on quite a large scale, was steadily increasing. Even the marquis de Mirabeau, that stout defender of the traditional values of French society against English commercialism and financial manipulation, was busy in 1763 forming a company to mine lead at Glanges in the Limousin. Associated with him were three dukes, four more marquises, four counts or countesses and a baron.[43] Meanwhile Voltaire stressed

---

[41] J. E. Norton, ed., *The Letters of Edward Gibbon*, 3 vols, 1956, i, 139–40.

[42] Châteauveron, *L'Ecole de l'administration maritime ou le matelot politique*, The Hague, 1763.

[43] G. V. Taylor, 'Types of capitalism in eighteenth-century France', *E.H.R.* lxxix, 1964, pp. 478–97. In 1756 the Abbé Coyer's book *La Noblesse commerçante* had advised French noblemen to follow the English example and engage in commerce. The resulting controversy has been studied in E. Depitre, 'Le système et la querelle de la *Noblesse Commerçante*, 1756–59', *R.H.E.S.* ii, 1913, pp. 137–77; and H. Levy-Bruhl, 'La noblesse de France et le commerce à la fin de l'ancien régime', *R.H.M.* viii, 1933, pp. 209–35. But there were in fact examples of aristocratic traders and industrialists during the first half of the century, even in a province as traditionalist as Brittany. See *Comité des Travaux historiques et scientifiques: notices, inventaires et documents*, vii, 1922, p. 47 and ix, 1925, pp. 3–15. On noblemen in coal-mining see M. Rouff, *Les Mines de charbon*, 1922, p. 182. Bonnassieux and Lelong (see below, p. 119) show that noblemen normally acted as commercial and industrial spokesmen for their localities.

once again, in his account of England's success in the Seven Years War, the thing which in his view lay at the root of everything: the fact that the English representative system gave stability to the nation's finances and flexibility to its commercial structure.[44] Even English writers, Madame du Deffand averred in a letter to Voltaire, were superior to those in France: they wrote out of conviction and not just to gain notoriety.[45] She had perhaps been talking to Wilkes during his exile in Paris.

But as the year wore on and the English seemed to be so much less successful than the French in defying governmental authority, the mood changed. The virtues of the English system—or at any rate some of them—were still held in some esteem, but the English themselves were no longer seen as true to them. They had been irredeemably corrupted and cowed, said Pernin des Chavanettes in his *New History of England*, and George III's ministers had been able to reduce parliament to complete docility. The liberty of the people was nothing but an empty phrase and the doughty champions of freedom had been brought low by the very thing for which they had once been admired—their consuming interest in money and trade. 'When the love of gain takes control of a man,' pronounced Pernin sententiously, 'it is rare indeed for him to desert his golden calf in order to dedicate himself to an abstraction which won't even give him a return on the money he spends defending it.'[46] Even the seemingly anglophile arguments of Châteauveron had a somewhat similar sting in their tail. Commerce, he concluded, had made the English masters of the world; but in doing so it had turned them into slaves.[47] It seemed that the marquis de Mirabeau's prediction was coming true: having had their society torn apart by the conflict between the love of money and the love of liberty, the English had now to watch helplessly while the one snuffed out the last vestiges of the other.

While Englishmen of weight and substance saw their representatives corrupted and their liberties eroded, rogues and vagabonds were allowed more licence than was compatible with a truly liberal society. 'If there is liberty at all in England,' said Fougeret

---

[44] Voltaire, *Oeuvres complètes*, xv, 367.

[45] Marie de Vichy, marquise du Deffand, *Lettres à Horace Walpole 1766–1780 et à Voltaire 1759–1775*, 2 vols, 1864, ii, 449.

[46] Pernin des Chavanettes, *Nouvelle histoire d'Angleterre*, 6 vols, Amsterdam, 1765, vi, 191.

[47] Châteauveron, *Matelot politique*, p. 238.

de Montbron scornfully, 'it is liberty for the *canaille*.'[48] When Charles-Marie de la Condamine, of the French Academy of Science, visited London soon after the peace, George III received him and his colleagues very graciously; but in France the visit was remembered not for the royal reception but for the noisy crowd which followed La Condamine through the streets of London jeering at his physical disabilities.[49] What was even more infuriating, from the French point of view, was that French rogues when in England shared the immunity allowed to English rogues. In the autumn of 1763 two London agents of the French foreign office, de Vergy and d'Eon de Beaumont, tried to blackmail their own government; and when this was parried d'Eon de Beaumont brought proceedings against the French ambassador for conspiring with de Vergy to murder him. Throughout the whole squalid scandal the English government insisted that the liberties of England prevented it from handing the two men over to the French for punishment; and yet when Englishmen living in Dunkirk offended against French law the English demanded exemption for them on the grounds that the peace treaty had provided for Englishmen to visit Dunkirk to see that the fortifications were demolished. 'It is hard', the French foreign secretary told Hertford angrily, 'that the King of England should oblige the King of France to keep his bad English subjects whom he desired to get rid of, and yet would not restore to him his own bad subjects, whom he desired to have in order to inflict on them the proper punishment.'[50]

There was nothing inconsistent in thinking at one and the same time that the English had betrayed their traditions of liberty and that they gave too much licence to the 'inferior orders' and to the demagogues who stirred them up. Englishmen themselves, true

---

[48] Fougeret de Montbron, *Préservatif*, p. 45.
[49] Boswell, who met La Condamine in London, said that he was very old (in fact he was sixty-two) and had to use an ear trumpet. It was this that brought forth the jeers. Boswell, *London Journal* p. 278; P. J. Grosley, *Tour to London*, 1772, p. 85.
[50] P.R.O. S.P. 78/265 fo. 143. For English reactions to the d'Eon affair see Add. 32, 952, fos 110–11; *C.H.O.P.* i, nos 1087, 1118, 1284, 1521, 1651. See also the collection of documents and other items on d'Eon in *H.M.C.* 39, *Hodgkin*, pp. 352–68. In 1836 Frederic Gaillardet brought out his semi-fictitious but fully documented *Mémoires du chevalier d'Eon*; and most writing on the chevalier has remained in this limbo between fact and fiction ever since. Louis XV's double espionage system, which was the real seedbed for the whole affair, is best studied in D. Ozanam and M. Antoine, eds, *Correspondance secrète du comte de Broglie avec Louis XV*, 2 vols, 1956–61.

to the traditions of Toland and the other radicals of the seventeenth century, believed that liberty was inseparable from
property and that unruliness among the labouring classes was an
opportunity for tyranny and not a guarantee of liberty. Even
'republican' Hollis, a radical whose ideas were so extreme that
he was generally regarded as an eccentric rather than as a serious
politician, declared that 'all commonwealths were founded by
gentlemen'.[51] And what was true of the radicals was also true of
those within the establishment who sought to hold them at bay.
In March 1765, when Newcastle and his friends among the old
Whigs came out against the government's Poor Bill, saying that
it was 'the most pernicious stretch of democratical inclination'
and would 'set all the counties of England in a flame',[52] it was not
because it gave more liberty to the poor themselves but because
it put more power in the hands of the country gentlemen. It was
these men of substance who were seen as the best hope for
liberty or the worst threat to stability, according to one's point
of view. And they themselves judged France in similar terms:
one traveller noted that 'I could never observe any extraordinary
poverty and misery among the lowest orders in France. It is the
next rank above them, the farmers, whose condition appears most
disadvantageous in the comparison with that of their fellows in
England.' As for the country gentlemen, many of them were
doomed to 'ragged idleness and sparse diet'.[53] Like that more
famous traveller, Arthur Young, he saw this lack of substantial
farmers and independent squires as the real threat to French
liberty.

Thus the debate which was going on within and between the
two countries in the 1760s was not about 'democracy' or 'popular
sovereignty' in the sense in which such terms have later come to
be understood. Rousseau's *Social Contract*, the first eighteenth-
century attempt to work out a theory of mass democracy, had
been published in 1762 but had so far had little influence. Indeed,
in Choiseul's eyes Rousseau was yet another incendiary inhabitant
of that literary underworld to which the English government was

[51] Cited C. Robbins, 'The strenuous Whig, Thomas Hollis of Lincoln's
Inn', *W.M.Q.* 3rd series, ii, 1950, pp. 406–53. The conservatism of the radicals
is superbly exemplified in Toland's remark, made in the dedication to his
Anglia Libera in 1701, that men of property were the truest lovers of
liberty and thus had a natural right to a share in government.
[52] Add. 32, 966, fos 146–7, 131.
[53] Add. 12, 130 (*Notes Made in a Journey through France, chiefly relating
to the picturesque circumstances of that country*), fos 177–8.

far too kind.[54] Many self-styled Patriots on both sides of the Channel used the language of democracy, but this does not mean that they were conscious precursors of a thing called the democratic revolution. They might talk of 'the nation' and its interests, of 'citizens' and their rights and duties, but they still assumed that society would remain strictly hierarchical and that the political nation would be restricted to men of property and substance. La Chalotais, though he was particularly adept at coining the terms that were to form the revolutionary vocabulary of the 1790s, was rigidly conservative in his view of society. He believed not only that the poor should stay poor but also that they should stay illiterate: one of his principal charges against the Church was that it undermined society by educating the labouring classes beyond their station in life. Voltaire, who agreed with him fervently on this point, once remarked to him that the monks who cheated gentlemen out of their labourers in this way should be yoked to the plough themselves.[55]

Nevertheless, the 1760s were a time of ferment, even if the end product was never intended to be anything as intoxicating as social revolution. The reason for the ferment was comparatively simple. The established order of things, associated on one side of the Channel with Whig corruption and on the other with royal favourites, Jesuit confessors and tax farmers, had been severely shaken by the Seven Years War. Those who had previously felt themselves outside that established order, strong in their positions in society but weak in their influence on government, now felt that the time had come to change the order of things in such a way as to make it wider and more representative of the political nation as a whole. Through no fault of their own, most of them were desperately parochial and limited in their outlook: their claim to be Patriots, to speak for the *patria* itself, could not conceal the fact that they understood far less about the needs of central government than did the corrupt oligarchs or clerical bureaucrats whom they sought to displace. Indeed, the very corruption of government had alienated it from local magnates in technical as well as personal terms. It seemed to be run by a separate breed of men, cut off from the rest of society by the fact that they had invested in office rather than in land or trade;

[54] Deffand, *Lettres à Walpole*, i, 98.
[55] Cited F. de la Fontainerie, *French Liberalism in the Eighteenth Century*, New York 1932, p. 39.

and independent men had no desire either to know them or to understand the craft they plied. Consequently the first and crucial question raised by the Patriot assault on the seats of power was simply this: did they have the knowledge or the ability to occupy them? Could they replace the men they were hounding from office so enthusiastically? It may be exhilarating and even thera-peutic to pile your sins onto a scapegoat and drive him into the wilderness, but it is less exhilarating to discover later that he was the only efficient beast of burden that you had. This was the point that Newcastle and Hardwicke and their Whig friends made with monotonous regularity, both to their king and to their fellow politicians. They might be corrupt and they might be factious; they might even be unpatriotic. But good government could not continue without them.

Surprisingly enough, one of the clearest statements of this particular difficulty came not from the displaced oligarchs of England but from one of the triumphant Patriots of France. In the summer of 1763, just as the *parlements* seemed to be carrying all before them, one of their supporters wrote apprehensively in his diary:

> The destruction of the Jesuits, which is bound to take place within a few years, will mean that the Dauphin will come to the throne without having this shrewd body of men, expert at political affairs and all that they involve, to turn to for advice. All that will be left will be the *parlements*; and if their authority and so-called rights are undermined, then there will be nothing to stop the complete triumph of despotism. If on the other hand the *parlements* stand together and take strong measures to oppose this triumph, then the result will be a revolution throughout the country—an extremely dangerous development which will lead the English and other countries to take advan-tage of it and seek a pretext for war.[56]

Many of the Patriots who pushed their way into government office in the 1760s saw this problem, in some cases more clearly than those who had brought them there. Within a few months of his appointment, L'Averdy broke completely with the irrespon-sible and unconstructive slogans of the opposition and immersed himself in painstaking and enlightened administrative reforms which in some ways carried on where Bertin had left off. Indeed,

[56] E. J. F. Barbier, *Chronique de la Régence et du règne de Louis XV*, 4 vols, 1847–56, iv, 465.

Bertin had not really left off at all: he was replaced as controller-general, but he continued to be a member of all the important royal councils for the next seventeen years and was in effect minister for economic affairs. This was the great strength of the French system of government, that it could have it both ways. George III had to choose between men like Grenville, efficient administrators but uninspiring politicians, and men like Pitt who could charm the House of Commons but could do nothing about an administrative problem except shout at it. Louis XV, on the other hand, could have men of both sorts in his administration, even if it meant that they quarrelled with one another for much of the time. While Choiseul and his cousin Choiseul-Praslin presided over the glamorous departments of government—the War Office, the Admiralty, the Ministry of Foreign Affairs—and preserved the popular image of a patriotic and dashing administration, men like L'Averdy and Bertin and Trudaine analysed the fiscal and economic structure of France and moved tentatively towards the complex and usually unpopular reforms which it demanded. Sometimes the two sides hamstrung each other, as when L'Averdy's tax exemptions for newly cultivated waste lands led to a sharp drop in timber supplies for Choiseul's programme of naval expansion; but for the most part the system worked surprisingly well. If the upheaval of the 1760s was to resolve itself into a new and better order of things, two requirements had to be met: the aggrieved local interests had to be represented in central government and some at least of their representatives had to understand and work at its problems. In France there was some chance that both these things might be achieved.

In England there was less, as the split between Grenville and Pitt showed. Grenville thought that it was the business of a Patriot politician not just to represent those who had previously felt excluded from central government but also to face the problems of that central government, even if he was dubbed a tyrant for his pains. For him patriotism was not just a way of rallying the opposition but also a way of running the government—running it by transcending the corrupt and lax system of management with which the Whigs had been satisfied. Though not corrupt himself, he had plenty of corrupt followers: he was, after all, concerned to create a new governing party out of the most unpromising and disparate ingredients, a task which called for vigilant and unscrupulous use of government patronage. But he also drew to him men who thought that the important thing in politics was not the striking of attitudes but the actual business of carrying on the government. Many of them were talented and hardworking administrators, the nearest thing to professional civil servants that this amateurish age had so far produced. For them the aftermath of war was not just a problem but also an opportunity—an opportunity to create a new and more efficient machine of government. While their king wanted to overthrow the old Whig establishment for a negative reason, because it had been factious and unpatriotic, they welcomed its demise for a positive reason. They wanted to put in its place a new and more efficient administrative structure, not just for England but for the whole of the British empire. 'The people of North America at this time', wrote one of their number, a governor of the colony of Massachusetts Bay, 'expect a revisal and reformation of the American governments and are better disposed to submit to it than they ever were or perhaps ever will be again. This is therefore the proper and critical time to reform the American governments upon a general, constitutional, firm and durable basis.'[57]

But the most colourful and influential of all the patriot politicians stood squarely in the path of all administrative reform. In the first few months of the new reign, while he was still in office, Pitt had been well aware of the financial and administrative needs of the empire he was conquering. He realized, for instance, that there would have to be an increased military and civil establishment in America and that this would have to be paid for by means of new taxes, some or all of them presumably levied in America itself. But once out of office, he conveniently forgot all this. Proposals for an increased establishment suddenly became dangerous and unconstitutional devices to swell the government's powers of patronage, while the new taxes became mere instruments of tyranny. Choiseul and L'Averdy, or the two wings of the French administration which they respectively epitomized, at least had the sense to quarrel in private; but Pitt and Grenville were forced, by the nature of the English system, to quarrel very much in public.

However much they might quarrel, however difficult it might be to reconcile the aspirations of opposition patriotism with the

[57] Cited E. S. Morgan and H. M. Morgan, *The Stamp Act Crisis*, Chapel Hill 1953, p. 19.

realities of government patriotism, there was at least one thing which in both countries revealed how much the different wings of the Patriot movement had in common. This was the consideration of the alternative. For in both countries there *was* an alternative: in many people's eyes an obvious and inescapable alternative. In France the dauphin, undisputed heir to a king who was already well past middle age, was known to be the implacable enemy of Choiseul and all he stood for. When he came to the throne, it was confidently assumed, there would be no more talk of Patriot politics, no more conciliation of the *parlements* and no more hounding of the Jesuits. The present king of France might be prepared to experiment with a new sort of government, but his successor was determined to return to the traditions of the past. One day the Patriots would find that same past which they thought they had transcended waiting round the corner for them as their future.

In England the future was less certain. Opposition politicians had always looked to the future king, to the Prince of Wales, as the man who would sweep away existing evils and bring them to power. In the present situation it would have been natural for the Whigs to look to the Prince of Wales to do away with Grenville and Pitt and bring back Whiggism; and this was precisely what Newcastle instinctively sought to do. But it would hardly have been practical politics, since the Prince of Wales was only a year old. Instead Newcastle and the Whigs turned to Cumberland, the king's uncle and the living symbol of the old Whig establishment. It was a forlorn hope, for Cumberland was not the heir to the throne: he might succeed in dragging the past into the present, but he could hardly guarantee to make it the future. There was, however, one moment when it seemed that he might come very near doing so. In the spring of 1765 the king fell ill. Whatever his illness was, and most people in politics thought it was more serious than was given out, it was alarming enough to make him desperately anxious to provide for a regency for his infant son in the case of his own death or incapacitation. Bute, who still had some influence over the king and over his mother the Dowager Princess of Wales, entered into secret negotiations with Cumberland. The aim of these negotiations was not only to divide effective political power between the two men in the event of a regency but also to bring to power then and there an administration composed of their respective followers.

This plan, which had the enthusiastic support of the king and came very near to success, would have restored the Whig establishment to power and ended the Patriot dream once and for all. So serious was the danger that it did what countless pious conciliators had failed to do over the past four years: it brought about a reconciliation of Grenville and Pitt.[58] Together they fought off the threat, but only for a short time: in July 1765, after making an unsuccessful effort to detach Pitt from Grenville, Cumberland determined to bring his Whigs back to power on their own, with himself in such a commanding position that one distinguished student of the period has said that he was 'in effect Prime Minister'.[59] It was said by a contemporary that Cumberland was convinced that now Pitt and Grenville were united 'the whole government of the country would fall into their hands'[60] unless they were challenged immediately. Thus by the autumn of 1765 there was, in England as in France, an outright confrontation between the Patriots on the one hand and the traditional political establishment, protected by a royal figurehead, on the other. The only difference was that in England the royal figurehead had actually got himself into power, whereas in France the dauphin was still waiting impatiently for his father to die.

Then, within the space of two months, the whole situation in both countries was completely changed. On 31 October 1765 the duke of Cumberland complained of a headache and within a few minutes was dead of a brain haemorrhage. In Paris the dauphin's death was expected at any moment, since he had been seriously ill for some weeks; and at the end of October William Cole, who was visiting the city, took care not to have his new coat fully trimmed, so that it would serve him as mourning in due course. He was anxious to pay proper respect to the dauphin who was, he said, 'of a most amiable character . . . consequently maligned, hated and abused by the deistical philosophers and their faction'.[61] He was soon to have the chance, for the dauphin finally died on 20 December 1765. In both countries the traditional political forces had suffered a blow from which they were never to recover. So, as it turned out, had relations between the two countries. The confused and uncertain aftermath of one war was

---

[58] Jarrett, 'Regency Crisis', p. 311.
[59] *Letters from George III to Lord Bute*, ed. R. Sedgwick, 1939, p. 242n.
[60] Robert Jephson to John Hely Hutchinson, 12 June 1765, *H.M.C.* 27, 12th Rep., ix, *Donoughmore*, p. 255.
[61] Cole, *Journal 1765*, p. 93.

over: the developments which were to lead to the next were already under way. In the changed situation resulting from the deaths of Cumberland and of the dauphin, these developments were to shatter the Patriot movement and remould the social forces that had gone to make it up.

4   *The Patriot dream*

*I*n 1765 the monks at the Abbaye aux Hommes at Caen commissioned from the painter l'Epicie a picture of their founder,
William the Conqueror, to go in their refectory. It was an
enormous and melodramatic piece of work showing William at
the moment of his triumphant landing in England; and it was
such a tremendous success at the Paris salon, where it completely
dominated the whole exhibition, that it had to be kept on by
popular demand while the monks ate under an empty wall.[1]
Meanwhile Pierre Belloy, an ex-lawyer who had so far failed
dismally in his efforts to make a living by writing plays, suddenly
struck lucky with *The Siege of Calais*, a piece which rang with
contemptuous defiance of the English. If fashionable Paris was
anything to go by, France had had enough of being humiliated
by England and wanted to recall past glories and dream of future
ones. In the comparatively cool and sequestered world of the
government officials and the economic theorists there might still
be those who were ready to learn humbly from the English—in
July 1764 the inspectorate of manufactures sent Gabriel Jars over
to study the English iron industry and 'find out above all why this

[1] D. Diderot, *Salons*, ed. J. Seznec and J. Adhemar, 4 vols, Oxford, 1957–67,
ii, 41, 183.

industry is so much better developed in England than in France'[2]
—but the mood of the country as a whole, if such a thing could be
gauged, was more bellicose. If the dauphin's death sealed the
triumph of patriotism it was the swashbuckling Patriot politicians
like Choiseul, rather than the patient administrative reformers like
L'Averdy, who were likely to be the beneficiaries.

Choiseul had certainly achieved great things within the past
two years. His attempts to found a new French colony in Guiana
had been sadly unsuccessful and even the colonies France had kept
by the peace of 1763 had suffered some disastrous setbacks, as
when a plague of ants devoured the sugar crop on Martinique
and St Lucia in 1764 and 1765. But Choiseul's commercial policies
had proved successful all the same and French trade had revived
dramatically. The government's contacts with the great merchant
firms of the Atlantic ports were very close—indeed, if a Patriot
minister meant one who had the confidence of the commercial
classes, then it could well be argued that Choiseul deserved the
title more than did Pitt—and government policy showed a real
appreciation of the needs of the colonial trade. It was also
extremely enlightened. Le Mercier de la Rivière, intendant of
Martinique from 1759 to 1764, was by common consent one of the
most brilliant administrators of his day and his achievements in
the French West Indies were praised by advanced thinkers all
over Europe. And it was the French, rather than the English, who
first embarked on the essential task of dismantling the overregulated mercantilist system which often stifled the very trade
that it was supposed to protect. Those on the spot had been
pressing for this ever since the end of the war—Bute received
representations for a free port in Dominica as early as February
1763—but it was Choiseul's edict of April 1763, allowing foreign
ships to carry certain goods to and from the French colonies, that
was the first significant breach in the old colonial system.[3]

[2] Jars's instructions are quoted by Bacquié, *Les Inspecteurs*, p. 44. See
J. Chevalier, 'La mission de Gabriel Jars dans les mines et les usines
britanniques en 1764', *Transactions of the Newcomen Society*, xxvi, 1947–49,
pp. 57–68. Another anglophile scientist, Jean Hellot, did much to make
Jars's visit a success: see A. Birembaut and G. Thuillier, 'Les Cahiers du
chimiste Jean Hellot', *Annales*, 21ᵉ année, 1966, pp. 254–91.

[3] On colonial policy see C. L. Lokke, *France and the colonial question
1763–1801*, New York, 1932. Many of the relevant documents are printed in
L. C. Wroth and G. L. Annan, eds, *Acts of French Royal Administration
concerning Canada, Guiana, West Indies, Louisiana prior to 1791*, New
York 1930. See also J. de Maupassant, *Un grand armateur de Bordeaux:
Abraham Gradis, 1699?–1780*, Bordeaux, 1917, and L. P. de May, 'Le Mercier
de la Rivière', *R.H.E.S.* xx, 1932, pp. 44–74.

Choiseul was not just concerned to rebuild French maritime supremacy in order to take part in a peaceful commercial rivalry with the English. He was engaged in the much more specific and much more serious task of preparing for a war of revenge. Though France had been forced to make a humiliating peace, her chief minister had no intention that it should be a permanent one. Time and time again he warned the king that England would always be his most dangerous enemy;[4] time and time again he cut through administrative difficulties in order to ensure that France had the naval resources to challenge England successfully when the time came. New schools of naval construction and seamanship were set up under government auspices and great efforts were made to improve the system of timber requisitioning upon which the French navy depended. Nine new ships were launched in 1763, three times as many as in the previous year, and within a few years Choiseul had increased the navy's complement of ships of the line by a half, as well as multiplying the number of frigates several times over. The provinces of France, especially those semi-independent provinces whose *parlements* Choiseul was accused of conciliating, were prevailed upon to contribute heavily to the naval programme; and as a result the new fleets included ships like the *Languedoc*, of eighty guns, and the *Provence*, of sixty-four, named after their donors.[5]

Even though he had converted his invasion barges into timber boats, in order to supply the dockyards with their essential needs, Choiseul had by no means abandoned the idea of invading England —in time of peace if necessary. Even before the treaty of Paris was signed French agents in London were reminding their superiors that English intransigence in the negotiations left France with no alternative but to prepare for a new war. In the autumn of 1763 d'Eon de Beaumont was ordered to map areas suitable for a surprise landing; and when he rendered himself useless by plunging into blackmail and conspiracy another agent was recruited who sent back well over a hundred plans and memoranda describing the southern counties of England in detail. Plans to land 60,000 men at Barnstaple reached an advanced stage and

[4] *Mémoires du duc de Choiseul*, ed. F. Calmettes, 1904, pp. 381–414.
[5] V. Brun, *Guerres Maritimes: Port de Toulon*, 2 vols, 1861, i, 449. See also P. Charliat, *Trois siècles d'économie maritime française*, 1931; P. W. Bamford, *Forests and French seapower*, Toronto, 1956; C. Aboucaya, *Les intendants de la marine sous l'ancien régime*, Gap, 1958.

the idea of an invasion of Ireland was frequently put forward. All these projects postulated a surprise invasion without a declaration of war; such things were impossible in the middle of a war, said one planner disarmingly, because the English would be in a state of readiness, and the officers involved did not seem to find this unduly dishonourable. The crushing of the English was an end that justified any means. 'The determination to abase the power of England,' wrote one nobleman as he outlined a plan for a simultaneous invasion of England and Ireland, 'must surely be the guiding passion of every true Frenchman.' Only Louis XV himself, more scrupulous than his subjects, was shocked by some of the ideas put forward.[6]

French domestic policy, like French foreign and colonial policy, tended to reflect contempt rather than admiration for the English and their so-called 'free' institutions. Duhamel du Monceau, an inspector of the French navy and an expert on forestry, coal-mining and farming as well as on naval architecture, had been well known in the 1750s for his treatises on English agriculture and his general enthusiasm for all things English; but his chief occupation in the early 1760s was the editing of a series of manuals designed to challenge the tradition of secrecy on which England's industrial superiority rested. They were produced by the French Academy of Sciences and they provided, for the first time, full and detailed descriptions of the various processes used in industry.[7] Meanwhile an edict of March 1763 announced that in future the French government would make less use of the system of commercial privileges, not in order to exchange it for the English system of patents but in order to work towards a more open exchange of technical information. In England such moves were being made only by private bodies such as the Society of Arts, which tried to persuade inventors to make their ideas freely available in return for a premium from the society. The pioneers of the new technology had their problems in both countries, but at least in France there was a reasonable chance of financial

[6] P. Coquelle, 'Les projets de descente en Angleterre', *R.H.D.* xv, 1901, pp. 433–53, 591–624 and xvi, 1902, pp. 134–57. On Louis XV's scruples see the same author's 'L'espionnage en Angleterre pendant la guerre de sept Ans', *R.H.D.* xiv, 1900, 508–35. See also M. C. Morison, 'The duc de Choiseul and the invasion of England 1768–70', *T.R.H.S.* 3rd series, iv, 1910, pp. 82–115.

[7] See A. H. Cole and G. B. Watts, *The Handicrafts of France as Recorded in the Descriptions des arts et métiers* (Kress Library of Business and Economics publication no. 8) Boston, Mass., 1952.

backing: in the 1760s Nicholas Cugnot got French government support for a steam engine which worked extremely badly, while in England James Watt could get no support for a steam engine which promised to work extremely well.[8]

The reforms undertaken in France in the 1760s were too extensive and too disparate to fit into any consistent pattern, either of anglophobia or of anglophilia. Some were based on a study of English practice—while the Department of Bridges and Highways sent off for information on English regulations about the width of wheel rims, the French treasury set Moreau de Beaumont to work to study English taxation—but very few of them were inspired by unqualified admiration for English institutions. The really significant thing is that there were so many of them. While England was so torn apart by the consequences of victory that she could scarcely pass a single enactment without repealing it within a year or so, France was goaded by defeat into a sustained burst of administrative activity. The collection of the direct taxes was rationalized and many exemptions done away with—except that of the *bourgeoisie* of Paris, who were powerful enough to ensure that they kept all their exemptions. An extensive programme of municipal reform was carried out, even though much of it was to be abandoned in the 1770s. Edicts were issued approving officially what had long taken place unofficially: the participation of the nobility in trade and industry. Guild privileges were broken down and the manufacture and circulation of all sorts of commodities, from textiles and leather to porcelain, were freed from existing restrictions.[9] And at the same time the intendants in the provinces carried on with a programme of day-to-day administrative duties which would have been unthinkable in England: surveying the harvest for tax assessments, arranging pensions and other assistance for the needy, running courses in midwifery and public health, hearing tax appeals, setting up public workshops for the unemployed, inquiring into the state of local industries, distributing free supplies of new crops like potatoes or madder and dealing with natural disasters of one sort and another. These came thick and fast: cattle plagues, diseases among dogs and cats and fowls and then, from 1765 onwards,

[8] S. T. McCloy, *French Inventions of the Eighteenth Century*, Kentucky, 1952, p. 37; A. Wolf, *History of Science, Technology and Philosophy in the Eighteenth Century*, 1952, p. 554. On Watt, see below pp. 134, 257.
[9] For a summary of the reforming edicts see J. Godechot, *Les Institutions de la France*, 2nd edn, 1968, pp. 16–23.

a series of extremely bad harvests followed by epidemics of influenza.[10] And in spite of it all the French government did its job sufficiently well for the 1760s to be looked back to subsequently, by people all over France, as 'the good old days' before the country's troubles really began.

By the time of the dauphin's death, at the end of 1765, things were just beginning to go sufficiently well for some credit to be reflected on the government. For years past it had seemed that France must either put up with the traditional power structures, Jesuits and all, or risk the humiliating and perhaps dangerous experiment of copying the English. A popular song of the Seven Years War had attributed what it called the 'decadence' of France largely to the financiers and the Jesuits, and had suggested the hanging of the latter as the best remedy;[11] but few of those who sang it would have agreed with Voltaire and the other anglophiles that the cure for absolutism and clericalism lay in adopting the parliamentarian and protestant institutions of England. And now, it seemed, the choice had been triumphantly avoided: France had a government which had chased out the Jesuits and had started to demolish some of the more oppressive features of the old system, but which was nevertheless determined to defy rather than to imitate the self-satisfied tradesmen across the Channel. With the death of the dauphin that government came of age. It was no longer an ephemeral unstable thing, a dashing war minister keeping himself in power on borrowed time by opposing the known wishes of the heir to the throne: it was there to stay. It was the future as well as the present. The dauphin's widow remained true to the Jesuits and did her best to shield her son, the future Louis XVI, from the pernicious doctrines of the

[10] V. R. Gruder, *The Royal Provincial Intendants: a governing élite in eighteenth century France*, Ithaca, 1968, is concerned with social origins rather than administration; but the full range of the intendants' responsibilities, especially in the field of social welfare, can be seen in S. T. McCloy, *Government Assistance in Eighteenth Century France*, Durham N.C., 1946—an invaluable book which corrects the popular view that the *ancien régime* was a callous tyranny. On the epidemics of the 1760s see G. Fleming, *Animal Plagues*, 1871 and P. M. Bondois, 'La protection du troupeau français au xviii⁰ siècle: Lépizootie de 1763', *R.E.H.S.* xx, 1932, pp. 352–75. For a typical account of the subsequent nostalgia for the 'good old days' of the 1760s see Y. Lemoigne, 'Populations et subsistances à Strasbourg au xviii⁰ siècle', *Mémoires et documents publiées par la Commission d'histoire économique et sociale de la révolution française*, xiv, 1962, pp. 13–44 (English translation in J. Kaplow, ed., *New Perspectives on the French Revolution*, New York 1965, pp. 47–67).

[11] P. Barbier and F. Vernillat, *Histoire de France par les chansons: 3, du Jansénisme au Siècle des Lumières*, 1957, p. 154.

'enlightened' philosophers and their disciples in the government; but it must have been clear to her, by the time she too died in March 1767, that she had been fighting a losing battle. Even the collective voice of the assembled clergy of France, when it condemned the philosophers in its 1765 assembly, was of little account. The Patriots had won and the traditionalists, the clericals, the Jesuits had lost. Indeed by 1769 Madame du Deffand thought that the Jesuits were in such desperate straits that they were even reduced to intriguing with the English ambassador's wife against the triumphant Choiseul.[12]

The crowning irony in all this was that very word 'patriot', which had by now come to be generally accepted as the label for all those who supported 'enlightened' policies and politicians, was itself a borrowing from the political vocabulary of England. In the year of the American revolution d'Holbach declared grandly that 'true patriotism can only exist in countries where free citizens, governed by just laws, live in happiness and unity and strive to deserve the esteem and the affection of their fellow-citizens';[13] and it was no doubt comforting for the French to imagine that their patriotism was descended directly from the patriotism of ancient Rome, the sturdy republican devotion to the good of the *patria*, without having been sullied by any sinister connections with England. This was why Leblanc and d'Argenson went out of their way to deny the similarities between ancient Rome and contemporary England.[14] By the 1760s learned societies were offering prizes for discourses on the special nature of French patriotism and at least one writer undertook to define the precise difference between French patriotism and English.[15] But there was no hiding the fact that Patriots in French politics and Patriots in English politics had a great deal in common— including that streak of passionate national pride and fire-eating xenophobia that made them hate one another so cordially. They both claimed to represent the hitherto unrepresented, the great mass of their fellow-countrymen whose interests were neglected by a narrow and corrupt political establishment; they had both

[12] Deffand, *Lettres à Walpole*, i, 183.
[13] For this and other uses of the word see under 'Patriotisme' in P. Robert, *Dictionnaire alphabétique et analogique de la langue française*, 1951–64.
[14] See above, pp. 20–21.
[15] Basset de la Marelle, *La Différence du patriotisme national chez les Français et les Anglais*, Lyon, 1762.

been brought to power as a result of the Seven Years War, which had exposed the weaknesses of the establishment they challenged; and they had both been divided, by the effects of that same war, into the political Patriots and the administrative Patriots, the strikers of attitudes and the solvers of problems. The great difference between them—and it was to prove to be of momentous importance—was that in France the two kinds of Patriots worked reasonably harmoniously together, each supplanting the old order in his own way, while in England they quarrelled so violently over the carcass of the old order that they drove it almost to the point of resurrection.

The first flicker of resurrection seemed to have stopped the quarrel dead in its tracks: no sooner did Pitt and Grenville realize that there was a real chance of Cumberland bringing the old Whigs back to power in May 1765 than they staged a dramatic reconciliation scene. But as a political force the reconciliation did not prove particularly effective or particularly permanent. It could not prevent the entry of the Cumberland Whigs two months later and it seems to have been of surprisingly little account when the real moment of truth came for English politics with the death of Cumberland at the end of October 1765. If George III himself is to be believed, his Whig ministers 'from the hour of the duke of Cumberland's death' were clamouring to get Pitt into the ministry. Soon they were even prepared to make him head of it. By February 1766 Lord Rockingham, the first lord of the treasury, was saying that 'he wished to God Mr Pitt would fix up some plan for carrying on administration and putting himself at the head of it'.[16] Of Grenville there was little or no mention: most people in politics seemed to assume that the answer to the country's problems lay in a coalition between the old Whigs—the Rockingham Whigs, now that Cumberland was dead and Newcastle too old to be a leader— and Pitt. Less than a year earlier all the talk had been of the independent backbenchers rallying round Grenville and Pitt in their joint stand against the Whigs. What had happened in those few short months to change the political situation so radically?

There were various possible answers to this question, some of them in terms of the personalities of politics and others that were

[16] *Letters from George III to Lord Bute*, p. 242; *Chatham Correspondence* ed. W. J. Taylor and J. H. Pringle, 4 vols, 1838–40, ii, 397.

involved with the great questions of national policy—above all with the question of relations with France. The Whigs themselves, goaded by the unfamiliar and unpleasant experience of being out of power, had been tempted during the past few years to pose as radicals and reformers in order to boost their own political stock. If Grenville was going to beat them at their traditional game of patronage politics, then they would out-manoeuvre him at his own game of Patriot politics. And it was Rockingham, the present first lord of the treasury, who had encouraged this radical pose and given his support to the small group of extremists who adopted it and who were regarded rather disdainfully by Newcastle and Cumberland as 'the young men'. They included people like Sir William Meredith, whom Newcastle had always regarded as a Tory, and they even gave their support to such wild and eccentric country gentlemen as Nicolson Calvert. Newcastle had always insisted that they would achieve nothing because they lacked 'the weight of nobility'; but under Rockingham's leadership they had come to dominate the party and Cumberland's death seemed to be the signal for them to take it over altogether.[17] And Pitt was their natural ally because he and they had stood together against Grenville's controversial measures —above all, against the Stamp Act.

Grenville's plan to raise money in the colonies by means of a stamp duty on legal documents was accepted eagerly and almost unanimously by the English parliament when it was first put forward in 1764. It was only later, after the Americans had countered the Act itself with a trade boycott which injured English commercial interests, that Pitt and the radical Whigs suddenly discovered the iniquities of the Act and mounted a strenuous and ultimately successful campaign against it. The repeal of the Stamp Act in 1766 by the Rockingham administration won Pitt's gracious approval, but it still left unsolved the problem of American taxation—a problem which worried him more than it worried most other politicians since he had been one of the first to see the need to maintain and finance an increased military establishment in America in order to guard against a French war of revenge. No English government was prepared to abandon either the military establishment or the intention of

[17] Jarrett, 'Regency Crisis', pp. 293–4; D. H. Watson, 'The rise of the opposition at Wildman's Club', *Bulletin of the Institute of Historical Research*, xliv, 1971, pp. 78–97.

raising the revenue for it in America itself. It was for this reason that the repeal of the Stamp Act was accompanied by a Declaratory Act which specifically reserved the right of the home government to tax the colonists if it saw fit. From the very beginning the progress of the American revolution clearly revealed the truth which Horace Walpole was to underline at the moment of its culmination in the summer of 1776: the distrust of Americans by Englishmen and of Englishmen by Americans sprang from, and was conditioned by, the distrust which both of them felt for the French.

The issue which was at stake between Grenville on the one hand and the fortuitous Pitt–Rockingham alliance on the other was not whether Anglo-American unity against France was necessary but how it could best be achieved, whether by coercion or by conciliation. Because of his links with the francophile Bedford group Grenville was often accused of underrating the danger from France, of alienating the colonists without realizing the opportunities he was presenting to the national enemy across the Channel. And yet some of his policies, such as the free trade policies of Bedford himself, were more likely to improve relations between England and the colonies than was the stubborn mercantilism of Pitt. It was just that Grenville happened to believe, rightly or wrongly, that England could only stand firm against France if she governed her colonies effectively and asserted her right to make them pay for their own defence. At first most people in England agreed with him; then, when American resistance seemed to jeopardize England's trade and even England's security, his policies were rejected. And Cumberland happened to die just at this moment of rejection, just in time to allow his erstwhile followers to climb on the anti-Stamp Act bandwagon and push through policies which he would have regarded with contempt. Richard Jackson, London agent for the colony of Pennsylvania, declared in July 1766 that if Cumberland had not died, 'instead of a repeal of this Act, there would have been a number of regiments in America before this'.[18]

There was another reason for Grenville's isolation, more potent in the final analysis than all the considerations of policies and party groupings. This was the simple fact that he had offended

[18] Cited M. G. Kammen, *A Rope of Sand: the colonial agents, British politics and the American revolution*, Cornell, 1968, p. 123.

the king. In the first place his insistence of having control of all
patronage, which was essential if he was to build a new governing party out of nothing, seemed to George III to be impertinent
and irritating in the extreme. In the second place he had had the
crowning effrontery to survive an attempt by the king to remove
him. In the spring of 1765, when he had encouraged negotiations
between Bute and Cumberland aimed at forming an alternative
administration, George had never dreamed that Grenville would
prove both indispensable and irremovable. For this he never
forgave him. When he did finally manage to get Grenville out, it
was for good. A few months earlier all the court gossips in
France had assumed that Choiseul would fall from power when
Madame de Pompadour, the royal favourite who had supported
him, died in April 1764. They were proved wrong: Choiseul's
position in the country as a whole was quite strong enough to
make up for an adverse turn of events at court. Grenville, on
the other hand, was summarily dismissed by an infuriated king
in the middle of the parliamentary recess, even though he still
had a strong position in parliament. The contrast between the
courtly politics of France and the parliamentary politics of
England was not always as clear-cut as it seemed.

With Grenville thus deserted and the Whigs thus divided, all
roads led to Pitt. For him the death of Cumberland was even
more of a release than it was for the radical Whigs who were
running so excitedly to meet him. He had always hated the man:
in the 1750s he had suggested that Cumberland intended to usurp
the throne and Cumberland for his part had refused to carry out
his duties as commander-in-chief if Pitt were in power.[19] Newcastle subsequently deluded himself into thinking he had got the
two of them to cooperate against Grenville, but in fact they were
only trying to outmanoeuvre one another, each seeking to pull
the Whig party in his own direction. When it seemed that
Cumberland was about to win the tug-of-war Pitt was so
frightened that he even made up his quarrel with Grenville; but
now that the danger from Cumberland was past there was no
longer any need for Grenville. The Grenville brand of Patriot
politics, which had tried to translate into administrative terms the
desire of the independent gentlemen to reduce government

[19] Stanhope, *History of England from the Peace of Utrecht*, 7 vols, 1836–54,
iv, 19; G. S. H. Fox-Strangways, Earl of Ilchester, *Henry Fox, first Lord
Holland*, 2 vols, 1920, ii, 38–41.

expenditure at all costs, was hopelessly discredited because it seemed to have divided Englishmen against one another and given Frenchmen a handle against them. It was time for Pitt to peddle his own brand, which had always sought to unite all Englishmen, on both sides of the Atlantic, in warlike gestures against the hated French. In England, as in France, 1765 was the year of the swash-buckling Patriot politicians rather than the well-meaning adminis-trative reformers.

All roads might lead to Pitt, but they would have some difficulty in converging. William Knox, a Grenville man and a keen fiscal reformer, had written from Paris back in 1763 that France could do great things if she had men like Pitt in her government. One of the people to whom he wrote it, Governor Lyttelton of Jamaica, agreed eagerly: if she were properly governed France, with her great resources, could challenge Britain again 'before we shall have paid off such a part of our great debt as I believe every good Englishman would wish we should before we engaged again in a new contest'. Pitt meanwhile was opposing all Grenville's efforts to pay off those same debts; and by 1766 Lyttelton, a member of a prominent Patriot political family, was horrified to find Pitt challenging the Stamp Act. He was sure, he told Knox, that the great man had been misled and was basing his case on incorrect information.[20] Like many others, he instinctively looked to Pitt as the hammer of the hated French; but his attitudes to fiscal and administrative questions pointed in quite another direction. And this was also true of commercial policy: if England had lagged behind France in the liberalization of trading regulations it was largely due to the influence of diehards like Pitt. Pitt had conquered an empire for the sake of the old commercial system, with colonies serving as sources of raw materials and as markets for manufactured goods, and he intended that it should remain that way. Ever since the peace of Paris the campaign for a system of free ports in the West Indies had been gathering force, gaining much of its support from those places that Pitt regarded as his own Patriot political territory: Bristol, Liverpool, the City of London. Edmund Burke, private secretary to Rockingham when he came to power in 1765, set himself to organize this campaign in the interests of the Whigs, just as he organized the similar campaign against the Stamp Act; but he found it quite impossible to win over Pitt. 'The great

[20] *H.M.C.* 55, *Various collections*, vi, *Knox*, pp. 87–9, 92.

D

Commoner sets his face against it', he told a friend in April 1766.
'I went down to Hayes with a very respectable merchant of
Lancaster, to talk him, if possible, out of his peevish and perverse
opposition to so salutary and unexceptionable a measure. But on
this point, I found so great a man utterly unprovided with any
better arms than a few rusty prejudices.'[21] The Free Port Act
was in due course passed and proved a great success; but Pitt's
'peevish and perverse opposition' did not augur very well for his
future efforts as a Patriot minister. He might wish to lead his
countrymen against the French, but it was by no means easy to
see how he would pull together all the threads of domestic, commercial, fiscal and colonial policy which were needed for the
task.

When George III summoned Pitt to form an administration in
the summer of 1766 he made it clear that such an administration
ought to concern itself with 'destroying all party distinctions and
restoring that subordination to government which can alone
preserve that inestimable blessing, Liberty, from degenerating
into Licentiousness'.[22] Pitt accepted the task and as a first step
took a peerage, becoming the earl of Chatham, and installed
himself in the rather aloof and secluded post of lord privy seal.
From this lordly eminence he could preside over the more
workaday departments of government, selecting men from all
parties to fill them and giving to them himself, as part of his own
personal charisma, that coherence and unity which in the bad
old days sprang from party allegience. Burke, that vehement
advocate of the old party system, called the Chatham administration 'a tessellated pavement without cement';[23] but both George III
and Chatham himself, both the Patriot King and his Patriot Minister, believed that the cement would be provided by a common
devotion to the *patria*, to the good of the country as a whole and
to the policies which were in its true interest. 'Not men but
measures' had been a Patriot slogan for nearly half a century.
Burke dismissed it as cant and even Canning, by no means a
supporter of the old Whig orthodoxy, was to declare forty years
later that it was like supposing 'that it is the harness and not the
horses that draw the chariot along'. He was also to insist that in

---

[21] E. Burke, *Correspondence*, ed. T. W. Copeland *et al.*, 9 vols, Cambridge
and Chicago 1958–70, i, 251–2.
[22] Fortescue, i, 385.
[23] Burke, *Select Works*, i, 145.

moments of national crisis it was particularly absurd to hope that the salvation of the country could spring from 'this or that measure, however prudently desired, however blameless in execution'. It must come from 'the energy and character of individuals'.[24]

The point about the newly-created Earl of Chatham was that he was, at any rate in his own eyes and in those of a few faithful disciples like the Earl of Shelburne, at one and the same time the energetic individual and the fount of prudent measures. In France it might be necessary to separate the energy and the prudence, to have a Choiseul to provide the former and a L'Averdy to provide the latter. But the English political system could and would produce a truly patriotic administration, combining the patriotism of character and the patriotism of measures. After the false start under Grenville (who, in Chatham's eyes, had been so pettifogging over measures that he had forfeited the confidence of men of character) the Patriot movement would at long last prove that it could produce a viable alternative to Whiggism and could translate into reality the famous dream of Bolingbroke, which had been the inspiration of the Patriot movement on both sides of the Channel:

> The true image of a free people, governed by a PATRIOTIC KING, is that of a patriarchal family, where the head and all the members are united by one common interest . . . instead of abetting the divisions of his people, he will endeavour to unite them, and to be himself the centre of their union: instead of putting himself at the head of one party in order to govern his people, he will put himself at the head of his people in order to govern, or more properly to subdue, all parties.[25]

Bolingbroke's flight of fancy had been based on one fundamental fallacy: the idea that a nation—or, for that matter, a family—is by definition united by a common interest which is discoverable and can be followed in practical politics. Whig government had been based on the alternative proposition, that societies and families and other social units contain contradictory and centrifugal interests which can at best be held in balance, made to cancel one another out. The Whigs, like their counterparts in the traditional political establishment of France, were

---

[24] Speech of 8 December 1802, *P.H.* xxxvi, 1080.
[25] *The Patriot King*, 1752, p. 162; reprinted in E. N. Williams, *The Eighteenth-Century Constitution*, Cambridge 1960, pp. 85-6.

realists and argued from the postulate of divergence, the conviction that human beings will in the natural course of things
disagree and must have agreement imposed on them if there is to
be any sort of order in society. The Patriots, on the other hand,
were idealists and postulated convergence: they thought that
human beings would automatically come to agree as to their
common interest if only they had someone to lead them to it.
This belief was now to be tested, as the Patriot administrations in
the two countries struggled to discern and pursue that will-o'-
the-wisp called the national interest.

The death of the French dauphin had had a less traumatic effect
on political life in France than Cumberland's death had had in
England, largely because the dauphin's enemy was already in
power. Choiseul had been successfully defying the heir to the
throne for seven years, whereas Cumberland, although only
prospective head of a Regency Council rather than prospective
king, had been an effective obstacle to Pitt right up to the moment
of his death. But the dauphin was to have his moment of triumph,
even if it was posthumous and more than a little qualified. Louis
XV, usually a rather indolent and easygoing person, was coming
to realize that he must exert himself and make a personal stand
against the *parlements*. The *parlement* of Rennes in Brittany
had by this time reached a state of scandalous insubordination:
having torn down the texts of a royal edict it had resorted to a
strike—traditionally the most extreme weapon in the *parlement*'s
armoury—and had brought the administration of justice to a
standstill in the province. In May 1765 it was dismissed and
a commission sent down to take over the running of the law
courts and inquire into the whole affair. A particularly ominous
development was the apparent determination of the *parlements* to
go beyond the mere resistance to taxation and to seek an extension
of their already considerable administrative authority. They
claimed a right to pronounce on ecclesiastical matters and when
the king produced a ruling, in September 1765, that the bishops
alone had such a right, it was openly challenged. The comte de
Saint Florentin, who as secretary of the king's household had
responsibility both for Church affairs and for Brittany, received
seditious anonymous letters which were attributed by handwriting
experts to La Chalotais. La Chalotais was arrested and quickly
established himself as a martyr for freedom on a scale only to be
equalled by John Wilkes. In spite of royal prohibitions, the

parlement of Paris produced remonstrances about the Breton affair and insisted once again that all the *parlements* were branches of the same single and indivisible representative body of France— a claim which, as Hertford told his government, was 'another strong symptom of that spirit of liberty which has been for some time very apparent in this kingdom'.[26]

Thus by the time the dauphin died there was every reason to think that he might have been right, that the king would do well to assert his existing authority in Church and state before it was too late. After a short pause, in order to observe the outward forms of national mourning for the dauphin, the Paris *parlement* returned to the attack in February 1766 and the king determined to act. On the evening of 2 March he issued orders for two regiments of guards to be posted at the *parlement* and in the streets leading to it; and the following morning he rode down in solemn procession to conduct his court of *parlement* in person. By a stroke of amazing good luck the procession met a priest carrying the sacrament to a sick man, so that the king was able to make the dramatic gesture of stopping his own procession and kneeling in the road as the other went by. The crowd cheered him. For a brief moment the remote and unpopular king of Versailles had become the people's darling again, as he rode out to defend those religious forms which still meant more to the ordinary Frenchman than the slogans of the *parlements*. When he got to the *parlement* he had all its various chambers assembled before him and told them roundly that all their recent pronouncements and pretensions were unconstitutional and must be expunged from their records. 'I shall not tolerate in my kingdom,' he declared, 'the formation of an association which would cause the natural bond of similar duties and common responsibilities to degenerate into a confederation for resistance.'[27]

The significant thing about this spectacular show of royal authority, which became known as the 'session of the scourging', was that Choiseul continued in office after it. His enemies constantly accused him of suborning the *parlements* against the king and it was to be supposed that if this were indeed so the king's belated show of firmness would result in his dismissal. But it did

---

[26] P.R.O. S.P. 78/261 fos 310–11.
[27] A contemporary account of the episode is printed, together with a translation of the declaration itself, in Rothney, *The Brittany Affair*, pp. 173–8.

not. Choiseul's administration continued to respect the rights of the *parlements* and other local bodies which claimed to exercise administrative and other rights *under* the crown; but there was no question of admitting any rights as *against* the crown. There was nothing new in this: Choiseul's public and private utterances, and in particular his letters to Voltaire, had always shown quite clearly where the line was to be drawn between cooperating with the *parlements* and conciliating them.[28] The administration not only respected the rights of existing representative institutions: it even created new ones. Both Cambrai and Lorraine were constituted in 1766 as *pays d'états*—that is, as provinces having the coveted privilege of holding local estates to run local affairs and uphold local rights. When Corsica was taken over by the French crown in 1769 Choiseul campaigned vigorously for an assembly to be constituted there and he drew up long and detailed agenda for its first session.[29] In France as in England the Patriot minister had been forced or required to respect the wishes of a king who had had a sudden burst of energy; but this did not necessarily mean the abandoning of principles. If previously there had been patriotism from weakness, there was now to be patriotism from strength.

Whatever else patriotism from strength might imply, it certainly implied a strong line in foreign affairs. Ever since the signing of the peace treaty Choiseul had been warning the English that he would regard the return to power of Pitt as an unfriendly gesture which would make it difficult to preserve good relations between the two countries. Far from rebuffing this as unwarranted interference by one country in the internal affairs of another, the Bute and Grenville administrations had done their best to soothe and reassure the French: 'there is not the least room for uneasiness on this head', the secretary of state had told the ambassador in Paris in May 1763.[30] Nevertheless Choiseul's agents in London had kept him carefully informed of every intrigue and every negotiation which even remotely involved Pitt; while in Paris, Horace Walpole reported, it was only necessary to drop the slightest hint that the great man might come back to office in order to create an apprehensive silence throughout a whole

[28] P. Calmettes, ed., *Choiseul et Voltaire d'après les lettres inédites du duc de Choiseul à Voltaire*, 1902, pp. 181–3.

[29] T. E. Hall, 'Thought and practice of enlightened government in French Corsica', *Am. H.R.* lxxiv, 1969, pp. 880–905.

[30] Egremont to Bedford, 20 May 1763, P.R.O. S.P. 78/257 fo. unnumbered.

company.[31] Now that the blow had fallen, Choiseul continued to feign alarm. 'The only thing which I fear,' he told the French *chargé d'affaires* in London, 'is that this really unpatriotic man may try to establish himself by a brilliant move and that this would be a war with France and Spain.'[32]

The brilliant moves of the newly created earl of Chatham were not in fact going very well. He had castigated his predecessors for throwing away the friendship of Prussia, England's ally during the war; but now that he was back in power he was forced to realize that it was Prussia that had thrown away England. The king of Prussia was primarily concerned with Poland and he had no intention of involving himself again in alliances in the west of Europe which might prejudice his ambitions in the east. Like Choiseul, he had kept himself very fully informed about English internal affairs; and the conclusion that he had reached, rightly or wrongly, was that Chatham was nothing but the tool of Bute and was reverting to the traditional Tory policy of commercial expansion rather than alliances on the continent.[33] It was the Cumberland Whigs, rather than Chatham, who had been ever since 1763 the advocates of 'proper alliances upon the continent, to support the particular interests of this country and the general system of Europe';[34] and they had denied that they wanted to go back to the now useless expedient of an alliance with Austria. They had gone to great pains to cultivate the German princes and had made much of the future duke of Brunswick when he had come to London in January 1764 to marry George III's sister.[35] In these circumstances it was comparatively easy for Choiseul to convince the powers of Europe that Chatham was untrustworthy and that his only concern was commercial aggrandizement rather than the European balance of power. The Chatham administration's first resort to force, which took the shape of sending a flotilla to the Falkland Islands to contest the

---

[31] Walpole, *Memoirs of George III*, ii, 163.

[32] Choiseul to Durand, 24 August 1766, cited J. F. Ramsey, *Anglo-French Relations 1763–70, University of California publications in history*, xvii, 1939, p. 146. See also Add. 32, 258, fo. 403 (Guerchy's report to Praslin, 11 March 1766) and the letters printed (though unfortunately without proper references) in C. de Witt, *Thomas Jefferson, étude historique sur la démocratie américaine*, 1861.

[33] Frederic II, *Mémoires*, ii, 429. See also the copies of correspondence between Frederick and his London agents in Add. 32, 309.

[34] Newcastle to Bentinck, 4 December 1764, Add. 32, 964, fos 187–8.

[35] See Add. 32, 955, fos 109, 130–1, 144, 166, 168, 170, 247.

Spanish claims there, seemed to confirm this impression. Choiseul had told the Spaniards as long ago as July 1765 that Chatham was going to return to power and that once this happened France and Spain 'could scarcely expect to keep the peace for more than a year'; and now it seemed that he was being proved right. He refused to support Spain against England over the Falkland Islands, saying that the French navy was not yet ready, but he made it clear that the two countries would have to stand together against Chatham in due course.[36]

One European ally that England had been particularly concerned to cultivate, ever since the days of Grenville's government, was Sweden. Grenville had always been anxious to base his foreign policy on commercial and industrial needs—he made a practice of collecting information on such matters from his consuls abroad, although this information was now conspicuously neglected by Chatham—and he saw that the trade in iron ore made a treaty with Sweden essential.[37] Such a treaty was finally signed in February 1766 and Chatham's secretary of state, the earl of Shelburne, proposed to use it as the basis for an elaborate system of northern alliances, to counteract France's 'southern system' of alliances with Spain and Austria. According to the French agent in London, he was boasting on the very day of his appointment that this northern league was already being formed;[38] but in fact it never existed outside the imaginations of Chatham and his disciples. Sweden turned steadily away from England and towards France until finally, in 1772, a political revolution in Stockholm made French influence there paramount. England could not agree with Russia as to what to do about Sweden, any more than she could agree with Prussia as to what to do about Poland. In the Baltic, as in other parts of Europe, the foreign policy of the Chatham administration was a failure. All it produced was distrust—European distrust of an England that sought to use Europe for her own commercial and colonial ends.

[36] Ramsey, *Anglo-French Relations*, pp. 146, 180.
[37] Grenville's concern for trade is shown very clearly in Spencer, *Diplomatic Correspondence of Sandwich*. The fact that Chatham's interest in such things could sometimes flag is shown by Add. 41, 340, fos 128–31—a long and informative letter to him from a Danish merchant in Geneva, which is endorsed 'unopened when received in the Museum'. On the importance of Geneva in English policy at this time see E. E. Rovillain, 'L'Angleterre et les troubles de Genève en 1766–67', *Zeitschrift für Schweizerische Geschichte*, vii, 1927, pp. 164–203.
[38] Durand to Choiseul, 3 August 1766, cited Ramsey, *Anglo-French Relations*, p. 192.

This distrust, assiduously cultivated by Choiseul and his successors, was to enable France to fulfil in the next decade her long cherished ambition of fighting England without having to fight England's continental allies at the same time.

Even more useful to France that the distrust between England and Europe was the distrust between England and America. In a long memorandum which he presented to Louis XV in 1765, Choiseul had insisted that England would always be France's chief enemy, that many centuries would pass before it was possible to make a lasting peace with her and that in the end she would be humbled by a revolt of her American colonists. He did not, however, expect to see this American revolution in his own lifetime and in the short term he was more interested in weakening England by exploiting her precarious political situation, produced by the increasingly bitter conflict between rival pressure groups, and her equally precarious financial situation, the result of her immense national debt.[39] What he does not seem to have appreciated was the close connection between these three factors. It was precisely the anxieties about the national debt, working themselves out within the context of pressure group politics, that brought about a revolt in America within a decade. The agents of the French secret service in America, briefed to collect information rather than to foment revolt, were to find themselves overtaken by their own long-term objective.

It was natural enough for any power to hope for revolution in the colonies of its enemies. While Choiseul was sending Lieutenant Pont-le-Roy and the baron de Kalb and other agents to America to look for signs of discontent, the English government was studying a scheme by a disaffected Frenchman to raise a revolution in the Spanish colony of Mexico.[40] But the French interest in America was given added importance by the fact that neither Englishmen nor Americans were agreed as to how best it should be countered—whether by allaying colonial fears or by strengthening colonial administration. One man who thought that both things could be done at the same time was Benjamin Franklin, Pennsylvania's agent in London. Franklin was a Patriot of the

[39] Choiseul, *Mémoires*, pp. 381–414.

[40] The plan for a Mexican revolution was first considered by the British government in October 1766 and was raised again a few years later when relations with Spain were bad: see *C.H.O.P.* iii, no. 393. On French agents in America see Ramsey, *Anglo-French Relations*, pp. 164–6; F. Kapp, *Life of John Kalb*, New York, 1884; *Am. H.R.* xxvi, 1921, pp. 726–47 and xxvii, 1921, pp. 70–89; Durand to Choiseul, 1 January 1768, Add. 32, 309, fo. 21.

most idealistic kind. He not only believed in Bolingbroke's dream
of a coherent and transcendent national interest: he also believed
that such an interest could transcend the Atlantic itself and unite
England and her colonies in one integral imperial union. He had
opposed Grenville's Stamp Act because it was a selfish and shortsighted attempt by a particular group, the landed men of England,
to keep down their own tax liability; but he had not been
particularly impressed when an equally selfish group, the business
interests that had been hit by the trade boycott, got it repealed
but failed to tackle the problem of imperial government. Now
he hoped for great things from the Chatham administration. He
dined alone with the two secretaries of state, Shelburne and
Conway, in August 1767 and was impressed by their determination to tackle the colonial problem. At the same time Durand,
Choiseul's agent in London, was doing his best to win over
Franklin and ensure that he received a flattering welcome in
France, where he went the following month. Franklin was not
to be won: 'I fancy that intriguing nation would like very well
to meddle on occasion,' he wrote, 'and blow up the coals between
Britain and her colonies; but I hope we shall give them no opportunity.' Even when the French royal family behaved with
ingratiating condescension to him at Versailles he was not
impressed. 'I would not have you think me so much pleased with
this king and queen as to have a whit less regard than I used to
have for ours,' he told a friend. 'No Frenchman shall go beyond
me in thinking my own king and queen the very best in the
world, and the most amiable.'[41]

Here, united in the person of Benjamin Franklin, were all the
ingredients of the Patriot political philosophy: a determination
to rise above particular interests and seek the common good, an
intense loyalty to the Patriot King and to his Patriot minister
and, above all, a healthy distrust of the French. And yet a dozen
or so years later Franklin was to be found at the court of the
French king, signing treaties with him to further an open rebellion
against George III and generally behaving in a manner which
Chatham openly denounced as unpatriotic to the point of treason.
It is possible to argue that this transformation was the result of
common ideals which Franklin had always shared with 'enlightened' thinkers in France. It is certainly true that many such
thinkers admired him as a new Prometheus, a man who had

---

[41] C. van Doren, *Benjamin Franklin*, 1939, pp. 364–7.

brought down fire from heaven by flying his kite in a thunder-storm; and it is also true that Maximilien de Robespierre, some years before he became a leader of the French revolution, was a passionate defender of Franklin's lightning conductors.[42] But in the final analysis it was the negative reasons rather than the positive, the things which divided him from the English rather than the things which united him with the French, that led Franklin to become the apostle of revolution in France. Like many organisms in the created world, revolution in the eighteenth century propagated itself by division. If it became international, it was because it failed to be national, because its aspirations of unity led only to division and civil war. It is the failure of patriotism, rather than the search for democracy, that is the key to the revolutions of the late eighteenth century.

If they were to aspire to national unity the Patriot ministers of the late 1760s would have to heal divisions which were bewilderingly complex in their origins and nature. Many people thought of them as economic divisions: a writer in the *London Chronicle* in May 1765, who gave himself the rousing pseudonym of 'Britannicus', attacked the widespread idea that there were two rival interests in the kingdom, one the landed interest and the other the trading interest. It was this myth of inexorable economic division, he insisted, that was at the root of the country's troubles. People must realize that all economic groups were interdependent: 'the prosperity, happiness and safety of this nation must ever depend on our rejecting all ideas of separate interests in the community.'[43] But the sad thing was that the healing of this particular division, the rejection of this particular myth, seemed only to be possible at the cost of opening up new ones. Sir George Savile, member of parliament for the county of Yorkshire from 1759 to 1783, was a great apostle of economic interdependence, a man for all interests. Newcastle considered him to be 'among the first of the nobility'; the independent country gentlemen of Yorkshire thought of him as one of them-selves; the trading towns of the county found in him an indefatigable spokesman for their interests. Yet one of his clearest statements of the doctrine of interdependence was made in the context of the widening gulf between the interests of England and those of her colonies. '. . . from the local situation of the chief

[42] *Ibid.*, p. 659.
[43] *London Chronicle*, 16–18 May 1765.

part of my landed estates there are but few persons in England
that will be more immediately affected by the increase or decay
of your trade,' he wrote to a friend in the colonies in 1768. 'But
do you think that because of that consideration that I shall be at
any loss to choose my side if matters shall be insolently driven
up to extremity by you?'[44] Nothing could have illustrated more
clearly the interdependence of land and trade, the unreality of
talking of country gentlemen and merchants as two distinct
species; but at the same time nothing could have foreshadowed
more vividly the split between England and America.

In France there was the same contradictory relationship
between economic divisions and geographical ones, the same
tendency for the one only to be healed at the expense of the
other. The distinction between the feudal world of land and the
'bourgeois' world of trade, which seems so real if one reads the
social theorists or the historians who believe them, becomes
extremely shadowy and blurred if one looks at the realities of
French provincial life in the eighteenth century. In Languedoc,
for instance, the nobility gave a clear lead in organizing the whole
economic activity of the province. The local Estates, as well as
the *parlement* at Toulouse and the sovereign courts at Montpellier
and Montauban, produced a formidable mass of legislation dealing
with all sorts of things from the building of roads and canals to
the abolition of the common lands. They subsidized industrial
research and they encouraged local industry (which ranged from
coalmining and glassmaking to silk and wool textiles), to break
free from the control of the central government. Together with
the Estates of Provence and Dauphiné they sought to control
and regulate the trade of the river Rhône, centred on the great
trade fair at Beaucaire; and their influence even extended to the
profitable trade with the Levant which was of vital importance
for all three provinces. Many noblemen in Languedoc ran their
own estates and drew only a small part of their income—in some
cases as little as 8 per cent—from seigneurial dues. For many of
them the chief use of feudal rights was to enable them to undermine feudalism: they exercised them in order to buy in land and
go over to large-scale capitalist farming. They were steadily taking
over the rights as well as the obligations of their peasants and on
many estates these peasants were in effect wage labourers. In the

[44] *Commons 1754–90*, iii, 406. For Newcastle's view of Savile see Add. 32,
965, fos 40–41.

three provinces of Languedoc, Provence and Dauphiné noblemen were liable for *taille*—the primary form of direct tax, which according to theorists was not paid by the nobility—on part of their land and this in itself forced them to produce proper accounts and run their affairs in a businesslike manner. There was very little in this south-eastern corner of France to suggest a society that was about to split apart into feudalism versus the *bourgeoisie*; but there was a great deal to suggest a country where central control of the peripheral provinces was about to break down, just as England's grip on her peripheral colonies was threatened in the same way.[45]

Superimposed on these general problems were two specific problems which came to a head in the two countries at more or less the same time and faced Chatham and Choiseul with difficulties which were remarkably similar in their complexity and their intractability. The first problem concerned the supply of corn and the conflict of interests which it created between producers and consumers. Just as Dr Johnson put the political aspect of the Patriot movement in its worst light with his famous remark that it was 'the last refuge of a scoundrel', so Byron put its economic and social aspects in the worst possible light with his lines:

> For what were all these country patriots born?
> To vote and hunt and raise the price of corn?[46]

The earlier part of the eighteenth century had indeed seen many years of low corn prices, with resulting agrarian depression and even periods in which small proprietors could not get enough for their crop to cover their necessary capital outlay for the following year. In such circumstances small landowners were hard hit, since they might well be impoverished by one year's glut in such a way as to prevent them from recouping their losses

---

[45] J. Albisson, ed., *Loix municipales et économiques de Languedoc* 7 vols, Toulouse 1780–87; L. Dutil, *L'État économique du Languedoc à la fin de l'ancien régime 1750–89*, 1911; P. A. Robert, *Les Remontrances et arrêtés du parlement de Provence au xviii° siècle, 1715–90*, 1912; E. Appolis, *Un Pays Languedocien au milieu du xviii° siècle*, Albi, 1951; A. Soboul, *Les Campagnes montpelleraines à la fin de l'ancien régime*, 1958; R. Forster, *The Nobility of Toulouse in the Eighteenth Century: a social and economic study*, Baltimore, 1960; R. Baehrel, *Une Croissance: la Basse Provence rurale*, 1961; E. Le Roy Ladurie, *Les Paysans de Languedoc*, 2 vols, 1966; G. Chaussinand-Nogaret, *Les Financiers de Languedoc au xviii° siècle*, 1970. On Dauphiné, see below, p. 208n.

[46] Byron, *Poems*, ed. V. de Sola Pinto, rev. edn, 3 vols, 1968, i, 507.

during subsequent years of high prices. The famous economic theorist Quesnay put the problem neatly in his apothegm: 'Low prices and a good harvest do not constitute riches; high prices and a poor harvest constitute misery; high prices and a good harvest constitute prosperity.' In other words, there *was* a need, in the eyes of many people on both sides of the Channel, to keep up the price of corn in order to ensure a decent living for those who grew it. French observers, especially those hostile to the English system, were fond of stressing that the English parliament ever since the days of William III had kept up the price of corn artificially as a sop to those Tory or Patriot country gentlemen who would otherwise have had economic grievances to add to their political ones. There was some substance in the charge that the Patriots were born to raise the price of corn; and a Patriot minister might therefore be expected to raise it still further.[47]

The chief instrument of this policy, which was a system of bounties on the export of corn, had fallen into disuse by 1766. The bounties had not been paid for ten years or so and the amount of corn actually sent out of the country had become almost negligible. Home demand was rising steadily and the price of grain, like the price of almost everything else, had gone up in response.[48] There had been sporadic food riots as a result—in Derbyshire in October 1764 colliers were forcibly seizing supplies of wheat and selling it below current prices[49]—but on the whole harvests were good enough to prevent any really catastrophic increase. In France a similar period of fairly good harvests had enabled the new policy of free trade in grain to work itself in, though not entirely without trouble. This policy, which in the eyes of Quesnay and his followers was by far the most important of the reforms of the 1760s, had been inaugurated by edicts in March and June 1763 which allowed the export of grain under certain conditions both from one province to another and from

[47] For a discussion of Quesnay's remark see B. H. Slicher van Bath, *The Agrarian History of Western Europe 500–1850*, 1963, pp. 105ff. A fairly typical French view of the corn bounties can be seen in *Faits qui ont influé sur la cherté des grains en France et en Angleterre*, an anonymous pamphlet published in April 1768.
[48] D. G. Barnes, *History of the English Corn Laws 1660–1846*, reprinted London, 1961, pp. 31ff.
[49] *Gent. Mag.* 1764, p. 543. It was also pointed out that in Yorkshire an association of gentlemen had been formed 'to raise a fund for the importation of corn from other counties, that the poor may be supplied at a reasonable price'.

France to countries abroad. These were followed by edicts allowing the export of livestock and animal foodstuffs and finally, in July 1764, came a definitive decree establishing free trade in grain. For a country where fear of famine was still so real that every locality watched over its own food supply with the jealousy of a squirrel guarding his store of nuts, this was an advance. But to Quesnay and his 'Physiocrat' followers it was still only a half measure, because it was geared to price levels: just as the English parliament had only given bounties for export when the price of corn fell below certain stipulated levels, so the French king now only permitted export at or below similar levels. The Physiocrats, as their rather pompous label suggested, believed in the rule of nature. They argued that the produce of the land was the only true form of wealth and that anything which shackled it was in the end a loss to the community. Only if food prices were allowed to find their own level would there be a proper relationship between the number of people growing food and the number of people consuming it. Artificial regulations merely produced artificial societies, with able-bodied men who ought to be tilling the land wasting their time instead on selfish and anti-social activities like commerce. 'Commercial men share in the wealth of nations,' said Quesnay indignantly, 'but nations do not share in the riches of commercial men. The merchant is an outcast in his own country . . . fortunes made in this way are underhand, knowing no king and no fatherland (*patrie*).'[50]

Whatever other differences there might be between English patriotism and French patriotism, the two movements seemed at least to share a common agrarian policy. In France, where the movement of grain had until now been restricted by a multitude of regulations, this policy took the shape of removing these restrictions in order that growers could reach the widest possible markets and not have to sell their produce locally at a loss. In England, where regulation had always been in the interest of the producer rather than the consumer, it was naturally more conservative: the country Patriots had only to maintain, rather than

[50] Cited Lüthy, ii, 22. On the physiocrats see G. Weulersse, *Le Mouvement Physiocratique en France de 1756 à 1770*, 2 vols, 1910; *La Physiocratie sous les ministères de Turgot et de Necker 1774–1781*, 1950; *La Physiocratie à la fin du règne de Louis XV*, 1959. See also R. Girard, *L'abbé Terray et la liberté du commerce des grains 1769–74*, 1924 and J. Airiau, *L'opposition aux Physiocrates à la fin de l'ancien régime*, 1965. The latter contains, p. 169, a useful summary of the free trade edicts of the 1760s.

raise, the price of corn and to see that the price of other things did not outstrip it. This last was their real concern. The inflation of the 1760s, which seemed to most of them to be the direct result of the Seven Years War and of the commercial greed which had prompted it, threatened to push up wages to a point where the production of corn at current prices was no longer profitable. Then rents would start to fall, the value of land would go down and the whole structure of society would collapse. And all because of the commercial men whose wars had produced, said the anonymous writer in the *Annual Register* in 1767, 'public poverty and private opulence, the fatal disease which has put a period to all the greatest and most flourishing empires of the world'.[51] Like their counterparts in France, the independent country gentlemen of England saw the traditional values of a landed society jeopardized by a catastrophic chain of events set in motion by mercantile ambition.

In fact the economic theories of Quesnay and his English admirers were wide of the mark, because the conditions that had produced them were changing. The long period of agricultural depression and low grain prices was giving way to a period of boom conditions and high prices. The chief problem of governments in the second half of the century was to become more and more the protection of the consumer rather than of the producer. Physiocrats on both sides of the Channel, and especially Arthur Young in England, would go on arguing for the next twenty years that wages were being artificially pushed up, largely as a result of the undue growth of trade and industry, far beyond what was justified by the increase in the price of basic foodstuffs. In 1769 Young attacked the French government for encouraging industry and thus creating urban centres which appeared to add to the country's population and prosperity, but in fact only robbed farmers of their labourers; and two years later he inserted into the second edition of his *Farmer's Letters* a diatribe against that other dire result of economic expansion, the love of luxury among the poor. 'It may be said,' he wrote, 'that wheaten bread, that beef, that mutton, that sugar, that butter, are dear; but do not in the height of an argument jumble these and the necessaries of life together.' Like his counterparts in France, Young believed that the golden age of agrarian prosperity could only be regained if labourers would refuse to be tempted by the new towns and

---

[51] *Annual Register*, 1767, pt. ii, p. 171.

would content themselves with wages which were just sufficient to buy them the bare necessities of life.[52]

But the Physiocrat myth of agrarian prosperity was dissolving almost as fast as the Patriot myth of political purity. There was an exceptionally bad harvest in 1766 and Chatham faced widespread food riots almost from the moment he took office. In September he got the king to sign a proclamation against forestalling, a venerable medieval remedy which even Chatham can hardly have expected to work now. It did not. He then imposed an embargo on corn exports, infuriating the landed men by doing so through the Privy Council rather than through parliament. The duke of Richmond declared angrily that 'nobility will not be browbeaten by an insolent minister',[53] and the opposition set to work to prove that such an embargo was unconstitutional. The riots continued, in spite of Chatham's insistence to Shelburne that special commissions must be set up to try offenders and mete out exemplary punishment; and when the king opened parliament on 11 November he spoke warningly of the 'spirit of the most daring insurrection' which had spread throughout the country.[54]

While in England the summer of 1766 was too wet, in France it was for the most part too hot and dry. But the result was the same: an insufficient harvest and food riots. By 1767 there was a serious threat of famine and epidemic in many parts of France, especially in the Orléannais and in the areas around the great clothmaking centre of Troyes. Extensive relief works were undertaken by the government, but in spite of all that could be done children died in great numbers of cold and hunger and disease.[55] The Physiocrats were still confident that free trade would in the end solve all problems; and Turgot, an enthusiastic Physiocrat who was *intendant* of Limousin, busied himself distributing copies of Le Trosne's *La Liberté du commerce des grains toujours utile et jamais nuisible*. Others were less enthusiastic. The *parlement* of Paris demanded that the king should take immediate action to safeguard the city's bread supplies and the government started

---

[52] Young, *Letters concerning the French Nation*, p. 37; *Farmer's Letters*, 3rd edn, 2 vols, 1771, i, 205.
[53] A. G. Olson, *The Radical Duke: career and correspondence of Charles Lennox, third duke of Richmond*, Oxford, 1961, p. 30.
[54] *Chatham Correspondence*, iii, 98; *P.H.* xvi, 236.
[55] C. Bloch, *L'Assistance et l'Etat en France à la veille de la Révolution*, 1908; A. Colomès, *Les Ouvriers de textile dans le Champagne troyenne, 1730–1852*, 1943.

to look over its emergency plans for feeding the capital. These plans had been laid in 1765, when L'Averdy had made a contract with a man called Malisset whereby the latter had agreed to run a royal corn mill at Corbeil, buying in grain and milling it as necessary to be released for making into bread at times of shortage. Malisset was to have received a flat two per cent on all grain purchases; but it now transpired that there were irregularities in his management of the mill and that he had probably milked the system for a good deal more than his two per cent. His contract was cancelled, but by this time it was too late: rumours of his supposed frauds had been assiduously circulated and exaggerated until by the summer of 1768 it was being widely asserted that there was a deliberate plan, a *pacte de famine*, to make private profit out of public hunger. This was the burden of Prévot de Beaumont's hysterical pamphlet, *Horrible conspiration, ligue ancienne entre le ministère, la police, le parlement de Paris, contre la France entière, découverte en juillet 1768*, for which he was hastily imprisoned. The *parlements* were scandalized that they should have been accused along with the ministry they were attacking and they determined to take the law into their own hands. Led by the *parlement* of Rouen they suspended the laws allowing corn exports; and they did this on their own authority, in defiance of the king and his council. The government continued to fight a rearguard action, but it became steadily less convincing. On 23 December 1770, the day after the dismissal of Choiseul, a definitive royal edict ended the policy of free trade in grain. Patriot economics in France were only able to survive Patriot politics by a matter of hours.[56]

The second of the specific problems of 1766 was also a matter of squaring the particular interests of a group with the general interests of the country as a whole. But this time the group was much smaller and much more vulnerable: not the whole body of the landed proprietors but merely those favoured merchants and capitalists who had been granted chartered rights to trade with the East Indies. In France they were organized into the *Compagnie des Indes*, in England into the East India Company. The English company was immeasurably the stronger of the two, not

[56] Biollay, *Le Pacte de famine*; C. Bloch, *Le Commerce des grains dans la généralité d'Orléans 1768*, Orleans 1898; G. Bord, *Histoire du blé en France: le pacte de famine. Histoire-légende*, 1887. There is a useful summary of the *pacte de famine* scandal in D. Dakin, *Turgot and the Ancien Régime in France*, reprinted New York, 1965, pp. 98–103.

simply because during the Seven Years War it had defeated the French company and made its own influence paramount on the Indian continent, but also because it was a powerful force in parliament and a large-scale government creditor. To some extent the contrasting fortunes of the two companies during the Seven Years War had reflected the differences in their status. The French company was alternately exploited and neglected by the royal government and finally deserted by the French navy, while the English company was strong enough to dominate government policy and thus ensure its own victory. During the stormy autumn of 1763 it was widely assumed that the French company would be wound up, partly because its trading prospects were now so bleak and partly because it was associated in the public mind with the financiers and the Jesuits and all the other privileged groups that were now being hounded as scapegoats. In October Jenkinson's agents were passing back to him stories that the *Compagnie des Indes* was about to be taken over by Laborde, a political associate of Choiseul and banker to the king.[57] A meeting of the company's shareholders on 29 December 1763 failed to agree on anything except petulant recriminations and so Laborde stepped in unofficially. He advanced 3 million livres to facilitate the loading of three ships for China and four for the coast of Coromandel, in the hope that this would give the company time to get on its feet again. Meanwhile the shareholders turned their wrath on the comte de Lally, the Irish Jacobite commander who had had the misfortune to be in charge when things went wrong for the French in India. He was imprisoned in the Bastille, tried by the Paris *parlement* and finally executed in 1766.

The English were driven by more complex motives than the French, since they were seeking a scapegoat for victory rather than one for defeat. Their most notable victim was Robert Clive, the most spectacularly successful of the 'nabobs', or newly enriched East India Company servants. Fundamentally he was the symbol of that unbridled commercialism, that cancer of private profit feeding on public interest, which was such a favourite Patriot target. But there was more to it than that. The policy of territorial conquest in India, with which he was identified, had given a new edge to the fears of all sorts of people, many of them a good deal more worldly and sophisticated than the ordinary anticommercialist country landowner. People within the East

[57] Add. 38, 201, fos 181–4.

India Company itself, whether simple investors or active traders or unprincipled speculators, feared that the solid profits of trade would be jeopardized by the incalculable responsibilities of government. People within the government, and to some extent people within parliament as well, feared that the company's new territorial position would give it power without responsibility and would make it a kind of state within a state, governing others but itself ungovernable. And people who were within all three, whose financial interests in the company were constantly at war with their political position in parliament and their administrative responsibilities in the government, were at the very centre of the whole problem, holding the fate of the company—and possibly of the government as well—in their hands. One such person was Charles Townshend, Chatham's chancellor of the exchequer in 1766. Although deeply involved personally in East India stock speculation, he was committed by his ministerial and parliamentary position to support Chatham's grandiose plan to subject the company to governmental inquiry and, if necessary, to governmental control as well.[58]

In France there was no grandiose plan for the *Compagnie des Indes*. There was only a babel of quarrelling directors and shareholders, each convinced that his enemies were plotting the ruin of the company and that his own schemes could save the situation. Laborde seems to have had a genuine plan of reform, whereby the company would be saved by the same means that the English South Sea Company had adopted in 1719: it would turn itself from a trading company to a finance company, borrowing and lending money instead of buying and selling goods. It was this plan, taken over and adapted by the Genevese Isaac Panchaud, that led eventually to the establishment of a government-sponsored Discount Bank in 1776; but it did not succeed in solving the problems of the *Compagnie des Indes*. These continued to grow, feeding on the proposals and counter proposals that were supposed to solve them, until in the end the government withdrew the company's privileges by an edict of 15 August 1769. By further edicts, of 17 February and 8 April 1770, the company was called upon to hand over its assets to the king, who guaranteed payment of its debts. But its shares, now down to a

[58] L. B. Namier and J. Brooke, *Charles Townshend*, 1964, pp. 159–72. See also L. S. Sutherland, *The East India Company in Eighteenth-century Politics*, Oxford, 1952.

level where they yielded a dividend of between ten and twelve per cent, still found a ready market and the company continued to play an important, though no longer exclusive, part in the trade with the East Indies.[59]

While the French government started off without a definite plan but finished up with definite action, the English government started off with a plan and then found itself unable to act. There were personal reasons for this—Chatham himself fell ill, his spokesmen in the House of Commons quarrelled among themselves and his chancellor of the exchequer used his direct contacts with the East India Company directors to mislead and deceive his own leader—but the real reasons were more fundamental. Chatham's plans for the East India Company, like his plans for the American colonies and his plans to transcend the factious hubbub of party politics, collapsed because neither he nor anyone else could discover and define that 'national interest' before which the local interests and the factious politicians and the chartered companies were supposed to bow. Specific Patriot policies had had some measure of success, both in England and in France, and the 1760s had witnessed a genuine if rather sporadic shift in the political balance of forces in the two countries. The traditional power structures, the power structures to which the dauphin and the duke of Cumberland had been so devoted, would never again rule with the confidence and assurance that they had shown before the Seven Years War. Patriot politicians had succeeded in their primary aim of challenging the comparatively narrow circle of officeholders who had monopolized political power during the first half of the century. They had even managed to widen the circle here and there, to inject new blood into it, to change for the better some of its administrative practices. But they had not succeeded in their ultimate aim, the aim upon which their whole political philosophy and their whole political future depended. They had not shown how the circle might itself be dispensed with, how the good intentions of the outsiders might somehow replace the administrative experience of the insiders, how the country might by some miracle be persuaded to unify itself, discover itself, discipline itself and govern itself. They had supplanted the corrupt managers but they did not know how to supersede corrupt management.

The nature of the Patriots' political failure was reflected in the

[59] Lüthy, ii, 376–97.

mode of their political death, which was slow and lingering. One by one the members of the traditional power structures found their way back into the Patriot ministries which vilified them but could not do without them. Stage by stage the Chatham and Choiseul administrations changed their appearance, like a make-up artist's dream of Dr Jekyll dissolving into Mr Hyde. Having sabotaged Chatham's plans for getting revenue from the East India Company, Charles Townshend was forced to lay new taxes on the American colonists in his budget of 1767. He accompanied this with new proposals on colonial government which alienated other and more liberal members of the ministry such as Shelburne.[60] Within a fortnight the king was telling Chatham that the members of the administration regarded one another as enemies. Chatham lapsed into serious mental illness and his passionate admirer, the young duke of Grafton, who had come in as first lord of the treasury in 1776 after making it clear that he was the disciple of Chatham and Chatham alone, was left to hold the ministry together as best he could with little or no help from his hero. Chatham refused to advise on necessary changes, but when they were made he said that they betrayed the original aims of his administration. He resigned at the end of 1768 and bent his energies to attacking the remnants of his own ministry. By February 1770, when the exhausted and disillusioned Grafton resigned in his turn, the proud Patriot administration of 1766 was nothing but an empty shell into which the older and less idealistic politicians had crept back like hermit crabs.

Choiseul stuck it out longer than Chatham. The appointment of his enemy Maupeou as chancellor in August 1768 was a serious blow and by the end of the year Madame du Deffand, a close friend of the Choiseul family, was beginning to fear the worst.[61] Maynon d'Invault, a member of the Paris *parlement* whom Choiseul had brought in to replace L'Averdy, was brought down by the scandals over the grain supply at the end of 1769; and the new controller general, the Abbé Terray, soon declared himself as an enemy of Choiseul. There was a trial of strength between them early in 1770, when Choiseul was said to have asked Laborde

[60] Namier and Brooke, *Charles Townshend*, pp. 173ff: See also J. Brooke, *The Chatham Administration 1766–68*, 1956; P. D. G. Thomas, 'Charles Townshend and American taxation in 1767', *E.H.R.* lxxxiii, 1968, pp. 33–51; R. J. Chaffin, 'The Townshend Act of 1767', *W.M.Q.* 3rd series, xxvii, 1970, pp. 90–121.
[61] Deffand, *Lettres à Walpole*, i, 171.

to blackmail Terray by refusing him essential loans. The king backed Terray and Choiseul was forced to beat a retreat, pleading for Laborde and his fellow banker Magon de la Balue before the royal council in a manner which recalled Grenville's desperate support of Amyand that Choiseul had so disdained seven years earlier.[62] A few months later the Patriot minister put himself in an even more compromising position by leaving Paris, and thus disassociating himself from the government, just at the moment when the king was treating the *parlement* of Paris to another castigatory session which recalled that of 1766. Louis XV seems to have become convinced by now that Choiseul's encouragement of the *parlements* was a danger to the throne itself—he told the King of Spain that a 'spirit of independence' was gaining ground throughout France—and Choiseul's own behaviour seemed to bear this out.[63] He was finally dismissed on 22 December 1770 and his country house at Chanteloup, to which he was exiled, immediately became a place of pilgrimage for every opposition politician from the duc de Chartres, the most restless of the princes of the blood, down to the meanest member of the *parlements*. 'He received at one and the same time,' wrote Choiseul's admirer the comte de Cheverny, 'the homage of all men of good will and of all the discontented.'[64]

The collapse of the Patriot administrations, and the transformation of the Patriot ministers into opposition leaders, was more than a political phenomenon. In the last analysis the questions which it raised were not merely political questions but social and economic ones. It called into question not only the political acumen of the Patriots or of the kings they served, but the validity of the whole Patriot analysis of society and the categories upon which it was based. Were there really 'insiders' and 'outsiders'? Was it really possible to draw a line between the interests of those within the power structure and the interests of those independent men who did not need to rely on it? And if

[62] *Ibid.*, i, 244–6. See also Add. 9280, fo. 9.
[63] Louis XV to Charles III 21 December 1770, cited Ramsey, *Anglo-French Relations*, p. 227. For an account of Choiseul's equivocal behaviour when the king clashed with the *parlement* see Deffand. *Lettres à Walpole*, i, 279.
[64] Dufort de Cheverny, *Mémoires*, ed. R. de Crèvecoeur, 4th ed., 2 vols, 1909, i, 389. The exact reasons for Choiseul's fall have always been in dispute. Ramsey challenged the traditional view, that it stemmed from his desire for war with England over the Falkland Islands, and more recently it has been suggested that the whole episode was an economic crisis which turned into a political one: see J. F. Bosher, 'The French Crisis of 1770', *History*, lvii, 1972, pp. 17–30.

these distinctions were valid, then how were they related to that other distinction that the Patriots were so fond of denouncing, the distinction between the 'landed interest' and the 'moneyed interest'? These were the myths that had given birth to the Patriot dream. Now that it was dying they too were in danger of dissolution.

5   *The awakening*

*H*orace Walpole was depressed by the political developments of the early 1770s. 'It will be observed,' he wrote sadly about a Commons debate of February 1772, 'how much disposition was spreading towards all annihilation of patriotism.'[1] It was at first sight a rather strange judgment, since the thing on which he was commenting was the support given by two prominent Whigs, Burke and Dowdeswell, to Lord North's stand against giving further relief to the dissenters. And if the political vocabulary of the past thirty or forty years still had any meaning at all, this should surely have been regarded as a symptom of the annihilation not of patriotism but of Whiggism itself. It was the Whigs who had traditionally supported the dissenters, tearing down in George I's reign the barriers against them which the Tories of Anne's reign had so carefully erected; and it was the Patriots who had, under Bolingbroke's guidance, taken over the distrust of dissenters along with most of the other prejudices and principles of the country gentlemen. And since the North administration was supposed to be carrying on, however tenuously, the Patriot

[1] Walpole, *Last Journals*, i, 13.

ministers' original aims of rescuing the king and the country from
Whig dictatorship, why should its winning over of Burke and
Dowdeswell be regarded as a defeat rather than a victory for
patriotism?

The easiest and most tempting answer to this question, as to
so many others in the period, is that it is not worth asking, that
the use made of political terms—especially by a man as devious
as Horace Walpole—is of no significance at a time of such
political confusion as existed both in England and in France in
the years immediately following the collapse of the Chatham
and Choiseul administrations. Madame du Deffand spoke of
French politics in 1771 as a Tower of Babel in which nobody
understood anyone else and all politicians sought indiscriminately
to destroy one another;[2] and English politics were little better.
Burke's *Thoughts on the Cause of the Present Discontents*,
published just as North was taking over from Grafton, stressed
again and again the confusion and fragmentation of political
parties that had come about during the previous ten years.
Ostensibly it sought to show that this state of affairs had been
brought about by a sinister group of courtiers, who had used
the well-meaning aspirations of their king in order to destroy
their political rivals. They had brought one party after another
to power, it was asserted, and had then in each case used their
influence to undermine it and bring it into disrepute not only with
the king but also with the other parties in parliament. 'All sorts
of parties,' Burke alleged, 'by this means have been brought
into administration, from whence few have escaped without
disgrace; none at all without considerable losses.'[3] But, however
much Burke might project onto imaginary scapegoats the failings
of his own friends, it was in fact clear that he was surveying the
disintegration of the existing party system. What his sombre
picture of confusion really laid bare was not the infamy of
chimerical courtiers but the ineffectiveness of actual flesh and
blood party politicians—not least of those who boasted that their
patriotism raised them above party. If there was babel in Paris
and Versailles, then in London there was pandemonium. It
mattered little whose principles were being annihilated by whom,
since all principles were in any case in the melting pot.

And yet there was a pattern emerging, a pattern which did

---

[2] Deffand, *Lettres à Walpole*, i, 317.
[3] Burke, *Select Works*, i, 24.

much to justify Walpole's seemingly topsyturvy use of terms. It was emerging in much the same way and for much the same reasons as it had emerged in the original pandemonium: once the fallen politicians came to realize the extent of their fall and the sheer power of their adversary they saw the need to work together against him. For the thing that had really shaken even the most seasoned campaigners, in parliament and *parlement* alike, had been the speed and ease with which both George III and Louis XV had been able to enforce their authority in the dual crisis of 1770–71. In France the *parlements* were sent into exile within a month of Choiseul's fall and in their place the Chancellor Maupeou set up an entirely new system of courts known as the *Parlement Maupeou*. There was a ferocious outcry against this allegedly unconstitutional act and even the king's cousins, the princes of the blood royal, refused to take part in the ceremonies that ratified it. The members of the old *parlements* threatened what was in effect a general strike of the whole legal profession: not a single lawyer, they insisted, would stoop to take office in the *Parlement Maupeou*. But within a few months this brave show of defiance began to crumble: lawyer after lawyer came forward to fill the key places in the new courts. The princes made their peace with the king and even the duc d'Orléans, who with his son and heir, the duc de Chartres, was regarded by the extremists as their potential leader in a civil war, was having secret conferences with Louis XV by the spring of 1772.[4] For many years past it had been customary to speak of the king of England 'making a parliament'—that is, ensuring by a judicious use of crown patronage that the new parliament would do what his ministers told it to do—and now it seemed that the king of France was able to 'make a *parlement*' in an even more sweeping and absolute sense.

It was one particular aspect of the crown's 'making of parliament' in 1768 that lay at the root of the English aspect of the dual crisis. John Wilkes had returned from France in that year and had stood for the county of Middlesex, after failing to secure election for the City of London. He had been returned by a large majority but the House of Commons, under pressure from the king and his ministers, had declared that he was incapable of

[4] S.-P. Hardy, *Mes Loisirs*, ed. M. Tourneux and M. Vitrac, 1912, p. 342. Hardy was a Parisian bookseller whose diary (which is in the Bibliothèque Nationale, Paris: MSS Français 6687) covers 1764 to 1789. The part published by Tourneux and Vitrac ends in 1773.

taking his seat because he was still technically an outlaw. The electors of Middlesex had refused to elect anyone else and in the end, after three elections and three votes of the Commons against the admission of Wilkes, a government candidate called Luttrell was solemnly declared member of parliament for Middlesex, even though he had only polled 296 votes against Wilkes's 1143. It was this episode, and the widespread discontent and political agitation that sprang from it, that led Burke to say in his *Thoughts* that 'the true contest is between the electors of the kingdom and the crown; the crown acting by an instrumental House of Commons'. And having pushed his arguments thus far he took the next, the logical but extremely dangerous step: he pointed out that if the existing representative body could be controlled by the executive power then reference must be made to some wider representative structure. 'I see no other way for the preservation of a decent attention to public interest in the Representatives,' he wrote, 'but *the interposition of the body of the people itself*, whenever it shall appear, by some flagrant and notorious act, by some capital innovation, that these representatives are going to over-leap the fences of the law, and to introduce an arbitrary power.'[5]

This was a really astonishing suggestion for a Whig to make. The Patriots, for all their apparent radicalism and their refusal to accept existing political hierarchies, had at least taken care to base their politics fairly and squarely on property. They had claimed to speak on behalf of independent men of property and status, men who had a sizeable stake in society which entitled them to some political consideration. But now, it seemed, a prominent Whig spokesman was advocating the admission of the people in general, including perhaps many who had little or no property, to the ranks of the political nation. Burke fully realized the dangerous and indeed revolutionary nature of the step he was proposing—it was, he said, 'a most unpleasant remedy'—but he believed, or pretended to believe, that there was no alternative. 'Indeed, in the situation in which we stand,' he wrote, 'with an immense revenue, an enormous debt, mighty establishments, government itself a great banker and a great merchant, I see no other way'.[6] It was the sheer power of the government of the day, as revealed in the crisis of 1770–71, that seemed to him to make

[5] Burke, *Select Works*, i, 66, 78.
[6] *Ibid.*, i, 78.

the old patriotism outdated, to turn it into a genteel attempt to cure gangrene with lavender water, and to make a new concept of patriotism necessary. It was this new concept of patriotism that explained Walpole's changed use of the word in 1772; and it was this new concept, too, that led to the growth of revolutionary movements in America, in France and also to some extent in England as well.

There was no French equivalent to Burke's *Thoughts*: perhaps French politics would have developed along less violent lines if there had been. As it was, the propertied classes in France amused themselves with such professedly revolutionary but basically innocuous pastimes as freemasonry—which took a great leap forward in popularity following the establishment of the Lodge of the Grand Orient in 1771[7]—and only a small minority among them dared to think in terms of the 'interposition of the body of the people itself'. Malesherbes, a member of the Paris *parlement* and son of that Chancellor Lamoignon who had been supplanted by Maupeou in 1768, came near to it with his suggestion, made in a formal protest to the king in February 1771, that the Estates General should be summoned. The Estates General, the nearest thing France had to a national representative body, was traditionally organized in such a way as to give effective power to the nobility and the clergy; but since it had not met since 1614 it was by no means certain that if it did meet again it would do so under the old forms. Malesherbes, who had already appeared more than ten years earlier as an advocate of a widely based national assembly, was in fact suggesting something which might in the end prove as revolutionary as Burke's proposed interposition of the people.[8]

As heralds of a new and more democratic age Burke and Malesherbes were not particularly convincing. Both were in the last analysis spokesmen for the privileged and the propertied rather than for the people as a whole: their apparent enthusiasm for a wider franchise and a broader basis of representation was to prove very short-lived. But what was really important was not

[7] The literature on the real or imagined impact of freemasonry on French eighteenth-century politics is enormous. For a discussion of its nature and value see J. M. Roberts, 'The origins of a mythology: freemasons, Protestants and the French Revolution', *Bulletin of the Institute of Historical Research*, xliv, 1971, pp. 78–97.

[8] J. M. S. Allison, *Malesherbes, Defender and Reformer of the French Monarchy 1721–1794*, New Haven, 1938, p. 16. See also P. Grosclaude, *Malesherbes, témoin et interprète de son temps*, 2 parts, 1961–64.

the degree of conviction with which they put forward the new
patriotism but the degree of clarity with which they exposed the
inadequacies of the old. However much they might subsequently
try to forget it—and Burke tried very hard—they had seen for
one brief moment, illuminated by the glare of the 1770–71 crisis,
the simple fact that the existing political dialogue was unreal. Sir
Robert Talbot, in his *Letters on the French Nation* of 1771, put
his finger on the source of that unreality when he wrote: of the
parlements and their attacks on the financiers: 'Now half, at least,
of the grave personages who compose those august assemblies
consists of the sons, grandsons or heirs of men enriched by
finance. An office of Counsellor of Parliament, or of Master of
Accounts, is a kind of surtout which the financiers of one age
make their sons put on, in order to disguise and render them
respectable to the next generation.'[9] For years the Patriots had
talked of a gulf between the insiders and the outsiders, the officeholders and the independent men; but in fact that gulf had already
been turned into a communicating corridor, so many and intricate
were the bridges built across it by the ambitions of families anxious
for social advancement.

Talbot might well have gone further than he did, for the
members of the *parlements* were not only the sons and the grandsons of financiers: they were also in many cases the fathers and
the grandfathers of present or future ministers of the crown. The
ladder of social success, from the middle rungs of which the
parlements trumpeted so loudly their defiance of the government,
was in fact a ladder that had its top as well as its foot planted
firmly in the lush pastures of government patronage. When
L'Averdy in 1763 went straight from being the leader of the
opposition in the Paris *parlement* to being controller-general of
finances, the transition was hailed as a dramatic surrender by the
government; but in fact it was unusual only in its suddenness and
in the amount of publicity it received. Hardly a month went by
without some member of some *parlement* somewhere accepting
office under the crown and changing almost overnight from a
firebrand to a supporter of the establishment, just as in England
fiery and apparently 'independent' men in the House of Commons
were rendered docile and amenable by being appointed to government office.

In both cases a sceptic could be excused for thinking that the

[9] Sir Robert Talbot, *Letters on the French Nation*, 2 vols, 1771, ii, 99.

fiery speeches had been intended for no other purpose than to increase the speaker's nuisance value and thus to put up the price the government was prepared to pay in order to win him over. There were those who saw L'Averdy's conversion in these terms, just as there had been those who took such a view of the original entry into government service, back in 1746, of that archetypal Patriot, William Pitt. The vital difference between the two countries in this connection was that in France the conversion was for good: the *parlements* were not filled, as the English House of Commons was, with men who had started in opposition, gone into government and finally resigned and come back into opposition. It was for this reason that the French king's critics in *parlement* were almost all young men, with their careers to make. If they were at all able they were almost certain to be removed from the *parlements* by the time they were forty and transferred to an administrative post. It was only in England that opposition to the crown was the refrain, rather than merely the overture, of a man's political career.

The interpenetration of government and *parlement*—and thus the unreality of the French political dialogue—was seen most clearly in provincial government, which was at this time in the hands of thirty-four *intendants*—thirty-five after the taking over of Corsica in 1768—each of whom was responsible to the central government for the administration of a particular area known as his *généralité*. In 1763, when L'Averdy made his much acclaimed jump from the Paris *parlement* to the post of controller-general, at least twenty of the thirty-four were members of the Paris *parlement* and many of the remaining fourteen were either members of one or other of the provincial *parlements* or were closely related to those who were.[10] Relations at a local level between *intendant* and *parlement*, which might have been expected to reflect the dramatic conflicts at the centre between the king's government and the Paris *parlement*, were in fact very variable. It was provinces like Brittany, where there was a constant running fight between the *intendant* and the *parlement*, that caught the attention of the public at the time and have held the attention

[10] This association between the *intendants* and the *parlements*, which receives surprisingly little attention in Gruder's analysis (see above, p. 77n), can be seen in detail in J. F. Bluche, *L'origine des magistrats du parlement de Paris au xviii* siècle (dictionnaire généalogique)*, 1956—an invaluable book which lays the foundations for a structural school of French eighteenth-century history analogous to that established by Namier in England. See also the same author's *Les magistrats du parlement de Paris au xviii* siècle*, 1960.

of historians ever since; provinces like Languedoc, where Guignard de St Priest was *intendant* continuously from 1751 to 1785 and worked in the closest harmony with the *parlement* of Toulouse and the sovereign courts of Montpellier and Montauban, have received much less notice. Seen through the eyes of the pamphleteers and the writers of memoirs and the collectors of gossip, French eighteenth-century history appears as a violent clash between the government and the governed, a meaningful political dialogue which culminated in revolution—which was of course how the so-called Patriots in the *parlements* and elsewhere hoped it would appear. But seen through the eyes of ordinary people running their daily affairs, seeking the best form of investment for their wealth and the most promising careers for their sons, it appears very differently. The realities of family advancement and investment, which determined the structure of politics in any country at this time, made nonsense of the carefully nurtured myths of party politics.

In the context of France these truths are only just becoming evident, as a result of the detailed work which is at last being done on the structure of French politics in the eighteenth century. The structure of English eighteenth-century politics, on the other hand, has been revealed in great detail by the work which has been done over the past forty years under the impetus of Sir Lewis Namier. The first result of Namier's researches was to expose the mythical nature of the Whig view of the period, the view that saw eighteenth-century politics as a struggle between two distinct and disciplined parties over great issues of principle; but they have also cast doubts on the truth of the Patriot assertion that the political nation could be divided into the sinister network of government patronage on the one hand and the sturdy independent men on the other. However sturdy and independent a man might be, however much the landed nature of his property might free him from the need to seek crown favour or watch the fluctuations of government stock, he might still have sons to provide for. It was no accident that Sir Roger de Coverley, the great fictional archetype of all eighteenth-century independent gentlemen, was presented by his creators as a bachelor, with no family to advance. Real live gentlemen could seldom afford Sir Roger's lofty contempt for government office: their real complaint was not that patronage existed but that they were being excluded from it.

Namier directed attention in particular to that segment of political life which was the subject of so much controversy both in England and in France in the 1760s, the segment made up of merchants and bankers who entered political life in order to advance their business interests. He introduced the subject by quoting from *Seasonable Hints from an Honest Man*, a pamphlet written by John Douglas in the first few months of George III's reign to put the Patriot point of view. 'Men who are in trade, and who get themselves elected, only to be in the way of their trade' were, in Douglas's view, the chief threat to the independence of the House of Commons: they would 'assist in involving the nation in dangerous projects, and ruinous expense'[11] and would do as much or perhaps more harm than the placemen who were the traditional cause for Patriot complaint. Namier then went on to examine twenty-two merchants and bankers of the City of London who were particularly deeply involved in lending to the government and in exploiting government contracts, to show that most of them either sat in parliament or sent their sons into it, unless they were ineligible because they were of foreign or Jewish descent. But these men formed only the hard core of that 'commercial interest' of which Douglas and his readers among the country gentlemen complained so bitterly. By common consent that interest was at least three times as large as the inner group examined by Namier; and the real question in English politics, the question that underlay both the anticommercialist reaction of the early 1760s and the subsequent conflicts over American taxation or East India Company speculation, was whether or not a line could be drawn between the 'commercial interest' and the independent landed men who attacked it so violently.

It was at this point that the Patriot myth was most vulnerable, precisely because it was at this point that it divided into two. According to Grenville and his supporters the real Patriots were the independent landed men, who had resisted both the Whig attempts to restore the old oligarchy and the attempts of the commercial men to create a new plutocracy; but according to Chatham and his friends, including many who had been Whigs but now joined him in opposing Lord North, true patriotism lay in defending the vital overseas empire against the shortsighted landed men who would put it in jeopardy for the sake of a few

---

[11] L. B. Namier, *The Structure of Politics at the Accession of George III*, rev. edn, 1957, p. 45.

E

thousand pounds of revenue from the American colonists. Who, then, were the commercial men and who were the landed men? Were the landed men represented by the old original Tories, the men who according to Pitt's boast of November 1762 'had been of the denomination of Tories but during his share of the administration had supported government upon the principles of Whiggism and the Revolution'?[12] This certainly squared with the traditional Whig picture of the Tories as archaic and bucolic rural boobies, but it did not square with the economic and geographical facts. Great cities like Bristol and Liverpool, where Toryism was predominant among the richest and most influential inhabitants, could hardly be dismissed as mere outposts of petty squiredom.

Individual Tories could be as surprising as the places they came from. Matthew Brickdale, the rich clothier and undertaker who represented Bristol from 1768 to 1774, was a diehard Tory, as his father had been before him; and it was only when the city chose the Whig Burke in his place that it began to think that its commercial interests were being neglected in parliament.[13] Bamber Gascoyne, a rich brewer and landowner who was member for Liverpool from 1759 to 1761, certainly fitted the conventional picture of the Tory as a religious fanatic—in a letter to a friend he once dismissed the enemies of his beloved Toryism as 'Whigs, Quakers, Presbyters, the Devil, etc.'—but he could not really be called archaic or bucolic.[14] His successor Sir William Meredith was regarded by Newcastle as such a violent Tory that he could not be trusted with any local influence at all; and on occasion he could certainly exercise the privileges of his rank as ruthlessly as any French nobleman. Yet he was a determined spokesman for Liverpool's trading interests, especially with the West Indies. When the thorny question of rice exports from Carolina to southern Europe and Africa came up in the Commons it was Meredith who produced an extremely able report on the whole matter.[15] Sir William Codrington, member for Tewkesbury from

---

[12] See above, pp. 56–7.
[13] On these suspicions and the extent to which they were justified, see P. T. Underdown, 'Edmund Burke the Commissary of his Bristol constituents', *E.H.R.* lxxiii, 1958, pp. 252–69. On Brickdale see *Commons 1754–90*, ii, 115–16.
[14] *Commons 1754–90*, ii, 486–91.
[15] *Ibid.*, iii, 130–3; Add. 38, 200, fos 47–8; *Commons Journals*, xxix, 605–6, 625, 958. See also 'Sir William Meredith's confession of faith', an extremely interesting document printed in *H.M.C.* 35, Kenyon, pp. 497–8. On Meredith's privileged position, see the petition of Miles Button Allen (Add. 38, 341, fo. 157) who was in prison because of what he insisted was a false accusation by Meredith and had no redress because of the latter's privilege of parliament.

1761 to 1792, might seem at first sight a more typical Tory country gentleman, concerning himself only with his position as a Gloucestershire squire and busy in the Commons with turnpike acts and other local matters. Yet he owned plantations in Barbados and Antigua and he was the brother-in-law of the Whig financial and commercial expert William Dowdeswell—himself a man who ought to have been a Tory if he had paid attention to his landed position and to the traditional categories of political mythology.[16] Even Sir Roger Newdigate, one of those bucolic Warwickshire gentlemen whose inadequacies in parliament irritated Samuel Garbett so much, was actively concerned in developing coalmines on his estates at Bedworth and linking them by canal to Coventry.[17]

Quite apart from any question of political labels, the economic interests of the so-called 'independent country gentlemen' made it difficult for them to stand aloof, either from the commerce and industry of the country or from the contacts with government and policy making which such pursuits necessitated. The Foleys of Worcestershire and Herefordshire were traditionally a great Tory family, champions of the land and of local agriculture; but they were also great industrialists, controlling a network of iron foundries and forges which stretched throughout the Severn valley.[18] Even those landed men who did behave feudally did not always do so in the interests of what is generally thought of as the feudal society. George Warren, a gentleman with extensive estates in Lancashire and descended on his mother's side from the earls of Cholmondeley, was one of the most indefatigable practitioners of feudalism in the kingdom. In his manor of Stockport he resurrected and utilized every archaic toll and due that he could discover, but the purpose of it all—a purpose in which he was eventually thwarted by his aristocratic rival, the duke of Bridgewater—was the development of his coalfields and other industrial resources.[19] Indeed, it has been suggested that the real inspiration for the apparently bourgeois process sometimes known as the industrial revolution came not from a separate and

[16] *Commons 1754–90*, ii, 231–2, 333–5.
[17] *Ibid.*, iii, 196–9. For Garbett's complaints, see above, p. 32.
[18] B. L. C. Johnson, 'The Foley partnerships: the iron industry at the end of the charcoal era', *Ec.H.R.* 2nd series, iv, 1952, pp. 322–37; R. G. Schafer, 'Genesis of the Foley partnership', *Business History*, xiii, 1971, pp. 19–38.
[19] *Commons 1754–90*, iii, 607–9.

distinguishable 'middle class' but from enterprising country
gentlemen and from the land agents of great noblemen.[20]

In England, as in France, investment in government finance
was more widespread than the mythical Patriot antithesis between
rascally stockjobbing financiers and self-sufficient rural squires
would suggest; and dabblers in French government stock, as well
as in English, were found in some surprising places. Shrewsbury,
described by Namier as 'an independent borough which acknowledged no patron but chose its members usually from among old
Shropshire families',[21] was represented in the 1760s by Robert
Clive, symbol of the hated speculators of the East India Company,
and Thomas Hill, an international financier who carried on lucra-
tive dealings in all sorts of securities, including French government stock, but was nevertheless classed as a Tory by all the
political analysts of his day.[22] Whether the Tories and the Patriots
knew it or not, the financiers were amongst them. In the English
parliament, as in the French *parlements*, there were men who were
the sons and the grandsons of financiers and who had by no means
severed their connections with the source of their family's wealth.

But the existence of commercial and financial interests amongst
independent men did not necessarily preclude all Patriot politics,
even if it did make nonsense of much of the traditional Patriot
mythology. What really mattered was the direction in which the
influence was exerted—whether it was used to impose the iron
will of a monolithic government on all the economic activities of
the governed or whether it formed a means whereby the economic
needs of the governed could mould and make more flexible
the policies of the government. It is always difficult to assess the
actions, and even more difficult to assess the motives, of men who
stand at the meeting place of forces as powerful as those of
government and of the governed; and it is easy to assume that
such men were in fact the lickspittle court lackeys that they were
popularly supposed to be. It is sometimes assumed, for instance,
that because the French *Bureau de Commerce* functioned fairly
smoothly and without any great controversies or confrontations

[20] Recent work on the agrarian, and even aristocratic, origins of the
'Industrial Revolution' is too extensive to be summarized here. Perhaps the
best tailpiece is provided by S. D. Chapman: 'Indeed, the longer one looks
at the early cotton industry under the microscope, the less revolutionary
the early phases of its life-cycle appear to be' ('Fixed capital formation in
the British cotton industry 1770–1815', *Ec.H.R.* xxiii, 1970, pp. 235–66).
[21] Namier, *Structure*, p. 240.
[22] *Commons 1754–90*, ii, 225–8, 625–7.

its representative members, the *députés de commerce* from the twelve greatest commercial cities of France, from the province of Languedoc and from the French West Indian islands, must therefore have been mere cyphers.[23] Unlike English members of parliament, the *députés* received a salary to indemnify them for the time they spent on the *Bureau*'s business instead of on their own affairs; and this certainly gave the government a greater hold over them than the English government had over members of parliament. But then the *Bureau* was not supposed to be the counterpart of parliament. In effect the function it performed was the equivalent of the whole process which in England stretched from the lobbying of members of parliament right through to the much more difficult task of influencing the Board of Trade. It is not surprising, therefore, that commentators as knowledgeable as Postlethwayte should consider that it produced a more genuinely representative commercial policy than was possible in England.[24]

When the deputies did clash with those they were supposed to represent it was not always clear who stood for the government and who for the governed. In 1768 Philibert Simian, deputy for Marseilles, was called to account by the Marseilles chamber of commerce and stoutly defended by the central government; but his alleged neglect of duty concerned not the trade of the city as a whole but the particular privileges of the chamber and the money it was owed by the government. Ministers had already tried to flatter the chamber by reminding it of the great funds it controlled and the great fiscal powers it enjoyed; and now it was these things, rather than the trade of the city as a whole, that brought about a confrontation. Nor did Simian survive the confrontation for very long. In 1772, while on an extended visit to the city, he suddenly decided that he ought to retire. The royal governor of Provence talked about getting him replaced by one Arnaud, a candidate known to be unacceptable to the chamber; but the central government had learned its lesson and decided to confirm the appointment of the chamber's chosen candidate Rostagny. Rostagny remained on amicable terms with

<hr>

[23] See, for instance, J. F. Bosher, *The Single Duty Project*, 1964, p. 28, where they are described as 'officials of the Crown with the duty of expressing their collective opinion'.

[24] See above, pp. 29–30. The working of the *bureau* can be studied in P. Bonnassieux and E. Lelong, *Inventaire analytique des procès-verbaux du conseil du commerce et du bureau du commerce, 1700–91*, 1900.

the chamber until 1791, when the revolution abolished both deputies and chambers.[25]

The ordinary Marseillais might have been forgiven for wondering who exactly did represent them, the oligarchic chamber or the allegedly unrepresentative deputy. If so they were not alone in their feelings of frustration. Mr Birkbeck, agent of the English government in the port of Marseilles at the time of the Simian quarrel, told his superiors angrily: 'I do not wonder that our nation is so badly served and so often cheated by those they employ, when so little regard is paid to the remonstrance of those who do their duty and would serve their country. The form of office is the devil; for want of proper care of our seamen there are now within these twelve months 150 entered into the French service in this one port.'[26] The sense of being cut off and ignored, of being at the wrong end of a long line of corrupt and unrepresentative bureaucrats, was not peculiar to France. On both sides of the Channel independent men suspected that those who should have made their needs known to the government were failing in their duty.

From all this confusion, from all this recrimination and counter-recrimination as to who was the sturdy independent Patriot and who was the servile creature of the government, one essential political fact emerged: if the existing political dialogue was to continue it must either change its name or change its nature. In the crucial years between 1770 and 1774 there was something like a mass desertion from the ranks of opposition to the ranks of the government. French lawyers who in 1770 were preparing to live or die with the firebrands in the Paris *parlement* had discovered by 1774 that they had no defence against a government which could abolish their offices—and thus devalue their family's chief investment—except to take back those offices on the government's own terms. English politicians who in 1770 had been determined to break Lord North at all costs had found out exactly the same thing and for exactly the same reason. And, more important still, men who previously had thought that their way of life enabled them to scorn officeholders and ignore the

[25] J. Fournier, *La Chambre de commerce de Marseille et ses représentants permanents à Paris, 1599–1875*, Marseille, 1920, pp. 131–62; G. Rambert, *Histoire du Commerce de Marseille*, 6 vols, 1949, –iv, 250–5, 322, 328. Rambert concludes that all the deputies in this period, apart from Simian, were zealous defenders of the city's interests.
[26] *C.H.O.P.*, ii, no. 1337.

need to influence or participate in government were beginning to find that their trade or their investments in government stock or even their landed interests necessitated, whether they liked it or not, some sort of bridge between them and the central government. Finally, there were signs of a reaction against the restive and disruptive attitudes which had dominated the politics of both countries ever since the Seven Years War. English Tories, in particular, began to find their innate conservatism stronger than their hatred of particular Whig governments. Sir Walter Blackett, who came of an old Tory family with lands in county Durham and an important interest in the coal trade, was a notable example. Throughout the 1760s he had voted against government after government on all sorts of issues, culminating in that of John Wilkes and the freeholders of Middlesex; but in November 1770 he stood up in the Commons and confessed the error of his ways. He had had a change of heart, he said, 'upon one morning when I was walking alone in the Tuileries'. From that moment he swung steadily over to the side of North, to such an extent that in 1775, when 1210 of his constituents signed a petition against the American war, he refused to present it, bringing forward instead one in favour of the war. It contained 169 signatures: the triumph of minority over majority was even greater than in the business of Luttrell and Wilkes.[27]

What, if anything, Sir Walter had seen in the Tuileries to make him change his political attitudes was never revealed. When Lord St Vincent walked through the Tuileries gardens a couple of years later all he noticed was 'the interruption of too many of the votaries of Venus, for the most part of the lowest class';[28] but even such unflagging votaries as might still have been around to disturb an early morning walk could hardly have wrought such a dramatic change unaided. The political situation in Paris that summer, described by Madame du Deffand as so tense that it must explode within a matter of months, may have played a part. Support for Wilkes, which in England might seem like a lofty constitutional duty, no doubt looked rather different in Paris where the protagonists of the *parlement* were still flourishing the remnants of a shipload of handkerchiefs *à la Wilkes*, printed with his address to the electors of Middlesex, which had

[27] *Commons 1754–90*, ii, 94–6.
[28] Add. 32, 192, fo. 12.

been imported some months earlier.[29] Englishmen in France, like Frenchmen in England, tended to see their own discontents as less dignified when they were mirrored in the antics of the other nation.

Whatever Sir Walter Blackett's motives may have been, whatever connection there may have been between his retreat from Patriotism and the similar retreat that took place in France, the question posed by his desertion and the desertion of so many others was clear enough. Who was to replace them? The events of the 1760s, in spite of or perhaps even because of their confused nature, had at least kept alive the old Patriot myth that there were sturdy independent men within the political nation who could be relied upon to counterbalance the forces of government and thus give meaning to the political dialogue. But now Lord North and Chancellor Maupeou between them were calmly demonstrating the myth's falsity. Patriot and officeholder, like Punch and Judy, had been abusing one another and battering one another for a decade. Now the suave manipulator of both stepped into view holding a puppet in either hand. If the show was to go on, if it was to remain credible and meaningful, then some new figures would have to be found whose strings could not be quite so easily jerked by the government for its own purposes.

Few people—least of all Burke himself—really thought that such figures should be sought outside the ranks of the existing political nation, that 'the body of the people itself' should be allowed a say in the country's affairs. Nor was there as yet any general acceptance of the idea that dialogue and balance should be a permanent part of political life. In the *Thoughts* Burke made the remark that 'he that supports every administration, subverts all government';[30] but he did not mean by this that every government should have its opponents, that there should always be a shadow government waiting in the wings to take over when the political pendulum made its next swing. He meant, on the contrary, that the pendulum could only be brought to rest and a permanently acceptable government formed—a Whig government, needless to say—if men realized that other sorts of governments should not be supported. Similarly, Choiseul and his friends did not want to oust Maupeou as part of a continuing process of democratic alternation by means of which they would themselves be ousted

[29] Bachaumont, iv, 80.
[30] Burke, *Select Works*, i, 80.

in their turn. They wanted to oust him for the same reason that Burke wanted to oust North—because he was allegedly running the country in a way which offended against traditional constitutional principles to which a return must be made. In each country the opposition was faced with the same dilemma: it had to seek new allies in order to assert old principles. And it had to do so at the end of a decade which had demonstrated both the disunity of the governed and the ubiquitous influence of the government.

In the case of England there was one obvious quarter in which the necessary 'new forces' might be sought: the American colonies. Even Horace Walpole, who was certainly not one to underrate the graces of European society or to overrate the homespun virtues which the colonists were supposed to typify, found himself almost overawed when he contemplated the future potential of the New World. 'The next Augustan age will dawn on the other side of the Atlantic,' he told Sir Horace Mann. 'There will, perhaps, be a Thucydides at Boston, a Xenophon at New York, and, in time, a Virgil at Mexico and a Newton at Peru. At last, some curious traveller from Lima will visit England and give a description of the ruins of St Paul's like the editions of Balbec and Palmyra.'[31] The one philosopher who existed in reality rather than in Walpole's imagination, Benjamin Franklin of Philadelphia, was certainly made very welcome by radical thinkers in England. A group of them who called themselves the Honest Whigs and who met at St Paul's coffee house had particularly close contacts with him. One night in September 1769, when Boswell was there with Franklin and several others, the company agreed despondently that parliament corrupted every man who went into it, however independent he might have been before. The conclusion that Boswell drew from this sad observation was that they might just as well elect men who were already bad, so that the good men could be saved for something else.[32]

But for what else? That was the real question, both in England and in France. If existing representative and would-be representative bodies, parliament and *parlements*, were nothing but offshoots of the power structure, then it might be necessary not only to enlist new forces but also to create new bodies. In France

[31] Walpole, *Letters*, ix, 100.
[32] C. van Doren, *Franklin*, p. 401. See also V. W. Crane, 'The Club of Honest Whigs: friends to science and liberty', *W.M.Q.* 3rd series, xxiii, 1966, pp. 210–33.

there was talk of newly constituted assemblies, both at a national
and at a provincial level; and in England the furore over the
Middlesex election had set on foot a movement to form extra-
parliamentary bodies which later came to call themselves
'associations'. One obvious solution, which would kill several birds
with one stone, lay in the formation of an Imperial Parliament
such as the one that the Quaker merchant Thomas Crowley
outlined to Chatham in 1770.[33] Many opposition leaders, including
Burke himself, had some degree of interest in schemes of this sort.
James Burgh, a dissenting schoolmaster and a keen member of
the Honest Whig club, made the really crucial point in his
Political Disquisitions, published in 1774. He argued very per-
suasively that the ending of parliamentary corruption at home
and the defeat of North's oppressive policy in America were
inseparable one from the other. North's objective, he asserted,
was not simply to tax America but to corrupt her: if he was
allowed to succeed independents would become as rare on the
other side of the Atlantic as they already were in England. It
behoved independent Englishmen to support the Americans if
they wished themselves to be saved from extinction. The
instrument of salvation, in Burgh's view, was a radical reform of
parliament. There must be annual parliaments and secret ballots,
together with a wider franchise so that all taxpayers could vote
and all counties be represented in proportion to the contribution
they made to government revenue. And just as North could only
be stopped by means of parliamentary reform, so reform itself
could only be achieved by grasping the opportunity offered by
America's resistance. Similar arguments were put forward in
Major John Cartwright's *American Independence the Interest
and Glory of Great Britain*, though here the solution was seen
in terms of two reformed parliaments, one on each side of the
Atlantic, linked by a federal union.[34]

This kind of reasoning—or, to be more exact, this particular
combination of reasoning and prejudiced suspicion—reflected
clearly enough the basic truth about the American crisis, which
was that it could no longer be solved by concessions over

[33] For an account of these proposals see *E.H.R.* xxii, 1907, pp. 756–8.
[34] The Commons House of the Assembly of South Carolina was so convinced of this mutual interdependence that it actually voted £1500 of public
money to support Wilkes and the radicals. See J. P. Greene, ed., *The
Nature of Colony Constitutions: two pamphlets on the Wilkes fund controversy by Sir Egerton Leigh and Arthur Lee*, Columbia, S.C. 1970.

taxation. North, indeed, was making more concessions than any other government had made since the crisis began: compared with Grenville or Townshend or even with Dowdeswell, chancellor of the exchequer under Rockingham, his taxation policy was conciliatory. What was less conciliatory, in American eyes, was his plan to establish a civil list in the colony of Massachusetts and thus insert into America the thin edge of that patronage wedge which was already working so startlingly well in England and in France. The power of the civil list had been demonstrated as recently as 1769, when in the middle of the great debates over the Middlesex election all the beneficiaries under the English civil list, from pensioners and placemen to contractors and tradesmen, had dropped all their other concerns to clamour for payment of their arrears.[35] Even North's tax concessions could be made to appear part of the sinister conspiracy of enslavement. Ever since the failure of Chatham's plan to nationalize the East India Company, India had been viewed by independent men on both sides of the Atlantic as a happy hunting ground for those speculators and profiteers who formed such an essential part of the corrupt network of government patronage. In the spring of 1772 the Commons passed a resolution condemning the servants of the company and also set up a committee of secrecy to inquire into its affairs. By 1773, when North's Regulating Act could be seen to be propping the company up still further, and doing nothing to curb the speculative frenzy which the committee was busy condemning, it was natural enough for suspicious Americans to see cheap tea from India as a device to enrich the company rather than as a conciliatory gesture to themselves.

The Boston Tea Party gave the final twist to this particular screw, since it produced a demand in England for just that sort of extension of governmental powers that seemed to justify the worst suspicions of the Americans. North gave in to the demand; and his measures tightening English control over Massachusetts were widely supported by men from all parties. Rose Fuller, normally a staunch supporter of government, led the tiny handful that opposed this legislation. 'You will commence your ruin,' he said, 'from this day. I am sorry to say, that not only the house has fallen into this error, but the whole people approve of the measure. The people, I am sorry to say it, are misled. But a short

[35] E. A. Reitan, 'The Civil List in eighteenth-century British politics', *H.J.* ix, 1966, pp. 318–37.

time will prove the evil tendency of this bill. If ever there was a nation running headlong to its ruin, it is this.[36] Four days later, on 10 May 1774, another nation was presented with the chance to run headlong to its ruin or its salvation, as the case might be: Louis XV of France died and was succeeded, as George II of England had been fourteen years earlier, by an idealistic and well-intentioned grandson scarcely out of his teens. As English politics responded to the challenge of the New World and French politics responded to the challenge of a new reign, the old confrontation between entrenched professional politicians and self-styled Patriots would be acted out yet again. But this time it would be something more significant and more deadly than the shadow boxing of the previous decade; and it would involve the two countries more deeply in one another by involving both of them more deeply in the outside world.

[36] Debrett, *Parliamentary Debates*, 1774, pp. 254–5.

6   *Citizens of the world*

*I*t was the winter of 1770–71 that really killed the Patriot movement in English politics, at any rate in the traditional form that
Bolingbroke and Chatham had known. The parliamentary session
that began in November 1770 with Sir Walter Blackett's dramatic
recantation ended, in May of the following year, with the Patriots
in despondent disarray, snapping at one another and at their Whig
allies with indiscriminate petulance. Moderates accused radicals of
undermining the social order; radicals accused moderates of selling
out to the government; everybody accused everybody else of
putting their own particular interests before those of the country.
Chatham's hopes of leading a truly national opposition to the
North administration, which had seemed so bright a year before,
now seemed merely laughable. He retired to his country estate in
despair, convinced that a new age of decadence and corruption
had extinguished for ever the spirit of independence upon which
he had built his political career.

His lieutenant and political heir apparent, the earl of Shelburne,
was more resilient. Three days after the end of the session he set
off on a lengthy tour of France and Italy which he subsequently

came to see as the turning point of his life, the moment of transition from his old view of politics to a wider and more 'enlightened' one.[1] Most English travellers of the period reckoned to go to Italy for their art and to France for their ideas; and Shelburne was no exception. Although he was deeply influenced by his meeting in Milan with Cesare Beccaria, whose theories of penal reform were later to be taken up by Shelburne's *protégés* Bentham and Romilly, it was in Paris that his horizons were really widened and his ideas 'liberalized', as he himself put it. It was six years since the text of the great *Encyclopédie*, the collective wisdom of the 'enlightened' philosophers of France, had completed publication; and it had made Paris the undisputed intellectual capital of Europe. Like many other historical phenomena, the enlightenment seemed simpler and less complicated to those who lived through it than it has seemed since to those who have sought to assess its precise implications. In retrospect, it may seem advisable for us to put inverted commas around the word 'enlightenment'—just as we are tempted to do the same for the word 'patriotism'—in order to show that we have grave doubts as to whether it really meant what it seemed to mean. But in the 1770s there were few such doubts. Most people accepted the fact that there was in Paris a group of thinkers who believed they could change the world for the better by applying their powers of reason to its problems; and most people were either profoundly excited or profoundly irritated by what this group had to say.

From 1771 onwards Shelburne was one of the excited ones; and the importance of his excitement lay in the fact that most of those upon whom the traditional Patriot movement had been built were among the irritated ones. In the first place, the enlightenment was international in its aspirations. In September of 1770, while Sir Walter Blackett was passing through the dark night of his political soul and wrestling with the temptations proferred by Wilkites and colonial rebels, the enlightened *intendant* of Limoges, Anne Robert Turgot, was writing to Dean Tucker of Gloucester to say that 'as a citizen of the world' he looked forward to the coming separation of America from England.[2] Turgot—who was one of the thinkers who particularly influenced Shel-

---

[1] Lord E. Fitzmaurice, *Life of William, Earl of Shelburne*, 2 vols, 1912, i, 424–30.

[2] The letter, dated 12 September 1770, was subsequently printed by Tucker as a testimony to his own impartiality when he came to write on the French intervention in America. See below, p. 176.

burne in the summer of 1771—meant what he said. He genuinely believed that colonies like those along the American seaboard were more trouble than they were worth to the European power that owned them. Separation was the best thing for them, for England and for the world as a whole. Four years later, when he was chief minister to King Louis XVI, he was to press for the abandonment of all French interests in America and for the concentration instead on the expansion of the East Indies trade.[3] But to the ordinary independent man in England, struggling to make the colonists pay their share of taxes and inherently suspicious of the intriguing French, such talk was mere cant. The Earl of Shelburne might listen to it if he wished, but he was unlikely to carry with him either those who had followed Chatham against the French in the brave days of the Seven Years War or those who had subsequently supported Grenville's attempts to impose proper discipline on the colonists.

Shelburne listened all the same. He listened to Turgot, to Malesherbes, to Holbach and to many others. He was made especially welcome at the home of Trudaine de Montigny, who had been since his father's death in 1769 the virtual head of the French *Conseil de Commerce*. Shelburne, who had begun his own political career with a brief spell as president of the Board of Trade, was impressed with Trudaine's efforts to build a bridge between the thinkers of the enlightenment and the day to day business of commercial policy. One of those who advised Trudaine was the Abbé Morellet, who had been commissioned by the French government in 1769 to draw up its ultimatum to the dying *Compagnie des Indes* and who had subsequently become closely associated with those merchants and financiers who were opening up a new and unregulated trade with the Indies. Shelburne was one of those whose political careers had been damaged when Charles Townshend blocked Chatham's attack on the East India Company; and he had also had his reputation compromised in 1769 when Laughlin Macleane, a reckless speculator in East India stock, defaulted on debts which Shelburne had agreed to underwrite.[4] It was not surprising, therefore, that the French thinkers found their English visitor ready to listen to their plans for a great expansion of the Indian trade, based on a free

[3] V. Confer, 'French colonial ideas before 1789', *F.H.S.*, iii, 1964, pp. 338–59.
[4] *Commons 1754–90*, iii, 93–4. On the East India speculations, see below, p. 159.

cooperation between the two countries instead of a cut-throat mercantilist competition between two monopolist companies. Two recently published books which were all the rage in Paris at the time, Raynal's *History of the Trade to the Indies* and Gaillard's *History of the Rivalry between France and England*, helped to drive home the lesson. Gaillard's work, which argued strongly for an end to the conflict which it described, was especially welcome to this group of philosophers and administrators who were seeking to create a new radicalism based on Anglo-French cooperation.

But the old chauvinism which had characterized the sturdy Patriots of the age of Choiseul and Chatham was not yet dead. It had plenty to complain about already in the policies of Lord North and Chancellor Maupeou, which were clearly aimed at a *rapprochement* between the two countries,[5] and it had no wish to see supposedly opposition politicians advocate the same craven and cowardly ideas. The Falkland Islands convention of January 1771, an Anglo-Spanish compromise settlement which had been made possible by France's retreat from the dispute, had already done much to strengthen the hands of the governments against their Patriot opponents. Chatham, in particular, found that his desperate attempts to discredit it merely added to his own unenviable reputation as a hysterical and outmoded xenophobe. During the next few years the two governments moved steadily nearer to agreement over such key issues as the 1772 revolution in Sweden and the Russo-Turkish conflict in the Balkans and the eastern Mediterranean. By 1772 George III himself was suggesting a formal alliance with France.[6] If patriotism had indeed come to mean opposition to the government at all costs, as Walpole seemed to think, then francophile Patriots in England, like anglophile Patriots in France, were a contradiction in terms.

Shelburne nevertheless continued to strengthen his links with the French enlightenment and in April 1772 Morellet came to England at his invitation.[7] Shelburne's retinue of radical philosophers was less impressive than Trudaine's, but it was impressive enough to stimulate and encourage his visitor. It included Richard

[5] B. de Fraguier, 'Le duc d'Aiguillon et l'Angleterre, 1771–73', *R.H.D.*, xxvi, 1912, pp. 607–27.
[6] The proposal was based on the old myth of the harmonious opposites: George III echoed almost exactly what Louis XIV had said in 1667 (see above, p. 5). Fortescue, ii, 429.
[7] Fitzmaurice, *Life of Shelburne*, i, 430ff.

Price, a dissenting minister who was making a name for himself as a financial expert and who was to produce in 1776 one of the key political tracts of the period, *Observations on the nature of civil liberty*. This work, like Burgh's *Political Disquisitions*, saw the Americans as the only reliable guarantors for England's existing political freedoms; but it also saw them as the instruments by which she would win new and far more important freedoms. It claimed full civil liberties for the dissenters, on the grounds that such liberties were the fundamental and inalienable rights of men as men, not something that particular men could acquire by virtue of a specific act of religious observance. Revolutionary ideas of this sort, striking at the very foundation of everything that traditional patriotism stood for, were freely discussed in Shelburne's circle, as was the even more revolutionary idea that the object of government was 'the good and happiness of the members, that is, of the majority of the members, of any state'. This doctrine was later to be taken up and systematically developed by another of Shelburne's tame intellectuals, Jeremy Bentham, whose *Fragment on Government* was also to be published in 1776, the year that produced so many radical utterances ranging from Price's *Observations* to the American Declaration of Independence. The challenge which such a doctrine presented to the political ideas of the independent English country gentlemen —and also, for that matter, to their counterparts in France—was less obvious and less emotive than that contained in Price's assertion of dissenters' rights, but in the end far more devastating. In the first place it implied that the business of governments was domestic reform rather than foreign war; in the second place it suggested that governments should act positively to change the societies entrusted to their care; and in the third place it indicated that such changes should take account not just of the particular rights of particular groups or interests but of the needs of the majority of citizens.

The originator of this disturbing notion, which Bentham was to sum up in his phrase about 'the greatest happiness of the greatest number', was Joseph Priestley, a dissenting minister and teacher who was building up for himself a reputation as a political theorist to equal the one he already possessed as a chemist and physicist. It was contained in his *Essay on the First Principles of Government*, which had appeared in 1768 and had helped to draw him to the attention of Shelburne. In July 1772 the latter asked him to be his librarian; and this led to an association which lasted for seven years and was later described by Priestley himself in these words: 'In this situation I continued seven years, spending the summer with my family at Calne and a great part of the winter in his Lordship's house in London. My office was nominally that of librarian, but I had little employment as such. . . . In fact, I was with him as a friend.'[8]

Morellet, who had already translated Beccaria's treatise on crime and punishment into French, was anxious enough to discuss abstract questions of ethics and justice and human rights and wrongs; but he was even more concerned to push on with the discussions he had already had with Shelburne on commercial policy. Such questions could only be properly treated within the context of England's policy towards her colonies and of France's reaction to that policy; and so it was appropriate that Benjamin Franklin was of the party, to join in the general condemnation of North and of the baleful influence which the East India Company was supposed to be exercising over him. Like most other members of the group, Franklin was optimistic about the way things were going: he still believed that America's better self would be able to save England from her worse self, that the new forces and the new ideas represented by America would sweep away the old forces and the old ideas that were clustered around North. A year or so later, when he was just beginning to run into serious trouble with the English government, he could still write to a friend in America that 'the general sense of the nation is for us; a conviction prevailing that we have been ill used and that a breach with us would be ruinous to this country'.[9] It was in this comparatively serene mood, rather than in any petulant desire to seek French allies against English oppressors, that Franklin talked with the French apostle of a new kind of commercialism and of a new kind of internationalism. Morellet was not playing Choiseul's old game of suborning malcontents against the English; he was seeking out in England those same new forces which he thought he represented in France and which would transcend the chauvinistic power politics of Chatham and Choiseul.

The precise nature of these new forces, in hard economic or political terms, was not easy to define. They certainly did not

[8] J. Priestley, *Life and Correspondence*, ed. J. T. Rutt, 2 vols, 1831–32, i, 197.
[9] van Doren, *Franklin*, p. 456.

consist of the 'middle class' or the 'bourgeoisie', as opposed to the 'upper class' or 'feudal' elements of the old patriotism. The new, like the old, defied such classification. The one did not consist of landless entrepreneurs, any more than the other was made up of unenterprising landowners. The bourgeoisie of France in the strict sense of the term—that is, the freemen of the cities and towns of the kingdom—formed a series of privileged corporations whose outlook on almost all political and social questions was intensively conservative. Similarly, the borough corporations of many English towns were traditionalist and Tory in sympathy. The landowners, on the other hand, so far from being the collective incarnation of conservatism and hierarchy, were often both the source and the object of radical aspirations. Thus the Abbé Galiani, a violent opponent of Turgot who spoke in 1770 of war having been declared between 'the rural and the urban philosophers', said later that he resented the rural philosophers not because they were too conservative but because they were not conservative enough. If they had their way, he declared, they would overthrow existing hierarchies by creating a wealthy peasant class and thus re-establishing 'that equality of conditions which it has taken us six thousand years to destroy'.[10]

Shelburne himself clearly believed that it was possible to identify certain 'new forces' which would help him in his task of turning Chathamite patriotism into something more positive and more constructive. As long ago as 1762 he had abandoned the traditional mercantilist framework of Patriot politics, with its championing of the old industrial pattern of England centred on the woollen industry, and within a few years he was deeply involved as the political spokesman of newer and less privileged industries. He established particularly close connections with that same Samuel Garbett who complained in 1766 of the inadequate representation which his hardware interests in Birmingham had in parliament; and through Garbett he became concerned also with the Carron ironworks in Scotland. When Garbett brought forward proposals for a more general representation of industry and trade in parliament, it was Shelburne who championed them.[11] Moreover his links with the dissenters, which aroused deep suspicions among the independent country gentlemen, brought

[10] Galiani to Mme. d'Epinay, 5 May 1770 and 2 January 1773, cited J. Rossi, *The Abbé Galiani in France*, New York, 1930, pp. 35, 29.
[11] J. M. Norris, 'Samuel Garbett and the early development of industrial lobbying in Great Britain', *Ec.H.R.*, 2nd series, x, 1957–58, pp. 450–60.

him into contact with a whole network of people in the Midlands
and in the north of England who were in the forefront of industrial and technological development. William Wilkinson, an ironmaster like his more famous elder brother John, had been a pupil
at the Dissenting Academy at Warrington when Priestley was a
tutor there; and Priestley had married their sister Mary in 1762.
Their circle of friends and business associates included Josiah
Wedgwood the potter, John Smeaton the engineer, and John
Roebuck, one of the pioneers of the chemical industries and also
a partner in the Carron ironworks. Through them, as through
Garbett, Shelburne was brought into close political association
with Matthew Boulton, one of the most indefatigable lobbyists
of his time, and with his partner James Watt.[12] It was now nearly
a decade since Watt had made his crucial experiments on the
improvement of the Newcomen steam engine and he was beginning to despair of ever getting the new engine developed. In
1773 he told a friend that he was thinking of writing a book to
explain his discoveries to the world: if he was never going to get
any profit out of his invention at least he would get the credit
for it that way. If he had known that it was to be another seven
years before he saw any profits, he might have followed the
example of John Kay—the example that William Wilkinson himself followed in 1776—and fled from the frustrations of English
free enterprise to the comforts of French government regulation.[13]

This chain of associations and friendships and influences did not
amount to anything that could be called a party, or even an
organized and effective pressure group like those formed by the
East India or West India interests. To some extent it was a
substitute for a party: Shelburne was intelligent enough to see
that there was no future in the steadily narrowing horizons of
Chathamism, but he had not the confidence to launch out and
create a party of his own. And so he moved into this curious limbo
halfway between practical politics and intellectual day dreams.
His instincts were to be proved right in the long run: he had
more extensive contacts than any other politician of his time with
the ideas and people that were to mould the future. And yet he
was singularly bad at managing the present. He already had a

[12] E. Robinson, 'Matthew Boulton and the art of parliamentary lobbying',
H.J., vii, 1964, pp. 209–29.
[13] Cited R. E. Schofield, *The Lunar Society of Birmingham*, Oxford, 1963,
p. 70. On Kay in France see above, pp. 30–31.

reputation for deceit and devious dealings which isolated him from most other politicians; and now, as he gathered intellectuals and dissenters and hardware merchants around him, that isolation became more and more marked. It would only be broken if he was proved right, if the developments in America and in France did indeed lead to the triumph of new forces in those countries and thus in England as well.

The critical two years from 1774 to 1776 decided otherwise. As the Americans moved towards open rebellion, opinion in England hardened against them and against those who supported them. Even those who took their side did not always do so in a way which was calculated to forward Shelburne's enlightened dreams. Frederick Bull, a London merchant who was a dissenter and a supporter of the campaign for parliamentary reform, spoke vehemently in the Commons in 1774 in support of America's grievances; but the particular grievance he supported was that against the Quebec Act, the Act by which French Canadians were allowed to retain their Catholic religion and their French institutions. Like William Baker, member for Aldborough in Yorkshire and a prominent advocate of the American cause, he attacked the Act as a surrender to the sinister forces of popery and of French absolutism. Not surprisingly, Bull was to be one of Lord George Gordon's followers when in 1780 he stirred up the ugliest riots of the century in London in defence of Protestant bigotry.[14] Such men provided an unwelcome reminder of an unpleasant truth: the Americans themselves were not necessarily moved by the same high principles of tolerance and internationalism that inspired some of their loftier allies in England. The Quebec Act revealed once again the powerful current of francophobia that ran so strongly through English politics of the time. Of all the American grievances, the one that gained most sympathy among the English people as a whole was the one that was directed against the real or imaginary influence of France.

For the rest, there was little enthusiasm left for the colonists by the time the first shots were fired at Lexington in the spring of 1775. The American crisis, coming on top of the 1772–73 credit crisis, had undoubtedly led to recession and unemployment in many industries; but few industrialists were prepared to come to terms with the Americans on this account. Sir John Goodricke, member for Pontefract in Yorkshire, declared roundly that what

---

[14] *Commons 1754–90*, ii, 42–3, 129–30.

was needed was firmer measures against malcontents at home rather than concessions to the colonists. 'If artificial riots are not stirred up among the people,' he wrote, 'they will not suffer for want of work merely on account of the continental colonies not taking our goods.'[15] John Wesley was not so sure that the riots were artificial and he was particularly worried that ordinary Englishmen seemed to direct their anger not against Lord North but against the king himself: 'They heartily despise his majesty,' he told the secretary of state fearfully, 'and hate him with a perfect hatred. They wish to imbrue their hands in his blood; they are full of the spirit of murder and rebellion, and I am persuaded, should the occasion offer, thousands would be ready to act what they now speak.'[16] But Wesley's reaction to the situation was not to preach concession but to demand sterner measures against the Americans. In this he was in accord not only with the bulk of the landed men—who were almost persuaded to swallow their dislike of his religious ideas as a result—but also with the great industrial and commercial centres of the realm, almost all of which had by now come round to supporting the government. Only London and Bristol, where there were powerful interests that feared they would never recover the large sums owed to them by the Americans if war came, stood out in support of the colonial cause.

The really ironic thing, from the point of view of Shelburne and his internationalists, was that this hardening of the English attitude to the colonies was the direct result of improved trade with Europe. Some of the new industrialists, such as Matthew Boulton in Birmingham, already had long-standing associations with France and valuable markets there;[17] others found that such markets and such associations developed quickly as Europe recovered from the depression of the early 1770s. Years later, after the Americans had won their independence, Adam Smith told William Eden that the American trade was insignificant compared with the 'infinitely more advantageous' trade with Europe that could be opened up now that mercantilism could be dropped and

[15] *Ibid.*, ii, 509–10.
[16] Wesley to Dartmouth, 23 August 1775, *H.M.C.* 20, *Dartmouth*, iii, 220.
[17] E. Robinson, 'Boulton and Fothergill, 1762–82, and the Birmingham export of hardware', *U.B.H.J.*, vii, 1959–60, pp. 60–79. See also the comments of Josiah Tucker in his *Instructions for Travellers*, p. 23 (this work was printed in 1757 but not published: there is a copy in the British Museum, shelfmark 303.k.2).

free trade policies adopted.[18] What he did not point out was that the export trade in Europe which already existed before the American revolution had played an important part in precipitating that revolution and thus in making practicable the dismantling of the mercantilist system and the move towards Europe. England did not simply turn to Europe because she lost America; she also lost America partly because she turned to Europe. The more cosmopolitan and internationally minded the English industrialists became, the less inclined they were to give in to what they regarded as American blackmail. It was Matthew Boulton who organized, at the beginning of 1775, one of the most uncompromising of all the petitions from industrial areas against any concession to the colonists.[19]

The American crisis did not just make radical or enlightened ideas suspect in England; it also made them—or at any rate the politicians who expounded them—suspect in America as well. The agitation against the Quebec Act showed clearly enough what Americans thought of high-falutin' ideas like religious toleration and international understanding; and other indications suggested that they smelt out hypocrisy even in the opposition's apparent concern for America's liberties. Henry Cruger, a merchant of American descent who represented Bristol in the Commons from 1774 to 1780, was extremely wary of the Patriots, both old and new. 'America has long been made a cat's paw,' he told a friend in New York. 'On the ground of their calamities we fight our ambitious quarrels; and let who will gain the victory, New York will not be sixpence the gainer.'[20] In France, of course, this view of things was even more prevalent. The handful of men who believed that the English Patriots supported America for idealistic reasons was as nothing compared with the great mass of opinion which saw this support in quite different a light. 'Lord Chatham and his henchmen have deliberately stirred up the Americans,' reported France's ambassador in London in June 1775, 'and the tax on tea is nothing but a pretext: they are just making use of them.' If Chatham won the colonists to his side

[18] *Journal and Correspondence of William, Lord Auckland*, 4 vols, 1860–62, i, 65.
[19] Schofield, *Lunar Society*, p. 136. See also B. D. Bargar, 'Matthew Boulton and the Birmingham Petition of 1775', *W.M.Q.* xiii, 1956, pp. 26–39. M. Braure, 'Quelques aspects des relations commerciales entre la France et l'Angleterre au xviii⁰ siècle', *Annales du Midi*, 1953, pp. 67–80, shows that there was a sharp rise in British exports to Bordeaux, especially foodstuffs.
[20] *Commons 1754–90*, ii, 280–2.

he would then force himself into power, as being the only possible arbiter between the king and his American subjects; and then France would have reason to fear for her security. Six weeks later this same ambassador, the comte de Guines, warned his government that there was a growing conviction in England, both at Court and among the opposition, that a declaration of war against France was the only way to end the troubles.[21] George III had already pointed out that 'the gentlemen who pretend to be Patriots' were betraying their own principles by encouraging the colonists and thus weakening the country's unity in the face of its enemies;[22] and even those Patriots who were supporting the Americans were doing so, for the most part, out of aggressive francophobia and not out of any internationalist belief in the universality of 'the democratic revolution'. Patriotism in England, it seemed, was reverting to type.

George III had fears that it might do so in France as well. 'No one can foresee who will have credit with his successor,' he wrote when he heard of Louis XV's fatal illness, 'consequently whether the duration of peace can be long expected.' His ambassador in France assured him that the new king was noted for his 'love of justice, a general desire of doing well, a passion for economy, and an abhorence of all the excesses of the last reign'; but the English Court nevertheless waited anxiously while Choiseul made his bid for power.[23] The new queen of France, Marie Antoinette of Austria, was generally thought to be Choiseul's friend since he was the champion of the Austrian alliance which she represented; and he also had the support of most of the princes of the blood royal. At one time it seemed as if a Choiseul man, Breteuil, would be made foreign minister. In the end, however, Choiseul was sent empty away, back to his exile at Chanteloup, and a ministry emerged which was a combination of the traditionalist forces that had previously looked to the dauphin (the new minister of war, du Muy, had been a personal friend of the dauphin) and the more forward-looking men who considered themselves apostles of the enlightenment. The most important of these was Turgot, whose record as *intendant* of Limoges had won for him a reputation as the enlightened administrator *par excellence*. Louis XVI was reluctant to appoint a man whom he

[21] Doniol, i, 81–2, 116–17.
[22] Fortescue, iii, 48.
[23] *Ibid.*, iii, 104, 163.

had been taught to regard as a dangerous atheist, but in the end he gave in: Turgot took over as controller-general of finance in August 1774. English patriotism might be stubbornly refusing to respond to Shelburne's somewhat hesitant treatment, but at least French patriotism should take on a new and less chauvinistic appearance now that the self-styled 'citizen of the world' was in charge of things.

The citizen of the world had plenty of domestic problems to deal with before he could do anything about his internationalist aspirations. The first problem was what to do about the country's financial predicament; and this he dealt with in a letter which he wrote to the king on taking office. There would be, he promised, neither a government bankruptcy nor an increase in taxes. Nor would there be any extension of government borrowing: instead the deficit would be pared down by cuts in government expenditure, while the tax yield would be increased by more efficient collection and by the generally rising level of prosperity which his policies would produce. These policies were fundamentally those of the Physiocrats: the removal of trading restrictions, particularly those on the trade in foodstuffs, and the lessening of the burdens which bore upon the peasant. In this way Turgot hoped to produce a thriving agriculture which would in its turn stimulate the rest of the economy and in the end benefit the government's revenues as well. Then everything would fall into place: the conflicts which divided French society, even the conflict between crown and *parlements*, would lose their sting once the government was seen to be pursuing policies which aimed at the good of the whole country rather than the enrichment of the pressure groups that were popularly supposed to have been behind both Choiseul's administration and that of Maupeou. In the final analysis patriotism was a matter of caring for the land itself and for those peasant proprietors who cultivated the bulk of it.[24]

There was general agreement on both sides of the Channel that the poverty of the French peasant was at the root of France's problems. It was ninety years since La Bruyère had written his unforgettable description of the French peasantry, the blackened and scorched creatures who crouched like animals in the fields and only occasionally revealed, to the surprise of the observer,

---

[24] Dakin, *Turgot and the ancien régime*, passim. See also G. J. Cavanaugh, 'Turgot, the rejector of enlightened despotism', *F.H.S.*, vi, 1969, pp. 31–58.

that they had the faces and the voices of human beings; but still the majority of English travellers were appalled by what they saw. 'Most of their peasants make a wretched appearance and we scarce observed one among the lower class of a healthy manly figure, unless in the army,' reported Lord St Vincent after his tour of France in the winter of 1772–73. Sometimes there were impressions of a different sort, but they were invariably laced with a certain amount of surprise: whatever it was that they actually found, there was no doubt that what Englishmen expected to find in France was grinding poverty. In 1765 Thomas Pennant was staggered to discover in Burgundy 'an air of ease and contentment' and a general absence of those wooden shoes which he had been brought up to regard as the badge of continental enslavement. Eleven years later an English visitor riding from Dieppe to Paris noted with mounting surprise that 'all the people appear well clad and everything wears the face of plenty'. And as late as July 1789, on the very eve of that popular uprising which complacent Englishmen saw as the inevitable outcome of popery and tyranny, Dr Rigby was astonished to find that 'the general appearance of the people is different to what I had expected: they are strong and well made . . . Everything we see bears the mark of industry and all the people look happy . . . I will own I used to think that the French were a trifling insignificant people, that they were meagre in their appearance, and lived in a state of wretchedness from being oppressed by their superiors. What we have already seen contradicts this.'[25]

But English propertied complacency would not brook such contradiction and it continued to think that its own form of oppression was more efficient than that practised in France. In English eyes—and in the eyes of influential anglophiles in France —the French peasant was worse off than the English labourer because he was bound to his land by an anachronistic and ambiguous relationship which would never be tolerated by the more realistic land laws of England. Because of the taxes and tithes and dues he had to pay and because of his very limited capital resources, the peasant was unable to benefit from a good harvest to anything like the extent to which he suffered from a bad one. He was utterly vulnerable, exposed to every fluctuation of the

[25] La Bruyère, *Oeuvres complètes*, p. 333; Add. 31, 192, fo. 16; T. Pennant, *Tour on the Continent, 1765*, ed. G. R. de Beer, 1948, p. 42; Add. 12, 130, fo. 18; E. Rigby, *Letters from France in 1789, edited by his daughter*, 1880, pp. 11–12.

economy or of the weather. And his overlord was, therefore, just as vulnerable: in practice a feudal landlord could seldom dispossess a peasant simply because that peasant was too poor to farm his holding properly. The only way out, both for the peasant and for the lord, was the system known as *métayage*, whereby the lord advanced the peasant money to buy seed corn or implements, in return for an agreed proportion of the following year's crop. If that crop turned out to be a poor one, then there was no alternative for the lord but to throw good money after bad; no alternative for the peasant but to take on a further load of debt in an attempt to pay off the first. In this way master and man pulled one another down even as they sought to hold one another up. The master clung to his illusion of lordship, to the prestigious thing called *seigneurie* which meant so much to him, while the peasant clung even more tenaciously to his own particular illusion, the illusion that he owned the land he worked.

In one sense he did: he could bequeath it to his son and his rights over it were not terminable when his lease ran out, as was the case with the tenant smallholders who were his nearest equivalents in England. But on the other hand it was not his to dispose of as he wished: he could not, for instance, solve his problems by the outright sale of all or part of his land. There were some areas of France, especially in Languedoc, where there was a comparatively fluid land market and where peasant proprietors were being transformed into tenant farmers or hired labourers; but over most of the country there was a stricter observance of feudal law which kept the vast majority of small farmers suspended in that curious limbo known as peasant status, halfway between ownership and tenantry. As a result much of the land of France could never be properly cultivated because it was parcelled out among peasants who could neither be relieved nor removed. And for this reason tax anomalies, which existed in both countries, were far more serious in France than in England. The *taille* might often be less unfair than it seemed, because it was passed on from peasant to overlord, just as the land tax might often be more unfair because it was passed down from the rich squire who complained about it to the poor tenant who actually paid it. But in the end it was the land itself which paid the tax and which would return ever diminishing yields if it was not transferred into the hands of those who could afford to make the best of it.

In England such a process of land transference had been taking place for many years and had been greatly accelerated since the middle of the eighteenth century. Men who owned large estates had applied capitalist techniques to the management of their land and had aimed not at mere subsistence farming, not simply at producing enough of all the necessities of life to supply those who had lived on the land from time immemorial, but at the large-scale production of whatever commodity gave the best return on the money they had invested. These techniques, the techniques that led Oliver Goldsmith to write so bitterly of wealth accumulating and men decaying,[26] were both varied and complex; but fundamentally they relied on two devices, mortgage and enclosure. The growth of the credit structure in England, spreading outwards from the Bank of England and the great finance houses of the City of London to the banks in the provincial cities and market towns, meant that rich landowners found it easier to get richer. By mortgaging part of their land on a temporary basis they could raise the capital to make the whole estate more productive; by utilizing their influence in parliament they could promote Bills of Enclosure to sweep away the last relics of the old open-field system and make large-scale farming by modern methods possible. Strictly speaking an Enclosure Bill needed the consent of the owners of two-thirds of the land concerned; but in practice it was relatively easy for substantial landowners to push aside the objections of lesser men who had neither the money nor the legal knowledge to brief parliamentary agents, draw up petitions and manage all the tortuous details that were involved in fighting an Enclosure Bill in parliament.[27]

If this was the fundamental choice that lay before the men of the time, if every man and nation had to decide between feudalism and the freehold society, then few Englishmen had any doubts about what their choice should be. As Goldsmith pointed out with savage irony in his *Distresses of a Common Soldier*, an Englishman could suffer all the abominable cruelties and humiliations which the propertied classes could inflict upon him and yet still say at the end of it all: 'I hate the French because they are all slaves and wear wooden shoes.'[28] As for the idealistic and mainly

[26] Goldsmith, *Collected works*, iv, 289.
[27] For details see O. C. Williams, *The historical development of private bill procedure and standing orders in the House of Commons*, 1948.
[28] Goldsmith, *Collected works*, ii, 464.

anglophile philosophers of the enlightenment, they were for the most part ready to agree with the English themselves in equating the freehold society with a free society and the feudal society with an unfree and impoverished one. All the things which Voltaire had originally held up for admiration in the 1730s were summed up in the concept of the freehold society. Even the particular instruments by means of which it was advanced had been given the seal of his approval: he had been rapturous in his praises both of the representative principle and of the credit structure which it sustained and which sustained it. Every English landlord who raised capital and applied it to the improvement of the land, every squire who promoted Enclosure Bills and failed to renew leases when they fell in, could feel that he was demonstrating those very freedoms that the great Voltaire wanted to carry over from England into France. All that Turgot had to do, it would seem, was to apply the lessons he had learnt from his English friends and from the anglophile intellectual tradition in which he had been bred. In this way he could build a freehold society in France and solve her economic, social and political problems in one grand gesture.

Previous attempts at agrarian reform in France could certainly be seen as having been anglophile in inspiration and intention. The agricultural societies which the government had sponsored in the 1760s had been largely concerned with the discussion and propagation of works translated from the English or advocating English methods of agricultural improvement.[29] The controller-general of finance and the French ambassador in London had even conspired together in the spring of 1763 to smuggle three Lincolnshire rams and six ewes into France for breeding purposes.[30] Later in the same decade a start had been made on a long series of edicts which sought to abolish communal grazing rights and authorize the enclosure of common lands by those landlords who had the resources to exploit them effectively. By 1771 the royal council had registered its approval of at least one major land redistribution, on an estate in Lorraine, that bore a very close

[29] E. Justin, *Les sociétés royales d'agriculture au xviiiᵉ siècle, 1757–93*, Saint-Lô, 1935.
[30] A. J. Bourde, *The Influence of England on the French Agronomes, 1750–89*, Cambridge, 1953, p. 188n. Some years later the French government granted some land near Dieppe to an Englishman named de Mante, so that he could breed sheep obtained in this way. While English travellers despised him as a turncoat, the English authorities suspected him of being the head of a spy ring. See Add. 12, 130, fo. 12; Stevens, viii, no. 759.

resemblance to an English Bill of Enclosure.[31] At the same time there had been a massive increase in poor relief: from the mid-1760s onwards *intendants* up and down the country had been busy organizing *ateliers de charité* (a new and more constructive alternative to the old *dépôts de mendicité*) and undertaking great new public works, from roadmaking to the draining of swamps, in order to put the unemployed to work. All these changes had been continued and even accelerated by the Maupeou administration and Turgot, as *intendant* of Limoges, had been closely involved in their execution.[32] All he now had to do was to keep up the impetus of a reforming process which was slowly turning the traditional French society of supposedly self-sufficient peasants into a society of capitalist landlords farming their lands by means of a pool of free but landless labourers. And like the English, the French were learning that a proper system of poor relief was the price that had to be paid for this pool of labour if it was not to turn into a breeding ground for brigands and vagabonds.

But there was an important difference between what was being done in France and what had happened in England: in France it was being done by the government and in England it had been done by the governed. In provinces like Languedoc, where the local *parlements* passed canal bills and turnpike bills and enclosure bills in very much the same way as the English parliament, the process of change was reasonably smooth because it was working in the right direction, starting from the needs of the capitalist land developer and ending with the enactments of an institution in which he was represented.[33] But in other areas it started from the enactments of an unrepresentative government and ended with the stubborn resistance of landowners who had no conception of capitalism. In his article on farming in the *Encyclopédie*, the great Physiocrat economist Quesnay had stated categorically that capitalism, in the sense of mortgaging existing assets to raise credit for future expansion and development, could never have the same central place in agriculture that it had in commerce and

---

[31] Bourde, pp. 207–8. See also G. Debien, 'Land clearings and artificial meadows in eighteenth-century Poitou', *Agricultural History*, xix, 1945, pp. 133–7; M. Bloch, *Les caractères originaux de l'histoire rurale française*, 2nd edn. 2 vols, 1955–56, i, 225–34; A. Davies, 'New agriculture in lower Normandy', *T.R.H.S.* 5th series, viii, 1958, pp. 129–46; M. Garaud, *Histoire générale du droit privé français*, 2 vols, 1953–58, ii, 373ff.; P. Butel, 'Défrichements en Guyenne au xviii*e* siècle', *Annales du Midi*, lxxvi, 1965, pp. 179–203.
[32] Dakin, *Turgot*, pp. 33–118.
[33] See above, pp. 94–95.

industry.[34] And in this contention, shared by most of the French agrarian reformers up to and including Turgot himself, lay the paradox of the whole Physiocrat school of thought. Underneath the anglophile belief in agricultural expansion, in the increased production of real wealth, lay a profoundly anglophobe suspicion of the only thing that could make such expansion possible—the extended use of credit facilities, both by governments and by individuals. As far as the Physiocrats were concerned, productivity must precede capitalism: the land must be made to produce more, so that industry and commerce might in their turn be stimulated and the economy expanded. They seemed to be incapable of conceiving that the process might be reversed, that the wealth accumulated in industry and commerce might be made available, by means of better banking and financing facilities, to help develop the full potential of the land.

Prejudices of this sort had a long ancestry, stretching back beyond the Seven Years War, perhaps even beyond the Mississippi crash; but however far back their origins lay it was certain that those origins were closely associated with France's contempt for her mercenary little neighbour across the Channel. However much they might be divided about other things, most Frenchmen were united in their dislike of the ridiculous little English frog that would eventually burst itself in its attempts to blow itself up to the size of an ox. Even as late as May 1776, when the fate of Turgot and of his proposed reforms was hanging in the balance, his colleague Vergennes at the Foreign Ministry was still prepared to expound the stock French view of England's credit-based economy. 'People can go on as much as they like about the wealth of England,' he told Beaumarchais, 'but I still regard it as an unnatural growth, a sort of bloated dropsy; I prefer the healthy plumpness of France, even if it does come from over-indulgence. At least it is real: fertile lands, valuable produce, hard cash. No amount of credit crises can bring that down.'[35]

Turgot's distrust of credit operations may have been less anglophobe, less prejudiced, than this; but it had nevertheless a decisive effect on his policies. He had assured the king that there would be no extension of government borrowing and he intended to keep his promise. When the need arose he could demonstrate considerable skill in the conversion of existing loans or the raising

[34] Lüthy, ii, 766.
[35] Vergennes to Beaumarchais 2 May 1776, Stevens, ix, no. 86.

of new ones; but the object of such manoeuvres was always to reduce rather than to increase the government's indebtedness. Above all he was anxious to free the government from its dependence on financiers, whether those of the General Farm or those rival groups who were so anxious to replace them. By this time the suppression of the General Farm would have cost something in the region of 92 million livres of long-term debt and a further 38 million of short-term,[36] but Turgot was nevertheless prepared to work towards it. Even his scheme for a Discount Bank, upon which he was still engaged at the time of his fall from power, was an attempt to weaken the grip of the credit manipulators by borrowing direct from the public. In this it was closer to England's unsuccessful Land Bank of 1696, the Tory scheme that failed, than it was to the Bank of England of 1694, the Whig scheme that succeeded. Ever since 1694 English society had been torn apart by the bitter conflict between the Whig financiers of the bank and the Tory landed men in the counties. Turgot, like all Physiocrats, saw this as the fatal weakness in the English scheme of things and was determined to avoid it. If the real landed wealth of France could be made the basis of a solid credit system well and good; but he was not prepared to countenance the artificial expansion of credit by financiers who wanted to pump up the French economy until it was as bloated as the English.

All this was sound traditional Patriot politics, the politics of those *parlement* leaders who had ranged themselves behind Choiseul in his attacks on the Jesuits and on the financiers and on the English. Indeed, many of Choiseul's followers were tempted to see Turgot as one of them, especially after he had advised the king to recall the *parlements* at the end of 1774. Like them, Turgot disliked the Jesuits and shared the anticlerical traditions of the Patriots; like them, he disliked the financiers and the unnatural English practices which they sought to introduce into France. Like them, he saw the land as the source of all wealth and wished to see the taxation of it reduced. But as the full range of Turgot's reforms became apparent, the old-style Patriots of the *parlements* saw that he was not the man for them. They had already opposed many of the agrarian reforms of the 1760s; and in some provinces they had even put up a spirited defence of peasant rights over the common lands, in the belief that an attack on *some* property rights would

[36] Matthews, *Royal General Farms*, p. 257.

sooner or later develop into one on *all* property rights. Now, as
Turgot proceeded to far-reaching reforms of the *taille*, to an
investigation into the perquisites of officeholders and the powers
of the town guilds, to the curtailment of seigneurial rights, they
saw their worst fears fulfilled. The things which for them had
been ends were for Turgot and his enlightened friends mere
beginnings: the expulsion of the Jesuits was not simply a successful *parlement* bid to monopolize the persecution of heretics, but
a chance to end the persecution of heretics altogether. The reform
of the taxation system was not just a means of allowing rich men
to stay rich, but a means of redistributing the whole tax burden
more fairly. And so with privileges, whether official or commercial or feudal: what had been intended as an attack on the central
government's abuse of them was rapidly turning into an attack
on the privileges themselves.

When Turgot fell from power in May 1776 it was as a result
of the king's failure to support him against the *parlements* over
two main issues: the proposed abolition of the trade guilds and
the scheme to replace the *corvée*, or obligation to help with the
upkeep of roads, with a road tax payable by all landed proprietors.
The third issue, which contributed to his fall but was in fact less
acute in 1776 than it had been a year earlier, was his reintroduc-
tion of free trade in grain. He had done this very cautiously and
had still kept a tight control over grain exports; but he was
nevertheless blamed on all sides when the price of bread started
to rise inexorably during the early months of 1775. His enemies
may or may not have had a hand in stirring up the very serious
food riots that took place that spring in and around Paris; but
they certainly did not scruple to use them against him.[37] A
virulent propaganda campaign was mounted against free trade
theories, against the Physiocrats who peddled them and thus
against the whole fabric of enlightenment ideas. This campaign,
which continued into 1776, provided the essential background for
the *parlements'* successful stand against his reforms.

Thus the fall of Turgot seemed to be the triumph of the old
chauvinistic patriotism of the *parlements* over the new enlightened
patriotism of the philosophers. Horace Walpole certainly saw it
in that light. 'I am totally altered,' he wrote early in April 1776,

---

[37] G. Rudé, 'La taxation populaire de mai 1775 à Paris et dans la région
parisienne', *A.H.R.F.* 1956, pp. 139–79 (English version in Kaplow, *New
Perspectives*, pp. 191–210).

F

when the conflict between the minister and the *parlements* was just coming to a head, 'and instead of being a warm partisan of liberty, now admire nothing but despotism . . . I think that the resistance of the *parlement* to the adorable reformation planned by Messrs de Turgot and M(alesherbes) is more phlegmatically scandalous that the wildest tyranny of despotism.' Six weeks later, when the news of Turgot's dismissal came through, he declared portentously: 'A great revolution has happened in France . . . Poor France, and poor England! Choiseul, if not Choiseul some Louvois or other, will rise out of this fall of patriotic philosophers; and then we shall be forced to see the wisdom of the Stamp Act, and of persisting in taxing America!' And later still, at the end of May: 'The stocks have taken the alarm, and the Ministers have felt it some time. The change in the French councils have changed the spirits of ours. I believe almost any peace would be welcome to them . . . now we tremble at France, which America enabled us to resist.'[38] His view of English politics had been growing steadily gloomier for some time: the parliament at Westminster seemed to him to get narrower and more parochial even as its problems got wider and more international. And now the *parlements* of France, which he had once hailed as a light to lighten the English, were showing themselves in the same colours. The challenge of the new reign had produced the same sullen response in France as the challenge of the New World had produced in England. What was the point of preaching enlightened reform and international understanding to institutions that represented only prejudice and privilege and narrow nationalism?

Some of the more optimistic among the radical thinkers consoled themselves by insisting that it was only the existing representative institutions that were wrong and that new institutions would produce new policies. Cartwright, who published in 1776 a second and even more radical work on parliamentary reform, thought that a national society to promote such a reform was the best solution. He approached Shelburne to ask him to support the plan, only to be told that 'it will not be easy to get any number of great men, though favourable in their opinions to such a scheme as yours, to be active and zealous in carrying it into execution'.[39] Sir George Savile, who had by this time come

[38] Walpole, *Letters*, ix, 340–42, 359–70.
[39] Price to Cartwright, 2 April 1776, *The Life and Correspondence of Major Cartwright*, ed. F. D. Cartwright, 2 vols, 1826, i, 95–6.

to regard the American revolt as 'justifiable rebellion' and parliament's reaction to it as selfish folly, realized nevertheless that he and his fellow radicals were very much in a minority, not only in parliament but also in the country as a whole. 'We are,' he declared in a memorable phrase, 'not only Patriots out of place, but Patriots out of the opinion of the public.'[40] 'The state of politics here is in every way disagreeable,' wrote one American agent to another at the beginning of 1777, 'four-fifths at least of the English people despise us, and look upon us as cowards, and assert that we shall be beaten before the middle of the summer. The friends of America, on the other hand, are discouraged; those of the minority who have espoused the cause of the people, find that this cause is on the side of their adversaries.'[41]

The philosophers of the French enlightenment had always seen clearly enough that those who espoused the cause of the people were by no means likely to find the people on their side. Horace Walpole might only now be waking up to the fact that despotism could sometimes be better than liberty, but the authors of the 'adorable reformation' had known it for a long time. Even as Walpole wrote his lament for Turgot, a boatman on the river Rhône was telling an English traveller what he thought about the crusade against superstition which Turgot and his enlightened friends had launched. 'He was very free of abuse on the Archbishop of Lyons,' the Englishman recorded, 'for taking away from the water men their tutelar saint St Nicholas and putting a stop to their processions. They had nobody, he said, now left to pray to. To be sure there was the *bon Dieu* still, and after him he knew there was the Virgin Mary; but it was a very bad thing to take away the water men's own saint; and the archbishop would not have done it, if he had not been to get something by it.'[42] Turgot and his fellow philosophers, busy reducing politics to a rational science, were not disposed to pay attention to objections of this sort. The more they hurried towards the proposition that man could live by reason alone, the more impatient they became with the unreasonable and the ignorant. The same impatience could be heard in the utterances of their counterparts in England. Even Richard Price, angry though he was about the artificial and exclusive political structure of the time, was very careful to

---

[40] Savile to Rockingham, 15 January 1777, Albemarle, *Memoirs of the marquis of Rockingham and his contemporaries*, 2 vols, 1852, ii, 305.
[41] Stevens, vi, no. 634.
[42] Add. 12, 130, fo. 66.

explain that the aim of parliamentary reform should be to lessen, not to increase, the deplorable political influence of 'the lowest of the people'. There might conceivably be a time, in the distant future, when the Age of Reason would be able to become the Age of Democracy; but for the time being it could not afford to permit the dissentient voices of those who doubted reason's supremacy.

The real issue here was not the widening of the franchise but the very existence of a political dialogue in any form. Later, during the nineteenth century, it was recognized in most countries of western Europe that the essence of democracy was the agreement to disagree, the readiness to concede that there could be more than one answer to a political problem, more than one candidate for the job of running the country; and historians in the nineteenth century were therefore tempted to think that the great reformers of the eighteenth century must have thought likewise. In fact, however, they did not. They were conscious that they were building a new world, a world which must be built according to very precise and rational principles. If they discovered that their neighbours were building their bit of it according to fallacious principles, then they must take action to prevent the whole edifice being put in jeopardy. Disagreement among speculative philosophers might be amusing and stimulating, but disagreement among practical engineers was merely dangerous. And the whole purpose of the enlightenment was to remove philosophy from the realm of speculation and to apply it to problems of social and political engineering. This was the point of view to which Horace Walpole had now been converted, the point of view which saw the existence of independent opponents to government as a menace rather than as a reassurance.

If Walpole's conversion had proved permanent—which it did not, since he needed a succession of such *crises de conscience* to keep him in reasonable spirits—he would have felt at home in England for most of the twenty years that he still had to live. While the War of American Independence did not push Englishmen into enlightened reform, it certainly did push them into a mood of strong reaction against liberty—or, at any rate, against the liberty of politicians to form an opposition to the government of the day. Patriotism in the sense that Walpole had used the word in 1772, a determination to keep the political dialogue going and oppose government measures whenever it seemed appropriate, was very much out of fashion by the end of the decade. Instead George III's definition of patriotism, a determination to support the king's government at all costs and quell the conflict of parties, had taken over. The *Annual Register* for 1776 confessed ruefully that there was a violent reaction in the country against party politicians and especially against those who continued to oppose the government 'whenever it was put upon an independent and respectable bottom'.[43] In 1777 the leaders of the opposition gave up altogether and ceased to attend parliament, since they could not speak for the government without compromising their principles nor against it without compromising what was left of their popularity. When they returned in 1778 they did not cut a very convincing figure: their friends in America had forfeited what little support they still had in England by signing an alliance with the French, while they themselves appeared in a very bad light when they voted with the government in March 1778 against a proposal to tax the incomes of the placemen whom the independents hated so much. Even Sir George Savile, for so long the darling of the independent gentlemen of Yorkshire, rallied to the side of the professional politicians on this occasion and voted against the measure.[44]

There was nothing really new in all this. The basic conflict in English political life had always been that between the professional politicians at the centre and the independent men throughout the country. All that had happened, in the twenty years between the Seven Years War and the War of American Independence, was that an attempt to resolve this conflict had failed. The Patriots had claimed to be able to impose the will of the independents upon the professionals, to create a political party which would truly represent the country and would end once and for all the disgusting squabble for office that had passed for political life during the reign of George II. But the squabblers had proved too strong and the independent men too weak. After all the Patriot efforts the professionals were still there at the centre, some of them decorating the administration of Lord North and the rest seeking to enter it by the old methods of apparent opposition and secret negotiation. 'It is clear,' wrote Lord Holland, '. . . that previous to, in, and about 1778, several negotia-

---

[43] *Annual Register*, 1776, p. 47.
[44] *Memorials and Correspondence of Charles James Fox*, ed. Lord John Russell, 4 vols, 1853–57, i, 175.

tions more or less distinct, and all very secret, were opened with different persons in the opposition.' The government's agent in these negotiations was William Eden, first lord of the Board of Trade under North, who was later to negotiate the commercial treaty with France in the interests of those same new industrialists whom Shelburne was cultivating. At this stage, however, there was no question of new forces, but only of old prejudices: when Eden approached Shelburne, he was told that 'Lord Chatham must be the dictator'.[45] The old patriotism might be a bit tarnished, but Shelburne had the sense to see that it was a safer card to play in the circumstances than the new patriotism of enlightened radicalism and dissenter industrialists.

Here was the real tragedy of the Patriot failure in England, the real impact of that long crisis that had begun with colonial victories over the French and was now culminating in a French alliance with the colonists. The traditional Patriots had been discredited, their vaunted independence shown up as illusory and their leaders revealed as hypocrites. But they would survive nevertheless. Their position and prestige in the counties of England, their great resources of landed and mercantile wealth, would guarantee them an influential part in politics whatever might happen; and the War of American Independence was generating a mood of entrenched conservatism which would enable them to establish their social supremacy even more firmly than before. But what of the newer forces that had been drawn into the conflict? What of the unenfranchised and the unrepresented, who had rushed so precipitately forward to greet the new dawn that was now clearly not going to break? They were not playing at being outsiders, as the independent gentlemen of England were: they really *were* outsiders. And outsiders they seemed likely to remain.

In France the year 1776 had a very different outcome. If in England it led men to rally round the old order of things, in France it provided the new order of things with an opportunity such as it had never had before. Turgot and his friends, for all their enlightenment and all their rationalism, were in the final analysis defenders of the old France, the France that looked to the land and scorned the unhealthy capitalist expansion indulged in by the English. They were, as Galiani said, rural philosophers.[46] Now

---

[45] *Ibid.*, i, 179–82.
[46] See above, p. 133.

it was the turn of the urban philosophers. The landed men had shot their bolt: never again would Louis XVI have a ministry that sought to solve France's problems by applying the pastoral panaceas of the Physiocrats. The international financier, that sorcerer-like figure so distrusted by the honest farmers of France, was about to demonstrate the power of his spells in France as well as in England. In January 1778 a French agent in London told Vergennes hopefully that this magical power of high finance was about to lose its strength, that the war with the Americans would render its talismans powerless.[47] He was a singularly bad prophet, for in fact the financial wizardry which he so much feared was about to transform both countries out of all recognition. While in England it produced what theorists later came to call 'self-sustained growth', in France it laid the foundations of many years of self-sustained strife.

[47] Garnier to Vergennes, 16 January 1778, Doniol, ii, 747.

7   *Necker and North*

*I*t was Maurepas, the ageing stage manager of most of Louis XVI's early administration, who gave a name to the new form of necromancy under whose spell France was about to pass. The country, he remarked, was tumbling straight from Turgomania into Neckeromania.[1] An obscure foreign banker called Jacques Necker was suddenly credited with the ability to solve almost overnight the problems that had for a whole generation defeated experienced bureaucrats and enlightened reformers alike. He seemed to be some kind of alchemist who had discovered a new version of the philosopher's stone and could conjure wealth and financial stability out of the air. And France was ready for alchemists: a society that clung so eagerly to the faith-healers and the occultists, to the Mesmers and the Cagliostros and the countless lesser charlatans of the back streets, was only too anxious to have its financial difficulties cured as magically and as painlessly as its bodily ills.[2] The Patriots had promised to rescue the country

[1] P. Jolly, *Necker*, 1951, p. 149.
[2] See R. Darnton, *Mesmerism and the end of the enlightenment in France*, Cambridge (Mass) 1968.

from the tax farmers, but had turned out in the end to be almost indistinguishable from them; the enlightenment had promised a new heaven and a new earth but had turned out to mean nothing but new taxes. So perhaps the bankers could perform the miracles they had always promised and float France to prosperity on the airy fabric of their credit operations.

The traditionalists were horrified to find that men like Necker were to be the ultimate beneficiaries of their victory over Turgot. Turgot himself had been bad enough, with his talk of world citizenship and his attempts to transcend the old rivalries with England; but Necker was a great deal worse. He was by birth a Genevese, but his father had once been secretary to George I's Hanoverian advisers and had subsequently been subsidized by the English government to set up a *pension* for English visitors to Geneva.[3] The great bankers of Geneva were the leaders not only of international finance but also of international protestantism: the rich Huguenot families who had settled there maintained their contacts, both social and financial, with their fellow refugees in London and Amsterdam and the other commercial centres of northern Europe. They also maintained, rather to the disquiet of many people in the French government, their contacts in France itself. Saint-Florentin, the secretary of state with responsibility for religious affairs, had written angrily in 1762 of the 'infinite number of people who seek to come back to France not so much to benefit commerce or maintain the population as to spread heretical religion and republican ideas which they have picked up during their stay abroad'.[4] Ever since Louis XIV had been forced to borrow from Huguenot bankers, thus putting himself in pawn to a financial network which swept round his kingdom in a great arc from Geneva to Amsterdam and London, the threat of international Protestant finance had loomed larger and larger in the minds of French Catholics and French chauvinists. And Necker was at the very centre of this menace: his firm, Thellusson Necker and Company, was one of the greatest Protestant banks of Europe and had intimate connections with the Huguenot bankers of London and, through them, with the English government itself. It was small wonder that the champions of the enlightenment—who had for several years been particularly incensed with Necker because of his opposition to

[3] Lüthy, ii, 229.
[4] *Ibid.*, ii, 93.

free trade in grain[5]—found themselves supported by Patriots and
even by tax farmers when they denounced him and his Genevese
friends. Disagreements about particular reforms were forgotten
while all Necker's enemies united to remind their countrymen of
what had happened the last time France gave herself over to a
financial wizard inspired from across the Channel. Jacques Necker
would finish up like John Law, being entertained ironically in
London to a performance of *The Alchemist* while France lay
in ruins.

The warnings were ignored: within six months of Turgot's
fall the unstoppable Genevese banker was in charge of French
government finance. Clugny, the *parlement* leader who had been
Turgot's successor as well as his victor, died in October 1776;
and after two days of rather delicate negotiation Taboureau des
Réaux, a member of the Paris *parlement* and an ex-*intendant* of
Hainault, was appointed controller-general. He was to be assisted
by Necker, who as a Protestant could not be made controller-
general but was given the post of 'director of the royal treasury',
subsequently changed to the simpler and more dignified 'director-
general'. No one doubted where the real power and influence
lay. Turgot, in a bitter letter to Condorcet, compared the whole
business to the doctrine of the Trinity: Maurepas presided over
financial administration like a rather neglectful God the Father,
Taboureau had all the meekness and mildness of God the Son,
Necker breathed over everything the mighty wind of God the
Holy Ghost. 'And you only have to read the Acts of the Apostles,'
Turgot added, 'to see what a commotion that produces.'[6]

The truth about Necker was a good deal less dramatic than
the fevered suspicions of his critics. He certainly had close links
with the financial world of London and he had probably made
use of these links in 1763 to speculate very profitably in Canadian
bills of exchange, which he bought up cheaply in the knowledge
that the English government was determined to press for their
payment.[7] During the years that followed he became banker and
chief financial adviser to a whole new world of commerce that
grew up around co-operation with England in India rather than
rivalry with her in America. While the *armateurs* of the Atlantic
ports supported Choiseul in his bellicose gestures against England

[5] Voltaire to Christen, 14 May 1775, *Voltaire's Correspondence*, ed.
T. Besterman, 105 vols, 1953–65, xci, 32.

[6] Jolly, *Necker*, p. 119.

[7] Lüthy, ii, 374–5. See also P.R.O. S.P. 78/266 fos 231–2.

and in his attempts to supplant her colonial power, the *indienneurs* concentrated instead on peaceful trade in the Indies, with the tacit approval of the English East India Company and often with financial backing which came, thanks to Necker's good offices, from the London Huguenot banking house of Bourdieu and Chollet.[8] But this was far from being an Anglo-Genevese financial conspiracy. There were a great many Englishmen and a great many Genevese who were opposed to it; and the English government often looked with suspicion on the *indienneurs*, especially after the ending of the French East India Company's privileges in 1769. During the 1770s the new unregulated trade between France and the Indies expanded enormously: by the time Necker came to power it was importing three times as much into France as the old French East India Company had done a decade earlier.[9] But the very size of this trade and the extent of the investment that went into it rendered talk of cartels and conspiracies absurd. There were indeed a few great concentrations of capital asociated with Protestant families, both in France and in Geneva; but there were also innumerable shareholders who had no connection with England or Geneva or Protestantism, just as there were many influential financiers and entrepreneurs who were Necker's rivals rather than his cronies.

One of these, Isaac Panchaud, had a far better claim than Necker to be considered as the centre of a shady Anglo-Genevese financial conspiracy. He had been born in London of a Dutch mother and a Swiss father, although his maternal grandmother was French—a Huguenot refugee from Languedoc. He set up as a banker in Paris in 1763 and remained there until his death in 1789, although his operations were on an international scale and he retained his rights as a British subject: many English travellers regarded his bank as a home from home and as late as 1777 Horace Walpole could still speak of him as 'an English banker at Paris'.[10] By 1769, when the old French East India Company entered its death agonies, Panchaud had emerged as the chief opponent of the tax farmers and court bankers who sought to make the company—and indeed the India trade as a whole—serve their own dominance of the financial scene. On 29 March 1769 he proposed to the shareholders that the company should follow the example set by

[8] *Ibid.*, ii, 44, 438–55.
[9] L. Dermigny, *Cargaisons Indiennes: Solier et cie, 1781–93*, 2 vols, 1960, i, 87.
[10] Walpole, *Last Journals*, ii, 71.

the English South Sea Company and by Law's Mississippi Company half a century earlier and concern itself with credit manipulation rather than trade. His plan to use the company's funds to float a discount bank was a deliberate challenge to a similar bank set up by Laborde and other court bankers in 1767; and as such it was supported by a group of opponents of the court, including influential members of the Paris *parlement*. And it was Necker who did more than any other man to secure the rejection of this plan.[11] The magnates of international Protestant finance were more concerned to fight one another than to conspire together against the traditional values of French society.

These divisions were even more apparent by the time Necker came to power in 1776. The trade to the Indies had proliferated and in proliferating it had become increasingly compartmented. Quite apart from the polarity between the associates of Panchaud and those of Necker, there was yet another powerful and somewhat mysterious group of investors associated with the Grand family, bankers in Switzerland and Holland as well as in Paris, and headed by Le Ray de Chaumont, *intendant* of the Hôtel des Invalides. They dabbled in all kinds of ventures from Indian commerce to freemasonry, and had links both with the forces of change—it was Le Ray who lent his house to Benjamin Franklin when the latter came to Paris at the end of 1776—and with some of the least reputable aspects of the old system. They were certainly involved with Malisset and may have had a hand in the shady transactions that led to the *Pacte de Famine* accusations.[12] It was perhaps understandable that traditionalists like the Marquis de Mirabeau should lump Necker, Panchaud and Le Ray together as 'international speculators', men without loyalty either to king or to country; but it is less understandable that subsequent historians should seriously imagine that these men were all fellow conspirators seeking to overthrow the monarchy and the society of the *ancien régime*. If they did indeed constitute an underworld it was an underworld more concerned with gang warfare than with a concerted attempt to topple the establishment. Even in London, supposedly one of the nerve centres of their sinister operations, they went their very different ways. Necker's friends, Bourdieu and Chollet, were involved with the French ambassador Guines, who was speculating unsuccessfully in English govern-

---

[11] Lüthy, ii, 376–97.
[12] *Ibid.*, ii, 384, 452–6, 613, 674.

ment stock, while Panchaud and his associate Theophilus Cazenove, banker at Amsterdam, strove to rescue something from the wreck of their carefully rigged speculations in East India stock. These had caused a great scandal, ruining William Burke and Laughlin Macleane, and through them compromising Edmund Burke and Lord Shelburne, but they hardly constituted an international conspiracy.[13] If anything they were even less successful than Choiseul's earlier attempts to rig the English East India Company, which were revealed to the English government by a disaffected French agent at about the same time.[14]

Necker's political importance, and his usefulness to the French government, had grown originally out of his contacts with this underworld of financial speculation. He had been in London at the time of Turgot's fall, having been sent there with secret letters from the king of France to the bankers Bourdieu and Chollet. By this time Guines had been recalled, having proved himself extremely clumsy in handling the delicate issues raised by the American revolt. After a long and spectacular battle in the French courts he had managed to shift the blame for the speculations onto his secretary. Officially the view of Choiseul and the anglophobes—that he had been framed by his secretary and by the rascally bankers of London—was vindicated; but serious doubts still remained and the case was kept open by the insistent demands of the bankers that Guines be made to pay the very large sums which he still owed them. It was Necker who succeeded in quieting these demands during his stay in London, thus removing a grave cause of embarrassment for the government of Louis XVI.[15]

The historian Edward Gibbon, who was Necker's host for part of his visit, had no idea that he was entertaining a powerful agent of international finance or a future minister of the French crown. He had once been passionately in love with Suzanne Curchod, the girl whom Necker had subsequently married, and as far as he was concerned the Genevese banker was simply a domestic figure, 'a sensible good-natured creature . . . who might read

---

[13] L. S. Sutherland and J. A. Woods, 'The East India speculations of William Burke', *Proceedings of the Leeds Philosophical and Literary Society*, xi, pt. vii, 1966, pp. 183–216.

[14] *C.H.O.P.*, iv, no. 650.

[15] Lüthy, ii, 414–17. See Guines's desperate letter to George III, 23 February 1774, in Fortescue, iii, 70. There is an account of the whole episode in P. Girault de Coursac, *Marie-Antoinette et le scandale de Guines*, 1962. See also *H.M.C.* 78, *Hastings*, iii, p. 170.

English husbands lessons of proper and dutiful behaviour'. He
was glad to see Suzanne so well bestowed, but he was far too
preoccupied with his own career—the first volume of his *Decline
and Fall* had just appeared and was enjoying a great success—to
think about that of his guest. A few months later, however, when
he was in Paris as the guest of the Neckers, he had a very different
view of things. 'My friend Necker,' he wrote, '(for I now esteem
and love him on his own account) is declared principal minister
of the finances, and though he has great obstacles to contend with,
his knowledge, his firmness and the purity of his intentions ought
to make us wish for his disgrace.' Gibbon, who was later to
produce the official English condemnation of French intervention
in America, saw clearly enough that an efficient reforming minister at Versailles was a much greater danger to England than the
latterday Louvois of Horace Walpole's imagination. As so often
before, France was most to be feared when she was most to be
admired.[16]

An even more impressive tribute of fear and admiration came
from Edmund Burke. He did not have such extensive connections
with the literary and intellectual world of Paris as Gibbon had,
but he was very conscious of the political importance of France
for England. 'England,' he once said, 'is a moon shone upon by
France. France has all things within herself; and she possesses the
power of recovering from the severest blows. England is an
artificial country: take away her commerce, and what has she?'[17]
Now, thanks to the work of Necker, France's powers of recovery
were more apparent than ever before and her opportunities for
taking away England's commerce seemed almost limitless. In
February 1780, when he came to introduce into parliament his
much-publicized plan for 'economical reform', Burke prefaced
it with a lavish and highly complimentary account of Necker's
achievements in France. They had banished for ever, he said,
that 'want of public credit' that had previously been France's
most serious disability; and they had laid the foundations for a
new and revitalized system of finances. Under Necker's wise
guidance Louis XVI had turned his back on 'arbitrary finance'
and had based his fiscal policy on equitable principles and open
consultation. 'These,' Burke concluded, with a bitter reference to

[16] *Letters of Gibbon*, ii, 109, 161–2.
[17] *Recollections of the Table Talk of Samuel Rogers*, ed. A. Dyce, 1887,
pp. 100–1.

Patriot disillusionment with George III, 'are the acts of a Patriot king.'[18]

There were those in France who agreed with Burke. One provincial governor told Necker that he would do everything he could to help him, since 'I am anxious that you should not encounter even the slightest obstacle at a time when you are performing miracles that are the wonder of all right thinking men and all good Patriots.'[19] Others were less sure that the patriotism was on the side of the king and his new minister: one commentator who became steadily more and more opposed to the Necker régime concluded finally that the banker's only talent lay in corrupting his patriotic opponents with bribes of one sort or another. 'Nothing is more striking,' he wrote bitterly, 'than the sight of so-called Patriots abandoning their zeal for their country for the sake of an invitation to the minister's dinner party.'[20] Others waxed even more furious and denounced Necker in the most sweeping terms. The philosophers of the enlightenment, still lamenting the fate of Turgot, were particularly violent in their criticisms and one friend of d'Alembert's spoke angrily of 'dismissals without compensation, reforms without profit, loans without limit'.[21]

It was the dismissals without compensation that lay at the heart of the matter, not only for Necker's management of the French finances but also for the whole political development of the two countries in the second half of the eighteenth century. Patriots on both sides of the Channel were caught in the same agonizing dilemma, the dilemma that had brought their political campaigning to an embarrassed *impasse*: the dilemma of government office and the means of reforming it. On the one hand they hated the jobbery and corruption that turned public office into the instrument of political management; on the other they were committed to the defence of all forms of private property, including that particular form of property which was involved when a man bought an office. They despised the professional traffickers in office, whether in the privately owned General Farms of France or in the publicly owned Customs and Excise service in England; but they could not and would not deny that a government office was something which had a specific value, an important and

[18] *P.H.* xxi, 6–7.
[19] Add. 24, 207, fo. 39.
[20] Lescure, i, 117.
[21] Add. 22, 111, fo. 31.

essential form of investment which ought to be available to all men of property. They therefore took refuge in an imaginary utopia, a dream world of their own devising in which all offices were freely negotiable and were held by independent men, men rich enough and highminded enough to act without fear and without favour. This, they told one another happily, would be the ideal world. Only a few among them had the intelligence or the integrity or the foresight to see that it would be, on the contrary, a farcical world of bumbling incompetence and amateurism. The bureaucrats knew this, but the Patriots did not. And even the bureaucrats did not have the courage to act on their knowledge until Jacques Necker transformed the whole political dialogue in France by basing his policies on the professional salaried adminis-trator rather than on the amateur fee-collecting officeholder.

Other aspects of Necker's policy involved England in the sense that they hardened France's attitude towards her: by committing France to vast government loans, raised by foreign and Protestant bankers, he made conventionally xenophobic Frenchmen even more xenophobic in their determination to resist this incursion of unnatural and unhealthy English methods. But his attempt to create a truly professional administration involved England in another and wider sense, because it was her problem as well as his. As Necker moved from strength to strength, abolishing one venal office after another and replacing them with salaried commissioners, he raised a new and disturbing question, a question that crystallized the half-understood fear and admiration of Gibbon and of Burke: could England afford to continue naked if France was to be clothed? Could she risk the perpetuation of amateur management if France was to move into the age of professional government?

It was a question that contemporaries found difficult to face, especially if they still clung to their Patriot aspirations. Even as they prepared to resist the machinations of English finance and the assertion of English authority in America, the Patriots in France still admired England as the country where the Patriot dream remained intact. The *parlement* of Paris, at the height of its attack on Turgot, was still speaking of England as the land which liberty had chosen for her last refuge;[22] and a few months earlier Jean-Paul Marat, in whose hand patriotism was later to acquire a far more radical meaning, produced a classical summary of old

[22] Flammermont, *Remontrances*, iii, 319.

style English patriotism. His *Chains of Slavery*, published during his stay in England in 1774–75, was a great deal less fiery than its title suggested: it lauded the principles of the English constitution, inveighed against the corrupting effects of the patronage system and advised the electors of England to choose mature and independent men as their representatives. Altogether it was a very worthy effusion, which would have done credit to Arthur Young himself. Even the Literary and Philosophical Society of Newcastle-upon-Tyne, a cautious and respectable body which was shortly to expel Thomas Spence for criticizing the institution of landed property, gave its blessing to it.[23] English radicalism, proudly standing guard over its independent and amateurish traditions, could hardly be expected to admire the professional radicalism of the new French government if the French themselves were still ready to praise the sturdy anachronisms of English country gentlemen.

And yet the fact remained that the independent Patriot cause in England was in a very poor way. Dr John Moore, comparing in 1779 the prospects for French Patriots and their English counterparts, pointed out that if the French took greater risks they also had greater prospects of reward—both in terms of honour and glory and also in terms of possible eventual achievement. Now that the war with the American colonists had made opposition to the government sound like support for rebellion, articulate Patriots found themselves shunned and derided. Those among them who persisted in their attacks on the government were more likely to be ridiculed than to be promoted. 'Modern Patriots,' wrote Elizabeth Montagu contemptuously, 'treat the constitution of England as apothecaries do their patients: they endeavour to give a motion every day and fancy that will carry off all distempers.' 'Let anyone recollect,' concluded Moore, 'the numbers who, with very moderate abilities, have crawled on their knees into office, and compare them with the numbers and success of those who, armed with genius and the artillery of eloquence, attempt the places by storm; if, after this, he joins the assailants, he must either act from other motives than those of self-interest, or betray his ignorance in the calculation of chances.' While the French looked to old-fashioned English patriotism for their salva-

---

[23] J. P. Marat, *The Chains of Slavery . . . to which is prefixed an address to the Electors of Great Britain*, 1774. See also R. S. Watson, *The history of the Literary and Philosophical Society of Newcastle-upon-Tyne*, 1897, pp. 15, 18.

tion from the new-fangled methods of Necker, the English themselves were watching it fade away in the face of the new-found power of Lord North.[24]

The Whig opponents of Lord North, anxious to take over the Patriot slogans as a means of getting themselves back into office, insisted that his administration was as newfangled in its way as anything that Necker was doing. The angry orators of the Rockingham party spoke of dangerous innovations, of new and diabolical principles of prerogative government by means of which North was undermining the fundamental Whig doctrines which had held sway ever since the Glorious Revolution of 1688. Horace Walpole, whose sudden enthusiasm for strong government in 1776 was now quite gone, was intensely worried by the fact that some of the proposed remedies were as new fangled as the disease, that some extremists wanted to resist the government's innovations by bringing in changes of their own. 'But surely, surely,' he wrote in transports of Whig anguish, 'it would be wise to restore the Constitution before we try experiments on it? . . . subvert the established forms, and great clamour would arise, and every evil produced by the change (and I suppose nobody is vain enough to hope to invent a system liable to no objections) would appear aggravated by comparison.' He then turned, as Whig politicians did so often at moments of crisis, to the example of France: he explained how in the 1760s, at the height of the *parlements'* attack on the crown, he had warned Elie de Beaumont that the *parlements* must moderate their policies so as to appeal to the nobility, rather than risk losing all by becoming too extremist. He seemed to think that Maupeou's coup against the *parlements* in 1771 had proved him right.[25] The subsequent twists and turns of French politics were conveniently forgotten, as was his own shortlived enthusiasm for Turgot's administrative despotism of 1776. Thus the French experience was used to point the Whig moral: liberty could only be preserved by moderate aristocratic government—Whig government, in fact—and not by radical reforms. Such reforms were equally dangerous whether they were inspired by tyrannous bureaucrats or by misguided demagogues.

At the root of all this Whig propaganda against North there

[24] J. Moore, *A View of the Society and Manners in France, Switzerland and Germany*, 2 vols, 1779, pp. 109, 110–11. For Elizabeth Montagu's remark see *H.M.C.* 58, *Bath*, i, p. 347.
[25] Walpole, *Last Journals*, ii, 286–8.

was a myth, a myth as potent and as self-perpetuating as the myth
of international financial conspiracy which sustained much of the
propaganda against Necker. It was the myth of innovation, the
doctrine which insisted that North was replacing traditional
Whiggism with something new and different. For Horace
Walpole and his Whig friends that something was, quite simply,
Toryism. In their eyes North was the exponent of a new and
resurgent system of Tory prerogative government which had
first been introduced into English politics by Bute and his Scottish
friends in the 1760s and which was now about to blot out Whig
liberties for good. Once this system had triumphed over the
Americans it would go on to assert its power over the English
as well. By the spring of 1778, when the alliance between the
French and the colonists made it seem likely that the ministry
might lose the war, Walpole had convinced himself that defeat
was equally likely to lead to the extinction of liberty. 'If the
acknowledgement of the independence of the Americans should
reconcile them, and thence produce peace with France, I am
persuaded the King will still think of satiating his vengeance on
what he calls *the English Rebels*,' he wrote gloomily. As English
enthusiasm for the war continued unabated, even after the
Spaniards and the Dutch had also come out in favour of the
colonists, Walpole's version of the innovation myth came to look
very like that peddled by his counterparts in France. Like them,
he began to see commercial speculators as the real culprits,
gambling away the solid security of a settled society for the sake
of quick profits. 'Thus the year finished with the outset of a
new war,' he wrote on the last day of 1780, 'yet the Scotch had
so infatuated and poisoned the nation, that the Dutch war was
popular, at least in the City, where the spirit of gaining had
seized all ranks, and nothing was thought of but privateer-
ing.'[26]

In fact there was very little about Lord North's system of
government that was new or innovatory. He had not salvaged
the wreckage of Chatham's Patriot ministry by making it more
Tory but by making it more Whig. He was a realist and he played
the political game realistically, concerning himself with men
rather than measures. The foundations of his success lay in the
skilful negotiations of 1770 to 1772—negotiations of which Sir
Robert Walpole himself might have been proud and which

[26] *Ibid.*, ii, 149, 341–2.

brought many Whig groups, including some of the Rockinghamites themselves, into his administration. Even his policies were
Whig, as had already been shown when the leaders of the
opposition hurried to his side in March 1778 to help him defeat
the proposal to tax income from sinecures.[27] The most controversial policy of all, the war against the American colonists, was
fundamentally a Whig policy because it was concerned to uphold
the principle which lay at the root of all Whig political philosophy: the supremacy of parliament. Throughout the 1760s
successive administrations had shaped their American policies to
suit the shifting moods of parliament: the passing of the Stamp
Act, the repeal of the Stamp Act, the passing of the Declaratory
Act, the framing of the Townshend duties had all been undertaken in response to the wishes of parliament. George III was
perfectly justified in writing to North in 1775: 'I am fighting the
battle of the legislature and therefore have a right to expect an
almost unanimous support.'[28] If he had been prepared to admit
that assemblies on the other side of the Atlantic had the same
rights, the same direct relationship with his executive power, as
the parliament at Westminster, he might have avoided this
confrontation with his American subjects. But he would not admit
this because in his view it ran counter to the principles of the
constitution which he had sworn at his coronation to defend. The
'revolution principles' of which his Whig politicians were so fond
of reminding him were based fairly and squarely on the
supremacy of parliament; and it was this supremacy that he and
Lord North were now asserting. It was traditional Whiggism, not
newfangled Toryism, that was called into question by the American revolution and its repercussions in England.

Radicals on both sides of the Atlantic saw this clearly enough.
While passionate orators in the colonial assemblies and in the
Continental Congress dismissed the Westminster parliament as a
narrow and unrepresentative collection of placemen, equally
passionate men in England were doing precisely the same thing.
William Mason, a prominent advocate of parliamentary reform,
summed up radical suspicions about the Whig opposition leaders
when he told a friend that the Rockinghams 'were brought up
under Mr Pelham, who was a sort of usher in the Orford School,
and taught the same grammar, and whom the duke of Newcastle

---

[27] See above, p. 151.
[28] George III to Lord North, 10 September 1775, Fortescue, iii, 256–7.

followed as far as he was able to spell'.[29] Horace Walpole, though he was on good terms with Mason, distrusted the 'associations' which the radicals were forming in order to press for parliamentary reform. He pointed out, quite rightly, that they might well become 'tribunals over parliament, to whom the people might appeal against parliament itself'.[30] Most of the associations, especially the original one formed in Yorkshire by Christopher Wyvill, represented substantial country gentlemen rather than 'the people' as a whole. They wanted more seats for the counties, combined perhaps with the disfranchisement of some of the rotten boroughs that propped up the patronage system, rather than that 'interposition of the body of the people itself' which Burke had so rashly advocated ten years earlier. Nevertheless they were quite frightening enough from the Whig point of view: they challenged the Whig assumption that the existing parliamentary system was a sufficient and effective guarantor of the constitution. More dangerous still, they insisted that parliament should be strictly answerable to those who elected it: they took up the demand, already put forward by the Wilkite radicals of the earlier 1770s, for imperative mandates. Electors, they argued, should only vote for candidates who would bind themselves to obey their constituents at all times and over all issues.[31]

It was Edmund Burke who stepped forward to defend the Whigs against this alarming distension of the genie he had so thoughtlessly unbottled in 1770. He had already proved a doughty champion of the independence of parliament, refusing either to obey his Bristol constituents or to admit their right to question his actions in the House of Commons. Now he showed that he was as devious as he was doughty. He outflanked the associations and regained the initiative for the Whigs by bringing forward a plan for 'economical', rather than electoral, reform. While admitting that parliament had become narrow and unrepresentative he denied that this was the fault of the electoral system. On the contrary, the existing electoral system was the best guarantee of the independence of parliament because it ensured

[29] Mason to Harcourt 13 April 1780, cited E. C. Black, *The Association: British extra-parliamentary political organization, 1769–93*, Cambridge (Mass.) 1963, p. 55. The reference is to the continuing influence of Walpole, created Lord Orford in 1742. The letter is quoted in Volume VII of the *Harcourt Papers*, edited by Edward William Harcourt in thirteen volumes and printed privately at Oxford from 1876–1903.

[30] Walpole, *Last Journals*, ii, 276.

[31] See I. R. Christie, *Wilkes, Wyvill and Reform*, 1962.

the election of substantial men of property rather than the upstarts and lickspittles who would be brought in under a system of extended franchises and imperative mandates. The trouble lay in the powers of the executive, not in the privileges of the electorate: constituencies sent honest men to Westminster, only to have them corrupted by government office or the promise of government office. Therefore the solution lay in cutting down the number of offices which the government had at its disposal. The royal household and other departments of government must be drastically pruned, thus achieving at one and the same time the reduction of government expenditure and the limitation of government patronage. It was these proposals that Burke introduced in his speech of 11 February 1780, the speech in which he praised Necker's achievements in France in such fulsome terms.

The kernel of Burke's argument, and indeed of the whole Whig case, lay in the distinction he made between 'reform' and 'innovation'. 'Reform' was a legitimate activity, aimed at correcting abuses which had crept into an originally sound political system. This was what he thought Necker was doing in France and what he thought the Whigs should do in England. Necker was restoring the representative nature of the French constitution, the original constitution which Louis XIV's despotism had overthrown, by means of the Provincial Assemblies which he sought to establish in various parts of France from 1778 onwards: the Whigs must do the same by restoring the original liberties and independence of parliament. Necker was pruning sinecures in France: the Whigs must do the same in England. Necker was challenging the sinister power of the Farmers General and the other financiers by bringing government finance out into the open and borrowing from the public at large: the Whigs must challenge Lord North's cabalistic coterie of government creditors by the same means. Ten years later, when he came to piece together his somewhat hysterical reactions to the French revolution, Burke remarked that during the last years of the *ancien régime* 'rather too much countenance was given to the spirit of innovation, which soon was turned against those who fostered it, and ended in their ruin'; but he still retained his 'high degree of respect' for Necker and by implication exempted him from his general condemnation of Louis XVI's ministers.[32] The others had behaved like Lord North, using unwarranted and unconstitutional powers of prerogative

[32] Burke, *Select Works*, ii, 155, 140.

government in order to bring in dangerous 'innovations'. Only Necker had trodden the true and respectable path of Whiggism, restoring the representative bodies which enabled men of property to balance and contain the power of the crown.

Burke had not simply got things wrong: he had got them completely upside down. The absurdity of his picture of North the innovator was only equalled by the absurdity of his picture of Necker the conservative. Although some of the fears which the traditionalists had about Necker in 1776 proved unjustified— he did remarkably little, for instance, to further the campaign for the toleration of his fellow Protestants in France—his administration proved nevertheless to be one of the most revolutionary France had known for at least half a century. His scheme for the establishment of Provincial Assemblies, beginning with the one set up in Berry by his decree of 12 July 1778, was on the face of it a continuation of experiments and suggestions made by traditional Patriot and *parlementaire* groups: a *corps administratif* had been set up in the Boulonnais in 1768 and councils of notables had been authorized in Champagne in 1776–77, while Choiseul himself had at the same time put forward a plan for provincial estates throughout France.[33] But as the numbers and the influence of the provincial assemblies increased, both during Necker's administration and afterwards, it became increasingly obvious that they were in fact the rivals rather than the partners of older representative institutions. They usually included equal numbers of clergy, nobility, townsmen and non-noble rural landowners, so that the point of view of the 'privileged' orders of the clergy and the nobility did not necessarily prevail. They soon became the counterparts of the associations rather than of parliament, as the secretary of the British embassy was to realize in 1787 when he pointed to the *parlements'* resentment of the provincial assemblies as the central fact in French politics.[34]

Necker's abolition of sinecures, like his experiments with the representative principle, sprang from political ideas that were far more revolutionary than Burke realized. He was not simply concerned with the number of government offices but with their nature: he systematically replaced *officiers*, venal officeholders who had bought their places as an investment, with *commis*,

---

[33] Godechot, *Les institutions de la France*, p. 20; A. Soboul, 'The French rural community in the xviii and xix centuries', *Past and Present*, x, 1956, pp. 78–95; Choiseul, *Mémoires*, pp. 436–44.
[34] See below, p. 233.

professional salaried officials whose appointments were terminable. The process had been started earlier, especially by Turgot, and Necker carried it on with unprecedented vigour, transforming and professionalizing the major departments of French government. At the same time he brought order and system and proper book-keeping into French government finances for the first time and was able to publish in 1781 a detailed statement of revenue and expenditure, a startling and unheard-of achievement which, as one contemporary English writer said, 'deserves the thanks of every honest man and real Patriot, French or English'. It could well be argued that he was guilty of sharp practice in ignoring the cost of the American war and concerning himself merely with 'ordinary' expenditure; but there can be little doubt that within its limits his *Compte rendu* represented a fuller and more accurate statement than any previous controller-general could have published after such a short time in office.[35]

The most revolutionary of all Necker's actions was the one for which he was most loudly praised by Burke, the extension of French government credit so as to replace 'arbitrary finance' with a more widely based system of public loans. Taking over the Discount Bank, which had originally been formed by his rival Panchaud during the last few weeks of Turgot's ministry, Necker put it into the hands of a consortium of bankers whose links with international Protestant finance were even more extensive than those of the bank's original directors. Panchaud was ejected and the other bankers associated with the project—Pache de Montguyon, Paul Schlumpf, Jean-Werner Marck, Etienne Delessert—found themselves joined by new directors whose connections with Switzerland and with protestantism were as close as their own: Jean Girardot, Louis Tourton, Jacques Rilliet and others. Only Le Couteulx and Company, bankers at Paris and at Rouen, represented the traditional forces of French Catholic finance.[36] Under its new directors, and with the active support of Necker, the Discount Bank set out to provide cheap credit and thus to

[35] The contemporary tribute was by Josiah Tucker, *Cui Bono*, 3rd edn, 1782, p. 28. For an account of Necker's reforms see J. F. Bosher, *French Finances 1770–95: from business to bureaucracy*, Cambridge, 1970; on the *Compte rendu* see R. D. Harris, 'Necker's *Compte rendu* of 1781', J.M.H. xlii, 1970, pp. 161–83. Not all contemporaries were taken in by the *Compte rendu*: Henry Ellis, who was in France at the time and was impressed by her political stability, reported nevertheless in May 1781 that there was widespread scepticism about the figures Necker had published. See *H.M.C.* 55, *Various collections*, vi, *Knox*, p. 176.

[36] Lüthy, ii, 457–63.

finance the new wave of public borrowing and the financial speculation which soon grew up around it. Its original connections with the *indienneurs* became more and more tenuous and it became almost exclusively concerned with pure finance. By the time he resigned in May 1781 Necker had raised well over 500 million livres worth of new government loans, much of it with the assistance of the discount bank and its directors. In the eyes of his enemies he had saddled France with an alien capitalistic oligarchy; and it was alleged that many of his loans, especially that of November 1779, were cornered by the sinister Swiss Protestants in advance so that ordinary Frenchmen had to buy stock at three or four per cent above par if they wanted to subscribe.[37]

This was Jacques Necker's alchemy, the philosopher's stone by means of which he paid for French intervention in the War of American Independence without levying any extensive new taxes. Like many other alchemical processes it was of dubious value because the running costs outstripped the worth of the end product: by the time he had finished Necker was borrowing more money to pay the interest on what he had already borrowed than to pay for the American war. Worse still, much of the debt which he was incurring was irredeemable. Instead of promising to pay interest at a certain rate until such time as the loan was repaid, he bound the government to pay annuities for life in lieu of both interest and capital. The statistical side of life insurance, the calculation of probabilities and of life expectancies, was still in its infancy; and consequently the annuity rates were pitched much too high. Canny Swiss bankers could buy annuities which yielded eight to ten per cent of the outright purchase money and then put them up as collaterals for loans at the normal going rate of four to five per cent. Nor did they have to worry about death wiping out their assets: they did not have to have the annuities on their own lives but could nominate the person or persons during whose lives they were to be paid. Healthy children—particularly girls, who could be expected to live longer than boys as long as they kept their virginity and avoided the perils of childbirth—found themselves the nominal recipients of vast sums of French government money. The Genevese bankers made it their business to select thirty stalwart girls and commit them to lifelong spinsterhood so that they could act as profitable channels for annuity

[37] *Ibid.*, ii, 465–87, 496–514.

payments. To Necker's infuriated opponents it seemed that his only achievement had been to put France's future in pawn to the 'Thirty Immortal Maidens of Geneva' and to the unprincipled foreign heretics who lurked behind them.[38]

In Necker's own eyes his achievements were somewhat different. The *Compte rendu* of 1781 claimed, with a certain degree of justification, that the French finances were now sufficiently reorganized and overhauled to function properly under normal peacetime conditions. It was only the extraordinary demands of the American war that had necessitated these enormous loans which had upset the balance of the budget. In the *Compte rendu* he had brushed all this wartime finance aside, presumably because he thought that the financial machine was now running well enough, thanks to his reforms, to get itself back into balance as long as peace came soon. But it must come soon: if he had any shred of political honesty left Necker must stake his political future on the demand for peace. If he really believed in his reforms he must demand the opportunity to complete them. He therefore told the king in the spring of 1781, just when the success of his *Compte rendu* had made his position apparently impregnable, that he would not continue in office unless he was given control over army and navy expenditure and a share in the ultimate decisions of peace and war. In effect he was demanding the greatest innovation of all, the one thing which politicians on both sides of the Channel abominated above everything else. He was asking to be prime minister. He was asking to be raised to that eminence which in France was associated with Richelieu and Mazarin and which in England had brought about the eventual downfall of both Sir Robert Walpole and the earl of Chatham. He was offending against one of the fundamental principles of aristocratic government, the principle which underlay traditional politics in the one country, Whig politics in the other and Patriot politics in both: the principle of collective leadership.

And so he fell. Maurepas, now at the very end of his days, was able to bring about one final transformation scene before he himself was carried off the stage for good. He pointed out to the king that neither the ministry nor the country would stand for such overweening arrogance and he hustled Necker into the wings, bringing on in his place the reassuring figure of Joly de

---

[38] *Ibid.*, ii, 473–4, 478–83. See also G. V. Taylor, 'The Paris Bourse on the eve of the Revolution, 1781–89', *Am.H.R.* lxvii, 1962, pp. 951–77.

Fleury, a man of impeccable *parlementaire* lineage and long experience as an *intendant* and *conseiller d'état*. Joly did what was expected of him in that he swept away many of Necker's administrative reforms and returned to the system of venal office-holding which bound together the interests of the government and of the *parlements*; but he could not escape for long the revolutionary implications of the policies of Necker and his colleagues. Within a few months of his appointment he was faced with the old dilemma: should he raise new taxes or new loans? After five years of Necker's painless miracles the country was in no mood to accept the sort of tax levels that the American war really required. When his plans for tax increases ran into violent opposition Joly turned instead to new loans; and by the beginning of 1782 he was easing himself back into the pattern already laid down by Necker. Advised by Panchaud, he floated a new loan which was officially limited to 70 million livres but which in the end ran to some 190 million. Once again the loans were irredeemable—stockholders could opt for annuities at varying rates according to the age of the person named—and once again they were raised from foreign and Protestant sources, though this time it was Panchaud's associates in Amsterdam, rather than Necker's in Geneva, who put up the bulk of the money.[39] Thus the evil that Necker did lived after him while the good, the schemes for professional administration and effective representative institutions, remained in a state of suspended animation during his reluctant retirement.

The good that Burke had tried to do in his schemes of February 1780, the schemes which had been prefaced with such generous praise for Necker's reforms, had always been of a more dubious nature. Almost every detail of the Economical Reform plans showed that they were concerned with making the king's patronage less extensive rather than with making his government more efficient. Unlike Necker, who had seen the inadequacies both of the traditional power structure and of the shadow boxing that the *parlements* put up against it, Burke had tried to reconcile rather than transcend the existing practices of the government and the existing traditions of the opposition. His proposals represented the lowest common denominator that could be reached between the interests of those who inhabited the power structure, whether North's officeholding Whigs or Rockingham's office-

[39] Lüthy, ii, 519–28.

seeking Whigs, and those who still called themselves Patriots and thought they stood outside it. And that lowest common denominator had been worked out only because both sides thought they needed it: the Rockinghams thought that they could not get back to power without using the Patriots, while the Patriots thought that their position in the localities could only be safeguarded by playing the Rockinghams' game in London. If anything happened to alter those convictions Burke's plans, like Necker's, would have to be put back into cold storage.

Events in London in June 1780, when law and order collapsed under the onslaught of a hysterical anti-Catholic mob, changed the policies of both Whigs and Patriots, because they changed the conditions that had created them. The Rockinghamite attack on North in parliament had already forfeited the support of many independent men when it had become obvious that its object was to coerce the king rather than to reform the administration. The independents were ready enough in April to vote for a resolution declaring that the influence of the Crown ought to be diminished, but they were less eager to countenance the open threats to royal power which Rockingham's followers produced during the ensuing weeks. By the time the Gordon riots broke out on 2 June many backbenchers were already convinced that they had been fooled into supporting a factious attempt to narrow the government rather than a patriotic attempt to widen it into the government of national unity which they wanted. The riots made that government of national unity seem all the more necessary, while at the same time making the Patriots' present tactics seem all the more questionable. Rockingham and his friends, 'the great barons' as Mason called them scornfully, had persuaded the associations to make great use of petitions to parliament; but now it was the petition against so-called 'Catholic influence', presented to parliament by Lord George Gordon's Protestant Association, that had sparked off the most dangerous riots in living memory. The doubts and suspicions which had already driven apart one Whig–Patriot alliance, in 1770–71, had now reappeared with even greater force. The alliance collapsed almost overnight, as the parties to it fell over one another to renounce the dangerous and divisive game they had been playing; and Burke's economical reform schemes collapsed with it.

There were other and less obvious reasons for the collapse. To some extent North had already outmanoeuvred Burke by setting up commissions to inquire into administrative practices and recommend reforms. The reports of these commissions were in the end to provide the basis for improvements which paralleled Necker's professionalization of government rather than Burke's desperate attempt to preserve its amateur status.[40] And the Whigs themselves were less eager to press for reforms now that the Gordon riots seemed to have made North more dependent on their support on less extreme terms. Horace Walpole reported excitedly that the government was so terrified by the riots that it was seeking a coalition with the Whigs; and by 8 June, after nearly a week of lawlessness and some 400 casualties, he noted that the Whigs themselves were equally terrified and equally eager for a coalition. 'Burke was almost frantic with passion', he wrote, 'and was constantly with Lord North, which occasioned reports that he and Lord Rockingham were coming into place'.[41] By 12 June the riots were at last under control and the earlier patterns of political conduct were beginning to reassert themselves; but nobody in politics would forget in a hurry the frightening moment when the political and social establishment itself had seemed about to fall. It was the memory of this moment which was to turn men against all talk of change, whether 'reform' or 'innovation', and make them determined instead to defend the existing system against all comers. Having defended it against rebellious colonists and religious fanatics they were not going to let it be undermined by factious politicians or misguided reformers.

Nor were they going to let it be undermined by the scheming French. One of the oddest arguments put forward against the proposals of Burke and others for the reduction of patronage was used by Dean Tucker in a popular and successful pamphlet: he insisted that 'if English pensions are reduced then the king of France might allot one sixth of *his* pension fund, £200,000, to be distributed among his trusty and well-beloved friends, the ring-leaders of the populace of Great Britain for the time being'.[42] Tucker cannot seriously have believed that either the holders or the seekers of sinecures were 'ring-leaders of the populace', still

---

[40] See J. E. D. Binney, *British Public Finance and Administration, 1774–92*, Oxford, 1958.

[41] Walpole, *Last Journals*, ii, 312. See I. R. Christie, 'The Marquis of Rockingham and Lord North's offer of a coalition, June–July 1780', *E.H.R.* lxix, 1954, pp. 388–407.

[42] J. Tucker, *Four letters on important national subjects*, 2nd edn, 1783, p. 38.

less that Louis XVI was likely to lead them into such a role by
the offer of French gold; and yet his ridiculous argument was
solemnly advanced and eagerly accepted. He had always been an
enemy of xenophobia—he proudly displayed at the head of his
works Turgot's famous 'Citizen of the World' letter of 1770—and
he expressly denied having 'an inbred antipathy against France'.[43]
And yet he had been sufficiently embittered by France's support
of the American colonists to make political capital out of this
accusation that she was also ready to suborn demagogues in
England itself.

Absurd though it was, the charge revealed only too clearly
the intricate and interconnected nature of the myths which had
come to govern political behaviour in the two countries. During
the twenty years which had elapsed since the glorious victories
of the Seven Years War and the triumphant peace treaty of 1763,
the English had been struggling to defend their political system,
based on the supremacy of the parliament at Westminster, against
threats from outside which seemed about to overwhelm it. In fact
these threats had been impersonal and inexorable: they had arisen
out of the inner conflicts between the system itself and the new
administrative and political and fiscal strains which the war had
imposed upon it. But they had gradually become personalized, in
the mythology of politics, into a series of scapegoats. Ambitious
sinecurists seeking to extend their rotten realm of patronage across
the Atlantic, greedy merchants creating colonial wars and colonial
problems for their own gain, sinister financiers keeping up their
interest rates by inflating still further an already bloated national
debt—all these and many others had been pointed out to the
independent members of parliament as being the real culprits.
Even the independent members themselves had begun to doubt
one another as it became clear that they were all caught up in
the tentacles of an expanding industrial and maritime empire. The
war with the colonists had at first cleared away the confusions
and the suspicions, since it enabled all the evil forces of innovation
to be identified with the rebels and their well-wishers in England;
but now that it was coming to an end it was creating more
problems than it had solved. The debate on the ending of the War
of American Independence, like the debate on the ending of the
Seven Years War twenty years earlier, made the selection and
isolation of scapegoats extremely difficult. But at least this time

[43] J. Tucker, *Cui Bono*, 3rd edn, 1782, p. 5.

there was one archetypal scapegoat who stood behind all the others, real and imaginary: the hated Frenchman. Whatever the reality of English politics might require in the 1780s, the myth that underlay them demanded constant vigilance against the French.

The myth had never taken much account of the reality. In the 1760s Englishmen had girded themselves against a Popish threat from a France in which there was, according to their own ambassador, 'a total dissolution of papal authority among all ranks of the people', while in the following decade they had seen the *indienneurs*, many of whom were hated in France for their association with foreign capital and English influence, as minions of a commercially aggressive French government.[44] Now, while extremists like Gordon howled for Protestant intolerance as a shield against a France which was in fact moving faster than ever before towards toleration of her own Protestants, men as supposedly moderate as Tucker talked of English radicals being pensioned by a French king who had in fact made greater inroads into the pension and sinecure system than had ever been contemplated in England. And as the myths wrapped themselves around the realities, so they obscured and distorted them until in the end they re-created them in their own image. The realities of English politics in the 1780s demanded ruthless and radical action. Shibboleths like the mercantilist system, the supremacy and self-sufficiency of parliament and the amateur traditions of public service had all been shattered by the very war that had been intended to defend them. Such advantages as England did enjoy had come about in spite of these shibboleths rather than because of them: economic growth was taking place in spite of the mercantilist system, while political regeneration was taking place in spite of the existing representative structure and in spite of the existing administrative machinery. These advantages could only be pursued if the old convictions were turned inside out, if unrestricted trade and new institutions and extended governmental powers were discussed constructively instead of being resented and rejected. In reality England's defeat in the War of American Independence was a salutary development, which opened up exciting new possibilities; but in the political mythology of the time it was a matter for sullen resentment, for reactionary xenophobia and for the rejection of all things French.

[44] P.R.O. S.P. 78/265 fo. 208; Fortescue, ii, 434.

The French experience was curiously similar. Just as English politics since 1776 had been dominated by a determination to preserve traditional English institutions from subversion by Frenchmen and rebels, so French politics had been dominated by a desire to humble once and for all the dangerous republicanism and commercialism of England. This had produced strange paradoxes on both sides of the Channel. While Englishmen persuaded themselves that they were defending freedom by seeking to make their colonists less free, Frenchmen insisted that they were defending true kingship by challenging the English king's authority in America. Sometimes they genuinely respected the very institutions they were helping to undermine—Beaumarchais, in London to establish secret contacts with the colonial malcontents, could still speak of the English constitution as mirroring the basic harmony and balance of the universe itself[45]—but for the most part they felt a grim satisfaction in seeing the English, who had always lived by rebellion, perish by rebellion. The French foreign office produced memoranda to show that England had been abetting revolts in other countries, as well as in her own, for at least two centuries; and as late as July 1777 the French foreign minister Vergennes said that the English would soon revert to type and join their own rebellious colonists in stirring up further rebellions in Mexico and other Spanish and French possessions on the American continent. Having convinced themselves that their intervention in America was a blow against republicanism rather than a betrayal of monarchy, French statesmen were careful to guard against its possible consequences. Vergennes told his subordinates in confidence that French policy must not aim at the independence of the colonists, while Choiseul, still trying to influence events from his exile, advised the government that whatever happened England must be allowed to keep both Canada and the Carolinas, so that the upstart colonists could be kept in their proper place and be subject to control from Europe.[46]

However much statesmen might try to guard against the diplomatic consequences of intervention, it was beyond their

[45] Stevens, ix, no. 862.
[46] *Ibid.*, vii, no. 586; Doniol ii, 460, 462–3; Choiseul, *Mémoires*, p. 432. See also L. de Loménie, *Beaumarchais and his times*, tr. H. S. Edwards, 1856; E. S. Corwin, 'The French objectives in the American Revolution', *Am.H.R.* xxi, 1915–16, pp. 33–61; E. S. Corwin, *French Policy and the American Alliance of 1778*, Princeton, 1916; S. F. Bemis, *The Diplomacy of the American Revolution*, rev. edn, 1957.

power to guard against all its political and social consequences within France itself. La Luzerne, French minister in Philadelphia, was said to have told Congress that if it intended to govern the continent it must be sure to keep the people poor. 'This, says he, is our maxim in France. . . Poor men make the most obedient subjects and the best soldiers.'[47] And indeed to many French intellectuals, idealizing their colonial *protégés* as simple pioneers contemptuous of riches, this perpetuation of poverty in America seemed a noble aim. The marquis de Chastellux wrote that the dignified bearing of American women reminded him of the uncorrupted peasants painted by Greuze. He was charmed by the open and innocent moral standards of the colonists, by the 'extreme liberty that prevails in this country between the two sexes, as long as they are not married', and by their enlightened attitude to unmarried mothers. 'With them vice is so foreign and rare,' he wrote, 'that the danger of example is almost non-existent; so that a mistake of this nature is regarded as would be an accidental illness.'[48] It was all very idyllic and very pastoral, a latterday garden of Eden in which mankind could renounce riches and all the corruption they had brought with them. 'It is perhaps in America,' wrote Louis Sebastian Mercier in 1778, 'that the human race is to be re-created.'[49] Philosophers like Diderot, who on the eve of the American revolution had prophesied that France was about to follow England into cultural and intellectual decline because of her obsession with commerce, took courage again when they saw the homespun farmers of the New World challenge the greedy merchants and devious financiers of the Old. As the self-appointed champion of Greuze, Diderot was delighted to find that the Americans were breathing life into the figures of noble and virtuous peasants with which that artist's paintings were populated.[50] However paradoxical the diplomatic consequences of France's intervention might be, its social effects were even more paradoxical: it strengthened the hold of those same traditional values which its financial results were about to shatter.

The supreme symbol of that paradox was Benjamin Franklin,

[47] Cited Corwin, *French Policy and the American Alliance*, p. 264.
[48] F. J. de Beauvoir, Marquis de Chastellux, *Travels in North America*, tr. and ed. H. C. Rice, 2 vols, Chapel Hill, 1963, i, 120, 228.
[49] Cited D. Echeverria, *Mirage in the West: a history of the French image of American society to 1815*, Princeton, 1957, p. 77.
[50] Diderot, *Salons*, iv, 111.

the second foreign miracle-worker to whom France had been introduced in the autumn of 1776. He arrived in Paris towards the end of December, some two months after Necker's appointment, and he delighted fashionable society with his fur hat and his simple clothes and his bluff manners. 'Figure me in your mind . . . very plainly dressed,' he wrote to a friend, 'wearing my thin grey straight hair that peeps out under my only coiffure, a fine fur cap, which comes down to my forehead almost to my spectacles. Think how this must appear among the powdered heads of Paris.'[51] There was indeed a gulf between the sturdy colonists and the powdered heads of Paris—at least one American agent protested violently the first time his French barber subjected him to the full treatment of hair powder and hair bags[52]—but it was not as wide as Franklin's carefully cultivated image was intended to suggest. He was in fact an experienced businessman and politician who had been in public life for nearly half a century, mixing with the rich and the powerful on both sides of the Atlantic; but if the French wished to see him as a remote rustic genius, drawing fire from heaven down his kitestring like a new Prometheus, he was quite happy that they should do so. He was well aware that French policy towards America was based on sound commercial considerations and that it was speculators like Le Ray de Chaumont who were building the real bridges between Philadelphia and Paris. It was the realists with their love of wealth, not the idealists with their love of poverty, who would make French aid for America a practical policy. The origins of that aid lay, as an English secret agent in Paris saw clearly enough shortly before Franklin's arrival, in the 'extensive and very profitable commerce to be carried on between the subjects of France and those of Great Britain now in rebellion'. According to this same agent, the list of those engaged in such commerce included not only Le Ray de Chaumont and Bourdieu and Chollet but also many of the most reputable firms at Bordeaux and Nantes, along with several English and American financiers who had been involved with Franklin himself in land speculation a few years earlier.[53] Franklin's miracles might appear different from Necker's, the product of lofty science rather than labyrinthine

---

[51] van Doren, *Franklin*, p. 571.
[52] Stevens, i, no. 44.
[53] *Ibid.*, ii, no. 131; no. iii, 291. See also R. W. van Alstyne, 'Thomas Walpole's letters to the Duke of Grafton on American affairs', *Huntingdon Library Quarterly*, xxx, 1966–67, pp. 17–33.

speculation, but they nevertheless came from the same conjuror's box.

The French were in fact caught in exactly the same situation as the English: they were engaged in a venture which would inevitably divide their society still further because it was the opposite of what they thought it was and would have results utterly different from those they expected of it. While the English had been plagued by nightmares, tormented by visions of their freedom and their wealth being snatched from them by absolutists at home and abroad, the French had been enjoying heady dreams of triumph over the sinister forces of commercialism. They had lost their awe of the English constitution, which one French commentator described as a municipal device more fitted for aldermen managing boroughs than for statesmen governing empires,[54] and they had lost their fear of the things with which England was associated in French minds. Linguet, a disgraced and exiled journalist, was able to charm his way back to popularity and even to royal favour with comfortable words about the American episode proving the superiority of land power over sea power, of agriculture over commerce, of monarchical institutions over republicanism.[55] It had in fact proved nothing of the sort: it had bound France to an extended credit structure and a new kind of capitalistic politics as surely as it had forced the English to reconsider their concepts of freedom and their ideas about wealth. But in both countries the realists who saw these truths were far less numerous than the dreamers who chose to ignore them; and the images of the dreams and of the nightmares were still powerful enough to befuddle the moment of awakening.

That moment came in March 1782, with North's fall from power. By this time the experience of Necker's successors was already proving that in France the new forces were too strong to be pushed aside; but in England North's successors still thought that they could put new wine in old bottles and contain within traditional Whig principles the far-reaching changes which peace with the colonists and with the French would involve. As dream gave way to reality, as politicians in both countries began to see that they could not emerge from the American revolution with the same concepts they had taken into it, there took place another

[54] L. G. Dubuat-Nancay, *Les Maximes du gouvernement monarchique*, London, 1778, p. 353.
[55] S. N. H. Linguet, *Annales politiques, civiles et littéraires*, 17 vols, London and The Hague, 1777–90, i, 7, 48, 276, 282; Lescure, i, 133, 237.

revolution which was smaller in scale but nevertheless extremely important for the two countries. This was in Geneva, where the radical party overthrew the oligarchic government of the city in April 1782 and appealed to the new administration in England for support against the threat of French intervention.[56] France had been concerned for many years in the politics of Geneva, giving both diplomatic and military support to the conservative forces there. They in return had given her financial support: the government which had now fallen had included most of the great bankers who had taken up Necker's loans. On the other hand the new and more radical government also had its share of financiers and capitalists, most of them eager to oust their rivals not only as the rulers of Geneva but also as the creditors of France. The conflict between the old and the new Geneva might well spill over into the politics of Paris and perhaps of London as well, now that the English had an opportunity to support revolutionaries against France for a change. Six years of revolution in America had served to make the international financial network indispensable on both sides of the Channel; and now six weeks of revolution in Geneva gave it the chance to propagate itself anew by means of its own divisions.

[56] See E. Chapuisat, *La Prise d'armes de 1782 à Genève*, Geneva, 1932.

8 The politics of capitalism

Optimistic radicals in Geneva and in London thought that they felt the same wind of change blowing through both their cities in the spring of 1782. The new and revolutionary government in Geneva sent one of its most talented members, Jacques-Antoine Duroveray, to establish contact with the new and apparently equally revolutionary government in London, a government which was committed to reversing both the domestic and the foreign policies of Lord North. Officially Duroveray was received by Charles Fox, who as foreign secretary was one of the leading Whigs in the new administration; but unofficially most of his closest contacts were with the friends and supporters of Lord Shelburne, the new home secretary. And Shelburne had never been a Rockinghamite Whig: more than any other man he had kept alive, since Chatham's death in 1778, the Chathamite or Patriot tradition of politics. Rockingham might be North's successor as first lord of the treasury and leader of the ministry, but the victory over North had not been simply a Whig victory: it had been the victory of a coalition of Whigs and Patriots, led by Rockingham and Shelburne respectively. Both groups had had programmes of reform, just as both had had plans to deal in a completely new way with the complex international situation of which America and France, and now Geneva as well, formed the essential elements. But whose programmes of reform, whose plans for realignment, were to triumph? It was a difficult and divisive question and one before which the hopes of the Genevese radicals were to melt away into disappointment and disillusion.

In the City of London and in the corridors of Whitehall there were men who understood the importance of Geneva and of the part it might play in England's relations with France and with America; but for most Englishmen it was a faraway city of which they knew little and cared less. They tended to associate it either with gin—which was a mistake based on a misreading of the French word for a juniper berry—or with the dissenters, whose theological ancestry could be traced back to Calvin's Geneva and whose ministers still wore 'Geneva gowns'. Not all Genevese were devout Calvinists and many of them had established for themselves international reputations in fields which had little connection with religion. They included such essentially secular figures as Theodore Tronchin, the fashionable doctor who was patronized not only by the king of France but also by most of the princes of the blood, and Jacques Mallet du Pan, once a pastor but now a journalist on an international scale whose activities covered Holland and America as well as England and France. Neither Tronchin nor Mallet du Pan bore the least resemblance to the ranting religious fanatic who came to mind when entrenched Anglicans thought about Geneva; but they did both come from families associated with international banking and finance. There was more truth even in the French myth about Geneva than there was in its English counterpart.[1]

The English myth was nevertheless powerful enough to make things difficult for Duroveray and for those other Genevese who followed him to England later in the year. The Rockingham Whigs were balanced on a razor edge as it was: if they did not produce dramatic changes quickly they would be accused of going back on their promises, while if they played with changes that were too dramatic they would incur those same charges of 'innovation' that they had levelled at North and at the over-

---

[1] Lüthy, ii, 177, 344–5. See also J. A. Galiffe *et al., Notices généalogiques sur les familles genevoises depuis les premiers temps jusqu'aux nos jours,* 7 vols, Geneva, 1829–95.

enthusiastic Patriots. And it was clear that involvement with Calvinistic and capitalistic foreign radicals would fall well within the category of changes that were too dramatic. Fox and his subordinates at the Foreign Office spoke kindly to their Genevese visitors, but it was clear that nothing would be done. Even Samuel Romilly, who was passionately devoted to the popular party in Geneva and had written articles in the London newspapers in support of it, confessed privately that the new administration could no more help Geneva than it could help an oppressed nation on the face of the moon.[2] As for Shelburne, who already had links with dissent and with Geneva, he was rapidly being made to realize the dangers of this sort of association. A few months later a vicious attack was made on him in the *Gentleman's Magazine*, alleging that for twelve or fifteen years he had been intriguing with dissenters and malcontents, both at home and abroad, in order to get himself into power. His links with Franklin, with Priestley, with the whole network of Calvinist agitators whom English gentlemen distrusted so deeply, were jumbled together as the groundwork for a farrago of charges which were as absurd as they were dangerous.[3]

Such accusations were dangerous for the same reason that they were absurd: Shelburne knew perfectly well that the support of the independent backbenchers must be his ultimate aim and that his patronage of intellectuals and internationalists could never be more than a means to that end. He refused, therefore, to sacrifice ends to means and he kept the clamorous Genevese carefully at arm's length, at any rate in public. They were potentially divisive and neither he nor the Rockinghams wanted to appear as the promoters of division. While the two wings of the ministry jostled for position on the central ground that lay between them, Geneva was left to her fate. On 2 July 1782 the armies of France and her allies entered the city and restored the conservatives to power. Duroveray and some of his colleagues escaped across the lake in a small boat and took refuge in the nearby principality of Neuchatel, which was part of the dominions of the Protestant king of Prussia. There they were joined by other refugees, most

---

[2] Romilly's articles were published in the *Morning Chronicle and Advertiser* for 8 and 11 January 1782. For his remarks on the impossibility of intervention see his letter to his sister, 20 May 1782, printed in part in *Lettres de Jean Roget, 1751–1783*, ed. F. F. Roget, Geneva, 1911, pp. 229–30. Jean Roget, a Genevese radical, was married to Romilly's sister Catherine.

[3] *Gent. Mag.* 1783, p. 22.

of whom had links with the great banking houses of Germany and Holland and England. If the diplomatic pattern of Europe was about to revert to a confrontation between the Catholic powers on the one hand and the Protestant powers on the other— and there were many who thought that it was—then the conflict between the old and the new Geneva would have its part to play in such a situation. Just as the identity of interests between the Catholic powers of France and Austria and Spain was buttressed by increasingly complex connections between all three of them and the financial resources of the old Geneva, so the new Geneva offered to provide a basis for an Anglo-Dutch-Prussian combination relying on the money markets of London and Amsterdam and of the cities of north Germany. Once England made up her mind, once her political situation resolved itself in such a way as to make definite policies towards America and Europe possible again, she would find that those policies would have to take into account the Genevese problems which she had temporarily brushed aside.

The beginnings of a revolution in English politics came with the death of Rockingham, which took place on the day before the French marched into Geneva. He was only fifty-two and it was sad that he should have been allowed a mere twelve weeks in power after sixteen years in opposition; but whatever one may feel for the man himself it would be unrealistic to see his ministry as a vigorous thing cut off tragically in its prime. It was in fact an administration based on a pretence which was already beginning to wear thin, a pitifully transparent pretence of unity among men and unanimity over measures. At first sight the achievements of the Rockingham government were impressive, especially since it had only lasted for twelve weeks. It had given legislative independence to Ireland, it had made drastic reductions in the patronage of the crown and it had begun negotiations for an end to the war with America. But in every case the measures had created more problems than they had solved—problems, moreover, that exposed both the negative nature of Whig philosophy and the confused loyalties of the Whig party itself. The Irish were free to pass laws for themselves, but there was little agreement in England as to how those laws should be integrated with the ones passed at Westminster. The recognition of American independence had been agreed in principle, but it was by no means clear what use should be made of this concession in the delicate task of separating the Americans from their French allies and getting the best possible terms from both. The influence of the crown had been reduced, but only the most optimistic Whigs could imagine that this would of itself restore the prestige of parliament or solve the intractable administrative problems with which the country was now faced. These problems demanded the closing of options which the Whigs would rather have left open and which could be closed more easily now that Rockingham was dead.

The real issue that divided Englishmen in the summer of 1782, and for many years to come, was the question whether the new situation in which they found themselves should be regarded as a misfortune or an opportunity. Most of them regarded it as an unqualified disaster and would have agreed with the pamphleteer who compared the country to 'a person who has embarrassed all his circumstances by exceeding his income, or by engaging in projects beyond his abilities to accomplish' and who now 'endeavours to retrieve his affairs by lessening his expenses'.[4] The backbenchers had been saying for years that the projects of the commercial men were beyond the country's abilities to accomplish and that the colonial expansion which was supposed to be enriching England was in fact bringing about her ruin. Now they took a gloomy pleasure in being proved right; and they demanded drastic reductions in government expenditure and in government commitments. Above all they demanded an end to those institutions and abuses by means of which monied men insinuated themselves into political life. It was for this reason that the abolition of the Board of Trade and the exclusion of government contractors from the Commons, two measures taken by the Rockinghams, were so popular. One excited lady even told her friend that she had heard that there would be a rebellion if the Bill to exclude contractors was not carried.[5] Burke had indeed hit on a rich vein when he pointed the Rockingham Whigs towards 'economical reform': as well as apparently fulfilling their promises to end the corruption and intimidation of parliament, it also pleased all those who saw the defeat in America as a signal for a general disengagement from the politics of capitalism. A dozen years earlier

[4] W. Playfair, *The Increase of Manufacturers, Commerce and Finance, with the extension of civil liberty proposed in regulations for the interest of money,* 1783, p. 1.
[5] Mrs Thrale to Fanny Burney, 24 April 1782, *Diary and Letters of Madame d'Arblay, 1778–1840,* ed. C. Barrett, 6 vols, 1904–05, ii, 81–2.

Burke had foretold that the great threat to liberty and to the balance of the constitution would come from the fact that the government itself was 'a great banker and a great merchant'; now he could claim to be removing that threat by reducing the sphere of government and reminding all Englishmen, governors and governed alike, that they must henceforth cut their coat according to their cloth.

But in the final analysis the prophets of doom and the advocates of retreat were wrong: the need of the time was not to renounce England's position in international trade but to restore it. The Whigs were not simply dismantling a top-heavy and parasitical bureaucracy, as the enthusiasts for 'economical reform' seemed to imagine. They were also destroying what few foundations there were for an efficient and professional administrative system, a system capable of carrying into effect the policies required by the ever-widening complexities of world trade. Institutions such as the Board of Trade were not merely the tentacles of a capitalist despotism, devices through which the monied men squeezed the landed men; they were also the vital lifelines of a great trading empire. And, whatever the gloomy backbenchers might think, England still had a great trading empire: she had not lost her control over American trade simply because she had lost her control over great tracts of American territory. The Americans had to trade with someone, whether they were independent or not; and it was becoming increasingly clear that they did not propose to admit the French to the privileged positions from which the English had been temporarily ejected. Someone had to wake the backbenchers up to these facts, just as someone had to make them see the even more unpalatable truth which had been so blandly obscured by the 'reforms' of the Rockinghams: the country needed more government rather than less. Governmental responsibilities were growing at an unprecedented rate and it was no time to cut back governmental resources. The politics of capitalism made professionalism in government a necessity and not a luxury; and the politics of capitalism had come to stay, whether the country gentlemen liked it or not. Even the rulers of France, so long distrustful of the capitalist contagion which they sniffed from across the Channel, had now come to terms with it. They were ready and waiting to seize whatever the English rejected. And this, at least, was an argument that the entrenched opponents of capitalism were prepared to accept: the country gentlemen of Lancashire had already pointed out that attempts to get the new textile machinery banned would merely result in these machines being set up in France instead.[6] As so often before in the interlocking history of the two countries, the prejudices of chauvinism proved more powerful than the principles of economics.

It was upon Shelburne's shoulders that these burdens of persuasion and re-education fell. He took over from Rockingham as first lord of the treasury at the beginning of July 1782 and he remained in power until the end of February 1783; and during those eight months the whole tangled conflict between whiggism and patriotism was brought to a head, as were the conflicts within the ranks of the Patriots themselves. His ministry began with a confrontation between himself and Charles Fox over their respective views of kingship: Fox contended that the king must accept a new chief minister chosen by the Rockinghamite Whigs themselves, since they dominated the House of Commons, while Shelburne defended the king's undoubted constitutional right to choose whomsoever he pleased as his minister. Having vindicated the traditional concept of a Patriot king, the new first lord went on to refurbish the notion of a Patriot minister. He set to work to save what he could of the trading empire won by the first Patriot minister, his political mentor the earl of Chatham, while at the same time accepting the collapse of the territorial empire which it had brought with it. He also undertook the even more difficult task of winning back the country gentlemen from Whiggism and converting them to the need for a more positive kind of administrative reform than the Whigs had ever dreamed of. All the problems created by the Seven Years War, domestic as well as imperial, had now grown to maturity and were waiting to entangle Shelburne as he fought to end the War of American Independence. In making the peace treaties of 1783 he was battling with the legacies left behind by those of 1763; and in the end he was defeated by them. But the defeat, like the struggle, was on an epic scale.[7] It was not for nothing that Disraeli stressed the importance of understanding 'one of the suppressed characters of English history, Lord Shelburne'.[8]

[6] *Annual Register*, 1779, p. 233.
[7] V. Harlow, *The Founding of the Second British Empire 1763–93*, 2 vols, 1959–64, i, 312. For a less sympathetic view see J. Cannon, *The Fox–North Coalition*, Cambridge, 1969, p. 36.
[8] B. Disraeli, *Sybil*, 1845, chapter 3.

Most important of all, it was during Shelburne's administration that the dual revolution of western Europe was set once and for all on its final course. For more than thirty years England and France had been convulsed by political and social and economic changes which sprang, directly or indirectly, from overseas trade and the problems it had created. Their neighbours and their dependent territories had been drawn irresistibly into the same process: Geneva and Ireland and Holland and America and even Spain had all been affected. The war in America had been a dramatic manifestation of the process, but it had not been its culmination. That would depend on the peace and its consequences: it was what they brought out of the war, not what they had originally taken into it, that would shape the future of both countries and decide whether subsequent changes would break or merely bend their existing social and political framework. France had gone to war against arrogant commercialism and international finance, only to find herself a prisoner of these forces even in the moment of apparent victory. England had gone to war on behalf of the mercantilist system and the supremacy of parliament, only to find that in the moment of defeat she had to rethink her attitude to both these things. Adjustment, sometimes painful and radical adjustment, would be needed in both countries: but it would have to be one single process of adjustment and not two separate ones. Together the two countries must remould the international commercial and financial structure on which their own internal political structures ultimately depended. And it was Shelburne, the internationalist who eleven years earlier had responded so enthusiastically to the idealism of the 'citizens of the world', who must preside over the process.

Shelburne's counterpart on the other side of the Channel was very far from reverting to Turgot's ideas of international cooperation, but he was certainly beginning to have second thoughts about the War of American Independence. It was the re-emergence of old problems rather than the challenge of new ones which had led to this change of heart. By the early 1780s it was clear to Vergennes and to his colleagues at the French foreign office that their involvement in America had already led them to lose control over the new and threatening developments in Germany and in Poland. In the Near East the situation was even uglier: it began to look as if they had let Russia into the Mediterranean in their anxiety to oust Britain from the Atlantic.

This meant that France might well lose what influence she still had in India and other parts of Asia, while gaining very little by way of compensation in America. The triumphant Americans were already trying to make their French allies dance to their tune, a tune which was by no means in harmony with France's existing commercial interests. Vergennes had always known that the political consequences of the American rebellion might be uncomfortable for France and he now began to see that the economic consequences might be even more uncomfortable: the Americans seemed determined either to trade once again with the English or to trade with the French on terms that raised potentially explosive issues in French internal politics. How, for instance, could a profitable Franco-American tobacco trade be established without turning upside down the whole structure of the Royal General Farms and their monopolies? And if the trade with America went straight into the hands of the foreign bankers and speculators who had financed the war, as seemed extremely probable, how could this be prevented from having disastrously divisive social and political results?

The political and social divisions were already in evidence, widening and deepening as the country became more and more disillusioned with the American war. The period of economic expansion, through which France had been passing since the middle of the century, had ended with the war it had helped to produce: 1778, the year of intervention, was also the year in which the first unmistakeable signs of recession began to set in. By the time Vergennes and Shelburne started to thrash out peace terms France was in the grip of a full-scale agrarian depression, with steadily falling prices and steadily increasing unemployment. Industry in France was still heavily dependent on the country-side, for its materials and for its labour as well as for its markets; and so it too was beginning to follow the same downward spiral. Only international trade and finance, already widely hated as an unnatural and alien sector of the economy managed by Protestant profiteers, seemed able to confirm its unpopularity by preserving its buoyancy.[9] But even here there were serious divisions which had tended to crystallize out, in the course of the war, into a conflict between those capitalists who sought rivalry with England and those who sought co-operation with her. Franklin and his

[9] Lüthy, ii, 594. See also C–E. Labrousse, *La Crise de l'économie française à la fin de l'ancien régime et au début de la Révolution*, 1944.

friends had come to France to preach agrarian simplicity and brotherly love, but in the end they had only produced capitalist competition and social dissension. If they were to undo the harm they had done they would have to behave with singular saint-liness, bestowing their economic favours with no thought for themselves and out of a concern only for the country that had helped them.

Not surprisingly the Americans proved incapable of such altruistic conduct. Franklin had already negotiated secretly with the English on the basis of the cession of Canada, of which he knew Vergennes disapproved, and now he began to move towards the idea of a separate peace with England. Benjamin Vaughan, one of those dissenter merchants whose links with Shelburne had aroused such suspicion, was sent back to England from Paris to tell Shelburne privately of the American distrust of France. He also told him, in no uncertain terms, that America wanted to trade with England rather than with France.[10] The English for their part were able to show the Americans intercepted docu-ments which proved that France and her ally Spain were preparing to go back on their promises to America in order to get trading concessions for themselves. Gerard de Rayneval, Vergennes's chief adviser on commercial matters, made several secret trips to London and revealed clearly enough, as Shelburne told the king, that France was 'rather jealous than partial to America'.[11] Finally the English and American plenipotentiaries in Paris signed at the end of November 1782 the preliminaries for 'a Treaty proposed to be concluded . . . but which Treaty is not to be concluded until terms of a peace shall be agreed upon, between Great Britain and France'. On paper some shreds of Franco-American trust and cooperation had been preserved; but in reality there was very little left of it. One side of the Atlantic trading triangle had been broken and it was largely up to England to decide which of the others should triumph, whether Anglo-American capitalism should be turned against France or whether Anglo-French capitalism should be turned against America. Not for the first or the last time in her history England had to choose between turning towards Europe or turning towards her colonies

---

[10] Bemis, *Diplomacy of American Revolution*, pp. 224–31. On French fears of a revived and even strengthened Anglo-American trade see P. Legendre, 'Réactionnaires et politiques devant la crise coloniale', *R.H.* ccxxxi, 1964, pp. 357–76.

[11] Fortescue, vi, 125.

and ex-colonies. Not for the first or the last time she neglected, until it was almost too late, the possibility of doing both.

The situation was complicated by the fact that governments and the people they governed were often working at cross purposes. The French foreign office might have turned its back on the American alliance but there were plenty of influential people in France who still looked across the Atlantic for inspiration or for profit. The returning French noblemen who had fought with Washington's armies still wanted their plaudits, just as the powerful new commercial forces created by the war still wanted their profits. And financial necessity was already forging important links between the two groups: capitalists holding out hopes of quick profits soon came to terms with noblemen whose revenues were shrinking either because of adverse agrarian conditions or because of their own extravagance. By the spring of 1783, when the peace treaty with England was finally signed, Vergennes had come to believe that it was more important to restore relations with England than it was to flatter the new-born republicanism of America. The vital thing was to regain as much territory as possible without alienating the English—'to pluck the bird without making her squawk', as Rayneval put it[12]—and in this he seemed to have succeeded: Shelburne's government was prepared to work for a *rapprochement* with France at all levels, commercial as well as diplomatic, instead of reverting to the sullen xenophobia of the past. Vergennes later told one of his subordinates that Shelburne was the only Englishman he could trust, the only statesman who shared his own vision of the sort of co-operation that could and should exist between the two countries.[13] But it was hard to see how such cooperation could be achieved if hotheads like Lafayette went round boasting of their exploits against the king of England in America and making clumsy efforts to construct an exclusive Franco-American commercial relationship which cut across plans for free trade between France and England.[14] The understandable elation of those who

[12] Rayneval to Hennin, 26 January 1783, cited Bemis, *Diplomacy of American Revolution*, p. 252.
[13] Cited H. Doniol, 'Le ministère des affaires étrangères de France sous le comte de Vergennes: souvenirs de Hennin sur ce ministre', *R.H.D.* vii, 1893, pp. 528–60.
[14] F. L. Nussbaum, 'Vergennes and Lafayette versus the Farmers General', *J.M.H.* iii, 1931, pp. 592–613; L. Gottschalk, *Lafayette 1783–89*, Chicago, 1950, pp. 42–52, 68–72.

had won the victory rendered very difficult the task of those who had to build the peace.

The resentment which defeat had produced in England was an even more serious obstacle to *rapprochement* than the elation which victory had produced in France. Shelburne's management of the peace negotiations had been skilful and the terms he finally obtained from France were better than could have been expected when he first came into office; but he was nevertheless subjected to violent attacks when he brought his peace proposals before parliament at the end of January 1783. Fundamentally these attacks were self-contradictory: while North and his followers castigated the government for yielding too much to the American rebels, the Whigs, under the leadership of Fox, complained that the concessions were too little and too late. But politicians hungry for power cannot afford to be too fastidious about principles. Both Fox and North knew that Shelburne could destroy them if they stayed apart and that they could destroy him if they came together. They therefore worked doggedly to concoct a series of resolutions against the peace which would somehow reconcile their differences; and it was these resolutions, brought before the Commons on 21 February by Lord John Cavendish, which dealt the death blow to Shelburne and to the internationalism for which he stood. They were carried against him by 207 votes to 190 in the early hours of the following morning and two days later he resigned. The king accused him of betraying his own Patriot principles: if Patriot king and Patriot minister stood firm together they could defy the factious party politicians. But Shelburne, either from cowardice or from genuine constitutional scruple, thought otherwise; and so England's most internationally-minded statesman was abruptly removed from the scene in the middle of the greatest crisis England had ever faced in her relations with Europe and the world.[15]

Commentators buoyed up with rhetoric and principles and forgetful of the realities of power felt at the time, and have felt since, that the coalition between Fox and North was an unnatural and surprising one. But the two men had things in common which were far more important than the outworn arguments about America which had divided them in the past: they shared a passionate and urgent determination to preserve the existing

[15] For an analysis of Shelburne's fall and the vote of 18 February see J. Norris, *Shelburne and Reform*, 1963, pp. 263–70, 295–307.

structure of politics. No amount of Whig talk about Toryism and innovation could alter the hard fact that North was fundamentally a Whig politician, playing the old game in the old way that Fox and the Rockinghamites understood, while Shelburne was not. Whiggism stood for a balanced constitution, balanced between a relatively weak executive and a reasonably independent legislative. This balance did not simply permit the patronage structure from which the Whigs reaped such rich rewards: it necessitated it. If there was to be any sort of effective government within such a context it could only be brought about by career politicians harnessing parliament to the ministry by judicious distribution of patronage. And the idea of parties based on men rather than measures, coming together in the name of 'connection' and 'interest' rather than programmes of reform, was the best way of making that distribution both respectable and efficient. The Whigs had attacked North for using an illegitimate kind of party to harness parliament to his government, but they themselves had every intention of using what they regarded as a legitimate kind of party in order to harness government to the wishes of parliament. It seemed an important enough argument: each was accusing the other of putting the cart before the horse. But the cry of 'not men but measures', which Burke had opposed so bitterly when Chatham voiced it in the 1760s and which he opposed even more bitterly now that Shelburne was bringing it up to date in the 1780s, threatened to sweep away cart and horse alike by changing the whole nature of the harness. Fox and North had at least had in common a certain respect for the balance which they accused one another of upsetting. Shelburne, on the other hand, seemed to stand for a political system in which balance would be lost altogether, a system unified by professionalism and bureaucracy instead of being divided by amateurism and the cult of 'independence'.

Few contemporaries had any clear idea of what exactly Shelburne was planning. John Lee, solicitor-general in the Fox–North ministry, talked darkly of 'scholastic nostrums and the abstruse theorems of mechanism',[16] while Horace Walpole could see nothing to choose between Burke's proposals for 'economical reform' and Shelburne's advocacy of administrative and electoral reform. 'The whole scene of reformation,' he wrote disgustedly, 'was a mummery that at once insulted the nation, virtue and

[16] Cited R. W. Harris, *Political Ideas 1760–92*, 1963, p. 93.

charity, and enriched only the principal reformers.'[17] It has been left to the historians to reconstruct, from the papers Shelburne left behind him, the complicated and far-reaching plans which he was contemplating and to show how they would have eroded the old amateurism and established instead 'the paramountcy of the public interest'.[18] And very few Englishmen in 1783 were prepared to think of the public interest as something which could safely be entrusted to the government: it was, on the contrary, something which independent men in the counties and on the back benches of the House of Commons must defend *against* the insidious encroachments of government influence. Only papists and absolutists and Frenchmen—or their English admirers—could wish to strengthen central professional government at the expense of local amateur self-government. Shelburne had already shown what he was made of, in the opinion of his critics, by suggesting in 1780 that the English ought to set up an effective police force along the lines of the one which existed in France.[19] Now he was going further and seeking to impose French institutions on England—strong monarchy, centralized bureaucracy, governmental control of commercial policy—while at the same time allowing France to get away with more than she should have done at the peace conference. The fact that he had outmanoeuvred the French on many essential points, that his associations abroad were with critics rather than supporters of the French government, that his opponents were far readier to abdicate trading supremacy than he was, did nothing to save him. It was Shelburne the francophile, rather than Shelburne the administrative reformer or even Shelburne the king's friend, who was defeated in February 1783. However much North and his new Whig allies might disagree about the concessions to the Americans, they could and did agree to attack with all their force the concessions to the French. And it was here that they were successful: Lord John Cavendish's carefully worded strictures on French territorial and commercial gains won over just enough backbenchers to lose Shelburne his majority and his political future.

For several months the tide of political events in both countries ran strongly against *rapprochement*, as both governments retreated behind their walls of chauvinism to conduct the same

[17] Walpole, *Last Journals*, ii, 457.
[18] Norris, *Shelburne and Reform*, p. 293.
[19] *Ibid.*, p. 134.

sort of hunt for scapegoats that had taken place twenty years earlier, after the last peace treaty between England and France. The French controller-general launched an attack on the tax farmers, while the new administration in England set Edmund Burke to work to prepare a Bill for the regulation of the East India Company. The themes were familiar enough, but this time there were significant variations: neither country was as naïve as it had been in the 1760s, when mere uninformed prejudice had produced similar attacks on similar targets. Even the most bucolic Frenchman now knew that there were rival capitalists waiting to take over if the tax farmers were defeated; and early in 1784 a popular journalist spoke of *la Banque* and *le Commerce* as being rival forces just as sinister and dangerous as *la Finance*, the original network of tax farmers which they were seeking to supplant.[20] D'Ormesson's campaign against the Company of General Farmers aroused only the faintest echo of that wild popular enthusiasm which had been so evident in the 1760s. Most traditionalist Frenchmen watched with indifference as the king's minister tried to jump from the frying pan into the fire, from the clutches of *la Finance* into the scarcely preferable clutches of *la Banque* and *le Commerce*. The young Marquis de Lafayette, newly returned from his military exploits in America to lead the demand for an end to the tax farmers' tobacco monopolies, was an impressive and popular figure; but the commercial interests that lurked behind him were less so. If these interests had hoped to set up a profitable Franco-American trading network of their own on the ruins of the tax farmers' privileges, which were swept away by d'Ormesson's decree of 24 October 1783, they were to be disappointed. A week later d'Ormesson fell from power, brought down by the massive influence which the Company of General Farmers was able to exert at court, and the decree was revoked. Neither it nor its author were mourned for very long: Frenchmen were too cynical about their government's new masters to be particularly worried about the success of the old.

A fortnight after the fall of d'Ormesson the Fox–North coalition threw down a challenge to the East India Company which was in its own way as dramatic as d'Ormesson's challenge to the tax farmers. It laid before parliament two bills, one to set up a new Board of Control to supervise the company and the other to bring the officials in India under the authority of this same

[20] Bachaumont, xxv, 46.

board. Like the efforts of Lafayette and d'Ormesson against the
tax farmers, it was open to widely differing interpretations. At
one level it could be seen as an act of far-sighted statesmanship
which sought to create a new concept of public interest transcending both king and parliament: the members of the board were
to hold office for four years and were only to be dismissed in the
very exceptional case of an address of both houses of parliament.
There is no doubt that Burke, in drawing up the Bills, had been
determined to end what he saw as the 'rapacious and licentious'
rule of the company in India itself.[21] He felt, as he was to feel
more strongly still when he came to impeach Warren Hastings,
that England was responsible for the happiness of millions of
Indians and must transcend her own political squabbles in order
to shoulder that responsibility. In this cause he was prepared to
go back on his own earlier statements about government not
becoming 'itself a great banker and a great merchant', as well as
his more recent assertions of the sanctity of chartered rights.[22]

On the other hand the Bills could easily be seen as a retreat to
the patronage squabbles of the past rather than an advance to
the statesmanlike imperialism of the future. The ministry had
already dropped Shelburne's plans for free trade—the American
Intercourse Bill, only remaining relic of these proposals, had been
defeated in March—and had reverted instead to traditional
mercantilist policies. On 2 July an Order in Council, drawn up
with the help of Grenville's old adviser William Knox,[23] had
placed restrictions on Anglo-American trade which were reminiscent of the 1760s; and the patronage politics behind the India
Bills were reminiscent of the same period. The court of directors
of the East India Company contained men like the chairman, Sir
Henry Fletcher, and his supporter Jacob Wilkinson, both of
whom supported the ministry in the hope of advancing their own
careers; while the ministry itself had every reason to seek East
India Company patronage in order to make up for the crown
patronage which George III was deliberately withholding from it.
Burke's proposed board of control could well be represented as
an unholy alliance between the Fox and North parties and the
Fletcher and Wilkinson interests in the company. Pamphlets and
caricatures describing it in these terms were enormously successful

[21] Speech on India Bill, 1 December 1783, *P.H.* xxiii, 1350.
[22] See his speech defending charter rights in Africa, *P.H.* xix, 309, 313.
[23] See R. L. Schuyler, *The Fall of the Old Colonial System*, New York,
1945, p. 89.

and at the end of November the shareholders of the company led a successful revolt against Fletcher, getting him replaced by an avowed opponent of the ministry and of the Bills. Encouraged by this development, and by secret negotiations which he had been conducting with those who might form an alternative administration, George III took the very questionable step of informing the House of Lords that any peer voting for the Bill would be regarded as the king's enemy. In this way he was able to secure the ministry's defeat in the Lords, even though it still had a handsome majority in the Commons, and to dismiss it on 18 December 1783.[24]

In England as in France popular opinion refused to give the benefit of the doubt to the fallen ministers. Lenoir, lieutenant of police in Paris, was a friend and supporter of d'Ormesson's successor: it is probable, therefore, that his accounts of the popular enthusiasm which accompanied the change of ministers were exaggerated.[25] But there could be no doubt about the violence of the reaction against Fox and North in England. From all parts of the country petitions and addresses poured in on London, thanking the king for saving the constitution and the people from the sinister designs of the Whig politicians. More than two hundred such protestations were received, six or seven times as many as any other crisis of the period had produced. In constituency after constituency scandalized electors protested their loyalty to the cherished theory of constitutional balance and their determination as independent men to defend that balance against factious party leaders. Thomas Grosvenor, one of the acknowledged leaders of the independent backbenchers, held a series of meetings at the St Albans Tavern pledging support for 'the party who should, in the present distracted moment, manifest a disposition to union'.[26]

It was certainly a distracted moment in the political history of both countries; but the true nature of the present distractions was as unclear to contemporaries as the true nature of the present discontents had been to Burke when he wrote about them so

[24] For an account of the fall of the Fox–North administration, and in particular of the secret negotiations leading to it, see Cannon, *Fox–North Coalition*, pp. 128–44.

[25] R. Lacour-Gayet, *Calonne: financier, réformateur, contre-révolutionnaire, 1734–1820*, 1963, p. 68.

[26] *Annual Register*, 1784, pp. 265–72; Cannon, *Fox–North Coalition*, pp. 178–9. See also *Correspondence between William Pitt and Charles duke of Rutland 1781–87*, ed. Earl Stanhope, rev. edn, 1890, p. 7.

confidently thirteen years earlier. There was at any rate one root
cause to which most distractions and discontents could be
traced back: the discredit of existing representative or would-be
representative bodies. The *parlements* of France had been
taught a sharp lesson by the crown in the 1770s and since their
reinstatement in 1774 they had behaved with caution and circum-
spection: only in 1776, when they were assured of influential
support against Turgot from within the ministry itself, had they
reverted to their old bluster and bravado.[27] Their bluff had been
called and they knew it. The events of the 1770s had shown that
they were part of the patronage structure and not doughty champions of the country against it; and those events had also shown
that they were divided among themselves almost as sharply as
the parliament at Westminster was divided from the colonial
assemblies on the other side of the Atlantic. The *parlement* of
Paris was as incapable of acting in unison with its so-called
colonies in the provinces as the English parliament was of representing the whole of the British empire. While the British theory
of empire had been dying its spectacular death amid the noisy
lamentations of Chatham and Burke, the *parlements'* theory of
the *union des classes* had been wasting away less dramatically but
just as surely. Centrifugalism, which the French had always seen
as the greatest danger of the English system and against which
they had sought to erect defences of centralism and even of
absolutism, seemed about to triumph in both countries. Neither
of them possessed, or seemed capable of creating, an institution
which could with confidence and credibility claim to represent
the whole political nation, either in social or in geographical
terms.

For the *parlements* the future looked bleak: if they were to
outbid the new Provincial Assemblies which were being used by
successive governments to cut the ground from under their feet,
they could only do so by the abdication, rather than the assertion,
of their powers. They were steadily being driven into the position
which was to provoke their final and suicidal act, the declaration
that they were not competent to approve new taxes and that the
government must therefore turn to that wider but more archaic
body, the Estates General of the realm. But English parliamentarians were made of sterner—or perhaps merely more illogical—

[27] See W. O. Doyle, 'The parlements of France and the breakdown of the
old regime', *F.H.S.* vi, 1970, pp. 415–58.

stuff. They had been driven back step by step in much the same way: first they had failed in their attempt to speak for the whole empire and then they had allowed this same attempt to drag them into a war which alienated them from their own constituents instead of vindicating their pretensions to imperial supremacy. They had abandoned the supremacy, renouncing their authority over the Americans and their legislative control over the Irish, but they had done little to repair the breach between themselves and those who had elected them. Pressure for parliamentary reform had come not from the unpropertied but from the existing electorate; but even so backbenchers who claimed to represent the independence of the country rather than the subservience of the patronage structure had allowed themselves to be headed off by the party leaders from any effective reforms. Now, with the king's new administration appealing over their heads to the country at large, their dilemma was exposed in its cruellest form. All the brave talk about 'a disposition to union' could not hide the fact that the independents must themselves unite either with a government that defied parliament in the name of the country or with an opposition that defied the country in the name of parliament. And yet in spite of all this they were a very long way from self-doubt or suicide. In England it was the king and not the parliament whose thoughts turned to abdication in the crisis of 1783.

The crisis had brought to power ministers whose very names recalled earlier confrontations between central authority and centrifugal tendencies. D'Ormesson was succeeded by Calonne, a champion of royal authority in the 1760s and probably the man responsible for Louis XV's sweeping declaration against the *parlements* in 1766.[28] Fox and North were replaced by a government led by William Pitt the younger, son of the man who had come forward, also in 1766, to save George III from the factious politicians. Experienced observers knew well enough that the appearance of such men was just another chapter in the story of court intrigue and power politics: Calonne had powerful friends among the financiers and courtiers who had brought down d'Ormesson, while the younger Pitt's spectacular emergence as first lord of the treasury at the age of twenty-four had been prefaced by secret negotiations with representatives of the king and of the East India Company. The new ministers were not

[28] Lacour-Gayet, *Calonne*, p. 22.

really the saviours of their countries from the machinations of nabobs and financiers and speculators. They represented only the triumph of one set of capitalists over another. But those who believed in the necessity for salvation found it necessary to invent saviours even if they did not exist. By the spring of 1784 Pitt had dissolved the old parliament and won himself a comfortable majority in the new one, while in the French countryside the peasants carved inscriptions in the snow and the ice in honour of the minister who had promised to mulct the financiers and the capitalists and the officeholders.[29]

The division between the country and the forces from which it hoped to be saved was in neither case a simple one. There were those who thought simply in terms of a 'landed interest' and a 'commercial interest' and believed that Pitt and Calonne had saved the former from being swamped by the latter. Certainly Pitt's refusal to work with North, which was one of the root causes of the divisions in English politics since 1782, sprang partly from a dislike of the financial and commercial potentates upon whom North had become dependent as a result of the war; and North for his part was prepared to defend the commercial interest, as when he pointed out that Pitt's proposals for parliamentary reform would give 'a decided superiority to the landed interest over the commercial' and must therefore be resisted.[30] But neither country was thinking in terms of what has since been called 'the class struggle', of middle-class money-grubbers in fustian ranged against indolent aristocrats in silks. Rather the reverse: the capitalist network was seen as especially pernicious because it included among its leaders some of the greatest in the land. In 1777 a French journal had launched a scabrous attack on an Englishman called Richard Smith, who had come to Paris after serving a prison sentence for the notorious corruption with which he had tried to buy his way into parliament. Having been thwarted in his efforts to put to political purposes the enormous sums he had brought home from India he took them instead to the French court, where he took part in marathon gambling sessions with the princes of the blood. Readers were told in

[29] *Ibid.*, p. 79. In both countries popular gratitude of this sort was normally directed at the king (and, in this particular case in France, at the queen as well). The fact that Pitt's name was linked with that of George III more frequently than Calonne's was with Louis XVI's shows the truth of Linguet's remark that French ministers, unlike their English counterparts, were anxious *not* to be talked about. See Linguet, *Annales*, ii, 461.

[30] Cannon, *Fox–North Coalition*, p. 92.

shocked tones how he had sat 'with his elbows on the table, in the most familiar manner' in the company of the king's brother the comte d'Artois and the king's cousin the duc de Chartres, later to become duc d'Orléans on the death of his father in 1785. In this way, the writer concluded angrily, the worst features of English life were being allowed to infiltrate into the French royal family and into the French nobility.[31]

Similar charges were being levelled at English princes and English financial adventurers. Much of Fox's unpopularity sprang from the fact that he could be represented as a kind of sinister political broker between the Prince of Wales, who had political influence but needed money, and the East India nabobs who had money but needed political influence. Certainly the prince's indebtedness had been as great a problem as East India policy for the Fox–North coalition: on 17 June 1783 Fox had predicted that the ministry would collapse the following day because of the difficulties it was running into on this score.[32] But at least in England the princes kept the monied men at arm's length. They might need their cash but they did not stoop to joining in their speculations. In France, however, there was a much closer connection between the court and the capitalists. The Prince de Conti had been involved in speculative operations with the Genevese bankers as long ago as 1769; and the comte de Provence, Artois's elder brother, had had his own direct contacts with American businessmen even before France openly intervened in the War of American Independence. From 1779 onwards Artois was borrowing on a large scale from the Genevese; and his financial agents, Antoine Bourbulon and Radix de Sainte-Foy and Pyron de Chaboulon, were drawing him deeper and deeper into speculative ventures. By 1781 these men, and especially Pyron de Chaboulon, were getting an even rougher handling from the pamphleteers and journalists than the unfortunate Richard Smith had received.[33]

Whatever doubts there may have been about the truth of such charges, there was no doubt about their political effects. If and

---

[31] Bachaumont, x, 328–9. On Richard Smith see *Commons 1754–90*, iii, 449–51.

[32] *Memorials and Correspondence of Fox*, ii, 114.

[33] Lüthy, ii, 398, 472–3, 511; Stevens, ii, no. 151, vii, no. 694; Lüthy, ii, 687, 691–3. On Provence see G. Walter, *Le comte de Provence*, 1950. V. W. Beach, 'The count of Artois and the coming of the French Revolution', *J.M.H.* xxx, 1958, pp. 313–24 is inaccurate and should be treated with extreme caution.

when all the excitement about princes and nabobs and speculators died down, Calonne and Pitt would still have to face the great issues of world trade and international finance, the issues which the events of the Necker and North régimes had helped to formulate and which the transient nature of subsequent régimes had left unsolved; and stories of capitalism and corruption in high places created an atmosphere in which a sensible approach to such matters became increasingly difficult. The French were still wary of England, even though they saw her as a less dangerous neighbour now that she had been stripped of her colonies, and they had watched with some revulsion her latest lurch into political instability. One English visitor to Paris at the end of 1783 found that the French all thought England was on the verge of a revolution; and a few months later Daniel Pulteney wrote to the duke of Rutland from France to say that 'sensible thinking people there all concur in wishing this Mr Fox at the devil, as he seems to them always embroiling matters without advantage to the kingdom or to himself'.[34] Pitt's victory brought some reassurance, though there were Frenchmen who found his drastic remedies almost as unpleasant as the disease they seemed to have cured: the duc de la Rochefoucauld, who was in England at the time of the election which unseated so many of Fox's supporters, was rather disturbed to see a substantial landowner rejected by mere 'farmers and freeholders' simply because he had voted for Fox and North.[35] The real problems which the two countries faced demanded cooperation between them, but the imaginary dangers which they thought they faced, dangers associated with the importation from the other country of unreal social values and subversive political influences, made such cooperation hard to envisage.

There was at least one person who imported himself into France from England in the autumn of 1783 and who could be said by his enemies to personify the unreal values and subversive influences. This was Etienne Clavière, one of the radical Genevese leaders who had escaped across the lake with Duroveray at the time of the French intervention. He had gone in the first place to Neuchâtel with the rest of the exiles and there he had met a young French journalist called Brissot de Warville and a notorious French nobleman called the comte de Mirabeau, the son of that marquis de Mirabeau who had defended the traditional values of

---

[34] Cannon, *Fox–North Coalition*, p. 163n; *H.M.C. 24 Rutland*, p. 92.
[35] Cannon, *Fox–North Coalition*, p. 214.

French society so vehemently. The younger Mirabeau was at odds with his father, who had had recourse to the traditional values of French society in order to get his son put in prison, and Brissot de Warville was at odds with almost everyone. Together they had reassured the Genevese radicals, Mirabeau insisting on his own ability to get the French government to change its policy and Brissot embarking on a work called *The Philadelphian at Geneva* in which he depicted the Americans and the Genevese as fighting shoulder to shoulder against the established order of Europe. The French government had remained unmoved by Mirabeau's memorandum on Geneva, even though he predicted dire consequences for France if she drove the radicals into alliance with England and the other Protestant powers, and so he had returned to his own affairs. The radical leaders had then decamped one by one to England, with Brissot in tow, and had become involved in complex negotiations with successive English governments for the establishment of a 'New Geneva' of radical exiles in Ireland. But by the autumn of 1783 it was clear that the scheme would almost certainly prove abortive and Clavière decided that it was time to turn from principles to practicalities. Some of his younger and more idealistic compatriots stayed on in England, attaching themselves mainly to Shelburne and to the dissenter industrialists of the Midlands, but he crossed to Paris with the avowed intention of making money. A royal decree promulgated at the end of September had enabled the Discount Bank to extend its credit operations and Clavière was convinced that this could be made the occasion for a speculative boom which would be as profitable —at any rate for those who got out soon enough—as Law's adventure over half a century earlier.[36]

Clavière's journey from London to Paris was symptomatic of convictions that were deeper and better informed than the hysterical imaginings of those who saw him as the bearer of subversive contagions from England. Panchaud himself had already argued, in a work published some months earlier, that French national credit was expanding steadily while that of England was shrinking. The Bank of England, he had averred, was already beginning to collapse under its own weight; the financial and economic future lay with France if only she would grasp it

---

[36] J. Bouchary, *Les Manieurs d'Argent à Paris à la fin du xviiie siècle*, 3 vols, 1939–43, i, 11–101; E. Dumont, *Souvenirs sur Mirabeau*, ed. J. Bénétruy, 1951, pp. 7–10; J. P. Brissot de Warville, *Mémoires, 1754–93*, ed. C. Perroud, 2 vols, 1910, i, 244–301.

—and if she would grasp also the politics of capitalism which
went with it.[37] Panchaud's financial optimism was matched by an
equally hopeful outlook on the part of French industrialists and
technologists: they were impressed with England's achievements
over the past few years but they did not doubt their own ability
to match them and possibly to outstrip them. They certainly did
not regard them as constituting an 'industrial revolution' which
had relegated France to an inferior and anachronistic position.
French industry had the advantage of an advanced technology—
was it not even now leading the way in ballooning, seemingly the
most exciting and significant invention of the age?—and it had
the advantage of comparatively low labour costs. All it needed,
in order to outstrip its English rivals, was a boost to industrial
investment and an end to restrictive guild practices and the
protected markets which sustained them. It needed, in short, a
government with a positive and expansionist economic policy.
While the peasants busied themselves carving out of the snow
their pious hopes that Calonne would save the country from the
capitalists, the capitalists urged him to join with them in saving
the country from itself.

On the whole Calonne made a good start on his ambiguous and
contradictory task. He had made a thorough study of contemporary economic theory and he was convinced that the secret of
national prosperity lay in the creation of capital and the creation
of demand. His close associate and adviser Dupont de Nemours
worked on the basis of the old Physiocrat maxim, that in order to
grow rich one must first spend, but he also brought with him
all the Physiocrat distrust of speculative capitalism, especially
when it was in foreign hands. New government loans were
floated, the first of them only a few weeks after Calonne's
appointment, and vigorous attempts were made to attract capital
away from speculative ventures into government stock and into
soundly based industrial investment. These two last were
inseparable one from the other, since Calonne's industrial policy
was firmly based on the French tradition of government support
and government subsidies. Loans to industry from the *Caisse du
demi pour cent*, which had almost ceased since the early 1770s,
began to be granted again on a large scale, especially to the textile
industries. The chemical industries, whose expansion was essential
if the increased amount of cloth turned out by the new machines

[37] Bachaumont, xx, 46–8.

was ever to be bleached and treated, were also given extensive support.[38] Above all, the iron and steel industries were the object of intense government scrutiny: the English ironmaster William Wilkinson, who had emigrated to France some years earlier, remarked prophetically that 'whenever Frenchmen relinquish their fiddling and dancing and cultivate the art of ironmaking &c, England will tremble'; and Calonne did his best to see that that day came soon. In conjunction with Vergennes and with the French ambassador in London he returned to the old practice of tempting skilled workmen to bring their secrets from England to France. He even interested himself in a German workman, dug up by the French resident at Rastadt, who claimed to have learnt the secrets of steel refining in England. By 1785 the new French iron foundries at Le Creusot were going into full production and Calonne had persuaded the king himself to invest heavily in them and in their associated enterprises.[39]

In all this Calonne was traditional enough: government support for industry was a time-honoured practice in France and there was nothing in it to endanger Calonne's image as the saviour of the country from the speculators. The same peasants who honoured him for his decree of 14 March 1784 taxing the financiers would also honour him for creating employment for them and for their children. One industrialist who was ennobled in 1787 was singled out for special praise because he provided work in his textile factory for children of five and six years of age;[40] and even those peasants who did not send their children to the factories were glad enough to earn extra money in the evenings by doing piecework at home.[41] 'The French,' one English visitor remarked in 1784, 'of all people are the most remarkable for subjecting to regulations whatever is susceptible of them';[42] they

[38] Lacour-Gayet, *Calonne*, pp. 150ff.; A. Saricks, *Dupont de Nemours*, Kansas, 1965, *passim*; Depitre, 'Les prêts au commerce', P. Baud, 'Les origines de la grande industrie chimique en France', *R.H.* clxxiv, 1934, pp. 1–18.
[39] H. W. Dickinson, *John Wilkinson*, Ulverston, 1914, p. 50; A.N. F[12] 1300; W. J. Pugh, 'Calonne's "New Deal"', *J.M.H.* xi, 1939, pp. 289–312. See also the account of the French iron industry in 1787 by 'Mr. William Wilkson' [*sic*] in S. Pollard and C. Holmes, eds, *Documents of European Economic History, vol. 1: The process of industrialization 1750–1870*, 1968, pp. 83–4.
[40] M. Reinhard, 'Elites et noblesses dans la seconde moitié du xviii° siècle', *R.H.M.C.*, nouvelle série, iii, 1956, pp. 5–37.
[41] See La Rochefoucauld's account in Pollard and Holmes, *Documents*, pp. 91–2.
[42] J. Andrews, *Letters to a Young Gentleman on his setting out for France*, 1784, p. 390.

were unlikely, therefore, to criticize Calonne for creating prosperity by the regulation of industry and by the extensive reforms
which he was carrying out in the machinery through which that
regulation was achieved.

But the harsh fact remained that capital tended to go where it
would earn the highest returns rather than where it would do the
most good. Some local authorities were still prepared to invest
their funds in deserving industries—the development of the
balloon by Montgolfier and his successors owed a lot to the
financial support given by the Estates of Languedoc[43]—and in
some areas, such as Dauphiné, there were still rich men who were
sufficiently public-spirited or sufficiently naïve to prefer local
investment to the attractions of the stock-market in Paris. But
even this cut both ways. Government inspectors sent out by
Calonne to teach new and more efficient methods found that it
was precisely in such areas that archaic practices were cherished
most tenaciously.[44] Only the richest and most enlightened noblemen could avoid the temptations of the speculative companies
while at the same time transcending the narrow horizons of small-
scale locally-based industry. Thus the duc d'Orléans, who was a
great deal richer than his cousins Provence and Artois, could and
did contribute to the growth of the textile and chemical industries in France as a whole while they were contributing merely to
the growth of the speculative bubble in Paris.[45] But even
Orléans could not finance the whole of French technological
progress. That needed the help of the professional financiers; and
they were not going to divert funds from profitable speculations
to new industrial processes unless they were convinced that there
was real money in it. Calonne did his best to convince them, by
getting the Academy of Science to report on new inventions such
as the marquis de Jouffroy's steam ship, in the way it had already

[43] Bacquié, *Les Inspecteurs*, pp. 36–7.
[44] P. Léon, *Les Techniques métallurgiques dauphinoises au xviiie siècle*
(*Histoire de la pensée, v*), 1961. See also, by the same author, *La naissance
de la grande industrie en Dauphiné*, 2 vols, 1954; 'Les essais de énovation de
la métallurgie dauphinoise à la fin du xviiie siècle', *Revue d'histoire de la
sidérurgie*, i, 1960, pp. 21–42; *Marchands et speculateurs dauphinois dans le
monde antillais du xviiie siècle: les Dolle et les Raby*, 1963. Much interesting
material may also be found in V. Chomel and H. Lapeyre, *Catalogue des
livres de commerce et papiers d'affaires conservés aux archives départmentales de l'Isère*, Grenoble, 1962.
[45] See B. Hyslop, *L'apanage de Philippe-Egalité, duc d'Orléans, 1785–91*,
1965.

reported on Montgolfier's balloon. But the reports were not convincing and the money was not forthcoming.[46]

Calonne trod his tightrope skilfully for two years and more. Up to the beginning of 1786 it was generally believed that he was struggling manfully against what one recent historian has called 'the rising tide of stock exchange speculation'[47] and straining every nerve to see that all available capital was put to sound and productive use. He held aloof from the great bull market in Discount Bank shares, which doubled their value during the year 1784, and in January 1785 he caused a fall in the shares by promulgating a decree forbidding the bank to increase its dividend. In order to hasten the flow of money back from Discount Bank speculation into government stock he then commissioned the younger Mirabeau to write pamphlets not only against the Discount Bank itself but also against the Bank of St Charles, a Spanish bank with which the Discount Bank did a lot of business in piastres and in Spanish government stock. These works had the desired effect of sending the shares down still further, even though Calonne had to disavow the work on the Bank of St Charles because of protests from the Spanish ambassador.[48] But disavowal or no disavowal his image was still intact: there was no shame in employing the magic name of Mirabeau to defend France against foreign speculators, even if this did lead to protests from foreign courts.

And yet things were not quite what they seemed. The scramble for Discount Bank shares in 1784 had been accompanied by a wave of resentment against the foreigners who were thought to have more than their fair share of control over the bank. Louis Pourrat, a banker from Lyon, tried to push through a motion excluding them from the board of directors. It was blocked; and those who blocked it, including particularly Panchaud and his Genevese associates, became more unpopular than ever. In the end Pourrat came to blows with Clavière, who was denounced by the newspapers as 'one of the Panchaud acolytes', on the floor of the stock exchange itself.[49] By this time it was obvious that Panchaud and Clavière had sold out at the height of the bull market and were now concerned to push the value of the shares

---

[46] See under 'Jouffroy' in Michaud's *Biographie Universelle*.
[47] Lüthy, ii, 691.
[48] *Ibid.*, ii, 687–705. See also F. M. Fling, 'Mirabeau and Calonne, 1785', in *Annual Report to the American Historical Association*, 1897, pp. 133–47.
[49] Bachaumont, xxv, 46, 93; xxviii, 42–3.

down. Hence Calonne's actions at the beginning of 1785 soon came to be interpreted not as the statesmanlike policies of a minister acting to curb speculation but as the irresponsible and corrupt behaviour of a minister running with the bears against the bulls. Mirabeau for his part came to be seen not as the worthy son of his father but as an unprincipled renegade who worked secretly for the very speculators whom he seemed in public to be castigating.

There was a certain truth in this view of things. Mirabeau himself told his English friends that his work on the Discount Bank was written to save Calonne and to avert a disastrous bankruptcy; what he did not tell them was that of its nine chapters six were composed by Clavière, two by Brissot and one by Dupont de Nemours—an interesting indication not only of Mirabeau's ability to pass off other men's work as his own but also of the relative amounts of speculator's propaganda, journalist's idealism and ministerial policy which its three real authors put into it.[50] In his attempts to control the great international speculators Calonne was like a very small man taking a very large dog for a walk: he did not know where he would find himself next. During the course of 1785 he broke his connections with Clavière and Panchaud, but this did not enable him to break his connections with speculation or with Geneva. He was caught on the wrong foot by the next pamphlet which Clavière promoted with Mirabeau's name on the title page, an attack on a company floated by Constantin Périer to supply water to Paris. Calonne was himself a large shareholder in this company—a fact which in itself was no more sinister than the king's investment in the Indret and Le Creusot ironworks, with which Périer was also associated— and his losses led him to threaten Clavière with police action. More important, they led him to depend more heavily than before on the activities of another group of Genevese exiles which was centred on Brussels. He was already linked with the bankers of that city via his friend and associate Micault d'Harvelay, the financier who had helped to bring him to power and whose widow he later married; and now these connections became stronger and more important. Duroveray and many other Genevese exiles had settled in Brussels and had formed a powerful

---

[50] Mirabeau to Romilly, 22 May 1785, Romilly, i, 247 (the editors are wrong in saying that the reference is to *De La Banque d'Espagne*); Dumont, *Souvenirs*, p. 13. See also Calonne to Vergennes, 21 June 1785, Add. 41, 170, fo. 5.

international combine called Senn Bidermann and Company, whose associated enterprises stretched from manufacturing industries in the Rhineland to commercial companies in Marseilles trading with India and with the Levant. It was the activities of this consortium that finally turned Calonne's management of foreign capitalism into foreign capitalism's management of Calonne.[51]

No nation likes to think of its destinies being manipulated by a group of foreign financiers, particularly when those destinies have in store one of the greatest revolutions of modern times. Once that revolution had taken place the morbid suspicions of the 1780s soon turned into the lurid delusions of the 1790s: the Genevese were seen not just as speculators but as conspirators, deliberately undermining France's government and society for their own profit and for the sinister ends of the foreign governments who paid them. The whole history of France since the 1770s came to be seen as the unfolding of a horrible plan whereby 'anglo-genevese conspirators' and 'foreign pensionaries of the English king' deliberately drove the country to financial and political and social collapse. Men who had been rivals all their lives, like Necker and Clavière, were represented as fellow-conspirators; and any revolutionary leader who had ever visited either Geneva or London was liable to find himself denounced as part of the same conspiracy.[52] And yet the two really vital points about the part played by the Genevese in the coming of the revolution were almost completely neglected: the fact that they were divided amongst themselves into two rival groups and the fact that their interest in France sprang from a disassociation from, and not an association with, her English rival.

As long ago as 1768 Necker had told one of his friends that in time of peace the realm of France offered the investor prospects as glittering as the kingdom of Peru had once presented to the Spaniards;[53] but this did not mean that he and his countrymen intended to exploit it and plunder it in the way the *conquistadores*

[51] Lüthy, ii, 658, 667–72, 680; Dermigny, *Cargaisons Indiennes*, pp. 242–7.
[52] See J–L–G. Soulavie, *Mémoires historiques et politiques du règne de Louis XVI*, 6 vols, 1801.
[53] Necker to J–L. de Luc, 28 November 1768, cited Dermigny, *Cargaisons Indiennes*, p. 193. It is interesting to note that for French traditionalists pre-conquest Peru served as a symbol of an ideal society uncorrupted by money and commercialism. See Huguet de Grafigny, *Lettres péruviennes*, 1747—a work which Mornet's researches (see above, p. 32n) showed to be extremely popular.

had exploited and plundered the Incas. Financial investment may
often involve low cunning, but it also involves high confidence.
To call it speculation instead of investment puts the emphasis on
the cunning, but it does not alter the fact that the confidence is
there as well. By the 1780s there were undoubtedly many
Genevese who could say, as Clavière said to a friend in Amsterdam
in January 1786, that their fortunes were inextricably bound up
with the fortunes of the kingdom of France.[54] They were hardly
likely to destroy deliberately the stability of the country in which
they had put so much faith and so much money. It was the clash
of forces and policies within the country itself, together with the
inability of the Genevese investors to take a consistent and united
line towards it, that led to the worsening of the situation. The
French made their revolution for themselves, but they made it
with Genevese money.

Although Calonne had quarrelled with Clavière by the end of
1785, his links were still with the new Geneva rather than the
old, with the exiles of 1782 rather than with those who had exiled
them. At the very beginning of his administration he had
supported a scheme put forward by Castries, the minister for the
navy, for the creation of a new French East India Company
backed by English money and operating under licence from the
English company; but when negotiations were opened in London,
first with the Fox–North coalition and then with Pitt, it soon
became clear that the plan would drive him into the arms of
Bourdieu and Chollet and the other London associates of his hated
rival Necker. Vergennes and his subordinates at the foreign office,
always more chauvinistic than their colleagues at the treasury,
were against the proposal in any case; and in the spring of 1785
Calonne rejected the plan and set up instead a company which
was a rival rather than a partner of the English in India. This
meant that the split between the old and the new Geneva was
projected into French trade as well as into French finance and
French politics: although secret negotiations with the English
company still continued for some months, a pattern steadily
emerged which made Calonne's company, backed by money from
the Genevese exiles in Brussels, the bitter rival of unprivileged
traders to India backed by Necker and Castries and their London
bankers.[55]

[54] Clavière to Cazenove, 13 January 1786, A.N. T^x 646/3.
[55] See J. Conan, *La Dernière compagnie française des Indes*, 1942.

It was this rivalry, together with that between Périer's water company and its competitors, that forced Calonne to seek wider and wider financial backing for his companies and then, having secured it, to manipulate the stock market according to the instructions of his backers. By 1786 he was irrevocably committed to a group of financiers who were determined to push up the price of their companies by any means. They were led by a Belgian banker called Seneffe, representing the heavy investments made by the Genevese exiles in Brussels, and by the notorious Pyron de Chaboulon, representing the equally heavy commitments of Artois and the other great princes and noblemen of the French court.[56] In 1785 the disreputable affair of the Diamond Necklace had dragged the queen's name into a scandal about an adventuress who tried to obtain very large sums of money by the most extraordinary of false pretences; and it was not long before the gossips of Paris were spreading stories of other members of the royal family who were trying to obtain even larger sums by even shadier means. Substantially the stories were true: men like Artois could not be shaken off as easily as Calonne had shaken off Panchaud and Clavière. The controller-general who had been welcomed by the French in 1783 as their saviour from the unsavoury activities of the capitalists was now presiding, whether he liked it or not, over some of the most unsavoury capitalistic activities France had seen since the days of John Law. And at the centre of it all, holding him prisoner as firmly as they themselves were held prisoner by their own speculations, stood the princes of the blood. They had come a long way since the days when their worst crime was to shock the journalists by allowing Richard Smith to sit with his elbows on their tables.

But this time there was no Smith at the table. The final irony about Calonne's ministry was that the anglophobia it generated was almost entirely unjustified. The capitalists with whom he worked were for the most part men who had deliberately decided to invest their money in France rather than in England, just as the industrialists he patronized were often men who had emigrated from England to France because they thought prospects were better there. Calonne and his economic advisers thought that French industry needed the stimulation of English competition, just as French agriculture needed the markets which England could provide for its wine and other products. They therefore

[56] Lüthy, ii, 691ff.

determined to drive the English into implementing at long last
the proposals for reciprocal trade which had originally been put
forward at Utrecht in 1713 and which the English parliament had
contrived to shelve for over seventy years. But the process of
implementation was not a particularly friendly one: Calonne and
Pitt knew that they needed one another but they did not know
that they liked one another. 'It is neither through magnanimity
nor a liking for France,' Gerard de Rayneval reported to the
French royal council in May 1786, 'that Mr Pitt is disposed to
brave the prejudices of his country to establish regular commercial relations with France. The fact is that he is convinced the
system of prohibition followed hitherto by England is without
real advantage for industry and commerce and prejudicial to the
revenue of the treasury. In reflecting on the interest of France,
the French government reaches the same conclusions as Mr Pitt
. . .'[57] The French government also insisted throughout the
negotiations that it was the English who were making difficulties
by pursuing protectionist policies. In 1785, just when France was
bringing pressure to bear on England by restricting her exports
to France, the French director of commerce blandly told the
English that in fact there was nothing unfriendly about this
because 'our prohibitive laws are hardly more than a façade and
we have a host of *magasins anglais* in all our towns and particularly in Paris'. English travellers in France also noticed these shops,
but they tended to attribute their existence to the ineffectiveness
of the French government rather than to its goodwill towards
England.[58]

Pitt's approach to the negotiations was equally ungracious. His
friend and colleague, the Duke of Rutland, a great industrialist
himself by virtue of his lands in the Midlands, presided over a
society of merchants and manufacturers known as the Anti-
Gallican Association;[59] and Pitt's own opinion of France, based
on the one short visit he made there in the autumn of 1783, was
not very high. He saw the need for free trade with Europe as
a whole but he very much resented France's attempt to short-
circuit it by securing reciprocal advantages for herself alone. He
felt that he was being forced into the negotiations by the threatening moves that France was making against him: her treaty with

[57] Printed in Pollard and Holmes, *Documents*, p. 122.
[58] Add. 38, 218, fo. 314; *H.M.C. 24 Rutland*, p. 247.
[59] *H.M.C. 24 Rutland*, p. 52.

Portugal in 1783, especially dangerous because Portugal's colonies were an important source of the cotton on which the industries of both countries relied, and her secret negotiations with the Dutch in 1784. The duke of Dorset, English ambassador in Paris, spent the summer of 1784 in a state of almost continuous apprehension about the Franco–Dutch talks, although in fact friction between the Dutch and the emperor made the Dutch alliance more of an embarrassment than an asset to France, since the emperor was Louis XVI's brother-in-law. And there were other things for the English to worry about. Jefferson had arrived in Paris with proposals for a Franco–American commercial treaty, while in Egypt the chevalier de Truguet was negotiating for concessions which would enable the French to establish a new and advantageous short route to India. The treaty which he signed with Bey of Egypt in February 1785 was later repudiated by the Sultan in Constantinople, but French schemes for the domination of the Near East continued for many years to worry the English and to threaten their position in India.[60] And on top of all this they were worried about French subversion much nearer home: in Ireland, where it had become almost an axiom that all troublemakers were financed by France, the lord lieutenant in Dublin heard with horror that an Irish Patriot leader called Sir Edward Newenham had invited Lafayette to visit him to continue in Ireland the work he had begun in America.[61]

Lafayette's visit to Ireland never took place, but English fears remained unallayed. The lord lieutenant passed on to the cabinet in London stories of French money being distributed and of Irish Patriots kneeling to drink Louis XVI's health. Even a visit to London by the duc d'Orléans in the spring of 1786 seemed to have an ulterior motive: he was there, the secretary for Ireland suggested, to stir up his crony the Prince of Wales to further unfilial and rebellious acts.[62] At the end of September 1786 the commercial negotiations were at last brought to a successful

[60] 'What a deplorable situation we are in;' the British ambassador in Brussels wrote to his colleague in Vienna in February 1784, 'we shall lose the East Indies for Holland and France are united to ruin our trade and in order to drive us out of the East Indies' (Add. 35, 531, fo. 62). On French designs on Suez see H. L. Hoskins, *British Routes to India*, 1928, p. 11. The comte de St Priest, French ambassador in Constantinople from 1768 to 1784, did much to popularize such schemes: see his *Mémoires sur l'ambassade de France en Turquie*, reprinted by the Ecole de Langues Orientales Vivantes, 1877.
[61] *H.M.C.* 24, *Rutland*, pp. 99, 107–8, 117–19.
[62] *Ibid.*, pp. 128, 130, 132, 300.

conclusion. A treaty was signed slashing import duties on English goods coming into France, mainly pottery and hardware and textiles, in return for reductions in the duty on French wines and brandy coming into England. But the atmosphere of suspicion and hostility persisted: even as the treaty was being signed there were dispatches on their way home from India to the French government warning that English pretensions and ambitions there had reached 'unheard of heights'.[63] The commercial treaty of September 1786 was the product of economic rivalry rather than of economic cooperation; and as far as the French were concerned its objectives were summed up by the stallholder at the fair at Guibray who told Arthur Young in 1788 that France was only importing English goods in order to learn how to better them.[64] But by the time the treaty came into force on 1 May 1787 Calonne had fallen from power and the whole framework of economic and administrative reorganization into which he had intended the treaty to fit was falling apart. His fall was the outcome of a dramatic and complex political crisis, a crisis which had come to be seen as the real beginning of the French revolution but which was itself precipitated by a confrontation between England and France. This confrontation, which took the form of a struggle for the control of the money market at Amsterdam, was to prove decisive in the international economic rivalry upon which the politics of capitalism depended.

[63] Cossigny to Castries, 5 September 1786, cited H. Furber, *John Company at work*, Cambridge, Mass., 1948, p. 303.
[64] A. Young, *Travels in France During the Years 1787, 1788 & 1789*, ed. C. Maxwell, Cambridge, 1929, p. 102. See also W. O. Henderson, 'The Anglo-French commercial treaty of 1786', *Ec.H.R.* 2nd series x, 1957, pp. 104–12; J. Ehrman, *The British Government and Commercial Negotiations with Europe, 1783–1793*, Cambridge, 1962.

9 *The moment of truth*

The Emperor Joseph II, head of the house of Austria and brother of Louis XVI's queen Marie Antoinette, was a stubborn and impetuous man whose inflexible policies tended to harm his allies more than his enemies. His visit to France in 1777 had done little to make the Austrian alliance any more popular there: he had proved an awkward and ungracious guest[1] and he got on badly with the king's brothers—especially with Provence, whom the Austrian ambassador had distrusted for some time. Joseph had however performed one important service for his sister. He had persuaded Louis to have the operation which enabled him at long last to consummate his marriage; but there were still scandal-mongers ready to whisper that the queen's children, now that they did begin to arrive, were the result of illicit affairs rather than of belated royal ardour. Supporters of the queen and of the Austrian alliance tended to attribute these scurrilous rumours, probably quite unjustly, to the machinations of Provence and Artois, whose apparently impotent brother had

[1] J. L. H. Campan, *Memoirs of the Private Life of Marie Antoinette*, 2 vols, 1823, i, 170–6.

so suddenly shown himself able to block their succession to the throne.[2] Tension between the Austrian and the anti-Austrian parties mounted and it only needed a quarrel over policy as well as over procreation to turn it from a court squabble to a national issue. Joseph precipitated such a quarrel in 1784 when he tried to make the Dutch open the river Scheldt, closed to navigation by international agreement since 1648. He hoped in this way to make his Belgian dominions more profitable by reopening the port of Antwerp, which had been cut off from the sea by the closure of the river; but since he possessed no effective navy he could do this only with the help of his French allies. France for her part had no wish to alienate the Dutch just when she was trying to detach them from the English alliance. It was an ugly dilemma and one which did not endear Joseph to those Frenchmen who saw their country's future in terms of economic rivalry with England rather than dynastic dependence on Austria.

The English watched the crisis develop with a certain amount of satisfaction but also with some anxiety: they had no wish to be pushed into war in support of the Dutch. George III questioned the French ambassador anxiously about the extent of Marie Antoinette's influence, while one of Pitt's junior ministers who took satisfaction in describing the divisions within the French government nevertheless feared that Vergennes would fall and the Austrians would have their way.[3] By the end of the year it seemed as though France had got the worst of both worlds, offending the emperor without reassuring the Dutch. 'The people of Amsterdam,' wrote the English home secretary smugly, 'repent having trusted to the friendship and support of France . . . I believe our late fellow subjects in America have as little cause to boast of the sincerity of the French as the Dutch have.'[4] But Vergennes hung on grimly and by the following summer he was having some success: Dorset, who had previously written only of the difficulties the French were encountering, had to admit at the end of May 1785 that 'a few millions of florins, I have reason to believe, are now the only subject of difference remaining to be settled'. In November the figure was finally settled at ten million, for which sum the emperor agreed to drop his claims.

[2] G. Walter, *Marie Antoinette*, 1948, pp. 228–32.
[3] Adhémar to Vergennes, 1 December 1784, cited Barral-Montferrat, *Dix ans de paix armée entre la France et l'Angleterre 1783–1793*, 1893, p. 45; *H.M.C.* 24 *Rutland*, p. 121.
[4] *H.M.C.* 24 *Rutland*, pp. 144–5.

France then signed her long delayed treaty of alliance with the Dutch, having assured them that she would pay part of the compensation for them. Dorset was away from Paris at the time and his secretary Daniel Hailes, who was much more hostile to France than was Dorset himself, took little pleasure in reporting to his government that Vergennes had achieved a great success 'that cannot fail of increasing his reputation'.[5]

Much as Pitt and his colleagues might resent this success there did not seem to be a lot they could do about it. Joseph had assumed from the start that England was now a second-rate power, since her defeat in America; and there were many Englishmen— including George III himself in his gloomier moments—who agreed with him.[6] If the country had welcomed Pitt as the Patriot champion against the factions in parliament it was not because it expected of him the bellicose patriotism of his father but because it looked for the more cautious patriotism of George Grenville. Even more than in the 1760s the country was conscious of its own divisions and its own weaknesses. There was a sullen hatred of France and an almost morbid suspicion of all her intentions: many Englishmen, from the foreign secretary downwards, feared that she had some ulterior motive in agreeing to such apparently unfavourable terms in the Commercial Treaty of 1786.[7] But there was little confidence in England's ability to wage war on her and little readiness to spend money on preparing for such a war. Pitt's business was with retrenchment, with ways of paying off the national debt rather than with ways of defending those Dutchmen who happened to hold a large part of it.

In France there was a much greater realization of what was at stake. Clavière had persuaded Mirabeau, at the very beginning of the crisis, to write a book attacking the emperor's claims; and it was Mirabeau who was to remind the Dutch, after the crisis was over, that England's thirst for power and for wealth had brought 'ruin to all parts of the globe and examples of crime and oppression which would have shocked even the Romans'.[8] Mirabeau had recently spent some months in England but he had

[5] Browning, i, 57, 82.
[6] J. Ehrman, *The Younger Pitt: the years of acclaim*, 1969, p. 476.
[7] *Ibid.*, p. 493.
[8] H. G. Riquetti, comte de Mirabeau, *Aux Bataves sur le Stadthouderat*, 1788, pp. 105–6. On Clavière persuading Mirabeau to write his *Doutes sur la liberté de l'Escaut, réclamée par l'Empereur* (French and English versions of which were published in London 1785) see Dumont, *Souvenirs*, pp. 48, 257.

shown little readiness to admire her or her institutions: he had
quarrelled with several of her leading figures and had finished up
by involving himself in an unsavoury court case at the Old Bailey,
after which his friends had had some difficulty in clearing his
name.[9] He had every sympathy with the desire of his capitalist
friends to oust the English from the money market of Amsterdam.
And the minister who was becoming increasingly dependent upon
those capitalists saw the point too: while Pitt buried himself in
financial matters and ignored the representations of the Foreign
Office about the importance of what was going on in Holland,
Calonne took an active part in building up a francophile party
in the Dutch Republic.[10] He was himself a northerner—he had
started his career as a member of the *parlement* of Flanders—and
he had always been conscious of the importance of Holland and
Belgium to France, even before he had established his close financial connections with Brussels. Another northerner, the *intendant*
of Hainault, published a book in 1787 in which he argued that if
the Dutch could be persuaded to withdraw their money England's
whole economy would collapse. Furthermore, he insisted, it was
becoming increasingly apparent to all sensible financiers, Dutch
or otherwise, that investment in France was now safer than
investment in England. 'He who lends to England,' the *intendant*
concluded, 'lends to a gambler who can only pay back if he wins;
he who lends to France lends to a man of real substance.'[11]

In a sense the crisis had indeed driven England into the position
of a gambler, a gambler who could afford to lay out only a small
stake on an outside chance. Since she could not afford to go to
war she must play France at her own game, the less expensive
but more risky game of building up a party in the Dutch Republic
itself. The Prince of Orange, Stadtholder of the Republic, was
George III's cousin and a symbol of the English alliance; but his
authority was severely limited by the rights and powers of the
seven provinces into which the republic was divided. The province
of Holland, in which the great commercial and financial centre
of Amsterdam was situated, was particularly powerful since it
contributed more than half of the country's revenue. It was

[9] See W. R. Fryer, 'Mirabeau in England 1784–85', *Renaissance and
Modern Studies*, x, 1966, pp. 34–87.
[10] A. Cobban, *Ambassadors and Secret Agents: the diplomacy of the first
earl of Malmesbury at the Hague*, 1954, pp. 120–1.
[11] Senac de Meilhan, *Considérations sur les richesses et le luxe*, Amsterdam,
1787, p. 492. See also L. Legrand, *Senac de Meilhan et l'intendance du
Hainault et du Cambrésis sous Louis XVI*, Valenciennes, 1868.

Amsterdam's eagerness to trade with the American colonists that had pushed the Dutch into war with England in 1780; and now the self-styled Patriots of Amsterdam seemed to want to copy the Americans as well as trade with them. If they had their way they would use the French alliance to teach the Prince of Orange the same lessons the Americans had already taught his cousin. Sir James Harris, English minister at The Hague, wanted to use English money to split the Patriot party in Holland and restore the Stadtholder's influence there. He was determined to beat the French at their own game of subsidizing subversion, to play and win in Holland the return match for what had happened in America.

Neither government was entirely happy about the policies it was pursuing. Vergennes had already had one war of intervention go sour on him and did not relish being dragged into another, while Pitt and George III doubted whether the sums that Harris was asking for—small though they were in comparison with the costs of a war—were really necessary. But towards the end of 1786 Pitt's attitude began to change and he became converted to Harris's views. The duc de Lauzun, an associate of Mirabeau and Panchaud who was in London at the time, got wind of the change and warned his government of it; but by the time his warning reached Paris the French government was falling apart. Vergennes died on 13 February 1787 and ten days later Calonne began to run into serious trouble when he put before an Assembly of Notables the next stages in his plans for financial stability and economic expansion. The struggles over the succession to Vergennes's post soon became merged with intrigues to oust Calonne as well. The controller-general was finally dismissed on 8 April 1787 and a ministry emerged headed by Lomenie de Brienne, archbishop of Toulouse and later archbishop of Sens. He was given the title of prime minister, which had not been used in France since Louis XV had declared his intention of being his own prime minister after the death of Cardinal Fleury in 1743. Brienne's appointment was generally seen as a victory for the queen and the Austrian party, who had been intriguing against Calonne for some time through his colleague Breteuil. Breteuil kept his post as secretary of state for the royal household and one observer wrote that in spite of rumours to the contrary there was complete harmony between the two men.[12] But this harmony did

[12] Lescure, ii, 179.

not last: Breteuil resigned after a few months and there was increasing friction between Brienne and the new foreign secretary, Montmorin, over the policy France should adopt in Holland. The queen and her friends had certainly scored a victory over Calonne and Artois and the speculators, but it was a victory they were incapable of exploiting. They knew that they disliked a foreign policy based on capitalism and republicanism—the king himself told Montmorin that he would rather lose control of Holland than keep it by such means[13]—but they did not know what to put in its place.

While French policies became more and more confused, Harris went from strength to strength. In February it had seemed to financiers as well as to diplomats that France was going to win: the French livre stood at an all-time high on the exchange markets of Amsterdam even after the news of Vergennes's death came through.[14] But by the summer things were moving in England's favour. The Patriots in Holland came out in open defiance of the rest of the republic and of the authority of the Prince of Orange; and when the Princess of Orange went to negotiate with them they took her into custody, albeit only for a matter of hours. This was extremely embarrassing for the French, not only because they did not want to appear as the allies of republican extremists but also because their diplomacy depended on keeping the friendship of Prussia—and the Princess of Orange was the sister of the new king of Prussia, Frederick William II. As the Patriots became increasingly unmanageable and the Prussians increasingly hostile, French policy collapsed. In September 1787 a Prussian army marched into the republic and the Patriot movement melted away before it. Thousands of Patriot refugees crossed into Belgium and some proportion of them (including, significantly enough, some prominent bankers) found their way to France. George III's speech at the opening of parliament on 27 November expressed satisfaction at the victory that had been achieved and members vied with one another to congratulate the government.[15] A few months later England formed a Triple Alliance with the Dutch and with the Prussians which was a striking contrast to the sorry state into which France's own system of alliances had fallen since the emperor's original claims on the Scheldt in 1784.

[13] Cobban, *Ambassadors and Secret Agents*, p. 139.
[14] J. Bouchary, *Le Marché des Changes à Paris à la fin du xviii° siècle*, 1937, p. 44.
[15] *P.H.* xxvi, 1224–54.

In France there was bitter recrimination. Those who had replaced Calonne naturally blamed him for everything: his financial and economic schemes had first led France into a disastrous commercial treaty with the hated English and had then led her into an equally disastrous and extremely undignified scramble for the favour of foreign capitalists. While William Eden, the man who had negotiated the commercial treaty, wrote to his friends back in England that 'there is not, I believe, any party or description of political observers in Europe who do not think and say that my situation here has eventually been instrumental in obtaining great and brilliant advantages for England', the wits of Paris were already commenting with savage irony on the 'garden of Eden' into which they had been led and the wiles of the 'new Adam' who inhabited it.[16] As for the queen, her friends reported that she detested Eden above all men:[17] his treaty had started the chain of events which the Austrian party had tried to prevent but for which it was now nevertheless getting the blame. Calonne and Artois and their raffish friends had frittered away the greatness of France with their over-ambitious speculations and their over-confident theories of economic growth and free trade, but it was the Austrian alliance that was the French people's chosen scapegoat for it all. Marie Antoinette had all the bitterness of a woman wrongfully accused.

The English took a calmer and more Olympian view of French politics. The *Annual Register*, noticeably affected by the mood of complacent superiority engendered by the Dutch victory, put it all down to France's convulsive and belated efforts to model herself on England. Readers were reminded that England's leading place in the affairs of Europe 'has given rise to a spirit of imitation which disposes them to copy us in all things, but principally in that in which we are most distinguished, the form of our government'. These efforts had been started by Necker's reforms— 'perhaps the greatest advance that ever was made by a king towards the establishment of a free constitution'—and the latest troubles were only to be expected, as the new wine reacted upon the old bottles into which it was poured.[18] Having been in the

---

[16] Eden to Rose, 27 January 1788, *Diaries and Correspondence of George Rose*, ed. L. V. Harcourt, 1860, p. 72; Barbier and Vernillat, *Histoire de France par les chansons: 4, La Révolution*, 1958, p. 17. The 'Adam' in question was of course Adam Smith.

[17] Add. 33121, fo. 5.

[18] *Annual Register*, 1787, pp. 176–9.

dark for so long, the French were bound to have difficulties as they struggled into the daylight of constitutional government and free institutions. But they would probably be all right in the end, as long as they were patient and were ready to ask for advice from across the Channel when they needed it.

Subsequent generations of Englishmen took this interpretation a stage further, by giving to it an economic as well as a political dimension. The England of the 1780s came to be seen as having industrial as well as constitutional lessons to teach the French: the superiority which had been so dramatically demonstrated in the great victory of 1787 was ascribed to the factories and the mines and the counting houses of England's newly industrialized economy. More specifically, it was ascribed to that most cherished of all the historian's clichés, the rise of the middle classes. The *Annual Register* thought merely in terms of England pointing the way from absolute monarchy to political liberty, but subsequent historians thought in terms of obsolete hierarchies giving way to social mobility. And the proof of it seemed to lie in the one thing to which the *Annual Register* paid curiously little attention: the actual manner of Calonne's fall. For Calonne had not fallen merely because of court intrigue. He had been dismissed after his reform proposals had been blocked by an assembly of notables which represented—on the face of things at any rate—the serried ranks of privilege. And while Calonne fell, Pitt stood: at the very moment when Calonne was fighting desperately for his reforms, Pitt was putting through parliament amid almost universal acclaim his Consolidation Act, a measure which reorganized and simplified the Customs and Excise. Pitt's legislation, like Calonne's plan for the simplification of French indirect taxes and the imposition of a single duty, was based on proposals that had been discussed in administrative departments for many years and had now been rendered urgent by the commercial treaty. While the hierarchies of feudal France prevented Calonne's free trade plans from working at all, the parliament of industrialized England made sure that Pitt's plans worked better than ever.[19]

[19] The view that England's industrial supremacy was something inherent and longstanding, a cause rather than an effect of the political developments of the 1780s, is challenged by F. M. Crouzet, 'Angleterre et France au xviiie siècle: essai d'analyse comparée de deux croissances économiques', *Annales*, xxi, 1966, pp. 254–91. A. Cobban, *The Social Interpretation of the French Revolution*, 1964, challenges the associated view that there was a 'middle class' which in England was able to make an industrial revolution but in France had no alternative but to make a political one.

But the problems of Calonne's dismissal and Pitt's survival, problems which historians have rightly seen as holding the key to the whole period, cannot be solved so easily. However enlightened his reforms may have been, Calonne was still a gambler, a man who played fast and loose with the fortunes of France and staked the credit of the government on his own speculative financial adventures. Mirabeau's devastating pamphlet on *The Denunciation of Stockjobbing*, which was published in March 1787 and played an important part in bringing about Calonne's downfall, contained a hard core of truth as well as a good deal of embroidery. It was Calonne's rigging of the stock market and his connections with the hated foreign capitalists, rather than his tussle with the 'privileged classes', that made him one of the most unpopular men in France. It was this that provided his enemies with ready listeners when they suggested that the blood he was spitting out (for he had just gone down with a chest complaint) was the blood of France which he had been sucking for so long.[20] The *parlement* of Paris was dominated by men who knew too much about his manipulations, men like Robert de Saint-Vincent who declaimed constantly and effectively against the speculators. Calonne therefore got the king to convoke an Assembly of Notables representing the country as a whole, a device which had not been used since the early seventeenth century, instead of submitting his programme of reforms to the *parlements* for registration. But Mirabeau's work ensured that the assembly was as familiar with the stockjobbing scandals as any *parlement* would have been; and in the end it was only the section presided over by Artois, Calonne's fellow speculator, that stood by him and his reforms.[21]

The reforms themselves were important and far-reaching: as well as his proposals for the abolition of existing internal customs barriers and the imposition of a single duty throughout the realm, Calonne suggested a general tax on all income from land, to be administered and collected by the landowners themselves by means of a complete system of provincial assemblies. The lands of the clergy and the nobility would have been liable for this tax, but on the other hand the privileges of these first two orders of

[20] Lescure, ii, 103.
[21] J. Egret, *La pré-Révolution française*, 1962, p. 189; P. Chevalier, ed., *Journal de l'assemblée des notables de 1787*, 1960; A. Goodwin, 'Calonne, the assembly of French notables of 1787 and the origins of the *Révolte Nobiliaire*', *E.H.R.* lxi, 1946, pp. 202–34, 329–77.

the realm would have been extended by giving them complete exemption from the *capitation* and other direct personal taxation. Although the proposals also included some old Physiocrat favourites, such as free trade in corn and the abolition once more of the *corvée*, it was the basic programme of tax reform and provincial assemblies that was the subject of the real argument between Calonne and his enemies with the Assembly of Notables. The object of the programme was clear enough: to sustain the government's credit by holding out prospects of increased revenues and thus of guaranteed repayment of government debts. Its effect was clear also: it would cut the ground from under the feet of the tax evaders, bourgeois as well as noble, by removing the archaic loopholes they had been exploiting for so long and subjecting them to a uniform tax based upon a proper assessment. Furthermore, it would make them into their own executioners by forming them into representative bodies in which details of the tax would have to be thrashed out in public. Some years earlier the comte d'Albon had written contemptuously of the English: 'More heavily burdened with taxes and debts than any other nation in Europe, the English are content with their lot and put up meekly with the most crushing impositions, simply because they still fondly imagine that they are taxing themselves and because their governments are cunning enough to keep alive this ridiculous illusion.'[22] Now the French also were to be put into the leading strings of a representative system, that shabbiest of all the English conjuror's bag of tricks. And they would not even have the consolation of having one single central representative body which could as least pretend to represent the whole country. They would be divided and ruled.

Since the threat was primarily a threat to landed wealth the counterattack came, naturally enough, from those who held such wealth. But this did not necessarily mean that it came merely from the 'privileged classes'. An eminent French historian has seen '*l'embourgeoisement progressif du sol*', the constant buying up of landed property by the middle classes, as a central feature of French economic and social history in the seventeenth and eighteenth centuries.[23] All over the country the distinctions between the different orders of the realm were becoming

[22] C. C. F. d'Albon, *Discours politiques, historiques et critiques sur quelques gouvernements de l'Europe*, Neuchatel, 1779, p. 49.
[23] H. Methivier, *L'Ancien régime*, 1961, p. 72.

blurred, as members of the middle class bought lands and became *seigneurs* while aristocrats turned themselves into businessmen in order to exploit the mineral and industrial resources of their land. For this very reason the outward forms which were based on the old distinctions were becoming increasingly irksome: histories of the French revolution are full of examples of middle class men and women who were turned into revolutionaries because they had been snubbed by noblemen or noblewomen whom they considered no better than themselves. By 1790 or so the memory of such experiences may indeed have led those who had suffered them to clamour for the abolition of nobility and privilege; but it was having a very different effect in 1787. They did not want to abolish these things but to enjoy them themselves. Jean Marie Roland de la Platière, a civil servant who considered that he had not been given that rank in society to which his talents and his high-sounding name entitled him, was filled with envy of those who were more successful. He hated John Holker, the expatriate Englishman who was his superior in the inspectorate of manufactures and who had been ennobled some years earlier; but the terms in which he attacked him did not suggest sturdy middle class contempt for the institution of nobility. Holker, he wrote, had come to France with a blind horse and an illiterate wife; his origins were 'lost among the vilest of the populace of Manchester' and it was scandalous that he should have been made a nobleman. 'The rank and privileges of a noble', wrote one English visitor, was 'the hobby-horse of every Frenchman.'[24] It was a hobby-horse that Roland and thousands like him were waiting impatiently to mount. In the meantime they were prepared to let the existing magnates of the land defend both the hobby-horse itself and the landed wealth which so often acted as a mounting block for it.

Meanwhile in England Pitt survived because he pleased the landed men and not because he was the representative of a new and middle-class order of things. The old landed families of England were prospering as they had never prospered before, particularly those few hundred greatest and richest families who owned between them about a fifth of all the land in the country. It was becoming increasingly difficult for any aspirant from the middle classes to buy his way even into the ranks of the gentry,

---

[24] Andrews, *Letters to a Young Gentleman*, p. 149. Roland's polemic against Holker is discussed in Bacquié, *Les Inspecteurs*, pp. 245–6.

let alone into the nobility. An outlay of some £30,000 was needed even for a modest estate; and the sort of estate that carried with it parliamentary patronage, and thus the chance of further promotion in the social scale, cost a great deal more. And the existing landed families made sure that their estates came onto the market only very infrequently: they could always have recourse to the favourite English device of mortgage if they needed ready money and there were no longer the civil commotions of the seventeenth century to bring on to the market the lands of those who had chosen the wrong side. 'The inflow of new families into the ranks of landowners was much lower between the 1730s and the end of the eighteenth century,' it has been concluded, 'than in the previous two hundred years.'[25] The old families had the land and the power and they intended to keep it. They also intended to keep if they could the existing structure of direct taxation, which was based on anomalies of assessment as absurd in their way as the exemption of 'noble land' from the *taille* in France.

In both countries the injustices of the taxes on land had to some extent been blunted by the provisions of countless sales and leases. Rents had been fixed which allowed for the tax payable, purchase prices had been agreed which took into account tax liability, non-nobles had bought 'noble land' in order to get the tax exemption it carried with it. Clever lawyers, whether they were working within the freehold society or within the feudal society, could and did ensure that their clients passed their tax liabilities on to someone else if at all possible. Failing that, there was always the time-honoured practice of tax evasion, which was carried on vigorously in both countries. Only the poor, who could not afford to employ either lawyers or tax evasion experts, paid as much as— sometimes more than—they were supposed to. For the rest, men of property and substance knew how to manipulate the system, whether they were noblemen or not. In many cases French noblemen, if they had actually paid all they were supposed to pay, would have paid more in direct taxation than their English counterparts: it was their manipulation of their assessments, rather than their exemptions and their privileges, that cheated the government of its money. It was for this reason that Calonne could with confidence offer *more* tax privileges for the clergy

[25] G. E. Mingay, *English Landed Society in the Eighteenth Century*, 1963, p. 39. The above paragraph is based on Mingay's conclusions.

and the nobility in return for the acceptance of a properly assessed general land tax; and it was for this reason that the 'privileged classes' could with confidence make political capital out of spurning the offer. The key to the situation was not that the 'privileged classes' had a vested interest in clinging to their exemptions, but that the propertied classes as a whole had a vested interest in avoiding at all costs a fair and effective system of assessment.

This fact was as central to the English situation as it was to the French. The battle which Pitt won so easily during the weeks when Calonne was losing his was in fact only half of the real battle: he had succeeded in rationalizing the system of indirect taxation but the anomalies of the land tax still remained. It was not until after 1793, when he found himself trying to finance a major war by means of a tax structure in which only a quarter of total revenue came from direct taxes, that he was able to fight and win the second half of the battle. And even then he had to adopt tactics which were strikingly similar to those used in France before the revolution. Just as Louis XIV and his successors had allowed particular classes or areas to buy exemption from particular taxes with a down payment, so Pitt offered to let land tax-payers redeem their future liabilities with ready cash. Only in this way was he able to dismantle the accumulated absurdities and injustices of the 1693 assessment and pave the way for a properly assessed income tax.[26]

Although the English might be in a position to wait until the 1790s for their properly assessed income tax, the French were not. From Necker's time onwards successive controllers-general had so inflated the level of government borrowing that the country now spent more than half of its annual revenue on paying interest on its debts. There was no question that the great majority of Frenchmen, from the vociferous anticapitalists like Robert de Saint-Vincent down to the poorest peasant, would have liked to repudiate the nation's debts and start again—if only a way could have been found to separate the sheep from the goats, the honest French investors who deserved to get their money back from the wicked foreign speculators who did not. Sensible and informed men, in government and out of it, knew perfectly well that such a process of winnowing was impracticable and they also knew that the withdrawal of foreign capital itself, quite apart from the

[26] See J. Steven Watson, *The reign of George III*, Oxford, 1960, p. 375.

withdrawal of French capital which would undoubtedly ensue, would do irreparable harm to France's economy and would undermine the prosperity of everyone in the land—even of those complacent agriculturalists who thought that they and they alone produced the real wealth of the country. Somehow the small minority that had a grip on reality must sway the great majority that lived by myth alone. They must make them see that France's troubles could no more be solved by chasing out foreign speculators than they had been solved in the past by chasing out the Jesuits. Even *le cadastre*, for all its terrors, was preferable to what Mirabeau later described in chilling tones as '*la banqueroute, la hideuse banqueroute*'. It was this choice between *cadastre* and *banqueroute*, rather than the question of privilege of taxation, which was the real financial issue underlying the crisis that began with the fall of Calonne and ended in revolution.

When Arthur Young arrived in Paris in October 1787, after an extended tour which had taken him through France to Spain and back, he found that people were already talking freely about the possibility of 'a revolution in government'. 'Such conversation never occurs,' he observed, 'but a bankruptcy is a topic; the curious question on which is, *would a bankruptcy occasion a civil war and a total overthrow of the government?*'[27] Talk of revolution was one thing: it could possibly mean something as drastic as what had happened in America or Geneva, but it was more likely to mean merely the replacement of one system of administration by another. Civil war was something much more serious, something which would destroy society as well as government. Men who could argue quite confidently about the need for revolutionary changes in the way the country was governed tended to lose some of their confidence when they realized that the country itself was in danger of splitting apart, that those who refused to pay more taxes might find themselves fighting those who refused to forfeit the money they had lent. Brienne had had as much trouble as his predecessor with the Assembly of Notables, dissolving them in May 1787 after they had rejected his own revamped version of Calonne's reforms. In June the ministry had made a show of firmness by issuing edicts establishing free trade in corn, setting up provincial assemblies and abolishing the *corvée*; but the crucial issue of the general land tax still remained.

[27] Young, *Travels in France*, p. 85.

France had still not decided between *cadastre* and *banqueroute*. The confrontation of the autumn of 1787 between the government and the *parlements*, which was nearing its climax by the time Arthur Young got to Paris, pushed the country one stage nearer to that decision and one stage nearer to civil war.

The confrontation with the *parlements* was precipitated by yet another government proposal for a general land tax, associated this time with a Stamp Act which would have made stamp duty payable on all kinds of documents from instruments of credit to advertisements in newspapers. These measures were linked with a thoroughgoing reform of finance and administration which was comparable to, and possibly inspired by, the reforms of Necker a decade earlier. Nor was the Brienne administration concerned simply with the machinery of government: it was also engaged upon a programme of social reform which included a very controversial edict granting a limited measure of civil liberty to French Protestants. It was perhaps this last enactment that led Burke to dismiss Brienne as one of the dangerous innovators of the 1780s, instead of according him the 'high degree of respect' which he bestowed upon Necker. For Burke had become convinced, long before he wrote his famous diatribe against the French revolution, that concessions of this sort by an established Church undermined not only the Church itself but also the society which it was supposed to sanctify. Worse still, they threatened political stability by allowing men who had previously been outside the political establishment to put pressure upon it. At the beginning of May 1789, just when the French were inaugurating their long awaited Estates General, Burke had to deal with a request from the dissenters of Bristol to support their campaign for increased toleration; and he dealt with it very harshly, saying that the dissenters had forfeited his sympathy by playing a prominent part in turning the country against parliament during the great crisis of 1783–84. In a letter to a friend a few months earlier he had made the point even more clearly: 'It was the present king and the present ministers,' he wrote, 'who have made and who continue this parliament out of doors.'[28] In Burke's view the balance between liberty and order was in danger, both in England and in France, because the disestablished were battering at the

[28] Burke, *Correspondence*, v, 470–2, 443.

doors of the establisment, because the country as a whole was raising a clamour which threatened to drown the voices of those who should speak for it. This was to him a denial, not an extension, of the representative principle. Ministers who encouraged it richly deserved to perish under the ruins of the establishments they were helping to destroy.

Burke had an absurdly exaggerated idea of the popularity of the *parlements*, as was to be shown in 1790 when he seriously suggested that if they had not been abolished 'the people might some time or other come to resort to them, and rally under the standard of their ancient laws'.[29] But it was nevertheless true that the nub of the situation in France, as in England, was the relationship between what Burke thought of as the parliament in doors and the parliament out of doors, the country's existing representatives and the country itself. When Brienne decided to enforce the registration of his tax edicts by *lit de justice* on 6 August 1787 he was in effect offering the *parlements* a choice of tactics: they could take their stand on their own existing powers or they could abdicate those powers and appeal to the country as a whole. Four years earlier the English parliament, a body with far more authority and prestige than the *parlements* of France had ever possessed, had stood at a similar crossroads and had decided to support its own dignity by defying a minister who claimed to represent the country's wishes as against those of parliament. And it had been defeated. In its defeat it had forfeited the last vestiges of that reputation which it had once enjoyed in France and which had already been seriously eroded by the American revolution: it was now regarded by almost all enlightened Frenchmen as a corrupt and unrepresentative body which was despised by those whose liberties it claimed to protect. It was hardly surprising, therefore, that the leaders of the *parlements* in the autumn of 1787 decided to take a different road. They decided to demand the calling of an Estates General.

In one respect at least the *parlements* were in a happier position than the English parliament: they could abdicate in favour of a body older than themselves. The estates general of France was a very ancient institution which had at one time regularly represented the three orders of the realm, although it had now been in abeyance since 1614. If the *parlements* were really committing constitutional suicide, then at least they were doing so for the sake

[29] Burke, *Select Works*, ii, 144.

of tradition and not for the sake of those 'innovations' which were the only alternative to parliament in England. Hailes did not believe that they were committing suicide at all: in his view it was the king's plan for provincial assemblies that was the real threat to the *parlements*, whose own device of an estates general was intended to save rather than supplant.

> The protection of the people from an increase of taxes is the ground . . . that has been artfully chosen by the parliament on which to rest their disobedience [he commented], but I have reason to think that the establishment of the Provincial Assemblies throughout the kingdom (a measure which could not be opposed by them in an open manner, on account of its extreme popularity) is the real, tho' concealed motive of their conduct. That innovation, which however it may be lightly treated with respect to its consequences to the constitution of the French monarchy by some individuals, seems, in general, to be allowed to be a change of great prospective importance.[30]

This much at least the *parlements* had in common with the Whigs whom they had once admired and who had once admired them: they were still fighting shoulder to shoulder in the battle against 'innovation'. Nor were they alone in the fight. From one end of France to the other the existing local institutions, and those whose interests were associated with them, took up the struggle against the new provincial assemblies. The demand for an Estates General, voiced in Paris by the king's leading opponents, was echoed by demands in the provinces for the revival and the extension of the powers of the old provincial Estates.

Both the ministry and the opposition were claiming to speak, each in its different fashion, for the France that had not yet spoken. The edict on provincial assemblies had been accompanied by provisions for the establishment of councils, elected by secret ballot, to represent village communities,[31] so that the government's proposals could well be regarded as being more genuinely representative than the demands of the opposition. Arthur Young certainly thought so: he considered that the new assemblies implemented the schemes put forward by French Patriots for many years past and that they enabled ordinary yeomen farmers

---

[30] Browning, i, 231–2. (Also printed in J. M. Roberts, ed., *French Revolution Documents*, vol 1, Oxford, 1966, p. 14.)
[31] A. Soboul, 'The French Rural Community of the eighteenth and nineteenth century', *Past and Present*, x, 1956, pp. 78–95.

to challenge the influence of local noblemen.[32] In some provinces,
notably in Normandy, the *parlements* found that local opinion
was so much in favour of the new assemblies that it was not worth
defying it. In others the opposition was more successful and
mounted vigorous campaigns on behalf of the ancient provincial
Estates.[33] The Estates of Provence, of Dauphiné and of Brittany
became the subject of particularly intense political debate—so
much so that the readiness of those provinces to support the wider
plan for an Estates General of the whole realm became more and
more uncertain. By supporting tradition against innovation, by
insisting on the need to go back to the hallowed origins of
France's political life, the opponents of the administration had
revealed the embarrassing fact that those origins lay in disunity
and separatism. At least the government, by looking forward and
by promoting change, was moving along those lines of convergence which had for centuries been steadily creating the French
nation out of a collection of disparate provinces. The opposition,
by looking back, was reopening the divergences and divisions of
the past. The France for which it claimed to speak was a France
which spoke with many different tongues.

Those who were conducting the chorus were able to produce,
by their sheer vigour and audacity, a certain impression of harmony. Before the *lit de justice* of 6 August 1787 the opposition
to the government was regarded by most people as coming from
a relatively small group of malcontents in the *parlements* who
were making a nuisance of themselves for the usual reason—
because they wanted to force their way into office. To some it
seemed that their ambitions were on a larger scale than those of
their predecessors, that they hoped to put up the value of their
offices in the *parlements* by claiming powers similar to those
enjoyed by the venal and corrupt parliamentarians of England;
but they did not appear as the spokesmen of a popular revolutionary movement, unless it was perhaps the popular dislike of
the foreign speculators. The hard core of opposition leaders in
the *parlement* of Paris—Duval d'Eprémesnil, Robert de Saint-
Vincent, Sabatier de Cabre, Adrien Duport—were sometimes
known as the 'American faction'; but this did not necessarily
imply either democratic intentions or popular support. Brissot

[32] Young, *Travels in France*, pp. 74–5.
[33] Egret, *Pré-Révolution*, pp. 212–23.

and Clavière were busy refurbishing the image of America, either
out of revolutionary idealism or from less lofty motives (for
Clavière and his associates were about to extend their speculations
to take in the American national debt as well as the French); but
their Gallo-American Society had little popular appeal and the
various works they published on America between 1786 and 1788
did not entirely succeed in recapturing that first vision of American pastoral simplicity which the French had once found so
appealing. France was by no means sure that she wanted to copy
America, or that she admired the 'American faction' for mooting
such an enterprise. But the *lit de justice* changed the picture, at
any rate in Paris. Crowds carried Duval d'Eprémesnil shoulder
high through the streets; and when the *parlement* was exiled to
Troyes for its contumacy its stock of popularity rose even higher.
In September, when it returned in triumph after persuading the
government to give in over the tax edicts, there were wild
outbursts of popular enthusiasm which provoked the troops to
open fire on the crowds—an ominous portent of things to come.[34]
If Arthur Young heard talk of revolution and civil war when he
got to Paris in October it was because the forces of opposition
had achieved a measure of coherence and popularity which might
yet enable them to divide the nation in their attempts to lead it.

Watching the scene from the British embassy Hailes was
anxious that the crisis should result in the perpetuation of division
rather than in the discovery of unity. The confrontation between
the French king and the Patriots of Paris had coincided with that
between the Dutch Stadtholder and the Patriots of Amsterdam;
and if the two conflicts were to merge, if the French Patriots
were to propel their king and their country into outright support
of the republicans in Holland, the outlook for England might well
be unpleasant. He sent the foreign secretary an analysis of the
situation which summed up in a masterly fashion the standard
reaction of an eighteenth-century government to the domestic
troubles of its neighbours:

I need not suggest to your Lordship's wisdom how much is to
be apprehended from a universal sense of the necessity of war,
and from that degree of unanimity that may arise from a
general notion (however ill-grounded) of injustice and provo-

[34] G. Rudé, *The Crowd in the French Revolution*, rev. edn, Oxford, 1969,
p. 29.

cation on the part of England. The distresses of the people may
be cheerfully borne; a ministry may be consolidated; and even
a failure, whether partial or general, in national engagements
may be palliated and, perhaps, excused should such a spirit be
ever raised in the public. I will venture to observe to your
Lordship, with the utmost deference, that it is the opinion of
many men of judgement and discernment here that, if France
were to remain a year or two longer undisturbed, the
necessity of contracting her expenditure might induce her to
direct the greater part of her operations of economy and
retrenchment to the War and Marine Departments, and thereby
render her much less formidable than she is at present.[35]

Arthur Young, as he travelled back from Paris to Calais at the
beginning of November, found that the national unity which had
seemed to be menaced by talk of civil war was now being
strengthened by talk of foreign war. 'The cry here for a war with
England amazed me,' he wrote when he reached Lille. '. . . It is
easy enough to discover that the origin of all this violence is the
commercial treaty . . . they would involve four and twenty
million of people in the certain miseries of a war, rather than see
the interest of those who consume fabrics prefered to the interest
of those who make them.'[36] There had indeed been bitter
recriminations about the commercial treaty, which had been
blamed for industrial recession ranging from the iron industry of
Hainault on France's northern frontiers to the cloth industry of
Carcassonne in the extreme south. But this was not the real reason
for the war fever: here, as in so many other things, Young's
picture of France was really a mirror image of his own prejudices. He hated to see capital being diverted from agriculture
to industry and so he had conceived the idea that many of
France's troubles sprang from that same industrialism which many
historians—including some who have made extensive use of
Young's observations—later came to see as being insufficiently
developed before the revolution. Some of the self-styled French
Patriots shared Young's prejudices: a few months later Brissot
was to preface one of his laudatory accounts of America with a
quite gratuitous attack on the industrialists of Rouen.[37] But this
did not mean that the chauvinism of 1787 had its origins in popular

[35] Browning, i, 249–50.
[36] Young, *Travels in France*, p. 94.
[37] J. P. Brissot de Warville, *New Travels in the United States of America
1788*, ed. D. Echeverria, Cambridge (Mass), 1964, p. 62.

resentment of the commercial treaty. France was on the verge of war not because of her commercial or industrial policy but because of a temporary identification between the diplomacy of international finance and the instinctive anglophobia of most Frenchmen. Even when the Dutch crisis cooled down, wider and deeper suspicions remained: it was believed, with some truth, that the English East India Company was preparing for war against France and that the English ambassador in Constantinople was seeking to set France against both Turkey and Russia.[38] Every other issue, domestic as well as foreign, was swallowed up in hatred of England.

> The differences between the Court and Parliaments, and even the great work of economy and reform are lost sight of by the public, and nothing is attended to but the grand question of war or peace [wrote Hailes]. I have been told, and I fear it is too true, that the ministers have no longer any confidence in what is said to them on the part of England; M. de Montmorin is said to have declared in a tone of resignation, that if the English were resolved upon war, they must have it.[39]

On the face of things it was not an auspicious moment for Mirabeau to launch a periodical devoted to reprinting items from English newspapers. And yet his *Analysis of English Papers*, which appeared twice weekly from the middle of November 1787 to the middle of November 1789, turned out to be a success. Even when they were hating one another particularly cordially, the English and the French remained intensely interested in one another. As the threat of war receded and the *parlement* leaders turned once more to their tussle with the government they were not disposed to revise their very low opinion of the present state of English parliamentary politics; but they had to admit all the same that the English had produced a prototype of such politics which they could not entirely reject, much as they might hope to improve upon it. They did not intend to copy the English revolution of 1688, any more than they intended to copy the American revolution of 1776, for the simple reason that they did not see themselves as revolutionaries at all: they were defending the

---

[38] On the suspicions about English intrigues in Constantinople see Barral–Montferrat, *Dix ans de paix armée*, pp. 300ff. On the extent to which the British East India Company was in fact preparing for war see C. H. Philips, *The East India Company 1784–1834*, rev. edn, Manchester, 1961, p. 67.
[39] Browning, i, 251.

traditional constitution of France against a government which was
seeking to impose arbitrary taxes in order to pay off foreign
capitalists. But the traditional constitution of France had been
neglected for a very long time. The Estates General had not met
for 175 years, while the provincial estates were for the most part
in a state of suspended animation. Even the actual composition of
a future Estates General was uncertain: the number of representatives accorded to the clergy, the nobility and the Third Estate had
varied in the Estates General in the sixteenth and seventeenth
centuries, just as it varied in those provincial Estates which were
still in being. France had a venerable tradition of representative
politics, but she did not have much recent experience of such
politics in action. She needed to look to England, if only to see
what to avoid.

On 19 November 1787, five days after the first issue of Mirabeau's new periodical, the government won a victory which
seemed to render nostalgia for the ancient constitution of France
and interest in the present constitution of England equally point-
less. At a special session of the *parlement* of Paris the king
announced that he would uphold the 'unchangeable principles of
the French monarchy' as laid down by his predecessor at the
Session of the Scourging in March 1766: all power lay in his
hands and the *parlement* of Paris had no right to tell him what
to do or to stir up the other *parlements* against his authority. The
Estates General would be summoned in due course, but not until
after the royal programme of financial and other reforms had
been put through. The Keeper of the Seals, who was the mouth-
piece for this vigorous assertion of royal authority, made special
mention of the edict for the toleration of the Protestants, which
had already aroused a good deal of opposition in Paris and was
to arouse more before it was finally registered by the Paris *parlement* a couple of months later. By thus stressing the reformist
nature of government policy the ministers divided their opponents
—Duval d'Eprémesnil campaigned energetically against the
toleration edict while Duport and others supported it—and
brought the initiative back into their own hands. First reactions
to this show of strength were uncertain: the stock market fell
heavily and there was talk of a change of ministry. But within a
few days subscribers began to come forward for the new government loan and people began to realize that the foreign Protestant
capitalists, distrusted though they were, might serve the ministry

in good stead. With Dutch bankers pouring into France and being welcomed with a new degree of toleration for their religion, Louis XVI's ministers had a new source of financial strength. By the end of November Dorset was writing home to say that 'from an appearance of much confusion everything seems now to denote an implicit obedience to the will of the sovereign'; and a few days later he was able to report that the new provincial assemblies had already agreed to increases in taxation that would bring in an extra fifty million livres a year.[40]

The most dramatic part of the day's proceedings on 19 November had been the intervention of the duc d'Orléans, who had sufficiently overcome his notorious shyness about speaking in public to defy his cousin the king and to tell him that his actions were illegal. Like the Prince of Wales's defiance of George III, this action was an almost inevitable product of the political structure of the time: the house of Orléans, cadet branch of the French royal family, was as natural a centre for opposition in France as the heir to the throne was in England. And since the days of the Regency the house of Orléans had also been associated with English influence. Contemporary publicists were always ready to bring charges of *anglomanie* against Orléans, just as nineteenth-century writers were later to see his role in the French revolution as an integral part of an Orléanist conspiracy, begun by his ancestor the regent, to undermine France with English ideas and English money.[41] Orléans had certainly visited London frequently during the past few years, buying a house there and spending a lot of time with the Prince of Wales. The two men looked out racehorses and mistresses for one another and Orléans was very fulsome in his praise of the prince's political stand against his father. Louis XVI certainly disliked his cousin's links with England and George III was said to have asked the French to stop Orléans suborning his son. But this did not mean that the two men were political allies, still less that they were part of an anglophile plot against France. The prince had in fact a very low opinion of his French visitor, while those associated with Orléans were even more contemptuous of the prince's Whig friends than they were of Pitt's government. The importance of the association lay in the suspicions it engendered rather than in the plans

---

[40] *Ibid.*, i, 270–2, 273–4. The royal declaration of 19 November 1787 is printed in Roberts, *Documents*, pp. 17–20.
[41] See above, pp. 13–14.

it concocted: the prince was disliked for importing the rakish frivolities of France and the duc d'Orléans was suspected of disseminating the subversive ideas of the English.[42]

Ideas, whether English or not, were becoming increasingly important as the struggle between the government and the opposition turned into one to woo the progressives and to pose as the champions of reform. 'The most sanguine of the young nobility', said Dorset in his report on the provincial assemblies, 'consider these assemblies as much more favourable to the cause of national liberty than they do the fruitless obstinacy and ill-timed resistance of the parliament in refusing to register new taxes at a moment when the nation was in the greatest distress for want of money.'[43] And there were other people as well as the nobility to consider. The clergy, some of whose members had been alarmed at the edict of toleration, were determined to preserve their position as a self-sufficient ecclesiastical establishment: their intransigent defence of their own tax privileges during the special assembly of the clergy which was convened on 5th May 1788 proved more of an embarrassment than an assistance to the opposition.[44] By the spring of 1788 the government was beginning to profit from a climate of opinion in which not only the provincial assemblies but also the mooted Estates General were seen as unifying and regenerating forces, as opposed to the divisive forces represented by Orléans with his aping of the irresponsible opposition politicians of England. Ideas which until recently had seemed exciting began to appear suspect, mere pretences to cloak political ambition: freemasonry and mesmerism seemed closer to esoteric absurdity than to eternal truth. There were worthier movements than these caught up in the tangle of societies which linked Orléans and the *parlements* with the radical intellectuals of Paris; but these too tended to lose more than they gained by the association. Even the marquis du Crest, who had tried to popularize Orléans's cause by employing 'progressive' writers and by publishing a work of his own on tax reform, found

[42] A. Britsch, 'L'Anglomanie de Philippe-Egalité, d'après sa correspondance autographe, 1778–1785', *Le Correspondant*, ccciii, 1926, pp. 280–95. For the Prince of Wales's real opinion of Orléans see *Correspondence of George, Prince of Wales, 1770–1812*, ed. A. Aspinall, 8 vols, 1963–71, i, 107–8, 110.

[43] Browning, i, 275–6.

[44] J. Egret, 'La dernière assemblée du clergé de France', *R.H.* ccxix, 1958, pp. 1–15.

himself dismissed from the duke's household at the end of 1787.[45]

Nobody was sure where it would all end. In April 1788 Hailes said that there was a general sense of 'disgrace and difficulties' and an eagerness for change which could only end either in anarchy or in a complete victory for the government. On 8 May, however, Dorset reported that the matter had been settled decisively in favour of the king: two members of the Paris *parlement* had been arrested and 'it is upon the whole imagined that the storm which seemed to threaten the internal tranquillity of this kingdom will blow over and that the examples lately made will have the effect of deterring others from shewing that spirit of opposition to the will of the sovereign, which, it is seen, does not fail to incur the severity of arbitrary power.' The two members were Duval d'Eprémesnil and a hitherto unknown colleague called Goislard de Montsabert; and their arrest had been as dramatic as Charles I of England's search for the Five Members of the English parliament a century and a half before. It came within an ace of being equally unsuccessful—the commander of the royal troops was reduced to hunting for the two men while they hid behind their friends—and it had the effect of turning them into national heroes as surely as Charles I had conferred that distinction on his own enemies in 1642.[46]

Immediately after the arrests all the *parlements* of France were forced by *lit de justice* to register edicts which in effect destroyed their own powers and set up instead a new system of law courts even more revolutionary than the *parlement Maupeou* of 1771. But it very soon became clear, in spite of this show of strength, that the king and his ministers lacked either the confidence or the unity which was needed if they were to brave the unpopularity they had incurred. In Paris the crowds were not particularly dangerous: after a day or so spent cheering the *parlement* and jostling those who had acted against it, they became quiet again.[47] But in the provinces things were uglier. There were troubles in Toulouse and Bordeaux and there was a significant hardening of separatist attitudes in the *pays d'états*, especially in Brittany and

[45] Bachaumont, xxxiv, 100; xxxvi, 88, 261–2. There is an extract from Ducrest's book in Pollard and Holmes, *Documents*, pp. 143–4.

[46] Browning, ii, 44. On Duval d'Eprémesnil see H. Carré, 'un precurseur inconscient de la Révolution: le conseiller Duval d'Eprémesnil', *Révolution Française*, xxxiii, 1897, pp. 349–73; 405–37.

[47] Lescure, ii, 253, 256.

Dauphiné. Louis XVI was learning in the 1780s the lesson that George III had learnt in the 1760s: conflict at the centre fed, and was in its turn fed by, conflict in outlying colonies and provinces. The realm of France was crumbling at the edges as surely as the British empire had crumbled a generation earlier.

There was discord at the centre to match the discord that had been created farther afield. Mrs Swinburne, an expatriate English-woman who was a personal friend of the queen, was convinced that Brienne had gone too far and had incurred the enmity of the king's family as well as of the king's enemies. Breteuil, who had by this time left the ministry and was turning the queen against it, was related to Duval d'Eprémesnil and was a secret supporter of the *parlements*. In June, after news had arrived of an open revolt in Dauphiné, Mrs Swinburne was sure that Marie Antoinette's influence was about to bring down Brienne. A few weeks later an equally serious revolt in Brittany caused wider repercussions at court: ladies in waiting found themselves dismissed because their husbands had shown sympathy for the Breton rebels, while the king had a furious quarrel with Artois for the same reason. And, of course, there were the usual suspicions of the English—'The Bretons expect to be helped by the English, which everybody agrees is but fair', remarked Mrs Swinburne—and the usual conviction that war against them would unite the nation: 'If the English declare war, they will give internal peace to France; they will increase their debt and get nothing but the shame of having shown a little poor spite, for their enmity will procure friends to France.'[48]

Once again these rumours and suspicions of English hostility had more force than foundation.[49] The English government was not in fact financing the Breton revolt, any more than the English opposition was doing anything to justify Louis XVI's order of April 1788 forbidding Orléans to re-establish his contacts with it. In fact both government and opposition had troubles of their own, seeking desperately to satisfy the forces of change while at the same time reassuring the conservatives. The dissenters, busy with their plans to celebrate the centenary of the Glorious Revolution by promoting a Bill to remove their civil disabilities, played off party against party in their search for support. The indepen-

[48] Add. 33, 121, fo. 5.
[49] See A. Cobban, 'The British Secret Service in France, 1784–92', *E.H.R.*, 1954, pp. 226–61.

dent gentlemen were becoming increasingly disillusioned with both Pitt and Fox and were talking of forming a 'third party'.[50] The industrialists, who figured in French political mythology as sinister potentates pushing their government into commercial treaties and trading wars, were in fact in a state of disarray after the collapse of their political pressure group, the General Chamber of Manufacturers, at the end of the previous year. There was a serious recession in the textile industry which had set the new cotton industries against the more traditional interests of the woollen manufacturers and had set both of them against the East India Company's imports of cheap cloth.[51] The East India Company itself, which the French saw as triumphant and aggressive, was in fact on the defensive against a virulent hatred of 'nabobs' which found its most powerful expression in the impeachment of Warren Hastings. There was no doubt that the English government took a certain satisfaction in France's troubles—Pitt told a colleague with some relief that 'the state of France, whatever else it may produce, seems to promise us more than ever a considerable respite from any dangerous projects'[52]—but this did not mean that it could or would do anything to promote them.

But the ironic fact remained that if Louis XVI's government gave in to the demands for the national regeneration of France they would put themselves into the hands of men who had international connections with England. However much the *parlements* might thunder against the foreign capitalists, it was still true that the demand for an estates general came not only from a disorganized majority anxious to avoid new taxes but also from a highly organized minority which saw representative government as the best guarantee for the national debt in which they had invested. Traditional France, the France which loyalist landowners still thought to be in control of things, might turn its face against such people and against the foreign alliances for which they stood; but traditional France had fewer options left open to it than it realized. If the queen were to succeed in her attempt to replace Brienne with some still more courtly traditionalist, some still stauncher advocate of the Austrian alliance, such a man would still need a financier to help him. If Brienne went

[50] The 'third party circular' of May 1788 is printed in L. B. Namier, *Monarchy and the Party System*, Oxford, 1952, pp. 22–4.
[51] For a summary of the 1788 recession and its effects see L. S. Pressnell, *Country Banking in the Industrial Revolution*, Oxford, 1956, pp. 453–5.
[52] *Diaries and Correspondence of George Rose*, p. 85.

I

there could no longer be any resisting the demand for an immediate Estates General; and if the Estates General met it would have to be managed by a man who had the confidence of those whose investments it was expected to underwrite.

In August 1788 the king suddenly and dramatically abandoned his position, announcing that he would convoke an estates general for the following spring. Brienne and his colleagues hung on for a few weeks but by the end of the month they were out and Necker had taken their place.[53] Many people had thought that Necker was finished politically because he had made a premature and offensive attempt to get back into power in April 1787, at the time of Calonne's fall; but the harsh truth was that he had survived his own blunders because he was indispensable. The convocation of the Estates General was in effect an admission that government credit was on the point of collapse. Only a man with the closest possible connections with government creditors, past, present and future, could save it. The precise reasons for the king's change of front were uncertain: some of his subjects thought of him as a well-meaning man who had finally granted his people's dearest wish, while others saw him as a realist who knew that the army could not be relied upon to put down the revolts in Dauphiné and Brittany, much less any subsequent troubles that might break out in Paris itself. The queen hinted at some great diplomatic coup, an acquisition of land in Flanders in return for helping the emperor against his rebellious Belgian subjects, which had failed at the last moment.[54] But whatever the motives, the consequences were clear enough. The choice between the *cadastre* and the *banqueroute* would now be made in public, by the Estates General of France and not by the ministers alone; and those within the ministry who wished to influence it must establish contact as soon as possible with those members of the opposition who wanted to do the same thing.

Such bridges would not be particularly easy to build. Samuel Romilly and Etienne Dumont, an English lawyer and a Genevese pastor who were both *protégés* of Shelburne, arrived in Paris in July 1788 to find the city sharply divided into the supporters of Necker and the supporters of Calonne.[55] Many of the latter were lying low and taking little part in politics, but their financial

---

[53] On Brienne's fall and the extent to which he was himself responsible for Necker's appointment see Egret, *Pré-Révolution*, pp. 315ff.

[54] Add. 33, 121, fo. 8.

[55] Dumont, *Souvenirs*, pp. 50-1.

interests were still identified with the international capitalism centred on the Genevese exiles of 1782, while the supporters of Necker still looked to Geneva itself and to London bankers like Bourdieu and Chollet. Romilly and Dumont were dazzled and delighted by the fashionable façade of the opposition, which they met in the drawingrooms and diningrooms of the men to whom they were recommended by their patron—Malesherbes, Morellet, Lafayette, de la Rochefoucauld, Dupont de Nemours, Mallet du Pan, Jefferson, Target and many others. But while these men wove beguiling fantasies about the long term effects of the Estates General and about the new era in human happiness which it would inaugurate, other and less reputable men were concerning themselves about the short term objective, the saving of the government and the country from bankruptcy. One of these men was the younger Mirabeau, whose pamphleteering had by this time brought him into such disrepute that Romilly and Dumont determined to have nothing to do with him; but Mirabeau turned up nevertheless and captivated them both. By the time they went back to England he had persuaded Romilly to write an account of the Bicêtre, which he later passed off as his own, and he had made Dumont promise to let him have a series of short articles on various topics.[56] He thus laid the foundations for a link between English political thought and French political action which was to have momentous consequences. Having undertaken the immensely difficult task of converting the Estates General of France to the politics of capitalism—a task made doubly difficult by the rival camps into which the capitalists were themselves divided—Mirabeau went on to turn difficulties into impossibilities by associating himself with the arrogant and self-deluding English.

Even before the announcement that the Estates were to be convoked the following year, Mirabeau had begun to moderate the violence of his attacks on Necker—because, as he later told Dumont, Necker's help was essential if the estates were ever to be called.[57] From July 1786 until January 1787 Mirabeau had held an obscure diplomatic post in Berlin; and he had returned from Prussia a devoted admirer of duke Ferdinand of Brunswick, a brother-in-law of George III and a great favourite with the Whig leaders since the 1760s. It was Brunswick who commanded the Prussian

[56] Romilly, i, 71; Dumont, *Souvenirs*, pp. 56–7.
[57] Dumont, *Souvenirs*, p. 53.

army in the Dutch republic in 1787, thus becoming a symbol not
only of the links between England and Prussia but also of the
association between both countries and the Dutch;[58] and by 1788
Mirabeau had dropped his anglophobia and was insisting that
France should abandon her alliance with Austria and join in the
Triple Alliance of England, Prussia and the Dutch republic. Now
that the Patriots in Amsterdam had lost, there was no point in
crying over spilt milk: France must get the strength of all the
money markets of northern (and Protestant) Europe around her
if she was to maintain her credit and avoid *la banqueroute*. Just
as the divisions between Calonne's backers and Necker's backers
must be transcended in order to save both from ruin, so the
divisions between France and her northern neighbours must be
transcended in order to promote the prosperity of them all. If
such policies also promoted the prosperity of Mirabeau, by transforming him from an opposition pamphleteer to a minister of the
crown, so much the better.

Mirabeau's first major attempt to influence the composition and
policy of the estates general was through the Society of Thirty,
a small club which met at the house of Adrien Duport.[59] Other
parlement leaders, such as Duval d'Eprémesnil and Sabatier de
Cabre, were also members, as well as Lafayette and several other
radically minded noblemen. By the time the society was formed,
early in November, 1788, the *parlement* of Paris had issued a
declaration demanding that the Estates should be constituted in
the same way as in 1614, with the three estates of the realm equally
represented and debating separately, so that the clergy and the
nobility, the 'privileged orders', should in effect have a double
voice against the single voice of the Third Estate. Since Lafayette
and his friends favoured the rival proposal, that the Third Estate
should have as many representatives as the other two orders put
together and should debate in common with them so that its
numerical superiority could count for something, the discussions
in the Society of Thirty must have been largely concerned with
this issue. But since Clavière and Panchaud were members as well

[58] On Brunswick's standing with the Whigs, see above, p. 89. Having
ended the Dutch revolution by means of an invasion and a stern manifesto
in 1787, he was to try the same devices on the French revolution in 1792—
with somewhat different results.
[59] See G. Michon, *Essai sur l'histoire du parti feuillant: Adrien Duport*,
1924. Egret is incorrect in stating (*Pré-Révolution*, p. 326n) that the title
'Société des Trente' was not used by contemporaries: see MSS Dumont, 35,
fo. 2: 'La Société des Trente a continué ses utiles assemblées'.

as Mirabeau the group could hardly have been allowed to forget that behind the question of representation lay the question of solvency: whatever dreams they might have for the future members must first of all ensure that the Estates met in a form which would produce a proper system of taxation and proper guarantees for the national debt.

Neither Mirabeau and the bankers nor Lafayette and the idealists found it particularly easy to convert the *parlementaires*.[60] The issue of tax privilege had largely been settled already: however the Estates were constituted it was extremely unlikely that the 'privileged orders' would make any serious attempt to defend their exemptions. Even the Abbé Sieyès, who was also a member of the society and whose pamphlet *What is the Third Estate?* proved to be the most influential of the many hundreds published that winter, admitted in his less rhetorical moments that tax privilege could often be a disadvantage to those who possessed it.[61] But the fact remained that an attack on the 'privileged orders' was the best means of deflecting attacks upon the capitalists and the government creditors. Sieyès knew perfectly well that his picture of the social divisions of France was distorted: the nobility were not all haughty playboys and the middle classes were not all thrifty toilers. In many cases it was the middle classes who were most stubbornly opposed to the reforms that the idealists were suggesting: in the legal profession, for instance, the judges and rich barristers were anxious to sweep away venality while the poorer and less privileged lawyers were anxious to keep it.[62] The *Cahiers de Doléances*, lists of grievances drawn up early in 1789 for the guidance of the deputies to the Estates General, were to show clearly enough that the propaganda of the pamphlet war had been based on crude caricatures rather than on social realities. But the crude caricatures were politically useful and politically powerful. While Sabatier de Cabre and the other conservatives of the *parlement* portrayed the nobility as a collection of honest and simple gentlemen defending traditional values against the parasitical capitalists of the middle classes, Mirabeau and his friends were pushed inevitably into an equally false position. Their picture of the Third Estate as the only bulwark

[60] See Mirabeau's letter to Lauzun, 4 December 1788, on his attempts to counter 'la tyrannie parlementaire' in the Society, *Mémoires de Mirabeau*, ed. Montigny, 8 vols, 1834–5, v, 200.
[61] See Behrens, 'Nobles, Privileges and Taxes', p. 458.
[62] P. Dawson, 'The Bourgeoisie de Robe in 1789', *F.H.S.* iv, 1965, pp. 1–21.

against reaction and privilege was as absurd and as potent as the
picture which Sabatier's journalist ally Rivarol painted of it, as
the dupe of sixty thousand government creditors who used it to
ruin France in order to get their money back.[63]

Behind the propaganda lay the reality: if the Estates General
failed to get off the ground there would be a bankruptcy. Ever
since the appointment of Necker there had been a fairly consistent rise in the price of government stock, but in the middle
of December this rise stopped suddenly, to be followed by a
dramatic fall. The reason was that a second Assembly of Notables,
called to consider the forms under which the Estates General
should be convoked, had failed to agree on the doubling of the
Third Estate's representation or the merging of the three orders
into one assembly. There was something to be said for the
arguments of the traditionalists—if France did really have an
ancient constitution it was foolish to prejudge the issue by
changing its forms before the Estates which was to regenerate
it had even met—but the intransigence with which these
arguments were put forward threatened to prove socially divisive
and politically disastrous. Dorset had already told his government
of fears that the clergy and the nobility might scuttle the Estates
altogether by refusing to take part in them; and now he reported
a drop of six per cent in the funds as a result of a remonstrance
which the princes of the blood had addressed to the king in
defence of the traditional forms of convocation.[64] This remonstrance indicated divisions at court as well as divisions in society,
for Provence and Orléans had refused to sign it. Provence had
supported the demands of the Third Estate in the Assembly of
Notables, while Orléans was reserving his position, ready to use
his popularity in Paris to his own advantage once the Estates met.
Meanwhile the geographical divisions of France served to darken
the prospect still further. Dauphiné, the province whose original
resistance was thought by many to have pushed the king into
calling the Estates, was quieter now; but in Brittany there was
something approaching civil war between the Third Estate and
the nobility—many of whom were impoverished country gentlemen who in England would scarcely have qualified for the vote.
And in Burgundy there was an even more candid admission of

[63] Lüthy, ii, 559.
[64] Browning, ii, 123, 127–8. The princes' remonstrance is printed in Roberts,
Documents, pp. 45–9.

separatism: the nobility of the local Estates there opened their proceedings with a speech saying how deeply they were distressed by France's troubles—and how determined they were not to become involved in them.[65]

For those who were involved in France's troubles there was at least one small consolation: England, the troublesome neighbour who was always suspected of causing and using the distresses of France, now had considerable problems of her own. Early in October Hailes told the foreign secretary complacently that England could congratulate herself on the prospect of France being weakened by internal troubles for many years to come;[66] but within a few weeks the reasons for his complacency were swept away. By the first week in November, just as the English were celebrating the centenary of their Glorious Revolution in 1688, it became known that George III was seriously ill. By the time parliament met on 5 December it was common knowledge that the illness had affected the brain and that the king was no longer capable of carrying out the functions of monarchy. Even in London it was difficult to reconcile conflicting reports and to find out exactly what was happening; for observers in France it was almost impossible. Thomas Coutts, an English banker in Paris, gave a ball to celebrate the king's recovery, only to find that in fact the royal malady was worse and malicious tongues were accusing him of celebrating prematurely the accession of the Prince of Wales to power.[67] Charles Fox, a politician whom the French had always regarded with a kind of fascinated horror, rushed back through France from his Italian holiday in order to help his master the prince to become regent. Louis XVI and Marie Antoinette asked Dorset to convey to the English government their solicitude and concern: whatever they may have felt about the political and diplomatic implications of the crisis they had had enough experience of intriguing princes to sympathize with the afflicted king and with his ministers.[68] For the rest, the French seemed to take it for granted that the prince would become regent

[65] *Discours prononcé par l'un de MM. les secrétaires de la noblesse . . . à l'assemblée de Dijon*, Dijon, 1788, p. 1. For events in Dauphiné see J. Egret, *La Révolution des Notables: Mounier et les Monarchiens, 1789*, 1950, pp. 7–49; and on Brittany the same author's 'Les Origines de la Révolution en Bretagne 1788–89', *R.H.* ccxiii, 1955, pp. 189–215. (English version in Kaplow, *New Perspectives*, pp. 136–52.)
[66] Browning, ii, 107–8.
[67] E. H. Coleridge, *The life of Thomas Coutts*, 2 vols, 1920, i, 262.
[68] Browning, ii, 112, 166.

and that Fox would take up again the sinister designs he had been
forced to abandon in 1783. As late as February 1789, when in fact
the crisis was over and the king restored to his senses again, anec-
dotes were still circulating in Paris about the prince's behaviour
now that he was regent.[69]

But the real significance of the regency crisis lay not just in
personalities, nor even in the sudden threat of political instability
in England on a scale comparable to that which already existed
in France. It lay in the fact that the fundamental weaknesses of
the British constitution were brought to light just at the crucial
moment, the moment when the French were debating whether
or not they should copy it. In spite of the years of anglophobia,
in spite of the commercialism and capitalism which many Frenchmen saw as the inevitable and unenviable accompaniment of
English parliamentary politics, there was still a residuum of real
regard in France for the freedom of the English. Although the
Cahiers de Doléances disagreed about many things, they did agree
on the need to secure in France those same liberties of the subject
which were so jealously guarded in England.[70] And while
ordinary Frenchmen saw England as a model of civil liberty,
many influential politicians saw her as a model of sound government as well—a country which, for all her faults, was able to
make proper use of the representative system and the broadly
based structure of government credit which it made possible.
Having arrived at the moment of truth in her own constitutional
development, France needed some point of reference, some existing pattern against which to measure her own achievements and
her own shortcomings. Before the critical winter of 1788–89 such
a pattern could still have been found in England; but what had
the English to say to the French now, now that their own
constitution had been shown to be so lamentably insufficient? Fox
had said that the prince had an imprescriptible hereditary right
to the regency, while Pitt had insisted that a regency could only
be set up on terms agreed by parliament. And nobody could say
which of them was right, because the constitution was silent upon
the point. Worse still, the Irish parliament in Dublin had supported
the prince's claim while the English parliament in Westminster
had rejected it: what would have happened to the constitutional

[69] Lescure, ii, 333. For later and even more exaggerated ideas on the
Prince's powers and principles see *ibid.*, ii, 524, 632.
[70] B. Hyslop, *French Nationalism in 1789 according to the General
Cahiers*, New York, 1934, pp. 92, 110, 171.

relationship between the two countries if the king had not recovered? As well as returning ambiguous answers to the central questions of sovereignty and succession, the much vaunted British constitution had returned no answer at all to vital questions about the relationship of one part of the empire with another.[71] As Sir Nathaniel Wraxall saw, the year 1789 was a moment of truth for the English as well as the French. Neither country was able to face its own dilemma without invoking, distorting and finally rejecting the things which the other had to teach it.

[71] See J. W. Derry, *The Regency Crisis and the Whigs*, Cambridge, 1963.

10 *The politics of chauvinism*

On midsummer day 1789, just as John Byng was painting his sombre picture of the impending English revolution, George III set off from Windsor to take a seaside holiday at Weymouth. At almost every stage the royal journey was marked by demonstrations of popular loyalty and affection for the king whose miraculous restoration to health seemed to have saved his country from political and civil strife. London had already shown its devotion to the king at a solemn service of thanksgiving at St Paul's Cathedral on 23 April, St George's Day; and now it was the turn of the countryside. Fanny Burney, travelling with the royal party as lady in waiting to the queen, saw 'faces all glee and delight' all along the roadside. Although the weather was dull and rainy the crowds grew bigger and more enthusiastic until at Winchester the whole city seemed to be out in the streets. At Romsey, where 'a band of musicians in common brown coarse cloth and red neckcloths, and even in carters' loose gowns, made a chorus of "God Save the King" ', the popular acclaim was such that it brought a lump to Fanny's throat.[1] There had been times

[1] *Diary and Letters of Madame d'Arblay*, iv, 290.

during the previous twenty-nine years when the politicians had succeeded in portraying the king as a malevolent tyrant, but now all this was forgotten. George III had at long last won that place in popular esteem which he had always thought he deserved, as the saviour of the constitution of 1688 from the wicked designs of factious men. For nearly three decades he had emulated the illustrious William III, encouraging his ministers to stand firm against party politics and to seek the support of the nation as a whole rather than of a mere majority in the House of Commons. And now at last he had succeeded: the alliance of Patriot king and Patriot minister, which had broken in the hands of Pitt the father, seemed now to have been realized with the help of Pitt the son. The constitution of 1688, for so long obscured by party politics, could now shine forth in all its splendour. Even Byng himself, for all his fears, was caught up in the general feeling that the centenary of the 1688 revolution would be marked by a return to its original principles.[2] It was regeneration, and not merely commemoration, that was in the air in the spring of 1789 as the English turned their attention to those centenary celebrations which had had to be shelved during the king's illness.

This mood was reflected in the even greater sense of national regeneration which marked the opening of the Estates General in France. The solemn and splendid scene at Versailles on 4 May 1789, when Louis XVI led the deputies in a service of dedication and consecration at the church of Saint Louis, gave rise to emotional outbursts of loyalty as striking as those which had been produced by the service of St Paul's eleven days earlier. Unlike the English, the French were not primarily concerned to give thanks for the preservation of their king—though they might well have done, for some weeks earlier Louis had been on the point of falling some forty feet from an unsecured ladder when a workman caught him in his arms and thus made a contribution of no little significance to the history of France and of the world.[3] But in both countries the safety of the king and the safety of his realm were still seen as inseparable: the impassioned cries of 'God Save the King!' and of 'Vive le Roi!' voiced something more than a devotion to the person of the monarch. They voiced hopes for the nation as a whole, hopes which could only be realized if the divisive forces which threatened both countries could be thwarted.

[2] See below, pp. 254, 256.
[3] Browning, ii, 183.

Just as those who cheered George III were celebrating the defeat of a factious opposition, so those who cheered Louis XVI were resolving to stand firm against the forces of faction within France. The marquis de Ferrières, who was sent into an ecstasy of patriotic loyalty by the magnificence of the occasion, took a solemn vow to dedicate himself to the overthrow of those sinister intriguers whose factiousness and self-seeking threatened to shatter the unity and dim the glory of his beloved France.[4] At the centre of all the enthusiasm of the spring of 1789 there stood the old myth of patriotism, newly resurrected after its apparent dissolution in the 1770s. While English publicists wrote that 'patriotism herself rises from her seat to pay the tribute of obeisance'[5] to Pitt's handling of the regency crisis, in France men began to speak of a *Parti Patriote* which would defend the French nation as a whole against the intrigues of particular interests or factious politicians.

Unfortunately the myth was as insubstantial now as it had been in the 1760s. John Byng, struck by the contrast between the glories of the 1688 revolution and the iniquities of contemporary politics, thought that all would be well if only the right people could get into parliament. Instead of the government being under the surveillance of honest and independent men who understood the social problems of the country, it was faced only with an opposition party that was as corrupt as the ministerial party itself. He was especially scathing about the tendency of the Whigs to worry more about Negro slaves and Indian princesses than about the plight of the English farm labourer.[6] In his view cant of this sort was all the more despicable now that the disputes over the regency had revealed the blatant ambitions which it had sought to cloak. Nor had the ambitious been abandoned now that the king's recovery had been announced: opposition politicians still talked darkly of the queen and her party holding the king in subjection in order to rob the Prince of Wales of his rights. As late as September 1789 one of the prince's followers said that George III was being 'carried about in a state of idiocy'.[7] But it was no good pretending that the independent men with their Patriot ideals could somehow sweep all this away. For the

[4] C. E. de Ferrières, *Correspondance inédite* 1789–91, ed. H. Carré, 1932, p. 43.
[5] Cited Derry, *Regency Crisis and Whigs*, p. 24.
[6] *Torrington Diaries*, ii, 108.
[7] Burke, *Correspondence*, vi, 27.

independent men took their stand firmly on amateurism in politics; amateurism in politics perpetuated the patronage structure; the patronage structure divided men into officeholders and officeseekers; and officeseekers would always cling to the heir to the throne as surely as officeholders clung to the reigning monarch. It was new life, rather than new truth, that had been breathed into the Patriot myth during the 1780s.

In France the position was even worse. The expectations which were being built upon the Patriot myth were far greater than they had been in the 1760s, and yet the amount of truth it contained was if anything less than it had been then. In the 1760s the marquis de Mirabeau and his followers had been able to write pityingly of the 'constant civil war' that existed in England between landowners, government creditors, industrialists and merchants;[8] but now they had less reason to pity their neighbours and more reason to pity themselves, for such divisions had become an inescapable part of French life and politics too. Sieyès and his fellow enthusiasts liked to declare that the Third Estate, the vast majority of the French nation, was united in a patriotic determination to end the rule of the 'privileged classes'; but the harsh truth was that these Patriots were themselves deeply divided over the vital question of the repayment or repudiation of the national debt. For many years French writers had pointed out how in England the development of a credit structure and the foundation of the Bank of England had divided the political nation far more sharply and far more dangerously than feudalism divided more traditional societies. Now they had to face the fact that similar things had come to pass in France since the financial manipulations of Necker and Calonne. The voice of the French nation could no more drown the articulate minority of government creditors in the Estates General than the voice of the English nation could drown the articulate minority of ambitious politicians in the parliament at Westminster.

The optimism of 1789 was confident enough to ignore these considerations, especially in France, because it was thinking in terms much wider than those of traditional patriotism. There were idealists in the Estates General for whom talk of national regeneration was not enough: in their view it was as parochial and as self-destructive to speak only of the good of France as it had been for the Burgundian nobility to speak only of the good of

[8] *Ephémérides du Citoyen*, iv, April 1767, pp. 194–5.

Burgundy. Lafayette, who had for several years kept a copy of the American Declaration of Independence in one half of a double frame in his study, was by this time thinking of filling the other half with something much grander than a declaration of the new-found constitutionalism of the French monarchy. Already the Patriots in Ireland were looking to him for guidance in their efforts to transcend their religious differences; perhaps soon Patriots all over Europe would unite to transcend the differences between their countries as well as the differences within them. Even England, poor deluded England whose revolution of 1688 had led her into a sterile backwater of party conflict, might be persuaded to leave the darkness of insularity for the light of universal truth. Since so many of the shortcomings of patriotism sprang from its chauvinistic nature they might well be purged by an approach which rose above nationalism as surely as it rose above provincialism. It was in this spirit that he was to lay before the deputies in July his draft for a *European Declaration of the Rights of Men and Citizens*, a document which was to be the Old World's answer to the challenge of the New, a worthy occupant for the other half of his double frame.[9]

There was not much response in England to Lafayette's visionary schemes: if fear of France had receded since 1787, so had admiration for her. The English were too busy worshipping the constitutional wisdom of their ancestors to interest themselves in the wisdom of what went on across the Channel. Even those who reacted against the atmosphere of national self-congratulation were still embedded deep in their habitual insularity. One of the supporters of Henry Beaufoy's Revolution Commemoration Bill did get as far as saying in the House of Commons that the measure 'would operate as a stimulus to our neighbours in their struggle for liberty'; but a more typical attitude to the centenary celebrations was that of Byng himself, who noted with approval a centenary ode which claimed to 'pity nations round, fast in chains of slavery bound'.[10] If the French really wanted recruits in England they would have to look for them among those who imagined that they felt the chains of slavery heavy upon them even in England.

Such people did indeed exist and they were for the most part the very people whom Byng accused of ruining the country.

[9] Dumont, *Souvenirs*, p. 269.
[10] *Torrington Diaries*, ii, 87.

While he was filling his journals with hostile accounts of the new machinery which was revolutionizing industry, one of the greatest pioneers of that same machinery was smarting under the snubs he had received from those who thought him socially inferior. 'Our landed gentlemen,' wrote James Watt to a friend in France, 'reckon us poor mechanics no better than the slaves who cultivate their vineyards.'[11] In France, on the other hand, Watt and his partner Matthew Boulton found themselves treated with the utmost respect. The French government welcomed them as distinguished visitors, whereas their own government seemed to regard them as unimportant hobbledehoys. 'Mr Boulton set out for London yesterday noon,' Samuel Garbett had written in 1785, when the industrialists were being called before the Board of Trade to give their opinions on questions of economic policy. 'I really will not go to play at Questions and Answers when I see that it's mere parade to give an appearance . . . Messrs. Watt, Reynolds, Wilkinson and Rathbone have knowledge and fortune which their dress don't indicate and therefore will too probably be treated slightly.' Another substantial industrialist, Thomas Walker of Manchester, found that the evidence he gave before the Board was later quoted against him in connection with the Irish trade proposals, although he had understood at the time that it concerned the cotton excise of the previous year. Nor were the opposition politicians any better than their counterparts in government: Charles Fox's xenophobic attack on the Commercial Treaty with France had shown a contemptuous disregard for the industrialists which had been much resented, especially in Manchester.[12]

The closer contacts with France which had been brought about by the Commercial Treaty had also exploded some of the myths about England's much-vaunted religious freedom. Lord Stanhope, moving the repeal of the Test and Corporation Acts in the House of Lords in May 1789, pointed out that by the terms of the treaty English Protestant dissenters would now be guaranteed a greater measure of civil liberty in France than they would enjoy if they

[11] Cited Witt Bowden, *Industrial Society in England towards the end of the eighteenth century*, New York, 1925, p. 155.
[12] Schofield, *Lunar Society*, pp. 237–50; 353; Witt Bowden, 'The influence of the manufacturers on some of the early policies of William Pitt', *Am.H.R.* xxix, 1924, pp. 655–74; *Letter from a Manchester Manufacturer to the Right Honourable Charles James Fox on his Political Opposition to the Commercial Treaty with France*, Manchester, 1787. See also F. Knight, *The Strange Case of Thomas Walker: ten years in the life of a Manchester radical*, 1957.

stayed in England—just as French Catholics who came to England would be in a better position than English Catholics. Sir Henry Hoghton, moving similar proposals in the House of Commons a few days earlier, had also drawn attention to the fact that France's treatment of Protestants was already more liberal in many ways than that of dissenters and Catholics in England.[13] And now, as France stood on the threshold of her great national regeneration, there might well be further reforms which would make England look by comparison like the last refuge of privilege and priest-hood. For Byng the threat of revolution lay in the fact that England was changing too fast, that the ancient rule of squire and parson was being challenged by the impertinence of capi-talists and sectarians; but there were also those who feared that she was not changing fast enough. If England presented an unchanging front to a changing world, if she tried to contain the new age of international capitalism within her traditional framework of landed supremacy and established religion, she might have in the end to break because of her refusal to bend.

Such ideas were not popular among politicians. The opposition Whigs were ready enough to make gestures towards the capitalists or the sectarians as long as it was safe to do so: Burke was anxious that the Prince of Wales should be gracious to Dr Priestley and to the manufacturers of Yorkshire for electoral reasons, but he stood out firmly against further toleration for the dissenters and against further political power for the industrialists.[14] As for admiration of France, response to stimulus from the Estates General, that was even more dangerous in a country still devoutly convinced of its own innate superiority to all foreigners. Only Shelburne, now raised to the new dignity of marquis of Lans-downe, clung still to his earlier role of 'citizen of the world' and patron of the new and radical forces in English society. It was to Lansdowne that Garbett had addressed his letter of 1785 about the Board of Trade's treatment of his friends; and it was to Lansdowne that Henry Beaufoy, author of the Revolution Com-memoration Bill and the attempt to repeal the Test and Corpora-tion Acts, looked as his political leader.[15] Since his resignation in 1783 the newly-created marquis had had ample time to interest

[13] *P.H.* xxviii, 16.
[14] Burke, *Correspondence*, v, 470–2; vi, 14–15, 23–4.
[15] Beaufoy, who had close links with the dissenters, had enlisted himself under Lansdowne's banner from the moment he had decided upon a political career. See *Commons 1754–90*, ii, 72–3.

himself in radical programmes and international affairs, for Pitt's government and Fox's opposition had both been equally careful to avoid any further involvement with him. As far as they were concerned he was a slippery and untrustworthy character, much too fond of using his commitment to measures as an excuse to avoid commitment to men. Oliver Goldsmith's memorable phrase about Burke needs only to be stood on its head in order to serve as an epitaph for Lansdowne: his fellow politicians never forgave him for giving up to mankind what they thought should have been kept for party.

Lansdowne's concern for mankind certainly seemed to have some sort of inverse relationship with his concern for party: the more isolated he became from the party politicians the more deeply he immersed himself in the abstractions of internationalism and radicalism. By 1786 he was telling his intellectual friends in France that he no longer counted for much in politics;[16] and when Etienne Dumont arrived in England early that year to act as tutor to his youngest son, Lansdowne gave up much of his time to him. Dumont was a young Genevese who was in sympathy with the exiles of 1782 and had been recommended to Lansdowne by their English friend Samuel Romilly. Romilly himself was on the fringe of that network of radicals and dissenters that stretched from the Scottish universities and the dissenting academies of the north through the Lunar Society of Birmingham to the intellectuals of London. He had originally come to Lansdowne's notice because of his strong views on criminal law reform; and the two men who had introduced him to the marquis were themselves representative of the wideness of the latter's circle. One was John Baynes, a Cambridge mathematician and Fellow of Trinity, and the other was Benjamin Vaughan, a unitarian merchant who had been a pupil of Priestley at the Warrington Dissenting Academy. Vaughan's political services to Lansdowne ranged from negotiating with the Americans in 1782 to editing a shortlived but very radical political journal, *The Repository*, in 1788. Contributors to *The Repository* included Franklin and Priestley; and Lansdowne got Dumont to approach Mallet du Pan to provide the 'Foreign Intelligence' from Paris. There were articles on the abolition of the slave trade, the reform of the criminal law and other aspects of the radical programme which 'Lord Shelburne's set', as Burke called them contemptuously, were working out. As well as

[16] Norris, *Shelburne and Reform*, p. 277.

abstract arguments there were practical examples: effective use
was made of the proceedings of a court which had fined a man
£5 for half murdering a child and yet had imprisoned for five
years another man whose only crime was to publish articles
against some foreign visitors and against the severity of the penal
code.[17]

One of the most internationally minded of all Lansdowne's
protégés did not, however, contribute to *The Repository*. This
was Jeremy Bentham, who had already spent several years
trying to bring his plan for the universal codification of laws
before the kings and emperors of Europe. Lansdowne had been
his friend and patron for more than seven years, but Lansdowne's
political associates had shown no interest in Bentham's ambitious
manifesto on *The Principles of Morals and Legislation*. Bentham
had tried to get it translated into French and had even visited
Russia in the hope that he might interest Catherine the Great
in it. He returned to England in February 1788, a month after
The Repository had been launched; but he had already rejected
Lansdowne's suggestion that he should serve him as a political
journalist and in any case he was looking to France rather than
to England as the most fruitful field for his activities.[18] By the
beginning of 1789 he had enlisted the help of Dumont in the translation and editing of his manuscrips—a task which the latter was
in the end to make his life's work—and he was sending Mirabeau
tracts on French politics for publication in France. Lansdowne
himself was also becoming more and more absorbed in French
politics and in the possible effects they might have on England.
In January 1789, the month in which he ceased to publish *The
Repository*, he told Bentham that he must continue his efforts to
get a hearing in France because forthcoming events there would
have important and beneficial repercussions all over the world. 'I
have long thought,' he wrote, 'that the people have but one cause
throughout the world. It is sovereigns who have different

---

[17] *Repository*, x (1 June 1788), 72–3.
[18] Bentham himself said later (Add. 33, 553, fo. 26) that his acquaintance
with Lansdowne dated from 1781; but in fact the two men had been in
touch since 1779: see Add. 33, 557, fo. 1; 33, 558, fos 325, 333. On the
politicians' lack of interest in the *Principles* see J. Bentham, *Works*, ed.
Bowring, 11 vols, Edinburgh 1838–45, x, 113, 124, 185 and U.C.L. M.S.S.
clxix, fos 124–5. Bentham's account of his refusal to act as a political
journalist for Lansdowne is in Add. 33, 553, fo. 27. For his attempts to get
a hearing in France see C. Blount, 'Bentham, Dumont and Mirabeau',
U.B.H.J. iii, 1952, pp. 153–67 and J. H. Burns, 'Bentham and the French
Revolution', *T.R.H.S.* 5th series xvi, 1966, pp. 95–114.

interests.' As the date for the opening of the Estates General came nearer he became more excited and more specific. 'I hope when you have given France a legislature,' he wrote to Bentham on 29 March 1789, 'you will suffer nothing to interfere and prevent your pen from enforcing these triumphs.'[19]

Two days after that letter was written Etienne Dumont set out on what was to prove one of the most dramatically abortive of all the missions from England to France during this period. It was completely unofficial and in a sense almost accidental: Dumont was merely a tutor whose employer, a retired politician with scarcely any influence in parliament, had given him leave of absence to go to France on business of his own. That business did not concern England or France but Geneva, where there had been yet another revolution at the end of January and the beginning of February 1789. Dumont had hoped that it would mean the triumphant return of the exiles of 1782, but to his disappointment they had only been allowed back on sufferance and had not been reinstated in their posts. Buoyed up with the internationalism and optimism of the Lansdowne circle, he had conceived the idea that the Estates General of France would right this injustice, that it would be only too glad to reverse the reactionary policy of previous French governments towards Geneva and thus demonstrate at the outset its enlightened attitude not just to France but to the whole of mankind. In the middle of February he had written excitedly to a Genevese friend saying that 'a person of great importance' had agreed to present the case of the Genevese radicals when the Estates General met; and a week later he had written to Lansdowne hinting that he might himself be allowed to go to Versailles to manage the whole business. Permission had been given and on 31 March 1789 Dumont and Duroveray left for France.[20] For a time they stayed with Clavière at his house near Paris, composing a memorandum on Genevese affairs with the help of Etienne-Salomon Reybaz, another of the

[19] Add. 33, 541, fos 1–4, 41–2. (Printed in part in *Works*, ed. Bowring, x 195, 197–8.) By this time Lansdowne saw a *rapprochement* with France, especially with a reformed and progressive France, as the best guarantee of his own return to power. 'I believe he would be a good minister for England with respect to a better agreement with France', wrote Tom Paine to Washington about Lansdowne in March 1789 (*Memoirs, Correspondence and Miscellaneous Papers of Thomas Jefferson*, ed. Randolph, 4 vols, Charlottesville, 1829, ii, 465).

[20] Dumont to Mouchon 16 February 1789, printed in J. Bénétruy, *L'Atelier de Mirabeau*, Geneva, 1962, p. 154; Dumont to Lansdowne, 24 February 1789, Bowood Papers (transcript in C.J.M., no. 18).

exiles of 1782.[21] Then they moved to Paris itself, to watch the elections for the Estates General, and finally on to Versailles in order to take part in the long awaited regeneration of France. They were not Frenchmen, it was true: but who could possibly object to that? They were citizens of the world, bringing with them both the blessings of freedom's traditional home in England and the hopes of its future home in Geneva.

But things were not at all as Dumont and his friends imagined. The visions of a new heaven and a new earth which seemed so bright in Lafayette's study or at Lansdowne's fireside were soon eclipsed by the political and financial realities that appeared when the estates general started to face up to its tasks. In the first place, very few deputies could pretend that those who had elected them had wanted them to busy themselves with schemes for universal perfection. The *Cahiers de Doléances*, lists of grievances which constituencies throughout the country had been required to draw up for the guidance of the government and of their deputies, were on the whole remarkably practical and down to earth in their demands. The very fact that the Government had asked all Frenchmen to state their grievances might well have been expected to produce radical demands even had they not existed before: if anything can reveal latent radicalism it is the deliberate canvassing of a whole nation. But even this challenge, this requirement that they should think up all the grievances they could, produced surprisingly little in the way of revolutionary fervour. The outstanding thing about the *Cahiers* was their conservatism: the great majority of them spoke in terms of an ancient constitution which should be respected rather than of an ideal constitution which should be constructed. There were demands for reforms, especially for an end to the sale of offices, but it was still presumed that these would take place within the existing structure of government. Some of the *Cahiers* of the nobility showed a readiness for change and, in particular, a readiness to give up tax exemptions; but those of the third estate were on the whole more traditionalist. Their grievances were the grievances of a possessing class, anxious to preserve what they had and the means whereby they had acquired it. The guild system, regarded by almost all enlightened thinkers as an obstacle to progress, was sturdily defended. Local complaints, sometimes even the defence of local

[21] *Réclamation des Genevois patriotes établis à Londres contre la nouvelle aristocratie de Genève*, Paris, 1789.

abuses, were constantly given preference over demands for abstract rights or general reforms. If the voice of the *Cahiers* was the voice of France, then it was parochial rather than universalist, specific rather than general, chauvinistic rather than cosmopolitan. Whatever else Frenchmen did or did not want their deputies to do, they certainly did not want them to import the traditional constitutionalism of England, the visionary radicalism of the Lansdowne circle or the Dumont concept of a revolution in foreign policy.[22]

The four Genevese and their friends back in England were not only wrong about the general attitude of the deputies and of those who had elected them; they were also wrong, disastrously wrong, about the specific attitude of the individuals through whom they hoped to work. Mirabeau, the 'person of great importance' whom Dumont had mentioned in his letter of February, needed the assistance of the Genevese, and in particular of Dumont, in order to write his speeches and edit the newspapers which he launched to project his own image; but he seems to have had little genuine interest either in the Genevese revolution or in the visionary schemes with which Bentham and others in the Lansdowne circle now began to bombard him. He wanted to establish an ascendancy in the Estates General in order to force himself into office, which meant that the English theory of a constitutional balance between the ministers of a king and the leaders of a representative assembly suited his book very well: it gave him a position from which he could on the one hand attack his rivals in the ministry as undemocratic and on the other attack his rivals in the assembly as irresponsible. Many other men who hoped to make political capital out of the Estates General had a similar interest in advocating some sort of constitutional balance. Whether or not Orléans himself had designs on his cousin's crown, there were almost certainly men in his *entourage*—including, some said, Mirabeau himself—who saw the Estates as a means whereby they could force the king to dismiss his present advisers and accept an Orléanist administration. They too must preach English constitutionalism in some form or other; but for all of them it was merely a means to an end. It certainly occurred to them that English ideas might serve them, but it did not occur to them that they might serve English ideas. Back at Lansdowne House the eager idealists scanned Dumont's letters (which were more like

[22] Hyslop, *French Nationalism according to the Cahiers, passim.*

the reports of a paid political agent than the jottings of a tutor on holiday) for evidence of a France dedicated to the service of a new and reformed version of English limited monarchy. When they did not find it they invented it, sending back letters of pious encouragement to Dumont and his friends and so contributing to a situation in which English radicalism and French conservatism became unwittingly dedicated to the destruction of themselves and of one another.[23]

The other individual through whom the Genevese hoped to work was Necker. During his previous term of office as controller-general Necker had shown over and over again that he was not prepared to take on the crusades which other people thought he should fight: hopes that he would champion the cause of his fellow Protestants or even his fellow Genevese came to nothing. He was as much dominated by his desire to retain power as Mirabeau was by his desire to seize it; and both men knew exactly which popular movements could be useful to them and which could not. Necker had found it advantageous to support the calling of the Estates General and the doubling of the Third Estate's representation, but this did not mean that he was prepared to back the unpopular constitutionalism of England or the irrelevant radicalism of Geneva. Radical Geneva was, in any case, not his Geneva: his Geneva was the Geneva of the old establishment, the financiers who had subscribed to his loans between 1776 and 1781 and would do so again if he could buttress French government credit with the confidence that sprang from a properly managed representative body. The time might come when he would need the financial backing of the new Geneva as well, so that he had the sense not to be too rude when Clavière and the others pestered him with representations on behalf of the exiles; but he was certainly not going to alienate his financial supporters of the old Geneva for the sake of a vision of universal radicalism propagated by the Lansdowne House intellectuals and their counterparts in France.[24]

[23] Dumont's letters to Romilly during this period are in MSS Dumont 17, fos 21–43. Parts of some of them are printed, together with Romilly's replies, in Romilly, i, 262–97. One very important letter, dated 1–3 June 1789, remained in private hands until it was published as *Lettre inédite d'Etienne Dumont sur quelques séances du Tiers Etat, mai 1789, publiée, avec introduction et notes, par J. M. Paris*, Geneva, 1877. Other relevant letters are in MSS Dumont 33, fos 55–6, 88–9, 95–6; Add. 33, 541, fos 51–2, 53–4, 55–6, 66–7, 79–80, 115–6; *Works*, ed. Bowring, x, 200–1, 212–17.

[24] See J. Martin, *La Polémique Necker–Dumont en 1789 avec documents inédits*, Geneva, 1927.

For the first month of their stay in France Dumont and his friends were what they thought they were: innocents abroad, highminded Genevese Patriots who had little political importance, either intentional or unintentional. Apart from one unpleasant incident when they were recognized as strangers and ejected from one of the primary assemblies in the Paris elections, they did not attract much attention.[25] But as soon as the Estates General opened at the beginning of May they were drawn inexorably into a central position in French politics, a position in which their well-meaning attempts to pursue their high ideals were bound to have unexpected and incalculable repercussions. The first issue which the Estates had to face was the checking of credentials: after a preliminary session, at which Louis and his ministers spoke a little about reform and a lot about money, the deputies were told to examine the returns and make sure everybody had been legally elected. The Third Estate returned next morning to begin this task in the great hall, in which the first session had been held; but the clergy and the nobility went to separate rooms and prepared to verify their own powers independently. The vision of the Estates General as a united assembly of the whole French nation was thus put in jeopardy at the very outset. If it was to be upheld the Third Estate would have to do absolutely nothing: even the act of examining their own credentials might be construed as an admission that they constituted a separate order. And so for six weeks there was deadlock. 'Everything is yet in suspense at the meeting of the States General in France,' the *Gentleman's Magazine* told its readers at the end of May; and a month later there was still nothing to report: 'The Assembly of the States General in France, from which high expectations had been formed, has now [June 22] been assembled forty-eight days, without having advanced a single step towards the grand business for which they were called together.'[26]

English observers found it difficult to sympathize with the policy of deliberate inaction upon which the Third Estate had embarked—it was as if the House of Commons had suddenly

[25] Dumont to Romilly, 28 April 1789, MSS Dumont 17, fo. 22. In his subsequent accounts of the primary assemblies, both in *Groenvelt Letters* (see below, p. 274n) and in *Souvenirs sur Mirabeau*, Dumont carefully concealed the fact that he was ignominiously ejected from the only one he actually attended.

[26] *Gent. Mag.* 1789, pp. 464, 560–1.

decided not to consider petitions about disputed elections until the House of Lords came to sit with them. Dumont himself, though he later pretended that he had always thought the Third Estate was right, had his doubts at the time.[27] He and his friends wanted to get things moving as soon as possible and they also wanted to bring together Mirabeau, the deputy who was supposed to be championing their cause, and Necker, the Genevese minister from whom they had hoped so much. They were worried by a confrontation which seemed to make such cooperation more and more unlikely. And to make matters worse they were receiving angry letters from their friends at Lansdowne House, who could not understand why the reforms upon which they had hoped to advise the French were being held up by what seemed to them a mere technicality. Both Bentham and Romilly were at work on manuals of parliamentary procedure, intended to give the French the benefit of English experience and English ideas on this matter, and they saw the delay over verification as further evidence of the need for their services. George Wilson, a friend of both men who was collaborating in the papers compiled for the edification of the French, was depressed by the truculence of the deputies in general and of Mirabeau in particular. 'As for Mirabeau,' he wrote to Bentham on 21 May, 'he is, I fear, an incorrigible blackguard and also very deficient in common sense.'[28]

By this time the Genevese were beginning to think that the achievement of their own aims and of those of their intellectual friends in England depended on wooing Mirabeau out of his truculence. He was essentially an isolated figure, a man without a party who had been rejected by his fellow noblemen—with the result that he had had to secure election as a deputy for the Third Estate—and was now widely distrusted by his fellow deputies, whom he had publicly described as a bunch of over-excited schoolboys.[29] But he was also tremendously forceful, a man who could not be ignored and who might yet come to control the situation if he could be persuaded to behave more sensibly and more tactfully. Towards the end of May Dumont decided to take him in hand: he walked him round and round the Trianon gardens and after a lengthy conversation he got him to agree to

[27] On 22 May Dumont asked Romilly if he did not think it would be better if the assembly was divided into two chambers, like the Lords and Commons in England: MSS Dumont 17, fo 27.
[28] Add. 33, 541, fos 51–2.
[29] Dumont, *Souvenirs*, p. 59.

take a more moderate attitude, both towards the deputies and towards the ministry. On 28 May, when Mirabeau adopted a surprisingly accommodating approach towards Necker's plan to end the deadlock between the orders, Dumont had reason to think that he had succeeded in taming Mirabeau and in reconciling him and Necker. Early in June Lansdowne and Romilly both received letters from Versailles to this effect. Within a few days, Dumont prophesied, Mirabeau would propose that the deputies should assure Louis publicly of their support for Necker. Then all would be well, Necker would 'become the Richelieu of the court in order to become the saviour of the people' and Dumont himself would be back in England within a fortnight or so.[30]

Never was confidence so lamentably misplaced. Mirabeau was by this time so dependent on Dumont's services as an unpaid editor for his newspaper and an unacknowledged writer of his speeches that he could not risk offending him unnecessarily. He therefore listened patiently to the homily in the Trianon gardens, but this did not mean that he would act on it unless it was in his interests to do so. He had other associates as well as the Genevese, associates who were pushing him in very different directions. Quite apart from his links with the Orléanists, which he took care to conceal from Dumont, there were his subsequent attempts to get on to terms with Lafayette, Provence and other possible members of a future administration. He was primarily concerned to replace Necker, not to assist him. Even his identification with the party of the government creditors, his determination to avoid a bankruptcy at all costs, did not mean that he was committed to any particular financier, be it Necker on the one hand or Clavière on the other. One of the things which irritated the Genevese about Mirabeau was his admiration for the marquis de Casaux, an eccentric friend of his father's who had some odd ideas about the English constitution and some even odder ideas about the acceptability of government bankruptcies.[31] They could not understand how the younger Mirabeau could still listen to these rusty old prejudices of his father's generation. They failed to see that the key to Mirabeau's character was his ambivalent attitude to his father and to everything his father stood for: no man could have become so emotionally involved in rebellion against his father

---

[30] *Ibid.*, pp. 59–60; Bowood Papers (transcript C.J.M. no. 22); *Lettre inédite d'Etienne Dumont*, p. 23.
[31] Dumont, *Souvenirs*, p. 103.

unless he had, at some level of consciousness, a desperate need for
paternal love and approval.

The ambivalence of Mirabeau's attitude made itself apparent
early in June, when Duroveray and Dumont took the next step
in their campaign by arranging a meeting between Mirabeau and
Necker. During the preliminary talks that led up to this interview
Mirabeau showed that he stood where his father would have
wished him to stand: he declared most vehemently that he would
defend the French monarchy with all his powers against the
'democratic invasion' with which it was threatened. But the meeting itself was a disaster. Necker seems to have behaved in a rather
pompous and condescending fashion—he may possibly have
thought, as one of the intermediaries certainly did, that Mirabeau
had simply come to sell himself to the government—and all
Mirabeau's aristocratic pride was aroused at being treated in this
way by an upstart Genevese financier. When Necker asked him
rather distantly whether he had a proposition to put to him he
replied that 'my proposition is to bid you good morning', and
stormed out of the room.[32] From that day onwards it was clear
that Mirabeau could now do little for Geneva, whatever he might
still be able to do for the English intellectuals who imagined he
was their spokesman, or for the French revolutionaries who
imagined he was their supporter.

The real danger was that his association with the English
intellectuals was beginning to jeopardize his chances of acceptance
among the French revolutionaries. Six weeks of impotence and
frustration had by this time discouraged the moderates in the
Third Estate and inflamed the extremists: men who might have
been content to get on with the practical business of the Estates
General had been turned by their enforced idleness into dreamers
of dreams and pedlars of slogans. By the middle of June, while
Mirabeau and his Genevese friends were still discussing the best
way of imposing English constitutional principles on the estates,
the radical members of the Third Estate were preparing to brush
aside ideas of constitutional balance and carry through a *coup
d'état*. Sieyès, who had always had the utmost contempt for the
English constitution, proposed that the discussions with the other
orders should be cut short and that the Third Estate should pro-
ceed to the examination of the electoral returns. On the same day,
11 June, Duroveray was violently attacked in the assembly, as a

[32] *Ibid*., p. 61; P. V. de Malouet, *Mémoires*, 2 vols, 1874, i, 276–82.

corrupt agent of the English government who had no right to sit with the representatives of the French nation. Mirabeau, who was apparently in the very act of receiving notes from Duroveray when the attack took place, managed to defend him and win the assembly over.[33] Dumont, who was impressed by Mirabeau's eloquence on this occasion, thought that their enemies had been silenced. But in fact he himself was even more vulnerable than Duroveray, since Lansdowne was paying him not with a salary but with a government sinecure; and he was in due course to be attacked equally viciously by the anglophobes.

Mirabeau's attempt to regain control of the situation foundered, like almost everything he did from this time onwards, because of the widespread suspicion that he was trying to foist English ideas and English practices on France. His proposed declaration of intent, aimed at protecting the prerogatives of the king and the existence of the three orders, was swept aside on 15 June; and two days later, when the assembly came at last to deciding what it should call itself now that it was going to recognize its own separate existence, his unpopularity proved decisive. Various attempts had been made to find a name which would respect the obviously conservative intentions of the *Cahiers* while at the same time rejecting any idea that the Estates General consisted of three separate orders debating independently. Sieyès had proposed 'Assembly of the known and verified representatives of the French nation', which had been countered by Mounier's more cautious but somewhat cumbersome formula 'Legitimate assembly of the representatives of the majority of the French nation acting in the absence of the minority'. Mirabeau suggested that they should call themselves simply 'The representatives of the French people' —a title which was triumphantly ambiguous and tactically irreproachable, since it could not be construed either as an assertion of unjustifiable claims or as a retreat from their present position. Ingenious though the suggestion was, it was attacked violently as an attempt to import into France the servile distinctions of England: Mirabeau's English friends might call themselves 'the people' or 'the commoners' as distinct from the nobility,

[33] The fullest account of this incident is in J. A. Creuzé–Latouche, *Journal des Etats-Généraux*, ed. J. Marchand, 1946, pp. 97–8. Mirabeau published the story, with a report of his own speech, in *Lettres à ses Commettants*, x, 13–24, Duroveray had indeed been given an English pension, of £300 a year, to console him for the failure of the plan to settle the Genevese exiles in Ireland. See also *H.M.C.* 24 *Rutland*, p. 130.

but proud Frenchmen would never do the same. Mirabeau vainly
tried to point out that the French were putting their own
construction on the word, that they were barking not at the
English but at their own reflection in the mirror of England. If
the French wanted to escape from their feudal servility they must
learn to use the word 'people' as proudly as the English already
did. His arguments were worse than useless: so far from reconciling the two extremes and promoting moderation, he only
succeeded in goading the assembly into an even more radical
decision. All three proposals were set aside and it was decided by
491 votes to 90 to adopt the title of 'The National Assembly'.[34]

This was a revolutionary act, even though it was not as yet a
revolution. By calling themselves the National Assembly the
members of the Third Estate had destroyed not just the form of
the Estates General, the division into the three orders, but the very
existence of the Estates General. They had usurped the prerogatives of the king and had called into existence a new and hitherto
unknown body to replace the one which Louis had summoned.
They had also rejected, significantly enough, any title which
contained the word 'representatives'. Even while spurning the
English they had taken a leaf out of the English parliament's book
and had claimed to act not as particular delegates obeying specific
instructions but as an embodiment of the national will, a 'grand
inquest of the nation' as the men at Westminster would have
called it. And in doing so they had put themselves in the same
dangerous position as the Whigs had been in five and a half years
earlier: if the king and his ministers could prove, as George III
and Pitt had proved in December 1783, that the sense of the nation
was on their side and not on the side of the majority in the
assembly, then the leaders of that majority might be destroyed
as Fox and North had been destroyed.

It was Mirabeau himself who saw the parallel most clearly and
who developed it later in his forceful speech of 16 July. In the
meantime other men, as conservative as he was but rather less
concerned with English politics, assumed that the king must now
dissolve the Estates—since some members of it had so clearly
ignored the instructions of their constituents—and summon a new
one. He must in fact 'go to the country' as the English would
have said.[35] But this was mere wishful thinking: it might make

[34] Dumont, *Souvenirs*, pp. 69–73.
[35] Malouet, *Mémoires*, i, 283ff.; Ferrières, *Correspondance*, p. 73.

sense politically but it made nonsense financially. Government credit, already wilting after the delays and the disagreements of the past few weeks, would collapse altogether if the estates were dissolved. The king's ministers knew this and most of the leaders in the newly created National Assembly knew it as well, especially as they had also declared on 17 June that taxes could only be legally collected as long as the assembly remained in session. There was no doubt that the king must make some response to the assembly's challenge—'if he did not', said Dorset, 'it will be little short of laying his crown at their feet'[36]—and that his response must repudiate their claim to speak for the nation whose representatives they declined to be. But there simply was not time for the response to take the form of an appeal to the people through fresh elections. In the last resort there was always the army: a few months earlier Dorset had told his government that it would be impossible for the French to assemble a large force that year because of all the new regulations that still had to be sorted out, but now he thought that the army might after all be effective because it was 'entirely devoted to the royal authority'.[37] But even a military *coup* against the assembly would take time to prepare. In the meantime something must be done quickly to regain the initiative for the king.

A fortnight earlier Louis's eldest son had died at the age of seven after a tragic and debilitating illness. Both the king and the queen were still overwhelmed by grief and were in no condition to deal coolly with affairs of state. When the royal council met on 19 June the king accepted a plan, put forward originally by Necker, for a special royal session of the Estates at which the king was to annul the proceedings of 17 June and then impose by his own authority a compromise settlement over the issue of separate or joint debating. The next day Necker had second thoughts and told Louis that the person who was advising him, and whose identity was a secret known only to Necker himself and to the king, now favoured a simple letter of invitation to the three orders instead. But it was too late: the assembly had already found itself excluded from its meeting place because of the preparation for the royal session and had assumed that it was about to be dissolved. The deputies were roused to new heights of revolutionary fervour by this apparent threat and they

---

[36] Browning, ii, 217.
[37] *Ibid.*, ii, 161, 217.

gathered in a nearby tennis court to take their historic oath never to separate until they had given France a constitution. When the council met again the news of this fresh act of defiance stiffened its resolve to squash the pretensions of the Third Estate. Louis was almost certainly influenced by the queen, who interrupted the council meeting to plead with him to take a strong line. Before the dauphin's death he might have told her not to meddle; now he was unable to do so. The royal session went ahead and the illegal actions of the Third Estate were duly annulled by authority of the king; but Necker's original proposals for a compromise declaration were dropped and Necker himself was not present. Instead the king personally told the assembled deputies that he was going to uphold the existing constitution, including the distinction between the three orders, and that if they would not help him he would carry on alone, since the *Cahiers* showed clearly that his intentions were in accord with the wishes of the greater part of the nation. It seemed that the days of hesitation and indecision were over and that France had a king at last.[38]

But in fact the royal session of 23 June was to usher in the destruction, rather than the restoration, of Louis's authority. He ended his speech by ordering the deputies to disperse and meet again the next day in their three separate rooms; but the Third Estate, together with some deputies from the clergy who had joined them over the past few days, ignored the command and continued in session after the king and his retinue had left. A visit from the king's master of ceremonies failed to budge them and Louis shrank from ejecting them by armed force. He therefore had to stand by while they made nonsense of his fine words and asserted once again, this time in even stronger language and with even firmer guarantees, the *de facto* existence of a National Assembly rather than an Estates General. After four days of tension, during which more and more deputies from the clergy and even from the nobility joined the assembly, Louis gave in and formally requested the first two orders to unite with the third estate and form one single assembly, 'in order to bring about more speedily the fulfilment of my fatherly good intentions'.[39]

Behind the scenes a less benevolent and more draconian form of parental discipline was being prepared. In public the king welcomed Necker back into favour and followed the policy of

[38] Roberts, *Documents*, pp. 109–23.
[39] *Ibid.*, p. 123.

co-operation with the assembly which his reinstatement implied; but in private there were frantic consultations with the army commanders to see whether it would be possible to subjugate by military force the assembly and its increasingly vociferous supporters in the streets of Versailles and Paris. Troops were concentrated in areas from which they could march on the capital and on 11 July Necker was suddenly dismissed and sent into exile. A new administration was set up under Calonne's old enemy Breteuil and under the maréchal de Broglie, commander-in-chief of the army. The royal troops began to close in around Paris and in the face of this threat the Parisians set up a provisional government and began to organize the defence of the capital. There was very little actual fighting, but what little there was had two dramatic results. In the first place it showed clearly that the troops could not be relied upon and in the second it brought about, on 14 July 1789, the fall of the Bastille. The storming of this ancient fortress prison was the result of a strange series of mistakes and misunderstandings; but once it had happened it provided a striking symbol of the triumph of ordinary citizens over the dark forces of arbitrary power. Back in the palace of Versailles Louis XVI abandoned, at any rate for the time being, his well meaning but rather querulous attempts to wield that arbitrary power. He dispersed the troops, recalled Necker and made his peace as best he could with the assembly and with the provisional government of Paris. 'The greatest revolution that we know anything of,' wrote Dorset to his government on 16 July, 'has been effected with, comparatively speaking, if the magnitude of the event is considered, the loss of very few lives: from this moment we may consider France as a free country; the king a very limited monarch and the nobility as reduced to a level with the rest of the nation.'[40]

While Dorset was relating the story of the French revolution to his superiors in England, Mirabeau was making yet another desperate attempt to assert the relevance of England to the French revolution. Over the past month he had managed fairly successfully to keep himself in the public eye and to live down his reputation as an anglophile reactionary. It was Mirabeau who defied the king's master of ceremonies on 23 June and it was Mirabeau who spoke most vehemently, during the tense days just before the dismissal of Necker, against the growing troop con-

[40] Browning, ii, 243.

centrations around Paris.[41] But there were still the old suspicions about the machinations of his Genevese friends. Surprisingly enough, these suspicions seem to have had some slight degree of justification, at least with regard to the crucial events between the 17th and the 23rd of June. Dumont subsequently stated quite categorically that Duroveray was the secret adviser who suggested the idea of a royal session to Necker and that he deliberately kept Mirabeau in the dark about his contacts with the ministry. At the time Dumont himself clearly knew more about the government's plans than would have been possible for a complete outsider. He told Romilly on 21 June that the Tennis Court Oath was a piece of hysterical folly: the deputies ought to have waited to see what the king's plans were before they made this ridiculous gesture 'against the king and against the nation'.[42] As to whether the Genevese themselves were acting 'against the king and against the nation', whether they were serving sinister ends of their own rather than the good of France as they saw it, this was a difficult question. Clavière the financier was probably more concerned with averting bankruptcy than with securing national liberty; but then so were many Frenchmen, inside the assembly as well as outside it. Duroveray the Genevese politician was probably anxious to maintain Necker in power, since neither a seizure of power by the assembly nor a royalist counter-revolution could be expected to do Geneva much good. But others as well as the Genevese wanted to seek the middle path which Necker seemed to represent between rebellion and reaction. As for Reybaz, he does not seem to have had any political axe to grind. Only Dumont, with his passionate and high-minded desire to use France as a guinea-pig for the constitution-building experiments of his friends at Lansdowne House, was following a line with which most Frenchmen were totally out of sympathy. Ironically enough, it was the most innocent of the four innocents abroad who was potentially the most dangerous.

This did not mean that he was a conspirator, even though his subsequent writings about this period of his life showed all the deviousness and inconsistency of the genuine conspirator.[43] What

[41] *Gazette Nationale ou Moniteur Universelle*, no. 10 (20 au 24 juin) p. 48; no. 15 (6 au 8 juillet) p. 68; no. 16 (8 au 10 juillet) p. 69.

[42] Dumont, *Souvenirs*, pp. 74–9; MSS Dumont 17, fos 29–31.

[43] When he wrote the *Souvenirs*, in 1799, Dumont was concerned on the one hand to disprove French charges that he had been part of a counter-

it did mean was that he was a powerful force working in exactly the opposite direction to that which he intended. He was a kind of burning glass, focusing the rays of anglophobia with devastating effect upon the hapless Mirabeau. Quite apart from Mirabeau's newspaper, the *Courrier de Provence,* which under Dumont's editorship advocated English constitutional theories and printed articles by English writers, there were constant references to England's achievements in the speeches Dumont prepared for Mirabeau to deliver in the assembly. Works by members of the Lansdowne House group were always being brought to Mirabeau's notice and it was one of these, an account by Romilly of English parliamentary procedure, that Mirabeau finally agreed to put before a committee of the assembly. The result was disastrous. 'We want nothing that is English,' shouted one deputy angrily, 'we have no need to imitate anybody.'[44]

revolutionary Anglo-Genevese conspiracy and on the other to allay English suspicions that he had been a rabid revolutionary. The result was a certain amount of intentional vagueness (he was quite unjustified, for instance, in pretending that he had to rely on memory and had little documentary evidence of his opinions and actions in 1789) and some glaring discrepancies, particularly as regards the events of May and June. These can be seen by comparing the *Souvenirs* with his letters of 1789, in MSS Dumont 17, 35 and in the Bowood Papers and also with MSS Dumont 8, 21, 35 and 45, all of which contain material relevant to his contribution to the *Groenvelt Letters,* which he and Romilly published in 1792. These too contained some distortions of the truth: the imaginary German traveller Henry Frederick Groenvelt was supposed to have watched the French revolution and then to have come to England, finding to his horror that many revolutionary changes were needed there also. Thus his account of events in France (written by Dumont) had to fit in with his account of abuses in England (written by Romilly). There is some truth in E. Halévy's remark (*The Growth of Philosophic Radicalism,* tr. M. Morris, 1928, p. 179) that *Groenvelt* was the first Benthamite book to appear; but it should also be pointed out that Benthamism itself was partly the product of the interaction between the Lansdowne group and the French revolution.

[44] Dumont recounted the incident later in his introduction to Bentham's *Tactics* (*Tactique des Assemblées Legislatives,* 2 vols, Geneva, 1816, i, 20). In the autumn of 1788 the Comte de Sarsfeld had asked Romilly to send him an account of English parliamentary procedure: Romilly had found to his surprise that no such account existed and had therefore written one himself. Sarsfeld received it in May 1789 but was too ill to translate it (he died at the end of the month) so that it was passed, via La Rochefoucauld, to Dumont and Mirabeau. It eventually appeared as *Règlements observées dans la chambre de Communes . . . mis au jour par le comte de Mirabeau,* 1789. It is clear from letters that passed between Bentham and other members of the Lansdowne group at the time Add. 33, 541, fos 51–2; MSS Dumont 33, fos 55–6; *Works,* ed. Bowring, x, 213–14) that the *Tactics* and the *Règlements* were the product of joint discussions and that the author of each had a part in the other—indeed, by 1791 Romilly was writing to Bentham about 'my part of the *Tactics*' Add. 33, 541, fos 292–3). As in the case of *Groenvelt,* it is important to remember that Bentham owed as much to the other members of the group as they owed to him.

K

It was imitation of the English king rather than the English parliament that Mirabeau seemed to counsel in his speech of 16 July, perhaps the most significant of all his anglophile utterances in the assembly. The deputies were trying to decide whether they should ask the king, in the name of the nation, to recall Necker; and this led Mirabeau to rhapsodize in general terms about the voice of the people and in more specific terms about the way in which the English constitution ensured that this voice would always be obeyed. He pointed out that in December 1783, when Fox and North had tried to ignore the voice of the people, George III had stepped in to restore the balance and defeat 'the aristocracy of the legislative'. Under the English constitution, claimed Mirabeau, the representatives of the people had almost supreme power as long as they respected the will of the nation but were reduced to mere impotent pygmies when they sought to promote instead their own selfish and partial interests. He buttressed his arguments with a scornful attack on those deputies —and there had been many during the past few weeks—who thought that their sudden emergence into freedom gave them the right to dismiss English constitutionalism as a spent force. 'England flourishes still,' he declared solemnly, 'for the eternal instruction of the world.'[45]

Mirabeau's basic theme was harmless enough, a mere restatement of the pious Patriot belief that honest independent men who stood for the whole nation could somehow be distinguished from dishonest rogues who worked only for their own ends. But in the context of July 1789 this particular variation was a dangerous one. Deputies who were already uncomfortably aware of the gulf between what they had done and what their *Cahiers* had told them to do were not going to be made any more comfortable by hearing that under a proper constitution the king would be able to appeal to the nation over their heads. They preferred to believe that the Parisian uprising, together with the growing unrest in the country as a whole, meant that the nation was solidly behind them and that the king's only possible function was to support them and not to supplant them. They were in no mood to be lectured by Mirabeau about the need for a royal veto or a balanced constitution. To them the theory of counterpoise was merely a theory of counter revolution, an affront to the majesty

[45] *Moniteur*, no. 19 (15 au 16 juillet) p. 84.

of the French nation which was so clearly revealing its faith in them.

The French nation's act of self-revelation was as closely involved with England and anglophobia as were the constitutional issues which it raised. The *Gentleman's Magazine* for July 1789 stated complacently in its report from France that 'all parties seemed happy and contented and the English constitution had all the appearance of being soon established'; but it also recorded, apparently without any sense of incongruity, that English manufacturers in Rouen were being attacked by rioters and that their looms were being taken out and burnt.[46] Industrial recession and unemployment, one of the basic causes of unrest in France, was already widely attributed to the malign influence of England operating by means of the Commercial Treaty; and the other chief cause, hunger, was soon to be associated in the popular mind with the same dark forces. Ever since the great storms of 1788, when crops had been flattened by hailstones so monstrous that they killed hares and partridges and tore branches from the trees,[47] France had faced an increasingly serious food shortage; and things had been made worse during the ensuing winter by a ferocious frost which had lasted for several weeks and had left behind it catastrophic floods in many parts of the country. Bread prices had risen remorselessly until on the eve of the Estates General men lucky enough to be in work had had to spend the bulk of their wages on the bare minimum needed to keep their families alive. Those out of work had only been saved from starvation by the efforts of private charities and of the government, which set up charity workshops in many areas. The presence of several of these in the environs of Paris, crammed with thousands of embittered men and women, had done nothing to reassure those responsible for law and order in the city. Necker had warned that the grain shortage might lead to a serious insurrection, but at the same time he had disarmed criticism by pointing out that his connections with England meant that he could always get corn from that source in an emergency.[48]

At the end of June 1789 the French government decided that it was time to act on Necker's suggestion. Pitt's administration

---

[46] *Gent. Mag.*, 1789, pp. 656, 661.
[47] There is a vivid account of the great storm in T. Blaikie, *Diary of a Scottish Gardener at the French Court*, ed. F. Birrell, 1931, pp. 215–16.
[48] Browning, ii, 124–5.

was formally requested to waive the export regulations in order
to allow France to buy 20,000 sacks of corn on the English market.
Instead of complying with the request on his own authority Pitt
referred it to the House of Commons, where there took place on
6 July an astonishingly pharisaical debate. One member thought
that while France was undoubtedly 'expiating her sins, for her
interference in America', she had not yet expatiated them enough
to deserve what he called this 'favour' of being allowed to import
English corn. Even those who approved of the idea did so with
egregious condescension: Wilberforce considered it 'a deed of
charity and benevolence which her distress claimed at our hands'.
In the end it was decided that corn prices in England were already
too high to risk letting grain out of the country; and a few days
later, when Pitt told the House about some corn merchants at
Shoreham who had fraudulently brought the price down in order
to export 8,000 sacks to Le Havre, he promised strong action
against them.[49] The French, accustomed to see the grain question
in terms of artificial shortages created for political ends, interpreted the English decision in their own terms: for months to
come there were accusations and counter accusations about shady
dealings with England. Both Necker and Orléans were at different
times charged with bribing the English to release or withhold
grain to fit in with their nefarious plans.[50] While revolutionaries
had visions of royalists creating shortages in order to bring the
nation to its knees, conservatives imagined that unscrupulous
agitators were using hunger as a means of producing unrest. And
in both cases it was the wicked English who were at the bottom
of it. By the end of July suspicions of this sort were so rife that
Dorset decided to write formally to the French government,
pointing out that England had acted with absolute propriety and
had even revealed to the French government an invitation she had
received to join in a plot to seize the port of Brest. The letter
only made matters worse: ulterior motives were invented for
England's apparent candour and the Brest conspiracy joined the
grain conspiracy in the mythology of the French revolution, both

[49] *P.H.* xxviii, 226–30.
[50] See *Dénonciation sommaire . . . contre M. Necker*, 1790; *Criminelle
Neckero–Logie*, Geneva, 1790. These and other attacks on Necker are
contained in the British Museum collection of revolutionary tracts, nos
768–9. On Rutledge, Necker's chief adversary, see R. Las Vergnas, *Le
Chevalier Rutledge*, 1932. The accusations against Orléans are summed up
in C. F. L. Galart de Montjoie, *Histoire de la Conjuration de L. P. J.
d'Orléans*, 3 vols, 1796, ii, 23–32, 330; iii, 26ff.

of them serving as examples of English guile and double dealing.[51]

Having asked for bread, the French found themselves given not stones but tourists. William Windham, who had tried to get the Commons to relent over the corn question and had in consequence been branded as a francophile agitator, came to Paris to get away from his own hostile constituents.[52] During August and September many more Englishmen arrived in the city, most of them filled with enthusiasm for the revolution. Having regarded the first six weeks of the Estates General with boredom and indifference, the English had now suddenly developed a consuming interest in French affairs. Enterprising impressarios were already at work on the spectacular re-enactments, such as the 'Amphitheatrical attack on the Bastille', which were to dominate the London theatre season that autumn. Opposition journalists had taken the opportunity to publish prints such as Gillray's *France freedom, Britain slavery*, in which Necker and Orléans were shown leading France forward into liberty while Pitt held Englishmen in chains. Other caricatures had linked Marie Antoinette and her Austrian advisers with Queen Charlotte, whose sinister German friends were supposed to be plotting to keep George III in leading strings and exclude the Prince of Wales from the succession. As far as Gillray was concerned they were all 'pests of France and Britain, German toad-eaters and German counsellors'.[53]

While some of the English visitors to Paris thought in terms of this rather crude parallelism, of Orléans succeeding where the Prince of Wales had so far failed, others saw the destinies of the two countries coming together at a loftier level. Romilly, who arrived in France in August, told Dumont that he thought of nothing else but the French revolution and its beneficent effects on England and on the rest of the world.[54] In due course he was to publish a book on the benefits which France would bring to England—the French example would lead, he thought, to penal reform, educational reform, parliamentary reform, reform of the

[51] Browning, ii, 250–4. The propriety of the British government's actions in this matter can be judged from Add. 28, 064, fos 114–24.
[52] See his letter to Burke, 15 September 1789, Burke, *Correspondence*, vi, 20–2.
[53] *Catalogue of Political and Personal Satires, British Museum*, ed. M. D. George, 1938, nos. 7561, 7546, 7548.
[54] Romilly to Dumont, 28 July 1789, Romilly, i, 272.

poor law and an end to every species of injustice and privilege.[55] For the moment, however, he was more concerned with the benefits that England could bring to France. Dumont, who had already assured Lansdowne that the French revolution was developing along exactly the lines he would have wished, now reported to him that Romilly was a valuable addition to the small band of anglophiles who were working behind the scenes to secure acceptance of the royal veto. Lansdowne himself, too worried about his wife's serious illness to give his full attention to politics, nevertheless did what he could by making Dumont over to Mirabeau as a full-time assistant and providing him with funds to draw on in Paris.[56] To the idealists of Lansdowne House it seemed that England and France might at last influence one another directly and positively instead of by the inverted and negative logic of the looking-glass. English experience and French enthusiasm might be fused in order to produce in both countries a new kind of society which could move forward in unity, instead of being constantly torn apart by convulsive spasms of repulsion and reaction. Englishmen and Frenchmen might be persuaded at last to behave like sensible beings instead of like dogs barking at their own reflections in a mirror.

It was a forlorn hope. Dramatic though they were, the events of 1789 were not dramatic enough to shake the English or the French out of their mirror-gazing habit. The French still saw their old fears reflected in England, fears of commercialism and corruption and faction, and now they saw new fears as well, fears of counter-revolution on the one hand and anarchy on the other. The English for their part soon reverted to a similar mood. By the time the summer visitors returned from Paris news was coming through of yet another uprising early in October, when the market women of Paris had swarmed into the palace of Versailles and overawed the assembly itself. It was widely believed that Orléans had stirred up this latest revolt in an attempt to seize his cousin's throne; and when Orléans arrived in London at the end of October he got a very cool reception. Officially he had come to discuss Belgium, where the emperor was facing a revolution as dramatic as the one in France; but in fact it was clear that

[55] S. Romilly, *Thoughts on the Probable Influence of the French Revolution on Great Britain*, 1790.

[56] Dumont to Lansdowne, 5 August, 12 August, 24 September 1789, Bowood Papers (transcripts in C.J.M., nos 27, 29, 32). See also Romilly's own letter to Lansdowne, printed in C. G. Oakes, *Sir Samuel Romilly*, 1935, pp. 386–90.

he was a political exile. George III said of the visit: 'I confess I attribute it to his finding his views not likely to succeed, or some personal uneasiness for his own safety.' The Whigs, who had been eager to congratulate Orléans earlier in the year as a successful brother-in-arms against wicked ministers and scheming German queens, now found it politic to avoid him if they could. The duchess of Devonshire, who was in France listening to all the gossip, became quite frantic with anxiety when she heard that the Prince of Wales was consorting with Orléans: 'Be on your guard, my dearest friend and brother,' she warned, 'for indeed he has heavy accusations and I fear proof against him.' George Selwyn, who had already seen the parallel between Orléans's ambitions and those of the prince, now reported that the former was 'universally despised and detested' in London. The popular prints no longer showed him as the liberator of France but as a cheap agitator tempting the fishwives of Billingsgate into excesses to match those of their counterparts in Paris. As to his official mission, that was treated with the same coolness: George III told him that England would not wish to see Belgium go the way of France, while Fox warned the Prince of Wales not to be drawn into any scheme to make him a figurehead in the Belgian revolution.[57]

The relationship between Lansdowne and Mirabeau turned sour in very much the same way as that between the Whigs and the Orléanists. The circumstances were different, in that the links were much closer and also much more idealistic, but the process was basically the same: like men caught in a nightmare they found that the more they tried to walk in step the more they ran away from one another in opposite directions. Mirabeau was suspected of being involved in the October uprising, so that his particular blend of French revolutionary zeal and English constitutional caution could now be seen, at any rate by his enemies, as the calculated policy of an Orléanist plotter. He was suspected of trying to topple the existing king while preserving the royal prerogatives intact for the convenience of the future king, whose minister he hoped to be. The more he and his high-minded English

---

[57] *The Later Correspondence of George III*, ed. A. Aspinall, 5 vols, Cambridge, 1962–70, i, 446, 451; *Georgiana: extracts from the correspondence of Georgiana, Duchess of Devonshire*, ed. earl of Bessborough, 1955, pp. 162–3; George Selwyn to Lady Carlisle, 21 August, 6 November, 19 November 1789, *H.M.C. 42, Carlisle*, pp. 666, 675, 677; *Catalogue of Satires, British Museum*, no. 7559; *Correspondence of George, Prince of Wales*, ii, 47, 57.

friends preached English constitutionalism the more they forged
a political weapon which, placed in the right hands and used in
the right way, would prove sharp enough to destroy them all.

Mirabeau's own destruction came swiftly. On 7 November a
deputy from Brittany, traditionally the home of anglophobia,
forced through the assembly a clause by which under the new
constitution no member of the assembly could be a minister of
the crown.[58] The proposal was clearly inspired by suspicion of
Mirabeau, who more than any other man sought to use promi-
nence in the assembly as a ladder to power in the ministry; but
it was also inspired by distrust of the English ideas he was
peddling. Constitutional theorists had once believed, in England
as well as in France, that the best way to ensure the sturdy
independence of the legislative was to separate it completely from
the executive in this way. In England, however, practical politicians had come to see that the presence of the king's ministers in
parliament was not just an extension of royal power but was also
a guarantee of parliament's own importance and of its place in
the running of the country's affairs. Experience might have led
the French to similar conclusions if they had given it the chance
to do so, instead of saddling themselves with a constitution based
on confrontation, rather than co-operation, between king and
assembly. But this is an academic question, just as it is an academic
question whether Mirabeau discredited English constitutionalism
or English constitutionalism discredited Mirabeau. The plain fact
was that both had been defeated. From this point onwards
France's revolution was to be inspired by the rejection rather
than the acceptance of the English example.

Mirabeau himself saw clearly enough what had happened: his
chances of getting into power on the shoulders of the revolution
were now very slender and he must turn instead to his plans for
promoting counter-revolution. He was already in touch with
Provence and with the queen, advising them on ways of putting
down the revolution by force, and now these contacts became
his main preoccupation.[59] Lansdowne, too, was a realist: he saw
that the reflected glory from France in which he had hoped to
bask might now prove more corrosive than warning. As more
and more pamphlets appeared in Paris attacking by name the

[58] *Moniteur*, no. 86 (7–9 Nov.) pp. 349–50.
[59] Mirabeau's counterrevolutionary correspondence with the Court is in
*Correspondance entre le comte de Mirabeau et le comte de la Marck,
1789–91*, ed. A. de Bacourt, 3 vols, 1851.

English and Genevese associates of Mirabeau, Lansdowne ordered
Dumont to return to England without delay. Dumont held out
for a few weeks, insisting that his patron's fears were exaggerated;
but in the end he too sickened of Mirabeau and of the company
he was now keeping. In the middle of March 1790 Lansdowne
learned with relief that Dumont was back in London. For all
practical purposes the English attempt to influence the French
revolution was at an end.[60]

But not everybody in the Lansdowne circle was as pessimistic
as Mirabeau and Lansdowne. Three days before the French
assembly's decision to exclude ministers, Dr Price had preached
an optimistic and even exultant sermon at his chapel in London.
It was a revolution sermon, part of those annual celebrations
which Lansdowne's friends in parliament had envisaged in their
Revolution Commemoration Bill. It was common knowledge that
Price, like most dissenters, thought that the 1688 revolution could
only be properly commemorated if it was completed—if the
narrow basis of parliamentary representation was widened and if
full participation in politics was allowed to all men of substance
and not just to Anglicans. Now he declared that the example of
the French, carrying through to their logical conclusions the
principles of elective monarchy proclaimed in 1688, must surely
shame the English into completing at long last what they had
started so gloriously a century before. Just as the French could
only carry through their revolution by looking to England, so
the English could only remain true to theirs by looking to France.
The time had come for the two countries to act upon one another
by the force of example rather than by the vehemence of reaction.
His suggestions were followed up: the revolution societies in
England established contacts with similar bodies in France and
plans were laid for closer affiliation between progressively minded
men in both countries.

It was this initiative, both the sermon itself and also the subsequent activities of the revolution societies, that produced a shatter-

[60] The particular libel which came into Lansdowne's hands was *Domine
Salvum Fac Regem*, probably by J. G. Peltier and published late in December. See Romilly, i, 294–5; MSS Dumont 17, fos 42–3. Lansdowne's increasing bitterness during the next few years, as he saw his francophilia turn
from an asset into a liability, is clearly reflected in Dumont's letters and
particularly in MSS Dumont 17, fos 88–91. But he did not go down without
a fight: in 1790 he made an impressive speech in the Lords tracing England's
unwarranted hostility to France back to 1786 and suggesting that it was a
cause, rather than an effect, of the excesses of the French revolution. See
P.H. xxviii, 939–48.

ing counterblast from Burke in his enormously influential
*Reflections on the Revolution in France and on the proceedings
in certain Societies in London relative to that event.* As with
Mirabeau's enemies in Paris, so with Lansdowne's enemies in
London: the weapon had been put into their hands and they
were not slow to use it. None used it more skilfully or with more
devastating effect than Burke. Ever since the catastrophic defeat
of the Whigs in 1783–84 he had been waiting for a chance to
re-establish the position of the Whig party as a moderate and
respectable party, the true guardian of property and constitutional balance against demagogy on the one hand and royal
tyranny on the other. In his view it was men like Pitt and Lansdowne, with their fraudulent claim to speak for the country as
a whole, who really threatened the balance of the constitution.
Whether it was sincere or whether it was mere humbug—and
privately Burke had no doubt that it was the latter—their support
for dissenters and industrialists and radicals of every hue could
only lead to the overthrow of the constitution of 1688. Given
proper support, the Whig party would do its duty and balance
out the power of the crown constitutionally within the context
of the existing parliamentary system. But if that system was to
be put in jeopardy by talk of change and reform, by the creation
of what Burke himself had already described as 'a parliament out
of doors', then the English revolution of 1688 would itself be in
peril. The very fact that France had so clearly rejected the existing English constitution meant that she would now welcome only
those Englishmen who were working for the overthrow of that
constitution. So far from representing the consummation of 1688,
as Price suggested, dalliance with France meant the rejection of
everything that glorious year stood for.

Burke had not paid much attention to French affairs during
the months leading up to the meeting of the Estates General. At
that time his main concern had been the overthrow of Pitt: it
was Pitt whom he described in January 1789 as the manipulator
of the 'parliament out of doors' and it was for their support of
Pitt, not of Lansdowne, that he castigated the dissenters in May
of the same year. But George III's recovery had destroyed all
Whig hopes for the quick overthrow of Pitt; and nobody had
been more demoralized by that recovery than Burke, whose
gloating pronouncements on the permanence of the king's sanity
had been particularly violent and particularly offensive. Now he

himself was widely regarded as a man driven to the edge of lunacy, a man whose obsession with his own political defeats had led him into hysterical and maniacal attacks on his king. When a madman called Frith threw a stone at George III in January 1790 it was Burke who appeared as Frith when the caricaturists came to illustrate the event.[61] He was in no position to try consequences with Pitt again—at any rate not until he had worked his own way back to respectability and acceptability. But at least he could make sure that the Whigs, and not Lansdowne, were accepted as the obvious alternative to Pitt if and when that minister did fall. There is no doubt that he was genuinely shocked by events in France from the summer of 1789 onwards; but on the other hand he was certainly not blind to the political use that might be made of Lansdowne's involvement in French affairs. His thundering denunciations of the French revolution in the *Reflections* sprang from calculation as well as from revulsion. It is interesting to note, for instance, that his first really violent outburst on French affairs was contained not in his early letters on the revolution in general, which were comparatively detached and moderate, but in a letter which he wrote to Sir Gilbert Elliot, Mirabeau's friend, on 3 January 1790. He had come across an account of Mirabeau's speech of 16 July 1789, in which George III was praised for championing the English nation against the Whigs in 1783–84, and it had aroused him to fury. He linked Mirabeau and Lansdowne, suggesting that both men were congenitally evil, the products of bad blood from which even time itself could never remove the taint. Within a few weeks he was hard at work on the *Reflections*; and when his friend Philip Francis returned his early drafts with the comment that publication would expose Burke to accusations of inconsistency, he was sharply told that this was unimportant when compared to the urgent need to bring to light the 'wicked principles and black hearts' of the Lansdowne circle. If the *Reflections* were the product of an obsession, it was an obsession with the evils of the marquis of Lansdowne as much as with the evils of the French revolution.[62]

In the event Francis's fears proved unfounded. Charges of inconsistency were indeed made—in February 1790, when Burke

---

[61] *Catalogue of Satires, British Museum*, no. 7624 (*Frith the Madman*). See also no. 7529 (*Cooling the Brain*) for earlier views of Burke as mentally disturbed.
[62] Burke, *Correspondence*, vi, 61–4, 88–92.

first expressed in parliament his doubts about the French revolution, the satirists were quick to note the contrast between his contempt for his own king and his concern for the king of France[63]
—but by the time the *Reflections* came out in November of that
year the mounting chauvinism of the time was swallowing
inconsistencies wholesale on both sides of the Channel. The
campaign for the removal of dissenters' disabilities had been
defeated in March; and the Anglicans had celebrated their victory
with prints which showed the dissenters plotting not only with
the whole National Assembly of France but also with Jews,
papists, atheists, Lansdowne supporters, Cromwellians and even
with a lady named Margaret Nicholson who had tried to stab
George III in 1786. These ill-assorted conspirators were shown
brandishing the anti-monarchial tracts of the English Civil War
—the very same tracts which Mirabeau and his Anglo-Genevese
friends had been accused of using in their campaign to undermine
the traditional values of France.[64] While the English viewed Lansdowne and the dissenters as the secret emissaries of a France which
had in fact rejected them, the French denounced them as the
apologists of a political establishment which was in the process
of disowning them. Such was the fate of internationalism in an
age of chauvinism, of hopes of convergence at a moment of divergence. Not that the divergence was to be merely momentary:
the two countries were to make war on each other for most of
the next twenty-five years, developing as they did so new variants
of their age-old dualism. But no amount of contrast and confrontation would ever take away their dependence upon one another
and the involvement which that dependence brought with it. Even
in their separation the two strands of the rope retained the twists
and kinks which revealed their common origin.

[63] See for instance *Catalogue of Satires, British Museum,* no. 7627
(Peachum and Lockett).
[64] *Ibid.,* no. 7628 *(The Repeal of the Test Act: a Vision).* On Mirabeau
and the Civil War tracts see Dumont, *Souvenirs,* pp. 110–1, 280–1.

Sources

This list is limited to those sources which I have found useful in tracing the impact of each country on the other. I have not tried to list basic sources for the history of England and France in this period, as this would have made the bibliography at least as long as the book. A bibliography of secondary works would have required even more space and would have been, I think, even more redundant: those books and articles which are directly relevant are listed in the footnotes, while the more general ones can be found in standard bibliographies. My debt to other books on the period—above all to H. Lüthy's great work, *La Banque protestante en France*, 2 vols, 1959–61—is, of course, enormous. If I fail to acknowledge it here it is not out of ingratitude but out of a desire not to repeat the material already contained in the notes, which form a kind of running bibliography of secondary works. Since this list is designed to complement the notes rather than to duplicate them, it is intentionally given a title more modest than that of 'bibliography'. Instead of trying to cover the whole field selectively, it tries merely to cover the essential ground in some detail.

A. MANUSCRIPT SOURCES

1. Public Record Office, London

Foreign Office papers: S.P.78/251–306, General Correspondence, France, 1761–78; F.O.27/1–33, General Correspondence, France,

1781–89; S.P.100/9, Letters of French ministers in England, 1744–74.

Chatham papers: P.R.O.30/8/6, 17–69, 101–03, 105–95, 264–71, 333–34, Correspondence of the elder and the younger Pitt; letters of Thomas Coutts; papers relating to taxation and to relations with France.

Calonne papers: P.C.1/123, includes material on commercial relations with England, 1783–87; P.C.1/125, includes correspondence with Pitt, Mirabeau and others, 1786–89; P.C.1/129, includes correspondence with the Polignacs, 1787–89; F.O.95/631, includes la Motte letters, 1787–88.

Treasury Solicitor's papers: T.S.11/995, 1116, 1128, food riots, 1766; T.S.11/178, 388, 389, prosecutions for libels on queen of France, 1784–86.

2. British Museum, London

The eighteenth report of the Historical Manuscripts Commissioners to the Crown contains (*Command Papers 1916*, vol. ix, app. ii, pp. 357–402) an important list of materials for diplomatic history, both in the British Museum and in the other collections covered by the work of the Commission up to that date. These include such major collections as the Newcastle papers (Add. 32679–33201) and the Hardwicke papers (Add. 35349–36278). I have not attempted to list these collections here, but simply to indicate volume by volume the miscellaneous materials on Anglo-French relations which exist in the British Museum's collection of Additional Manuscripts. Some of these are noticed in F. Braesch, *Rapport sur les documents conservés au British Museum*, 1907, but the greater part of them has been largely neglected, especially by French historians.

5425–30	Records of *vingtièmes* and other French taxes, 1784–87.
9280	Coxe papers, vol. cciii: Memoirs of French Court, 1771–73.
12130	Notes of a journey through France, 1776–77.
15467–68	Ecclesiastical revenues in France, 1760.
17976–79	Ecclesiastical revenues in France, 1760.
20821–24	Reports on population and resources of France, 1748–61.
20842	*Etat actuel du royaume de la Grande Bretagne*, 1756.
21513	Agreement between Mirabeau and his publisher, 1787, and other material on French affairs.
21514	Includes letters of Lalande, La Condamine and other French scientists.
21622	Pamphlets on French finances, 1763.
22111	Includes materials on Necker's first administration.

24207	Includes letters on French politics, 1779 and 1788.
25597	Papers on French finances, 1755–62.
26716	French ecclesiastical affairs, 1786.
27482–85	*Mes loisirs*, by Calonne.
27486	Anecdotes and memoirs by Calonne.
27487	Calonne's notes on various sovereigns of Europe.
28060–67	Official correspondence of the duke of Leeds, 1783–98.
28068	Enclosures in the duke of Leeds's correspondence, including an important memoir, dated 14 Oct 1789, advocating English aid for a counter-revolution.
28851	Papers on Richard Cumberland's secret mission to Spain, 1780.
29760	Includes letters of FitzJames in 1760s.
30002	Ricketts and Jervis correspondence: letters relating to France, 1779–96.
30271	Richard Garmston's tour to France, 1787.
31192	Lord St Vincent's tour to France, 1772–73.
32258–59	Deciphers of diplomatic papers: France, 1650–1804.
32309	Copies of correspondence of foreign ministers in London, 1766–72.
32922	Pitt–Choiseul correspondence, 1761.
33121	Mrs Swinburne's letters from Paris, 1788–89.
33125	Thomas Pelham's tour in southern France, 1777.
33538–41	Bentham correspondence, 1776–94 (in process of publication, under the general editorship of Professor J. H. Burns, University College, London. I have continued to cite the manuscripts because publication has not so far proceeded beyond August 1788. See below, p. 293).
33553	Includes Bentham's account of his relations with the Lansdowne family.
33557	Bentham family letter book, with details of outgoing letters.
34412–71	Auckland papers: includes correspondence between Eden and Rayneval from 1786 onwards.
34876–86	Gibbon papers: letters and journals. (The former have been published—see below, p. 297—but consultation of the manuscripts is still useful for the journals.)
35126–27	Correspondence of Priestley and others with Young.
35531	Letters of Sir Robert Keith on French threat in India.
35636	Includes Hanbury's letter on *La Richesse de l'Etat*.
36797	Bute's letters on activities of French agents in London.
38200	Bedford–Egremont correspondence on peace with France; Meredith's petition on Guadeloupe.

38201–06	Jenkinson correspondence, 1763–69.
38218	Liverpool papers: commercial relations with France, 1782–85.
38341	Papers on French finances and the *Compagnie des Indes.*
38373	Includes abstract of memoir by *parlement* of Bordeaux, 1764.
41170	Includes Calonne's letter to his colleagues about Mirabeau's *Caisse d'Escompte* and other papers on France.
41197	Letters on French occupation of Corsica.
41340	Includes Dombre's letter to Chatham in 1766.
41354	Letters to and from Wilkes during his exile in Paris.
42232	Includes tours in France, 1769 and 1777.

3. University College, London

Like the Bentham letters in the British Museum (see above, under Add. 33538–41), the Bentham papers at University College are in process of publication. The following are relevant to the questions raised in this book:

Case ix	Contains correspondence with Trail, Mirabeau and others at the time of the French revolution.
Case cxxxii	Letters written in 1819, containing account of the doings of the group at the time of the revolution.
Case clxvi	includes drafts on French finances, marked 'to Mirabeau'.
Case clxix	Drafts of outgoing letters.
Case clxx	Papers on France endorsed '*à Mirabeau*'.

4. Bowood Park, Wiltshire

The marquis of Lansdowne's manuscripts at Bowood Park include much material on Shelburne's relations with France and with the radical intellectuals of his time, as well as on his political career itself. In the early 1920s a large part of the collection went to the William Clements Library in the University of Michigan (see the *Bulletin of the Institute of Historical Research*, iii, 1924, pp. 77–80), but much important material remained at Bowood. I was unable to consult these papers, since at the time I was doing my research the muniment room at Bowood was under reconstruction; but by the courtesy of Monsieur Jean Martin I was able to make use of certified copies in his collection at Cartigny (see below, p. 291). Mr Charles Blount was kind enough to let me see his transcripts of the Bowood papers, which filled out the picture further.

5. Archives Nationales, Paris

Series F^4, F^{10} and F^{12} contain important material on the connections between administration, commercial policy and foreign

relations. F¹² 1300 and F¹² 1315a are particularly rich in papers
on the suborning of English workmen and other aspects of industrial espionage. Series AQ includes the papers of industrialists and
bankers who were involved with relations with England, such as
Laborde (further papers in T 1097), Feray and the brothers
Mallet. Clavière's papers, on the other hand, are in Tˣ646¹⁻⁵. See
also Sillery's journal, KK 641–46, on the estates general and the
National Assembly.

6. Bibliothèque Nationale, Paris

MSS Français 6687	*Mes loisirs* by S-P. Hardy, 1764–89 (see below, p. 298 for the published part of this journal).
MSS Français 10883	*Journal des états généraux de 1789.*
MSS Français 13713	*Journal des événements . . . par un clerc de procureur au Chatelet.* Covers April to October, 1789. Much malicious gossip, especially about Necker, but some genuine insights into the state of public opinion.

7. Bibliothèque Publique et Universitaire, Geneva

MSS Dumont 17	Dumont's letters to Romilly.
MSS Dumont 21	Drafts for inclusion in the *Groenvelt Letters.*
MSS Dumont 33	Letters to Dumont, divided alphabetically into five volumes.
MSS Dumont 34	Dumont family correspondence.
MSS Dumont 35	French version of Dumont's part of *Groenvelt Letters.*
MSS Dumont 45	Fragmentary biographical notes on Mirabeau.
MSS Reybaz 1	Letters from Dumont and others concerned in Reybaz's collaboration with Mirabeau, 1789.

8. Collection Jean Martin, Cartigny, Geneva

The private collection of Monsieur Jean Martin, a descendant of
the family into which Dumont's sister married. Includes Dumont's
correspondence with his family, with Necker and Mirabeau and
with many others; also certified copies of his letters to Lansdowne,
the originals of which are in the Bowood papers.

B. PRINTED SOURCES

I have tried to arrange this list in such a way as to facilitate
easy reference and to short-circuit the tedious task of pursuing
a string of shortened references back to their only begetter. I
have therefore abandoned subdivision and produced a single list
arranged alphabetically by author's name or, in the case of anonymous works, by the first main word in the title. Basic sources such
as periodicals, collections of laws and reports of debates are

omitted unless they are of a particularly specialized or ephemeral kind. Secondary works are only included if they incorporate a significant amount of primary material. In the case of standard collections of letters or memoirs I have followed the usage adopted in the footnotes, which is itself modelled on existing conventions. It would be perverse, for instance, to carry consistency to the point of listing Fortescue's *Correspondence of George III* under GEORGE III or Russell's *Bedford Correspondence* under RUSSELL.

ACCARIAS DE SERIONNE, J. *Les Intérêts des Nations de l'Europe développés relativement au commerce*, Leipzig, 1766.

—— *La Richesse de l'Angleterre*, Vienna, 1771.

AGNEW, D. G. A. *Protestant exiles from France*, 2 vols, s.l., 1886.

ALBEMARLE, G. T. KEPPEL, EARL OF. *Memoirs of the Marquis of Rockingham and his contemporaries*, 2 vols, 1852.

ALBISSON, J., ed. *Loix municipales de Languedoc*, 7 vols, Toulouse, 1780–87.

ALBON, C. C. F. D'. *Discours sur quelques gouvernements de l'Europe* Neuchâtel, 1779.

ALSTYNE, R. W. VAN. 'Thomas Walpole's letters to the Duke of Grafton on American affairs', *Huntingdon Library Quarterly*, XXX, 1966–67, pp. 17–33.

ANDERSON, J. *Observations on Means of Exciting a Spirit of National Industry*, Edinburgh, 1777.

ANDREWS, J. *Letters to a Young Gentleman on his Setting out for France*, 1784.

ARBLAY, MME D'. *Diary and Letters of Madame d'Arblay, 1778–1840*, ed. C. Barrett, 6 vols, 1904–05.

ASPINALL, A. ed. *The Later Correspondence of George III*, 5 vols, Cambridge, 1962–70.

—— *Correspondence of George, Prince of Wales, 1770–1812*, 8 vols, 1963–71.

AUGEARD, J-M. *Mémoires secrètes de J-M. Augeard*, ed. Bavoux, 1866.

BABEAU, A. *Les voyageurs en France*, 1885.

BACHAUMONT, L. P. DE. *Mémoires secrètes*, 36 vols, London and Amsterdam, 1777–89.

BAILEY, W. *The Advancement of Arts, Manufactures and Commerce, or, Descriptions of . . . the Repository of the Society for the Encouragement of Arts, Manufactures and Commerce*, 1772.

BAILLY, J. S. *Mémoires*, 3 vols, 1821–22.

BALDWIN, T. *Airopaidia*, Chester, 1786.

BANCROFT, G. *History of France and America's Common Action*, tr. A. de Circourt, 3 vols, Paris, 1876.

BARBIER, A. A. *Dictionnaire des ouvrages anonymes*, 4 vols, 1872–79.

BARBIER, E. J. F. *Chronique de la Régence et du Règne de Louis XV*, 4 vols, 1847–56.

BARBIER, P. and VERNILLAT, F. *Histoire de la France par les chansons*, vols iii and iv, 1957–58.

BARENTIN, C. L. F. *Lettres et bulletins de Barentin à Louis XVI, avril–juillet, 1789*, ed. A. Aulard, 1915.

BARNAVE, A-J-M-P. *Introduction á la Révolution Française*, ed. F. Rude (*Cahiers des Annales*, no. 15), 1960.

BARRUEL, A. *Memoirs illustrating the history of Jacobinism*, tr. Clifford, 4 vols, 1797.

BEARDE, DE L'ABBAYE. *Recherches sur les moyens de supprimer les impôts*, Amsterdam, 1770.

BEDFORD, J. RUSSELL, DUKE OF. *Correspondence of John, fourth Duke of Bedford*, ed. Lord John Russell, 4 vols, 1842–46.

BEIK, P. H., ed. *A Judgement of the Old Régime : being a survey by the parlement of Provence . . . at the close of the Seven Years War* (Columbia Studies in History, Economics and Public Law, no. 509), New York, 1944.

BENTHAM, J. *A Fragment on Government*, 1776.

—— *A View of the Hard Labour Bill*, 1778.

—— *Defence of Usury*, 1787.

—— *Introduction to the Principles of Morals and Legislation*, eds. J. H. Burns and H. L. A. Hart, 1970.

—— *Draft of a New Plan for the Organization of the Judicial Establishment in France*, 1790.

—— *Works*, ed. Bowring, Edinburgh, 1838–43.

—— *Correspondence*, vol. i (1752–76), ed. T. L. S. Sprigge, 1968; vol. ii (1777–80), ed. T. L. S. Sprigge, 1968; vol. iii (1781–88), ed. I. R. Christie, 1970.

BERGASSE, N. *Observations sur le préjugé de la noblesse héréditaire*, London, 1789.

BESENVAL, BARON DE, *Mémoires*, 2 vols, 1821.

BESSBOROUGH, V. B. PONSONBY, EARL OF. *Georgiana : extracts from the correspondence of Georgiana, Duchess of Devonshire*, 1955.

BIREMBAUT, A. and THUILLIER, G. 'Les cahiers du chimiste Jean Hellot', *Annales*, 21ᵉ année, 1966, pp. 254–91.

BLAIKIE, T. *Diary of a Scottish Gardener at the French Court*, ed. F. Birrell, 1931.

BLOCH, C. *Le Commerce des grains dans la généralité d'Orléans, 1768, d'après la correspondance inédite de l'intendant Cypierre*, Orléans, 1898.

—— *Les Contributions directes : instructions, receuil des textes*, 1915.

BLUCHE, J. F. *L'Origine des magistrats du parlement de Paris au xviiiᵉ siècle (dictionnaire généalogique)*, 1956.

—— 'Les magistrats du parlement de Paris au xviiiᵉ siècle', *Annales Littéraires de l'université de Besançon*, xxxv, 1960.

BONCERF, P. F. *Les Inconvénients des droits féodaux : nouvelle édition augmentée*, London, 1776.

BONNASSIEUX, P. and LELONG, E. *Inventaire analytique des procès-verbaux du conseil du commerce et du bureau de commerce, 1700–91*, 1900.

BOSWELL, J. *London Journal, 1762–63*, ed. F. Pottle, 1950.

BOULOISEAU, M., ed. *Cahiers de doléances du tiers état du bailliage de Rouen*, Rouen, 1957.

BOURNE, H. 'Correspondence of the comte de Moustier with the comte de Montmorin', *Am.H.R.* viii (1902–03) pp. 709–33; ix, 1903, pp. 86–96.

BRAESCH, F. *Finances et monnaie révolutionnaires*, 3 vols, Nancy, 1934–36.

BRETTE, A., ed. 'Relations des événements depuis le 6 mai jusqu'au 15 juillet, 1789: documents inédits', *Révolution Française*, xxiii, 1892, pp. 348–68; 443–71; 493–547; xxiv, 1893, pp. 69–84, 162–78.

BRISSOT DE WARVILLE, J. P. *Testament politique de l'Angleterre*, Philadelphia, 1778.

—— *Philadelphian à Genève*, Dublin, 1783.

—— *Mémoires*, ed. C. Perroud, 2 vols., 1910.

—— *Correspondance*, ed. C. Perroud, 1912.

      and CLAVIÈRE, E. *De la France et des Etats-Unis*, London, 1787.

BRITSCH, A. 'L'Anglomanie de Philippe-Egalité, d'après sa correspondance autographe, 1778–85', *Le Correspondant*, ccciii, 1926, pp. 280–95.

BROWN, J. *Estimate of the Manners and Principles of the Times*, 2 vols, 1757.

—— *Thoughts on Civil Liberty, on Licentiousness and Faction*, 1765.

BROWNING, O., ed. *Despatches from Paris, 1784–90*, 2 vols, Camden Third Series, xxvi, xix, 1909–10.

BURGH, J. *Political Disquisitions*, 3 vols, 1774–75.

BURKE. E. *Select Works*, ed. J. Payne, 3 vols, Oxford, 1878–1904.

—— *Correspondence*, ed. T. W. Copeland, *et al.*, 9 vols, Cambridge and Chicago, 1958–70.

BURON, E. 'Statistics on Franco-American trade 1778–1806', *Journal of Economic and Business History*, iv, 1931–32, pp. 571–74.

BYNG, J. *Torrington Diaries*, ed. C. B. Andrews, 4 vols, 1934–38.

Calendar of Home Office Papers, 1760–75, 4 vols, 1878–99 (vols i, ii, ed. J. Redington; vols ii, iv, ed. R. A. Roberts).

Calendar of State Papers: Acts of the Privy Council, Colonial Series, 1745–83, 2 vols, 1911–12.

Calendar of State Papers: Journals of the Commissioners for Trade and Plantations, 1759–1782, 4 vols, 1935–38.

CALONNE, C. A. DE. *De L'Etat de France, présent et à venir*, London, 1790.

CAMPAN, J. L. H. *Memoirs of the Private Life of Marie Antoinette*, 2 vols, 1823.

CARADEUC DE LA CHALOTAIS, L. R. *Essai d'éducation nationale*, s.l., 1763.

CARRE, H. 'La Chalotais et le duc d'Aiguillon' (prints the Fontette correspondence concerning the affair), *Mémoires de la Société des Antiquaires de l'Ouest*, serie 2, xv, 1892–93.

CARTWRIGHT, J. Take Your Choice!, 1776.

—— *The Life and Correspondence of Major Cartwright*, edited by his niece, F. D. Cartwright, 2 vols, 1826.

Catalogue of Political and Personal Satires, British Museum, vol. iv, 1761–70, ed. F. G. Stephens, 1883; vols v, vi, 1771–83, 1784–92, ed. M. D. George, 1935, 1938.

CHASTELLUX, MARQUIS DE. *Travels in North America in the years 1780, 1781 and 1782*, rev. edn. tr. and ed. H. C. Rice, 2 vols, Chapel Hill, 1963.

CHATEAUVERON, —. *L'Ecole de l'administration maritime ou le matelot politique*, The Hague, n.d. (1763).

CHEVALLIER, P., ed. *Journal de l'assemblée des notables de 1787*, 1960.

CHOISEUL, E. F., DUC DE. *Mémoires*, ed. F. Calmettes, 1904. (For the reservations which should be made about these memoirs, see P. Muret, 'Mémoires du duc de Choiseul', *R.H.M.C.*, vi, 1904–05, pp. 229–48, 377–99.)

—— *Choiseul et Voltaire d'après les lettres inédites du duc de Choiseul à Voltaire*, ed. P. Calmettes, 1902.

CHOMEL, V. and LAPEYRE, H. *Catalogue des livres de commerce et papiers d'affaires conservés aux archives départmentales de l'Isère*, Grenoble, 1962.

COLE, A. H. and WATTS, G. B. *The Handicrafts of France as recorded in the Descriptions des arts et metiers* (*Kress Library of Business and Economics*, publication no. 8), Boston, Mass, 1952.

COLE, W. *Journal of My Journey to Paris in the Year 1765*, ed. F. G. Stokes, 1931.

COLERIDGE, E. H. *The Life of Thomas Coutts*, 2 vols, 1920.

Complete Investigation of Mr Eden's Treaty, 1787.

Constitutional Queries Humbly Addressed to the Admirers of a Late Minister, n.d. [1762].

The Contrast; or, a comparison between our woollen, linen, cotton and silk manufactures, 1782.

CORNUAUD, I. *Mémoires*, ed. E. Cherbuliez, Geneva, 1912.

COYER, G. F. *La Noblesse Commerçante*, London, 1756.

CREUZE-LATOUCHE, J. A. *Journal des Etats-Généraux*, ed. J. Marchand, 1946.

CUMBERLAND, R. *Memoirs of Richard Cumberland, written by himself*, 1807.

DARIGRAND, J. B. *L'Anti-financier*, Amsterdam, 1764.

DAY, T. *A letter to Arthur Young Esq., on the Bill now depending in parliament to prevent the exportation of wool*, 1788.

DEFFAND, M. DE VICHY, MARQUISE DU. *Lettres à Horace Walpole 1766–80 et à Voltaire 1759–75*, 2 vols, 1864.

DE LA FONTAINERIE, F., ed. *French Liberalism and Education in the Eighteenth Century: the writings of La Chalotais, Turgot, Diderot and Condorcet*, New York, 1932.

DELOLME, J. L. *La Constitution de l'Angleterre*, Amsterdam, 1771.

DESAGULIERS, J. T. *The Newtonian System of the World the Best Model of Government: an allegorical poem*, 1728.

DIDEROT, D. *Salons*, ed. J. Seznec and J. Adhémar, 4 vols, Oxford, 1957–67.

DISNEY, J. *Memoirs of T. B. Hollis Esq.*, 1808.

DONIOL, H. *Histoire de la participation de la France à l'établissement des Etats-Unis d'Amérique*, 5 vols, 1886–99.

—— 'Le ministère des affaires étrangères de France sous le comte de Vergennes: souvenirs de Hennin sur ce ministre', *R.H.D.* vii, 1893, pp. 528–60.

DU BOUQ DE BEAUMONT, G. and BERNOS, M. *La Famille d'Orléans pendant la révolution d'après sa correspondance inédite*, 1913.

DUBUAT-NANCAY, L. G. *Les Maximes du gouvernement monarchique*, London, 1778.

DUFORT DE CHEVERNY, J. N. *Mémoires*, ed. R. de Crèvecœur, 4th edn, 2 vols, 1909.

DUMONT, E. *Lettre inédite d'Etienne Dumont sur quelques séances du Tier Etat, mai, 1789*, ed. J. M. Paris, Geneva, 1877.

—— *Souvenirs sur Mirabeau*, ed. J. Benetruy, 1951.

—— and ROMILLY, S. *Letters containing an account of the late Revolution in France, and observations on the constitution, laws, manners and institutions of the English . . . translated from the German of Henry Frederic Groenvelt*, 1792.

DUMONT, E., et al. *Réclamation des Genevois patriotes établis à Londres contre la nouvelle aristocratie de Genève*, 1789.

DUQUESNOY, A. *Journal . . . 3 mai 1789—3 avril 1790*, ed. R. de Crèvecœur, 2 vols, 1894.

D'YVERNOIS, F. *Le Gouvernement anglais et la Révolution Française: 'Les cinq accusations'*, ed. O. Karmin, Geneva, 1914.

Economie et population: les doctrines françaises avant 1800, bibliographie générale commentée (Institut National d'études démographiques), 1956.

EDEN, W. *Short Vindication of the French Treaty . . .*, 1787.

—— *Journal and Correspondence of William, Lord Auckland*, 4 vols, 1861–62.

ENGERAND, F. *Inventaire des tableaux commandés et achetés par la direction des bâtiments du roi, 1709–92*, 1901.

EON DE BEAUMONT, C. D'. *Lettres, mémoires et négotiations particuliers du chevalier d'Eon, ministre plénipotentiaire auprès du roi de la Grande Bretagne avec MM. les ducs de Praslin, de Nivernois, de Sainte-Foy, and Regnier de Guerchy . . .*, London, 1765.

Faits qui ont influé sur la cherté des grains en France et en Angleterre s.l., 1768.

FAUJAS DE ST FOND B. *Descriptions des expériences de la Machine Aérostatique de MM. de Montgolfier*, 1783.

—— *A Journey through England and Scotland to the Hebrides in 1784*, ed. Sir A. Geikie, 2 vols, Glasgow, 1907.

FAVART, C. S. *L'Anglais à Bordeaux, 1763.*

FAVIER, J.-L. 'Précis de faits sur l'administration de M. de Choiseul', *Révolution Française*, xxxvi, 1899, pp. 415–62 (prefaced, pp. 161–84, 258–76, 314–35, 411–15, by an account of Favier by J. Flammermont).

FERRIÈRES, C. E. DE. *Mémoires*, ed. Berville & Barrière, 2nd edn, 3 vols, 1822.

—— *Correspondance inédite*, ed. H. Carré, 1932.

FITZMAURICE, LORD E. *Life of William, earl of Shelburne, with extracts from his papers and correspondence*, rev. edn, 2 vols, 1912.

FLAMMERMONT, J., ed. *Remontrances du parlement de Paris au xviiie siècle*, 3 vols, 1888–98.

—— *Les Correspondances des agents diplomatiques avant la Révolution*, 1896.

FORTESCUE, SIR J. *The Correspondence of George III*, 6 vols, 1927–8.

FOUGERET DE MONTBRON, J. L. *Préservatif contre l'Anglomanie*, 'Minorque', 1757.

FOURNIER, —. *Mémoires secrètes de Fournier l'Americain*, ed. F. A. Aulard, 1890.

FOX, C. J. *Memorials and Correspondence of Charles James Fox*, ed. Lord John Russell, 4 vols, 1853–57.

FREDERICK II. *Mémoires*, ed. E. Boutaric and E. Campardon, 2 vols, 1866.

GALART DE MONTJOIE, C. F. L. *Histoire de la conjuration de L. P. J. d'Orléans*, 3 vols, 1796.

GALIANI, F. *Dialogue sur le commerce des blés*, London, 1770.

GARRETT, M. B. *A Critical Bibliography of the Pamphlet Literature published in France between July 5th and December 27th, 1788*, Birmingham, Alabama, 1925.

GEE, J. *Trade and Navigation of Great Britain Considered*, 1728.

The Gentleman's Guide in his Tour through France, 1788.

GIBBON, E. *The Letters of Edward Gibbon*, ed. J. E. Norton, 3 vols, 1956.

GILLE, B. *Les Sources statistiques de l'histoire de France: des enquêtes du xviie siècle à 1870*, Paris and Geneva, 1964.

GOLDSMITH, O. *Collected works*, ed. A. Friedman, 5 vols, Oxford, 1966.

GOYON DE LA PLOMBANIE, H. DE. *Vues politiques sur le commerce*, Amsterdam, 1759.

GRANGES DE SURGERES, —, MARQUIS DE. *Répertoire historique et biographique de la Gazette de France, 1631–1790*, 4 vols, 1902–06.

GREENE, J. P., ed. *The Nature of Colony Constitutions: two pamphlets on the Wilkes fund controversy by Sir Egerton Leigh and Arthur Lee*, Columbia, S.C., 1970.

GRENVILLE, G. and KNOX, W. *The Present State of the Nation*, 1768.

GROSLEY, P. J. *A Tour to London, or, New Observations on England and its Inhabitants*, tr. T. Nugent, 1772.

GUIBERT, J. A. H. *Œuvres militaires*, 5 vols, 1803.

GUYOT, P. and MERLIN, —. *Traité des droits, fonctions, franchises, privilèges et prérogatives annexées en France à chaque dignité et à chaque office*, 3 vols, 1786.

HARDY, S-P. *Mes loisirs: journal des événements tels qu' ils parviennent à ma connaissance* (1764–1773), ed. M. Tourneux and M. Vitrac, 1912. (For the complete diary, of which the published portion forms only part, see above p. 291.)

HAUSER, H. *Recherches et documents sur l'histoire des prix en France de 1500 à 1800*, 1936.

HAYEM, J., ed. *Mémoires et documents pour servir à l'histoire du commerce et de l'industrie en France*, 1913–1927.

HEZECQUES, C. A. F. F. DE. *Souvenirs d'un page*, 1873.

Historical Manuscripts Commission Reports: see in particular series 20 (*Dartmouth*), 24 (*Rutland*), 35 (*Kenyon*), 42 (*Carlisle*), 55 (*Various*), 58 (*Bath*), 68 (*Denbigh*), 78 (*Hastings*).

HORN, D. B., ed. *British Diplomatic Representatives, 1689–1789*, Camden Third Series, xlvi, 1932.

HOUTIN, A., ed. *Les Séances des députés du clergé aux Etats-Généraux de 1789: journaux du curé Thibault et du chanoine Coster*, 1917.

HUGUET DE GRAFIGNY, F. *Lettres péruviennes*, 1747.

Humble Petition of the Poor Spinners of the Town and County of Leicester, 1788.

HYSLOP, B. F. *A Guide to the General Cahiers*, New York, 1936.

Important Crisis in the Calico and Muslin Manufactory in Great Britain Explained, 1788.

Inventaires-Sommaires des Archives Départmentales. It is of course impracticable to list these extremely useful catalogues in full. I have made particular use of that for the department formerly known as the *Seine Inférieure* (*Archives civiles, série C–D*, vol. i, 1864), since it covers an area in which commercial and industrial policy was intimately bound up with relations with England.

JARS, G. *Voyages métallurgiques*, 3 vols, 1774–81.

JEFFERSON, T. *Memoirs, Correspondence and Miscellaneous Papers*, ed. Randolph, 4 vols, Charlottesville, 1829.

KENRICK, W. *Address to Artists and Manufacturers*, 1774.

KYNYNMOND, E., COUNTESS OF MINTO. *A Memoir of Hugh Elliot*, Edinburgh, 1868.

—— *Life and Letters of Sir Gilbert Elliot*, 3 vols, 1874.

LAFAYETTE, M., MARQUIS DE. *Mémoires, correspondance et manuscrits publiés par sa famille*, 6 vols, 1837.

LARDE, G. *Une Enquête sur les vingtièmes au temps de Necker, 1777–78*, 1920.

LA ROCHEFOUCAULD, F. A. F., DUC DE. *A Frenchman in England, 1784: being the 'Mélanges sur l'Angleterre'* . . ., ed. J. Marchand, tr. S. C. Roberts, Cambridge, 1933.

LEBLANC, J. B. *Letters on the English and French Nations*, 2 vols, Dublin, 1747.

LESCURE, M. F. A., ed. *Correspondance secrète inédite sur Louis XVI, Marie-Antoinette, la Cour et la ville, 1777–92*, 2 vols, 1866.

LE TROSNE, G. F. *De l'administration provinciale*, Basle, 1788.

Letter from a Manchester Manufacturer to the Right Honourable Charles James Fox on his Political Opposition to the Commercial Treaty with France, Manchester, 1787.

Letter to a Member of the P——t of G—— B——, occasioned by the privilege granted by the French king to Mr Crozat, n.d. (1713).

Lettre d'un patriote connu à un ancien magistrat sur les projets de l'Edit, concernant ceux qui ne professent pas la Réligion Catholique . . . où l'on démontre . . . le danger qu'il y aurait de leur accorder tous les avantages que l'on y propose, 1788.

LINGUET, S. N. H. *Annales politiques, civiles et littéraires*, 17 vols, London and The Hague, 1777–90.

LLOYD, C. *An Honest Man's Reasons for declining to take part in the new administration*, 1765.

MACKINTOSH, J. *Vindiciae Gallicae; Defence of the French Revolution and its English admirers* . . ., 1791.

MALLET DU PAN, L. 'Lettres inédites de Mallet du Pan à Etienne Dumont, 1787–89, publiées par A. Blondel,' *R.H.*, xcvii, 1908, pp. 95–121.

MALOUET, P. V. DE. *Mémoires*, 2 vols, 1874.

MARAT, J. P. *The Chains of Slavery . . . to which is prefixed an Address to the Electors of Great Britain*, 1774.

MARION, M., ed. *Les Impôts directs sous l'ancien régime . . . collection de textes*, 1910.

MARTIN, J. *La Polémique Necker-Dumont en 1789, avec documents inédits*, Geneva, 1927.

MATHIAS, P. 'The social structure in the eighteenth century: a calculation by Joseph Massie', *Ec.H.R.* 2nd series, x, 1957, pp. 30–45.

MATHON DE LA COUR, C. J. *Collection de Comptes Rendus, pièces authentiques, états et tableaux concernant les finances de France, 1758–87,* 5th edn, Lausanne, 1788.

MAUDUIT, I. *Considerations on the present German war,* 1760.

MAXWELL, C. *The English Traveller in France, 1698–1815,* 1932.

MENTION, L., ed. *Documents relatifs aux rapports du clergé avec la royauté de 1705 à 1789,* 1903.

MERCIER, L. S. *The Waiting City, Paris, 1782–88, being an abridgement of L. S. Mercier's 'Le Tableau de Paris', translated and edited by Helen Simpson,* 1933.

MIRABEAU, V. RIQUETTI, MARQUIS DE. *L'Ami des hommes,* 3 vols, The Hague, 1758.

—— *Théorie de l'impôt,* 1761.

—— and BAUDEAU, N. *Éphémérides du Citoyen,* 1767–68.

MIRABEAU, H. G. RIQUETTI, COMTE DE. *Considérations sur l'ordre de Cincinnatus,* London, 1784.

—— *Doutes sur la liberté de l'Escaut,* London, 1785.

MIRABEAU, H. G. *De la Caisse d'Escompte,* s.l, 1785.

—— *De la Banque d'Espagne,* s.l, 1785.

—— *Sur les actions de la compagnie des Eaux de Paris,* London, 1785.

—— *Lettre du comte de Mirabeau à M.... sur MM. Cagliostro et Lavater,* Berlin, 1786.

—— *Dénonciation de l'Agiotage,* s.l, 1787.

—— *Suite de la dénonciation de l'agiotage,* s.l, 1788.

—— *Aux Bataves sur le Stadthouderat,* s.l, 1788.

—— *Histoire Secrète de la Cour de Berlin,* 2 vols, 1788.

—— 'Quatorze billets inédits de Mirabeau à Etienne Dumont et à Duroveray, publiés par J. Martin', *Révolution Française,* lxxviii, 1925, pp. 289–311.

—— *Etats-généraux* (continued as *Lettres à ses commetants* and then as *Courrier de Provence*), 1789–91.

—— *Mémoires,* ed. L. de Montigny, 8 vols, 1834–35.

—— *Correspondance entre le comte de Mirabeau et le comte de la Marck, 1789–91,* ed. A. de Bacourt, 3 vols, 1851.

MOORE, J. *A View of the Society and Manners in France, Switzerland and Germany,* 2 vols, 1779.

MORE, H. *The letters of Hannah More,* ed. R. B. Johnson, 1925.

MOREAU DE BEAUMONT, J. L. *Mémoires concernant les impositions,* rev. edn., 5 vols, 1787–89.

MORELLET, A. *Mémoires,* 2 vols, 1823.

—— *Lettres de l'abbé Morellet . . . à Lord Shelburne,* ed. Lord E. Fitzmaurice, 1898.

MORRIS, G. *A Diary of the French Revolution,* ed. B. C. Davenport, 2 vols, 1939.

MURALT, B. L. DE. *Letters Describing the Character and Customs of the English and French nations,* 1726.

NAMIER, L. B. and BROOKE, J. *The History of Parliament: the House of Commons, 1754–90,* 3 vols, 1964.

NIVERNOIS, B. M. MANCINI, DUC DE. *Œuvres posthumes*, 2 vols, 1807.

OLSON, A. G. *The Radical Duke: Career and Correspondence of Charles Lennox, third duke of Richmond*, Oxford, 1961.

OZANAM, D. and ANTOINE, M., eds. *Correspondance secrète du Comte de Broglie avec Louis XV*, 2 vols, 1956–61.

PELTIER, J. G. *Domine Salvum Fac Regem*, 1789.

PENNANT, T. *Tour on the Continent, 1765*, ed. G. R. de Beer, 1948.

PERNIN DES CHAVANETTES, —. *Nouvelle histoire d'Angleterre*, 6 vols, Amsterdam, 1765.

PIDANSAT DE MAIROBERT, M. F. *L'Observateur Anglais* (later *L'Espion Anglais*), 10 vols, 1779–85.

PIGGOTT, SIR F. and OMOND, G. W. T. *Documentary History of the Armed Neutralities, 1780 and 1800, together with selected documents relating to the War of American Independence and the Dutch War*, 1919.

PINOT-DUCLOS, C. *Considérations sur les moeurs*, ed. F. C. Green, Cambridge, 1939.

PITT, W., the elder. *Chatham Correspondence*, ed. W. J. Taylor and J. H. Pringle, 4 vols, 1838–40.

—— 'Letters from William Pitt to Lord Bute, 1755–58', ed. R. R. Sedgwick, in *Essays presented to Sir Lewis Namier*, ed. R. Pares and A. J. P. Taylor, 1956.

PITT, W., the younger. *Correspondence between William Pitt and Charles, Duke of Rutland*, ed. earl Stanhope, rev. edn, 1890.

PLAYFAIR, W. *The Increase of Manufactures, Commerce and Finance, with the Extension of Civil Liberty, proposed in Regulations for the Interest of Money*, 1785.

POLLARD, S. and HOLMES, C. *Documents of European Economic History*, vol. i: *The process of industrialization 1750–1870*, 1968.

POSTLETHWAYTE, M. *Universal Dictionary of Trade and Commerce translated from the French of Monsieur Savary . . .*, 2 vols, 1751.

—— *Britain's Commercial Interests explained and improved*, 2 vols, 1757.

PRICE, R. *Observations on Reversionary Payments*, 1771.

—— *Observations on the Nature of Civil Liberty, the Principles of Government, and the Justice and Policy of the War with America*, Philadelphia, 1776.

PRIESTLEY, J. *An Essay on the first principles of government and on the nature of political, civil and religious liberty*, 1768.

—— *Life and correspondence of Dr Joseph Priestley*, ed. J. T. Rutt, 2 vols, 1831–32.

Rapport fait à l'Académie des Sciences sur la Machine Aérostatique inventée par MM. de Montgolfier, 1784.

RENOUVIN, P., ed. *L'Assemblée des Notables de 1787: la conférence du 2 mars*, 1920.

REYBAZ, E. S. *Un Collaborateur de Mirabeau; documents inédits précédés d'une notice par Ph. Plan*, Paris & Neuchâtel, 1874.

REYMOND, H. *Droits des curés et des paroisses*, 1776.

—— *Droits des pauvres*, 1781.

RIGBY, E. *Letters from France in 1789, edited by his daughter*, 1880.

RIVAROL, A. COMTE DE. *Mémoires*, 1824.

ROBERT, P. A. *Les Remonstrances et arrêtés du parlement de Provence au xviiie siècle, 1715–90*, 1912.

ROBERTS, J. M., ed. *French Revolution Documents*, vol. 1, Oxford, 1966.

ROCHEDIEU, C. A. *Bibliography of French translations of English works, 1700–1800*, Chicago, 1948.

ROGERS, S. *Recollections of the Table-Talk of Samuel Rogers*, ed. A. Dyce, 1887.

ROGET, J. *Lettres de Jean Roget, 1751–1783*, ed. F-F. Roget, Geneva, Basle and Paris, 1911.

ROMILLY, S. *Observations d'un voyageur Anglais sur la Maison de Force, appellée Bicêtre*, 1788.

—— *Règlements observés dans la chambre de Communes pour débattre de matières et pour voter*, 1789.

—— *Thoughts on the Probable Influence of the French Revolution on Great Britain*, 1790.

—— *The Life of Sir Samuel Romilly, written by himself, with a selection from his correspondence; edited by his sons*, 3rd edn, 2 vols, 1842. (More useful than earlier editions, since it contains, as an appendix to vol. i, important fragments from the journal of Romilly's friend Baynes.)

ROSE, G. *Diaries and Correspondence of George Rose*, ed. L. V. Harcourt, 1860.

ROTHNEY, J., ed. *The Brittany Affair and the Crisis of the Ancien Régime*, New York, London and Toronto, 1969.

ROUSSEL DE LA TOUR, —. *La Richesse de l'Etat*, 1763.

—— *Extraits des assertions dangereuses en tout genre que les soi-disant Jésuites ont . . . publiées . . .* Paris and Amsterdam, 1763.

ROZIER, F. *Nouvelle table des articles contenus dans les volumes de l'Académie royale des Sciences de Paris, 1666–1770*, 1775.

RUTLEDGE, J. *Dénonciation sommaire fait au comité des recherches de l'Assemblée Nationale contre M. Necker*, 1790.

ST PRIEST, COMTE DE. *Mémoires sur l'ambassade de France en Turquie (Publications de l'école des Langues Orientales Vivantes)*, 1877.

SCOTT, J. B. *The Armed Neutralities of 1780 and 1800: a collection of official documents*, New York, 1918.

SEDGWICK, R. R., ed. *Letters from George III to Lord Bute, 1756–66*, 1939.

SENAC DE MEILHAN, G. *Considérations sur les richesses et le luxe*, Amsterdam, 1787.

SHERLOCK, M. *Letters from an English Traveller*, 1780.

SMOLLET, T. *Travels through France and Italy*, 2 vols, 1766.

SOULAVIE, J. L. G. *Mémoires historiques et politiques du règne de Louis XVI*, 6 vols, 1801.

SPENCER, F., ed. *Diplomatic Correspondence of the Fourth Earl of Sandwich*, Manchester, 1961.

STEVENS, B. F., ed. *Facsimiles of MSS in European archives relating to America, 1773–83*, 25 vols, 1889–98.

SUARD, J. B. 'Lettres inédites de Suard à Wilkes, publiées par Gabriel Bonno', *University of California Publications in Modern Philology*, xv, 1932, pp. 161–280.

TALBOT, SIR R. *Letters on the French Nation*, 2 vols, 1771.

TEMPLE, W. *A Vindication of Commerce and the Arts*, 1786.

TENON, J. R. *Mémoires sur les hôpitaux de Paris*, 1788.

THICKNESSE, P. *Observations on the Customs and Manners of the French Nation*, 1766.

—— *Useful Hints to Those Who Make the Tour of France*, 1768.

Thoughts on the Use of Machines in the Cotton Manufactures, Manchester, 1780.

TOWNSHEND, J. *Journey through Spain in the years 1786 and 1787 . . . and remarks in passing through a part of France*, 3 vols, 1971.

TUCKER, J. *Instructions for Travellers*, 1757 (printed and circulated among friends, but never published).

—— *Four Tracts on Political and Commercial Subjects*, 3rd edn, Gloucester, 1776.

—— *Reflections on the Present Low Price of Coarse Wools*, 1782.

—— *Cui Bono*, 3rd edn, 1782.

—— *Four Letters on Important National Subjects addressed to Lord Shelburne*, 2nd edn, 1783.

VAUCHER, P., ed. *Receuil des instructions données aux ambassadeurs et ministres de France, xxv, 2: Angleterre, tome 3 (1698–1791)*, 1965.

VAUGHAN, B., ed. *The Repository; containing various political, philosophical, literary and miscellaneous articles*, 1788–89.

A View of the Internal Policy of Great Britain, 1764.

VOLNEY, C. F. *Considérations sur la guerre actuelle des Turcs*, 1788.

VOLTAIRE, F. M. AROUET DE, *Œuvres complètes*, 52 vols, 1877–85.

—— *Voltaire's correspondence*, ed. T. Besterman, 105 vols, 1953–65.

WALPOLE, H. *Letters of Horace Walpole*, ed. Mrs P. Toynbee, 16 vols, Oxford, 1903–05.

—— *The Yale Edition of the Correspondence of Horace Walpole*, ed. W. S. Lewis *et al*, London and New Haven, 1937– (in progress: 34 vols to date).

—— *Memoirs of the reign of George III*, ed. G. F. R. Barker, 4 vols, 1894.

—— *Last Journals*, ed. J. Doran, rev. A. F. Stewart, 2 vols, 1910.

WEDGWOOD, J. *Address to the Workmen in the Pottery on the subject of entering into the service of foreign manufacturers*, Newcastle, 1783.

WHATELY, G. *Considerations on the Trade and Finances of this Kingdom*, 1766.

WILSON, F. M., ed. *Strange Island: Britain through foreign eyes, 1395–1940*, 1955.

WITT, C. DE. *Thomas Jefferson, étude historique sur la démocratie américaine*, 1861.

WRIGHT, J. *Address to Parliament on the late Tax laid on Fustian and other Cotton Goods*, Warrington, 1785.

WROTH, L. C. and ANNAN, G. L., eds. *Acts of French Royal Administration concerning Canada, Guiana, West Indies, Louisiana, prior to 1791*, New York, 1930.

YOUNG, A. *Letters Concerning the Present State of the French Nation*, 1769.

—— *Travels in France during the years 1787, 1788 and 1789*, ed. C. Maxwell, Cambridge, 1929.

—— *Autobiography of Arthur Young with selections from his correspondence*, ed. M. Betham-Edwards, 1898.

Index